Painful Choices

Painful Choices

A THEORY OF FOREIGN POLICY CHANGE

David A. Welch

PRINCETON UNIVERSITY PRESS

PRINCETON AND OXFORD

Requests for permission to reproduce material from this work
should be sent to Permissions, Princeton University Press

Published by Princeton University Press,
41 William Street, Princeton, New Jersey 08540
In the United Kingdom: Princeton University Press,
3 Market Place, Woodstock, Oxfordshire OX20 1SY

Welch, David A.
Painful choices : a theory of foreign policy
change / David A. Welch.
p.   cm.
Includes bibliographical references and index.
ISBN 0-691-12340-3 (cloth : alk. paper)
1. International relations. 2. International
relations—Case studies. I. Title.

JZ1242.W45 2005
327.1′01—dc22   2004065770

British Library Cataloging-in-Publication Data is available

This book has been composed in Sabon

Printed on acid-free paper. ∞

pup.princeton.edu

Printed in the United States of America

1 3 5 7 9 10 8 6 4 2

For my students

CONTENTS

FIGURES AND TABLES

FIGURES

TABLES

ACKNOWLEDGMENTS

My recompense is thanks, that's all,
Yet my good will is great, though the gift small.
—William Shakespeare, *Pericles, Prince of Tyre*, 3:4

MANY PEOPLE have helped me with this book in many ways, large and small, wittingly and unwittingly. In particular I would like to thank those who have taken time to read and comment on drafts, share their expertise, or avail me of their dogged research assistance. These include, in strictly alphabetical order: Emanuel Adler, Aisha Ahmad, Alan Alexandroff, Nicole Anastasopoulos, Tarini Awatramani, William Berman, Steven Bernstein, Thomas Biersteker, Jim Blight, Robert Brigham, McGeorge Bundy, Marc Busch, Chester Cooper, Wolfgang Danspeckgruber, James Der Derian, Michael Donnelly, Peter Feaver, Michel Fortmann, Sir Lawrence Freedman, Aaron Friedberg, Aaron Gairdner, Gary Goertz, Ellen Gutterman, Michael Hart, Terry Hoppmann, Ole Holsti, Jeffery Kimball, Hiroshi Kimura, Masato Kimura, John Kirton, Bilge Kocyigit, janet Lang, Waleuska Lazo, Richard Ned Lebow, Fredrik Logevall, Gillian Manning, Ana Margheritis, Charles William Maynes, Robert McNamara, Kim Richard Nossal, John Owen, Louis Pauly, Yasuyo Sakata, Elias Scorsone, Scott Silverstone, Steve Smith, Janice Gross Stein, Sir Crispin Tickell, Ashwini Vasanthakumar, Geoffrey Wallace, Alexander Wendt, Melissa Williams, and Noboru Yamaguchi. I would also like to thank participants in seminars at the University of Arizona; the Thomas J. Watson Jr. Institute for International Studies, Brown University; Duke University; McGill University; l'Université de Montréal; the Center for International Studies, Princeton University; and the Munk Centre for International Studies, University of Toronto. Not least, I would like to acknowledge the generous financial and institutional support of the Social Sciences and Humanities Research Council of Canada; the Thomas J. Watson Jr. Institute for International Studies, Brown University; the Weatherhead Center for International Affairs, Harvard University; and the Center for International Studies, Princeton University. Any errors in this book are, of course, my own.

Chapter 3 draws upon previously published material: David A. Welch, "Remember the Falklands? Missed Lessons of a Misunderstood War," *International Journal*, vol. 52, no. 3 (Summer 1997), pp. 483–507; David A. Welch, "Culture and Emotion as Obstacles to Good Judgment: The Case of Argentina's Invasion of the Falklands/Malvinas," in *Good*

Judgment in Foreign Policy: Theory and Application, ed. Stanley A. Renshon and Deborah W. Larson (Lanham, MD: Rowman & Littlefield, 2003), pp. 191–215; and Masato Kimura and David A. Welch, "Specifying 'Interests': Japan's Claim to the Northern Territories and Its Implications for International Relations Theory," *International Studies Quarterly*, vol. 42, no. 2 (June 1998), pp. 213–244 (an earlier version of which appeared as CFIA Working Paper 97–3, Cambridge: Center for International Affairs, Harvard University, 1997). I would like to thank the editors for their forbearance.

Introduction

DURING THE 2000 U.S. presidential campaign, Republican candidate George W. Bush criticized the Clinton administration for overextending American commitments, failing to focus on key American interests, and burdening the U.S. military with tasks unrelated to its core mission. A president should authorize the use of military force, Bush insisted in the first of two presidential debates with Democratic candidate Al Gore, only "if it's in our vital national interests," when there is "a clear understanding as to what the mission would be," when the United States is "prepared and trained to . . . win," and when there is a clear exit strategy. "I would take the use of force very seriously," Bush asserted. "I would be guarded in my approach. I don't think we can be all things to all people in the world. I think we've got to be very careful when we commit our troops. The vice president and I have a disagreement about the use of troops. He believes in nation-building. I would be very careful about using our troops as nation-builders."[1]

In the second debate, Bush insisted that the United States should be "humble in how we treat nations that are figuring out how to chart their own course"—more respectful of the principle of state sovereignty, in other words—and he lambasted the Clinton administration for allowing the international coalition containing Saddam Hussein to weaken. "The coalition that was in place isn't as strong as it used to be," Bush complained. "He is a danger; we don't want him fishing in troubled waters in the Middle East. And it's going to be hard to—it's going to be important to rebuild that coalition to keep the pressure on him."[2]

With respect to the general principles of American foreign policy, in short, Bush promised restraint and selectivity. Bush would be a domestic politics president, most analysts surmised, as one might expect from a man without much experience of, interest in, or even knowledge of foreign affairs. Few international politics issues captivated him. Iraq was an exception. When host Jim Lehrer asked during the second debate whether Bush thought he could "get [Saddam] out of there," Bush replied, "I'd

---

[1] "Presidential Debate between Democratic Candidate Vice President Al Gore and Republican Candidate Governor George W. Bush, Clark Athletic Center, University of Massachusetts, Boston, MA, 3 October 2000."

[2] "Presidential Debate between Democratic Candidate Vice President Al Gore and Republican Candidate Governor George W. Bush, Wait Chapel, Wake Forest University, Winston-Salem, NC, 11 October 2000."

like to, of course, and I presume this administration would as well." But the main thing was containment. Bush would redeem Clinton's failed Iraq policy by reinvigorating multilateralism.

By the spring of 2003, the U.S. military had toppled Saddam's regime, having already toppled the Taliban regime in Afghanistan, and was heavily engaged in nation building in both countries.[3] Bush's call for humility, selectivity, restraint, and reinvigorated multilateralism had morphed into a doctrine of preventive war near-universally condemned abroad as dangerously unilateral.[4] While the American action in Afghanistan enjoyed considerable international support, the war in Iraq did not—in fact, the United Nations Security Council was strongly opposed. A domestic-politics president had suddenly become a foreign-policy president, indeed a national-security president broadly construed, largely unconcerned with multilateralism, and anything but humble. What had happened to provoke such a change?

The answer, of course, is 9/11.[5]

Now, at one level there is nothing surprising about this. 9/11 was the deadliest terrorist attack in history. By toppling both World Trade Center towers in the most horrific way imaginable—using hijacked airliners as weapons of mass destruction—Osama bin Laden's al-Qaeda network dealt the United States a psychological blow rivaled in American history only, perhaps, by the Japanese surprise attack on Pearl Harbor on December 7, 1941.[6] Suddenly the American people—and, of course, their president—felt acutely vulnerable in a way they had never felt before, and to an enemy they had hitherto underestimated. It would have been odd indeed if American foreign and domestic policy had not reflected the widespread perception in the United States that the world had changed both suddenly and profoundly. "A faceless enemy has declared war on the United States of America," Bush declared on September 12; "So we are at war."[7]

---

[3] "The theoretical pronouncements Bush had made about not nation building have been discarded almost wholesale in the face of the need to keep Afghanistan together. He was at times acting like the Afghan budget director and bill collector." Bob Woodward, *Bush at War*, p. 339.

[4] "National Security Strategy of the United States of America"; Ivo H. Daalder, James M. Lindsay, and James B. Steinberg, *The Bush National Security Strategy*, pp. 1–9.

[5] Throughout I will use this particular popular shorthand for the attacks mounted by al-Qaeda against the World Trade Center in New York and the Pentagon in Washington, DC, on September 11, 2001.

[6] As Bush confided to his diary on the evening of 9/11: "The Pearl Harbor of the 21st century took place today." Woodward, *Bush at War*, p. 37.

[7] Ibid., p. 41.

The problem, though, is that Osama bin Laden had declared war on the United States more than three years earlier—on February 23, 1998.[8] Al-Qaeda's first attempt to topple the World Trade Center had taken place eight years earlier. That attempt killed 6, injured 1,042, and caused "more hospital casualties than any other event in domestic American history apart from the Civil War."[9] American officials knew that the mastermind of the first World Trade Center attack, Ramzi Yousef, had plans to fly aircraft into government buildings.[10] Bush's own director of central intelligence, George Tenet, had told him even before the inauguration that al-Qaeda posed a "tremendous" and "immediate" threat to the United States.[11] The real puzzle is why American policy had not changed earlier to reflect the growing menace al-Qaeda had posed for almost a decade. "The question that would always linger," Bob Woodward later mused, "was whether they had moved fast enough on a threat that had been identified by the CIA as one of the top three facing the country, whether September 11 was as much a failure of policy as it was of intelligence."[12]

What is striking and surprising in retrospect, in other words, is not how dramatically American policy changed after 9/11 so much as how little it changed beforehand. Until 9/11, antiterrorism was a relatively minor concern in American foreign policy, largely handled as a routine security-intelligence issue—a matter of mundane police-work more than anything else. Terrorism was not an issue in the 2000 presidential campaign. Prior to 9/11, Bush had never even been briefed by his chief counterterrorism expert. The very first principals' meeting on the subject in the Bush administration took place only on September 4, 2001.[13] Everything changed after 9/11. The "War on Terror" became *the* central concern not only of U.S. foreign policy, but of American politics as a whole—a matter of the highest of high politics, to which everything else suddenly became secondary.

American policy toward Iraq changed fundamentally after 9/11, too.[14] Despite Bush's preelection hostility toward Saddam's regime, and despite the enthusiasm some of his officials felt for toppling Saddam from the very beginning of his administration, the fact is that Bush's Iraq pol-

---

[8] Simon Reeve, *The New Jackals*, pp. 194, 268–270. For further discussion, see National Commission on Terrorist Attacks upon the United States, *The 9/11 Commission Report*, pp. 47–48.

[9] Reeve, *The New Jackals*, p. 15. For further discussion, see *The 9/11 Commission Report*, pp. 153–173.

[10] Reeve, *The New Jackals*, p. 8.

[11] Woodward, *Bush at War*, p. 34.

[12] Ibid., p. 36.

[13] Richard A. Clarke, *Against All Enemies*, pp. 26, 237–238.

[14] Todd S. Purdum, *A Time of Our Choosing*, pp. 4–10.

icy remained Clinton's Iraq policy for more than a year and a half.[15] Officially, both presidents favored regime change, but in practice, neither felt the kind of urgency, and neither had the kind of unified advice, that made an energetic policy of regime change possible. Both simply hobbled along. But 9/11 shook everything up and gave the Iraq hawks the window they needed. "September the 11th obviously changed my thinking a lot about my responsibility as president," Bush later told Woodward. "Keeping Saddam in a box looked less and less feasible to me."[16] Once Bush had taken care of business in Afghanistan, he turned his sights on Saddam, despite the fact, with which Kenneth Pollack begins a book advocating a war with Iraq, that "[a]s best we can tell, Iraq was not involved in the terrorist attacks of September 11, 2001."[17]

While it is doubtful that anyone on September 10 would have agonized over the question of why American foreign policy had not changed significantly to meet the new transnational terror threat, anyone watching the news on the morning of September 11, 2001, would have felt that a dramatic change was certain. Anyone listening to the radio on December 7, 1941, would have felt the same way. But who would have anticipated Japan's fateful decision to attack Pearl Harbor in the first place? That signaled a change in Japanese policy of the first magnitude. Often the most interesting and the most momentous changes catch us by surprise. Moreover, they surprise us not merely because they seem to be such sudden, radical departures, but because radical departures strike us as so rare. Is there any way to improve our ability to anticipate such changes? Is there any way to enhance our understanding of dramatic changes (surprising or otherwise) and of the long periods between them?

My purpose in this book is to find out. I do so by developing and test driving a theory of foreign policy change. In this endeavor I was motivated by curiosity about three superficially different, but, at the end of the day, quite closely related concerns. The first was to see whether there is anything we can know with tolerable reliability about international politics *in general*. General, portable, parsimonious International Relations theory has been something of a Holy Grail at least since the behavioral revo-

---

[15] As Ken Pollack puts it, "the Bush administration turned out to be not too dissimilar to the Clinton administration in its final days." Kenneth M. Pollack, *The Threatening Storm*, p. 105.

[16] Bob Woodward, *Plan of Attack*, p. 27. On the internal disputes over Iraq policy and their evolution, see ibid., pp. 9–30, esp. p. 23: "The deep divisions and tensions in the war cabinet with Powell the moderate negotiator and Rumsfeld the hard-line activist meant no real policy would be made until either the president stepped in or events forced his hand."

[17] Pollack, *The Threatening Storm*, p. xxi. See also Clarke, *Against All Enemies*, p. 33.

lution, both in terms of its desirability and its elusiveness.[18] The failure of the grand-theory project to date has generated considerable criticism of the very idea, both among those who would describe it as desirable in principle but impossible in practice and among those who, in rejecting its very philosophical and methodological foundations, would insist that it is impossible even in principle. I began this project with a hunch that our disappointment with the search for general, portable, parsimonious IR theory may simply be an artifact of our having asked the wrong questions and having attempted to solve the wrong problems.

My second concern followed directly from the first. Suppose that a general (or nearly general) IR theory were possible after all; how far might we take it? What are its limits? What limits it? What might these limits say about the very philosophical questions that underlie many of the most active debates in IR theory today? I had a second hunch that, while a general IR theory might be attainable, it could never be perfect, and that as a discipline we might benefit from pondering its imperfections. In a very literal sense, in other words, I sought to conduct a study both of the possibilities *and* limits of general IR theory.

My third concern was whether a general IR theory could be useful both to analysts and to leaders. Here my feeling was that there are three quite different standards of usefulness. The gold standard is the ability to see into the future. The bronze standard is the ability merely to understand the past. There are good reasons to think the gold standard unattainable, but my third hunch was that we can do better than simple post-hoc explanation. The silver standard, as it were, would be to reduce uncertainty about the future. I wanted to see if a general IR theory could help us, if not predict important events in world politics, at least anticipate them, or be sensitive to the conditions under which they become more likely.

In the course of working on this project, not surprisingly, I encountered both gratification and disappointment. My own view, having now completed it, is that the effort proved largely successful and the disappointments instructive. Readers will, of course, judge for themselves. But I believe it shows that there are indeed grounds for thinking that we can

---

[18] I will embrace Hollis and Smith's useful practice of capitalizing the phrase when referring to the discipline (or using the abbreviation IR) and using lower case when referring to its subject matter. Martin Hollis and Steve Smith, *Explaining and Understanding International Relations*, p. 10. Behavioralism is a form of theory-driven empiricism employing the epistemology and methods of the natural sciences to seek lawlike generalizations, both explanatory and predictive, from quantifiable data. The phrase "behavioral revolution" denotes the social sciences' enthusiastic embrace of behavioralism in the 1950s and 1960s. Of course, some scholars working in a more traditional historical/interpretive mode sought general, portable theories as well; see, e.g., Hans J. Morgenthau, *Politics among Nations*.

generalize about important aspects of international politics in a way that helps us reduce uncertainty about the future as well as better understand the past.

I should note at the outset that this book constructs and explores *a* (fairly) general theory. The subtitle is *A Theory of Foreign Policy Change*, not *The Theory of Foreign Policy Change*. I do not wish to claim that this is the only one possible, even with respect to this specific problematique. The problematique itself is, of course, something that some readers will object to as falling outside the parameters of IR theory properly understood. Kenneth Waltz, for example, is keen to distinguish a theory of international politics from a theory of foreign policy.[19] I am less keen to make this distinction because if by a "theory of international politics" we mean a theory of behavior, this is precisely the wrong game to stalk, and our having stalked it thus far unsuccessfully, I argue, is the main reason for the widespread disenchantment with general IR theory. I am interested in a theory of change in behavior, not of behavior per se, so I am not in search of the conditions under which states will do specific things—thus I am not in pursuit of a theory of foreign policy strictly understood. But I am interested in changes in the behavior of states, not of systems, and so if we strictly insist that only purely systemic theories qualify as general IR theories, I would be wrong to characterize my project as I do. Lacking the capacity to imagine the justification for such a restriction, I feel comfortable with the characterization. A general theory gives us an explanation for why things happen that is not bound by time or place, and that is precisely what I offer here.

In addition to being quite general, the theory is both portable and parsimonious. A portable theory enables us to apply the explanation to a wide variety of specific cases that might seem on the face of things to differ significantly from one another. A parsimonious theory explains a lot of things in terms of a relatively small number of things. It is easy to see the attraction of this kind of theory. Thus when I suggest that Kenneth Waltz may have erred in seeking a general theory of international politics as he conceived it, I do not mean to quibble with his understanding of theoretical virtues. I merely mean to suggest that the quest for a general, abstract, parsimonious theory of international politics as he conceived it was hopeless from the beginning.

Why do I suggest this? And why do I seek instead a theory of foreign policy change?

There is too much variation in the things leaders of states seek, and in the imperatives to which they respond, for any spare theory to capture either the dynamics of international politics in general or the mainsprings

---

[19] Kenneth N. Waltz, *Theory of International Politics*, pp. 121–122.

of foreign policies in particular. This is because of the enormous complexity of, and variation in, the things that affect leaders' choices. Systemic imperatives, domestic political considerations, cultural attributes, ideologies, normative commitments, bureaucratic factors, and idiosyncratic personality traits can all influence the choices leaders make. Moreover, they do so haphazardly. This is not necessarily bad. It is one of the things that makes international politics so interesting. But it does mean that the kind of grand theory that presupposes the inputs of leaders' choices is bound to fail.[20]

Are there any constants of international politics, any fairly hard-and-fast regularities, upon which to build international "theory"? Two things stand out. First, people everywhere process information in more or less the same way. Human psychology in Japan is the same as human psychology in Europe. If we can identify the things leaders take into consideration in their deliberations, we can fairly confidently anticipate (within certain limits) how they will process them. Second, the ship of state is ordinarily ponderous, not nimble. It is insensitive to minor changes in the environment. It alters course only with great effort, and only when absolutely necessary. The state does not—because it cannot—constantly sample the outside world, adjusting and fine-tuning its behavior so as to optimize something (such as "power" or "the national interest"). The state is not like a variable-timing engine that continuously monitors and adjusts to its environment. Instead, it goes about its business today more or less the same way it went about its business yesterday, unless it has some very compelling reason to do something dramatically different. American policy toward Iraq between 1991 and 2003 provides a classic illustration. "We just fly missions and drop bombs from time to time," retired Army Colonel Andrew Bacevich mused in the year 2000, "because we've been doing it for ten years and no one can stop us from doing so."[21]

If we can be fairly confident most of the time that states will do today what they did yesterday, and that they will do tomorrow what they do today, it is not terribly important to know why any particular state does

---

[20] For further discussion, see Masato Kimura and David A. Welch, "Specifying 'Interests.' "

[21] Quoted in Thomas E. Ricks, "Containing Iraq: A Forgotten War," p. A01. If we wish to think in terms of similes, the state more closely resembles an interrupt-driven computer than a variable-timing engine. A computer processor operating at a 60 MHz clock speed will do precisely the same thing the next clock cycle that it did during the last—60 million times per second—until it receives a signal from an attached component, such as a keyboard, to do something different. It will then rise from its electronic slumber to comply. Even the fastest typist will convince a 60 MHz processor to do something different only once every 6 million clock cycles or so. While computers and states are both very status quo oriented, however, there is an important difference between them: to rouse the state, one must often pound both hard and repeatedly.

what it does, and there is no reason at all to try to determine why states in general do what they do in general. What we really need to know is: when can we expect them to do something noticeably different, and why?

I characterize the theory I develop here as a "loss-aversion" theory of foreign policy change because, as I will argue, foreign policy is most likely to change dramatically when leaders expect the status quo to generate continued painful losses. States will not alter their behavior simply to try to realize some marginal gain. The clearest signals of an impending change are desperation, stridency, and distress. The choice for change will often carry with it a risk of even greater loss—a risk of loss so great that, in many cases, no rational actor would accept it. The choice for change, in short, is commonly a painful choice.

I begin in chapter 1 by spending a little more time justifying some of these bold claims. In particular, I lay out a more careful defense of my view that a theory of foreign policy change is the appropriate game to stalk. In the course of this discussion I delve more deeply into meta-theory—the theory of theory, as it were—than some readers may care for, and if you have no more than a passing interest in this, you may wish simply to skim it. It is a necessary part of my argument, however, so I cannot afford to treat it too hastily. In chapter 2, I develop the theory of foreign policy change, drawing upon relevant work in organizational behavior, cognitive and motivational psychology, and behavioral decision theory. It is here that I begin paying close attention to limits. In the following three chapters, I "test drive" the theory in a series of structured, focused, comparative case studies.[22] In these chapters I try to bring the abstractions down to earth. Finally, in the conclusion, I comment on the theory's performance and limits and briefly address the practical policy implications of the study, which primarily concern strategic warning (in the security domain) and assessing the ripeness for negotiation and resistance points (in all domains).

While the book is clearly animated by an enthusiasm for the scientific project, my exploration of its limits reflects a pervasive theme: namely, that the science of international politics must somehow make allowance for the art. We must rediscover what scholars of International Relations knew before the behavioral revolution: that what happens in world politics is powerfully affected by the humanity of those whose choices shape it. Leaders have right brains as well as left. They are driven as much by passion as by reason. Moreover, international politics is a strategic enterprise not merely in the economic sense modeled so well by game theorists,

---

[22] For methodological discussion, see Alexander George, "Case Studies and Theory Development"; Alexander L. George and Timothy J. McKeown, "Case Studies and Theories of Organizational Decision Making," pp. 21–58.

but also in the classical sense, in which leaders sometimes attempt to mislead, lull, and outfox each other in high-stakes battles of wits. The kinds of events I seek to explain—and to help leaders anticipate—are therefore not the fully determined resultants of immutable physical forces, with which natural science grapples so well, but the willful choices of people acting in what they themselves perceive to be a fluid, dynamic, sometimes unpredictable environment. This places limits on the precision with which we can identify, measure, and forecast. It gives an advantage to the analyst who can combine knowledge and reason with less tangible abilities such as observational skill, insight, and empathy. It means that we must moderate our hopes and expectations for "testing" theory—Newton's experiments would have consistently failed if the bodies he pushed and dropped and threw had the will, capacity, and malice to misbehave—but since international politics is not an entirely capricious domain, and human nature is not infinitely malleable, we can still use evidence to distinguish better from worse statements about how the world works. We are not confined merely to interpreting it, or bearing witness to it. The middle-ground approach to epistemology I promote and defend in this book— "test driving" rather than "testing" theory; judging its performance, its comfort, and its fit-and-finish, rather than its "truth" or even, in comparative perspective, its relative usefulness—is as much, I contend, as the subject matter will allow.

This book, in short, is an attempt to make the case that we should be as scientific about the study of world politics as possible under the circumstances, and that while circumstances may not permit perfection, they are not quite so debilitating as many believe. As between theory and policy, in other words, we do not necessarily have painful choices to make.

Chapter 1

SURPRISE, ANTICIPATION, AND THEORY

IMPORTANT DEVELOPMENTS in international politics tend to catch us by surprise. The standard litany of examples is familiar. No one thought that the assassination of Austrian Archduke Franz Ferdinand in June 1914 would lead to a general European war within five weeks. No one predicted the Japanese attack on Pearl Harbor. No one forecast the end of the Cold War. No one predicted Saddam Hussein's invasion of Kuwait. Why is anticipating state behavior so difficult?

Part of the answer lies with the nature of the subject matter, and part lies with how we typically try to make sense of it. It goes without saying that predicting state behavior is not like predicting solar eclipses. Astronomers are good at predicting eclipses because they have a fair idea of how bodies in space move relative to each other, and they have no trouble getting the information they need through observation and measurement to project the relative positions of the Earth, the moon, and the sun well into the future. The forces that determine the motions of heavenly bodies are basically well understood. Not so for the behavior of states. Why not?

One reason we might call the *small-n problem*. A prediction is an inference from the general to the particular. It requires a prior understanding of the underlying relationships between two or more things, and that, in turn, rests upon our familiarity with them. There are billions of heavenly bodies for astronomers to observe, and while the attributes (position, mass, velocity) of individual heavenly bodies vary over time, heavenly bodies as such do not. They are all basically clumps of matter. But many of the international-political events that we would like to be able to anticipate occur only infrequently. Interstate wars, for example, are quite rare. Great Power wars are even rarer.[1] And wars are "alike" only in a very abstract sense. It is an open question whether the important similarities between, say, the Second World War and the Soccer War are anywhere near as numerous as the important differences.[2] We lump them together

---

[1] See Jack S. Levy, *War in the Modern Great Power System*; Melvin Small and J. David Singer, *Resort to Arms*; J. David Singer and Paul F. Diehl, eds., *Measuring the Correlates of War*.

[2] The Soccer War, or *Guerra de Fútbol*, broke out between El Salvador and Honduras shortly after the two countries had played a series of bitterly contested World Cup matches in the summer of 1969. There were more serious underlying causes of hostility, however, including a minor border dispute, economic grievances, and Honduras's involuntary repatriation of approximately 300,000 Salvadoran economic refugees. The war cost some 5,000

as elements of a single set ("interstate wars") through what is basically a dubious exercise in taxonomy. With so few cases, and with so much variation among them, it is hardly surprising that it is so difficult to determine the underlying relationships between wars and their possible causes. The same may be said for interventions, threats, alliances, alignments, customs unions, experiments in integration, and anything else not part of the routine, day-to-day foreign policy agenda.

A second problem we might call the *reflexivity problem*. Leaders of states make policy against the backdrop of a historical record to which they consciously react. They draw inferences or "lessons" from past experiences, or their subjective readings of history—not very rigorously or skillfully, I might add—in order to repeat earlier successes, and not to repeat earlier mistakes. The result is that something having happened once is often a reason for its being either more likely or less likely to happen again, depending upon how well things worked out the last time. Austria-Hungary, for example, pressed its luck too far with Serbia and Russia in 1914 in large part because it had gotten away with similar boldness six years earlier.[3] Britain tried to appease Hitler in the 1930s because British leaders felt that overly tough politics had led to World War I. Once Margaret Thatcher convinced the first President Bush in Aspen that Saddam Hussein was just like Hitler and that appeasement does not pay, Bush resolved then and there to roll back the Iraqi invasion of Kuwait.[4] The moon, of course, does not change its mind about where to go based on its experiences in earlier orbits. Unlike astronomical events, the underlying patterns of state behavior are constantly in flux as decision makers react willfully to history.[5]

---

lives. World War II lasted longer, had somewhat different causes, and cost approximately 35 million lives.

[3] In 1908 Austria-Hungary annexed Bosnia and Herzegovina, despite heated Serb protests. Serbia turned to Russia for support, which Russia declined to provide owing to its weakness at the time (Russia was still reeling from its defeat at the hands of the Japanese, and from revolution, in 1905). Russia's hesitancy led Austrian leaders to expect in 1914 that Russia would once again stand by while Austria smote Serbia for its support of Bosnian irredentists who were behind the assassination of Archduke Franz Ferdinand. Of course, precisely *because* it had dodged its responsibilities to Serbia in 1908, Russia refused to do so a second time.

[4] Jean Edward Smith, *George Bush's War*, pp. 65–72. There are circumstances, of course, when appeasement is a perfectly appropriate strategy, and in fact it has proven very useful to its practitioners from time to time. Britain, for example, used appeasement successfully to moderate tensions with the United States in the late nineteenth and early twentieth centuries. See, e.g., Antony Lentin, *Lloyd George, Woodrow Wilson and the Guilt of Germany*; William R. Rock, *British Appeasement in the 1930s*; Stephen R. Rock, *Appeasement in International Politics*.

[5] See generally Robert Jervis, "The Future of World Politics"; Yuen Foong Khong, *Analogies at War*; Richard E. Neustadt and Ernest R. May, *Thinking in Time*.

A third problem we may call the *theory/praxis problem*. In order to anticipate international political events, we need to have a theory in mind that tells us which indicators to look for and how to process them. Scholars of international politics think quite formally about theory. Practitioners do so less formally. But forecasting of any kind is, in some sense, theory-driven. The difficulty is that we derive and test theories about how the world works through observation and experience, but at the same time leaders of states make policy choices based in part upon the prescriptions of theory. Realist balance-of-power theory, for example, suggests that states will configure their alliances so as to balance stronger states or groups of states, much as Adam Smith's hidden hand is supposed to shape the behavior of firms in highly competitive markets. The theory provides both a description of state behavior and a prescription for state behavior. It tells us that states *will* tend to balance power, and that they *ought* to balance power if they wish to survive. Leaders who internalize the prescription—for example, nineteenth-century statesmen such as Austrian foreign minister Prince Klemens von Metternich, or British foreign secretary Viscount Castlereagh—will, not surprisingly, act in ways that appear to vindicate the theory.[6] What's more, scholars will count their actions as evidence for the theory.[7] But others, such as U.S. President Woodrow Wilson and French diplomat Jean Monnet, went out of their way to try to avoid balance-of-power politics because they thought it a source of great evil and suffering in the world. They spent a good deal of time and effort to craft policies and institutions designed to thwart it.[8] Their behavior, inspired by the Liberal normative ideal, will later be taken as evidence for Liberal theories and against Realist ones.[9] Neither balance-of-power theory nor Liberal theory is therefore truly general; they really explain only the behavior of those states whose leaders implicitly subscribe to them. But what predicts whether the leaders of any given state will be Realists or Liberals?

By the same token, Schellingesque theories of coercive diplomacy are borne out tolerably well by American foreign policy during the period in which Thomas Schelling and his students were actually shaping it.[10] As

---

[6] Henry A. Kissinger, *A World Restored*.

[7] Edward Vose Gulick, *Europe's Classical Balance of Power*.

[8] Arthur S. Link, ed., *Woodrow Wilson and a Revolutionary World, 1913–1921*; Margaret MacMillan, *Paris 1919*; Charles A. Kupchan and Clifford A. Kupchan, "Concerts, Collective Security, and the Future of Europe"; Karl W. Deutsch, *Political Community and the North Atlantic Area*.

[9] Michael Doyle, "Liberalism and World Politics," pp. 1151–1169; Bruce M. Russett, *Grasping the Democratic Peace*.

[10] Thomas C. Schelling, *The Strategy of Conflict*; Schelling, *Arms and Influence*; David Halberstam, *The Best and the Brightest*; Ted Hopf, *Peripheral Visions*.

general theories of how states respond to threats, however, the theories fail because not everyone has read and internalized Schelling. Certainly Saddam Hussein had not in 1991, which may help explain the spectacular failure of the United States and its coalition partners to get him to withdraw from Kuwait by means of threats alone under what were essentially near-ideal conditions for an exercise in compellence.[11]

Yet a fourth problem we may call the *degrees of freedom problem*. Heavenly bodies have no choice where they go. The set of things we need to know in order to fix the value of whatever it is we are interested in knowing about them is small. But the behavior of states is relatively unconstrained parametrically. Leaders of states almost always have a variety of options before them from which to choose a course of action, and no matter how well we specify the initial environmental conditions of choice, we cannot confidently predict which choice leaders will make solely on the basis of that information. This is true of any situation in which strategy is possible, even where the parametric constraints are quite clear. Take, for example, the game of chess. At any given time, we can specify precisely, and fairly succinctly, the complete list of permissible moves. But we can almost never know for sure which move a player will make. To predict a move a player will make in a game of chess requires detailed information about the player, not merely about the game. And even then, the fact that we may hold one move to be likely may be sufficient reason for a strategically sophisticated player not to make that move. Good players, in their genius and perversity, will set out to fool us. So will leaders of states from time to time. They will sometimes deliberately do what others consider unlikely in order to obtain the advantage of surprise. And in international politics, we have no way even of specifying the full set of possible moves.

A fifth problem we may call the *subjectivity problem*. Leaders of states make choices on the basis of how they see the world. Their view of the world may be quite different from that of other leaders, and from that of International Relations scholars. Consider assessments of the balance of power during the Cold War. With but few exceptions, Western scholars and policy makers generally considered the military balance unfavorable to the West. Soviet analysts and policy makers generally considered it unfavorable to the East. Similarly, Western estimates of Soviet economic capacity were systematically higher than the Soviets' own estimates. Not only were there striking differences in assessments based essentially upon "tangible" (i.e., quantifiable) indicators—such as numbers of tanks, artillery pieces, aircraft, and nuclear missiles—there were also wildly differing

[11] Janice Gross Stein, "Deterrence and Compellence in the Gulf, 1990–91." See also Troy S. Goodfellow, "An Empirical Test of the Theory of Compellence."

assessments (both self-assessments and assessments of the other) of so-called intangible power resources, such as strategic vision, will, credibility, and reputation.[12] Not surprisingly, predictions of state behavior that require as inputs objective values—such as the relative balance of power—will fail whenever the analyst's assessments differ significantly from those of policy makers, even in cases where policy makers internalize the prescriptions of the theory upon which the predictions are based.

A sixth problem we could call the *input specification problem*. To predict state behavior, we need to know two things: what leaders of states want (i.e., their goals or ends), and how they go about matching means to ends (i.e., their calculations). Contrary to popular belief, the specification of state "interests" appears to be an idiosyncratic process highly susceptible to random or arbitrary influences. Scholars and analysts are prone to making unwarranted assumptions or judgments about state interests, and about how leaders match means to ends.[13] Scholars and analysts alike, in other words, tend to make systematic errors about what states want and how they go about trying to get it.

Taking all of these problems into account, it is no wonder that international politics is so full of surprises. But there are those who would say: "The purpose of International Relations theory is not to predict—or, at least, not to predict specific events—but instead to explain broad patterns in classes of events (for example, arms races, power transitions, alignments, wars, cooperation).[14] Its aim is to show that certain kinds of events are more or less likely under certain circumstances, not that any specific event will or will not occur. The astronomical analogy is inappropriate: a better analogy would be to aviation safety. We know that plane crashes are more likely in bad weather than in good weather, but this knowledge will not enable us to predict that any particular plane flying in bad weather will crash. A theory of Great Power war may predict that wars are more likely during a hegemonic transition, or in a multipolar system, but it will not predict that a particular Great Power war will take place

---

[12] See International Institute for Strategic Studies, *The Military Balance*; Charles Tyroler, *Alerting America*; Committee on the Present Danger, *Can America Catch Up?*; Ray S. Cline, *World Power Trends and U.S. Foreign Policy for the 1980s*; W. Scott Thompson, *Power Projection*; Vladislav Zubok and Constantine Pleshakov, *Inside the Kremlin's Cold War*; Morton Schwartz, *Soviet Perceptions of the United States*; Melvyn P. Leffler, "Inside Enemy Archives"; William Curti Wohlforth, *The Elusive Balance*.

[13] I discuss the first claim more fully in the sections that follow, and the second claim in chapter 2; but cf. also Mark Blyth, "Structures Do Not Come with an Instruction Sheet."

[14] For enlightening views on whether the failure of scholars to predict the end of the Cold War constitutes an indictment of International Relations theory, see John Lewis Gaddis, "International Relations Theory and the End of the Cold War"; Ted Hopf, "Getting the End of the Cold War Wrong"; Richard Ned Lebow and Thomas Risse-Kappen, eds., *International Relations Theory and the End of the Cold War*.

during a particular hegemonic transition, or in any particular multipolar system.[15] While it would be nice for International Relations theory to offer policy makers a crystal ball, this is not what it is meant to do, and the expectation is unrealistic."

A second possible objection is this: "You are working with an inappropriate expectation about prediction, based on an inappropriate analogy to Newtonian physics. For reasons you yourself point out, the social realm is inherently unpredictable. International Relations theory should take its inspiration not from physics, but from evolutionary biology, which is not a predictive science. It can explain past events, but evolution is inherently unpredictable. The best we can do—and the most we should aspire to do—is to articulate plausible scenarios for how the world might unfold on the basis, in part, of local knowledge. We should abandon the quest for general deductive theory altogether."[16]

These are interesting and thoughtful objections. They raise three questions: whether the prediction of specific events is a *necessary* goal of International Relations theory; whether it is a *reasonable* goal; and whether it is a *desirable* goal. I would answer "no," "yes, within limits," and "absolutely," respectively.

Clearly we can articulate theories that will not help us predict the behavior of specific states. Kenneth Waltz's, for example, does not.[17] It aspires only to explain why balances will tend to occur and why Great Power wars are more likely in a multipolar than in a bipolar system. Its quite limited aspirations do not disqualify it as theory.[18] So the prediction of specific events is clearly not a necessary condition of International Relations theory.

It is also true that predicting specific events is an unreasonable goal in certain circumstances, as the aviation safety analogy suggests. We know a great deal about *how* bad weather can cause plane crashes—wind shear disrupts lift; ice build-up on the wings induces drag; hailstones damage compressor blades, reducing thrust; fog reduces the amount of time available to pilots in which to decide whether to abort an approach—but it is simply impossible to collect and to process all of the information that would be necessary to predict whether any particular plane flying in bad weather will crash. In principle, if we had all of this information, we might well be able to make such a prediction. But we will never have all of the

---

[15] A.F.K. Organski and Jacek Kugler, *The War Ledger*; Robert Gilpin, *War and Change in World Politics*; Waltz, *Theory of International Politics*.

[16] Here I am paraphrasing Steven Bernstein et al., "God Gave Physics the Easy Problems," much of which (especially pp. 43–53) I heartily endorse. As I shall make clear in a minute, though, I disagree with the punch line.

[17] Waltz, *Theory of International Politics*.

[18] See my discussion of this point in the introduction.

necessary information, so the hope is vain. All we can do is say that the danger of a crash is higher or lower in various circumstances, all other things being equal.[19]

But even in social and political life, there are times when we have good reasons for thinking a certain event more likely than an alternative, and occasionally we have good reasons for thinking certain events to be very highly likely indeed. We can often forecast election outcomes, for example, based upon combinations of historical voting patterns, economic and other conditions, and polling data. The forecasts are usually more reliable the nearer to the election, but sometimes we can be fairly confident of an election outcome months in advance, which is certainly a useful time horizon for a number of practical purposes. Obviously, elections occasionally fool us. A lot of people were surprised in 1948 when they woke up on the morning after election day to discover that Harry Truman had beaten Thomas Dewey after all. (None was as surprised as the staff of the *Chicago Daily Tribune*, whose morning edition headline on November 3 blared: "DEWEY DEFEATS TRUMAN.") Most people were probably surprised, too, that it took weeks to figure out who won the 2000 presidential election. Surprises such as these make politics exciting. But the general claim that we can never predict election outcomes with a useful degree of certainty is manifestly false.

This is why the analogy to evolutionary biology is instructive. It is true that evolutionary biologists are not generally in the business of telling us how species will evolve—which traits will appear or prove adaptive, which will prove disadvantageous and disappear, or how the interactions between various species and their environments will alter appearance or behavior. By and large they do not try to predict. But that does not mean that they never can. Evolutionary biology does, after all, give us a purchase on these questions. It tells us a fair bit about how context affects species. Because we understood something about evolution, for example, there was little mystery about what would eventually happen to "European" species of honey bees in Central and North America once African "killer" bees escaped in Brazil in 1957. We knew that African bees would slowly spread northward, invade European hives, dominate and mate with European bees, and pass on undesirable traits such as irritability, aggressiveness, and proneness toward swarming. Of course, the presence

---

[19] Note that constraints on the amount of information available is not the reason why many theories of international politics cannot generate specific predictions. No amount of additional information about the relative material capabilities of states will transform Kenneth Waltz's theory of Great Power war into a predictive theory. No amount of additional information about the relative capabilities of the United States and Iraq would have led theories of deterrence and compellence to predict that Iraq would refuse to withdraw from Kuwait.

of European bee genes in the mixed offspring has moderated some of the nastier traits of African bees. The 1960s' nightmare scenarios of giant swarms of lethal, vicious bees marauding the American landscape will clearly never come to pass. But Africanized bees have arrived in the United States, and the predicted evolutionary effects, for the most part, are indeed coming to pass—more than forty years after the first alarm sounded.[20]

With respect to the third question, the answer must surely be that prediction is a desirable goal, for two reasons. First, theories are more useful if, in addition to helping us explain events, they also help us foresee them. Scholarship serves policy best when it lengthens the shadow of the future. But in addition to this, prediction also provides the best possible test of theory. With loose concepts and vague postulates, any theory will be able to make post hoc explanations trivially easy, rendering the theory unfalsifiable. Consider the theory of deterrence and the question of whether Soviet Premier Nikita Khrushchev would attempt to deploy missiles secretly to Cuba.[21] In 1962 American policy makers and analysts widely agreed that Khrushchev would not attempt such a deployment because it would be "irrational" for him to do so in the face of American deterrent threats.[22] Such an attempt would trigger a grave confrontation in which Khrushchev could not hope to prevail, and thus he would have no choice but to back down. If the gamble were to pay off, Khrushchev would certainly stand to gain. But the cost/benefit calculus was clear: the deployment was a very bad gamble indeed. Nevertheless, Khrushchev gambled. Yet retrospective analyses had no difficulty whatsoever reexplaining Khrushchev's behavior as a rational gamble.[23] The very same concepts that led to a confident forecast that deterrence would succeed had no difficulty in retrospect accounting for its failure. If deterrence theory were specified pre-

---

[20] Mark L. Winston, *Killer Bees.*

[21] The relevant literature is voluminous. For discussion of rational deterrence theory in its more formal presentation, see Christopher Achen and Duncan Snidal, "Rational Deterrence Theory and Comparative Case Analysis"; George W. Downs, "The Rational Deterrence Debate"; Paul Huth and Bruce Russett, "What Makes Deterrence Work?"; Huth and Russett, "Testing Deterrence Theory"; Robert Jervis, "Deterrence and Perception"; Robert Jervis, Richard Ned Lebow, and Janice Gross Stein, *Psychology & Deterrence*; Jervis, "Rational Deterrence Theory"; Lebow and Stein, "Rational Deterrence Theory"; Lebow and Stein, *When Does Deterrence Succeed and How Do We Know?*; Lebow and Stein, "Deterrence"; Lebow, "Deterrence and Threat Assessment"; Scott Sagan, "History, Analogy, and Deterrence Theory"; Frank C. Zagare, "Rationality and Deterrence."

[22] Only Director of Central Intelligence John McCone and Senator Kenneth Keating (R-NY) predicted the deployment in advance. See generally James G. Blight and David A. Welch, eds., *Intelligence and the Cuban Missile Crisis*; Peter S. Usowski, "John McCone and the Cuban Missile Crisis."

[23] Arnold L. Horelick, "The Cuban Missile Crisis." Cf. also Raymond L. Garthoff, "US Intelligence in the Cuban Missile Crisis"; Mary S. McAuliffe, ed., *CIA Documents on the Cuban Missile Crisis.*

cisely enough to generate clear predictions, the Cuban missile crisis would have provided a valuable test of the theory. Instead, it simply provided an opportunity to reinterpret history so as to fit the theory.

It is, in any case, important not to misunderstand the nature of prediction. All predictions are probabilistic. It is never possible to predict events with absolutely perfect accuracy. This is as true for physics as it is for social science. The margins of error in physics are small; they are much larger in international politics.[24] For this reason, it is perhaps desirable to speak of anticipation rather than prediction. To be able to anticipate important world events is not to be 100 percent certain that they will occur. It is merely to have good reasons for believing them to be likely. We can expect no more, but neither should we seek less.[25]

The Case for a Decision-Based Theory of Behavior

It is clear that there are good reasons to search for theories that will help us anticipate state behavior. The question arises, however, what kind of theory might succeed, given the various problems I have identified? Practically speaking, is useful anticipation a hopeless goal?

I mentioned at the outset that important events in international politics surprise us partly because of the nature of the subject matter, and partly because of the way we typically attempt to understand it. The interactions between these make it difficult for us to anticipate the course of world events. What, exactly, are we doing wrong?

Contrary to an increasingly popular belief, the problem is not really in the particular vision of theory that has inspired much of the scholarship on international relations over the last few decades. This vision of theory is drawn from the natural sciences and has its roots in the positivist tradition. According to this vision, explanation consists in subsuming the particular under the general, and progress consists in extending the umbrella of explanation to cover an ever-increasing number of seemingly disparate phenomena. On this view, parsimony and portability are highly desirable attributes of theory. All other things being equal, better theories are simpler and cover a broader range of behavior.[26]

---

[24] In physics we can often attach meaningful numbers to our margins of error as well; in International Relations, we generally cannot.

[25] For related discussion, see Christopher J. Fettweis, "Evaluating IR's Crystal Balls."

[26] Imre Lakatos, *The Methodology of Scientific Research Programmes*, vol. 1; Imre Lakatos and Alan Musgrave, eds., *Criticism and the Growth of Knowledge*.

Among philosophers, positivism has fallen into a certain amount of disrepute.[27] The reasons for this have to do with its ontological and epistemological commitments, which some people would argue are difficult to vindicate in terms of its own rather demanding standards of knowledge and inference.[28] Critics of positivism in social science often attack what they see as its commitments to a rigid separation between observer and observed, to a sharp distinction between facts and values, and to a correspondence theory of truth.[29] They insist that there is no objective social "reality" independent of our experience or constructions of it, and hence objective "knowledge" of such a world is impossible. What passes for knowledge at any given time, many critics argue, is, in fact, distorted by unequal relations of power. For all of these reasons, the goal of "explaining" disparate social "facts" is illusory. We can, at most, "understand" the social world, by interpreting it.[30]

This is not my complaint. That is not to say that critics of positivism make no good points. We must all acknowledge that the world as it is, the world as it is studied, and the world as it is known are not, and cannot be, precisely the same things. We must also acknowledge that what scientists see depends in part upon how they look and what they look for. Thus we must concede to the critics that there is no perfectly objective world to be studied perfectly objectively, and that the quest for a body of statements about the world that corresponds precisely to that world is ultimately vain. But as far as I can tell, this is only to concede that error and uncertainty are unavoidable—and that is something all scientists who understand their work as falling broadly within the positivist tradition would readily concede anyway.[31] The crucial question is whether the error and uncertainty are tolerable, and that depends upon the answer to the question, "Tolerable for what?" Our fault tolerance will be much greater if we are grinding a mirror for shaving than it would be for the Hubble space telescope. Error and uncertainty are not always

[27] See, e.g., Hilary Putnam, *Reason, Truth, and History*; Richard Rorty, *Philosophy and the Mirror of Nature*.

[28] An "ontology" tells us what kinds of things exist. Positivist ontology refuses to acknowledge the reality of anything neither directly observable nor observable through its effects. "Epistemology" is the study of knowledge. Positivism holds that we can only know things through experience. Positivism therefore embraces the scientific method as a means of learning about the world.

[29] A correspondence theory of truth holds that true propositions "correspond" to objective features of the world: i.e., that there is a kind of one-to-one mapping between features of the world and (true) statements about it.

[30] The best entrée to these issues is Hollis and Smith, *Explaining and Understanding International Relations*.

[31] I make these points at somewhat greater length in my review of Richard Wyn Jones, *Security, Strategy, and Critical Theory*.

so radical as to undermine our confidence in any general statements about the world whatsoever, nor so pervasive that we have no grounds whatsoever for preferring one statement about the world (for example, that the Earth is round) to another (for example, that it is flat). Positive science is not quite the pristine activity that we would like it to be, but that is less a criticism of science than of our unrealistic expectations about it. Moreover, positivism has a number of compelling virtues. Chief among these are its demanding standards. The clarity of its rules of judgment and inference makes science a truly public activity and permits a genuine community of scholarship. It also provides built-in checks against the characteristic sins of its "postpositivist" competitors: vague standards of knowledge and inference, stealthy truth claims, idiosyncratic analysis, and no way of distinguishing good theory from bad.[32]

Nor is my complaint that positivism tends toward generalization and abhors the particular. To be able to speak at great length about an individual event is a fine thing, but it is surely even better to be able to relate it to other events in a way that reveals some deeper unity between them—especially if the discovery of patterns, trends, or relationships then permits forecasting. Parsimony, too, is a fine goal, though a greatly misunderstood one. Parsimony merely tells us that we should prefer the simpler theory to the more complex when each performs equally well. As such, it is an injunction against unnecessary overhead. But parsimony is rarely relevant to the study of international relations, since it is rarely the case that two competing theories perform equally well. Thus the occasion for employing the parsimony criterion as a tie-breaker almost never arises in practice.

So what, then, is my complaint? My complaint is that the inspiration of natural science has encouraged a preoccupation with relating behavior to environmental stimuli and constraints. Put another way, the positivists among us find Skinnerian behaviorism too alluring. When combined with the pursuit of efficiency and portability, this preoccupation generates a body of general, abstract, deductive theory ill-suited to explaining or predicting the behavior of actors operating in a context characterized by small-n events, reflexivity, subjectivity, willful strategy, indeterminate parameters, idiosyncratic preferences, and theory/praxis interactions. In such a context, the behavior of actors depends heavily upon how they construe the situations they face. The problem is that there is no necessary correspondence between those constructions and measurable parameters. The laws of physics may work very well for describing and predicting the movements of the planets, once we fix values for their masses, positions,

---

[32] For further discussion, see Steve Smith, Ken Booth, and Marysia Zalewski, eds., *International Theory.*

and velocities; but no matter how precisely we fix the masses, positions, and velocities of children on a playground, we will never manage a similar feat. I submit that states much more closely resemble children than planets.

The drawbacks of this impulse are amplified by the pervasiveness of the levels-of-analysis organizing device, which largely defines the lines of debate among International Relations theorists today.[33] Scholars who seek efficient theory relating behavior to environmental constraints are naturally drawn to ask whether the main pressures and constraints are to be found (for example) at the level of the international system ("all politics is power politics"), within individual states ("all politics is domestic politics"), within governmental institutions ("where you stand depends upon where you sit"), or within individual decision makers' heads ("personality is everything").[34] This is not necessarily a bad question to ask. But if we get hung up on it, there will inevitably be a lack of fit between theories organized along levels-of-analysis lines and the classes of state behavior they seek to explain wherever the states exhibiting the behavior in question respond differently to similar cues or respond to fundamentally different cues in the first place. Take, for example, the Crimean War, which arose out of a dispute between Louis Napoleon of France and Tsar Nicholas I of Russia over the disposition of Christian shrines in the Holy Lands, and over the protection of the Christian subjects of the Ottoman empire. Nicholas's policy was shaped primarily by his faith, by his role as spiritual head of the Orthodox church, and by his interpretation of treaties. Louis Napoleon's policy was shaped primarily by a domestic political imperative (placating the Ultramontanes) and a diplomatic goal (subverting the Holy Alliance). British policy was shaped at the elite level by a strategic concern (a desire to prevent Russian encroachment on the Turkish straits) mediated by a cognitive error (the misperception that Russia had such a goal), pushed along by a public inflamed by a Russian naval action (the attack on Sinope).[35] The war was, in short, the product of

---

[33] The classic statements are Kenneth N. Waltz, *Man, the State and War*, and J. David Singer, "The Levels of Analysis Problem in International Relations." Cf. also Jack S. Levy, "Contending Theories of International Conflict."

[34] On the relationship between levels of analysis and agent-structure interactions, see Hollis and Smith, *Explaining and Understanding International Relations*; Alexander Wendt, "Bridging the Theory/Meta-Theory Gap in International Relations"; Hollis and Smith, "Beware of Gurus"; Wendt, "Levels of Analysis vs. Agents and Structures: Part III"; Hollis and Smith, "Structure and Action: Further Comment." Explicit attempts to theorize across levels of analysis are comparatively rare. A prominent exception is Robert Putnam, "Diplomacy and Domestic Politics," which, notably, has not given rise to a rigorous body of theory, nor to systematic tests of propositions. See, e.g., Peter B. Evans, Harold K. Jacobson, and Robert D. Putnam, eds., *Double-Edged Diplomacy*.

[35] For discussion, see David A. Welch, *Justice and the Genesis of War*, pp. 48–75.

forces operating at all levels of analysis, and it provides equally good (or bad) evidence for any particular theory of war that would privilege causes at any one. If the Crimean War is typical of wars in general, then attempting to theorize about the causes of wars by looking for constraints at any particular level of analysis will not prove to be particularly productive.

One possible response is to ratchet back our aspirations—that is, to pursue highly contingent, middle-range theories with narrow scope conditions, rather than grand theories or theories articulated at higher levels of generality.[36] But this move is problematic, essentially because it would aggravate the small-n problem without giving us increased purchase on the other problems that I argued make prediction so difficult in international politics. In essence, the move retains the presumption that state behavior is best explained with reference to measurable parametric constraints, and it is this presumption, rather than the breadth of theory, that is the source of the difficulty.

A preferable response is to tailor theory to the subject matter—or, to put it another way, to identify the kind of theory for which the various obstacles to prediction I identified are not obstacles at all. This response points in the direction of decision-based theory.[37]

All state behavior is the product of human decisions. We talk about the interests, preferences, and behavior of *states*, but this is merely a convenient shorthand (and one I will freely indulge myself) for the goals and choices of individual human beings who make the decisions that result in the behavior we observe.[38] If various aspects of the ways in which leaders of states make decisions frustrate the attempt to predict state behavior by looking for patterns in the environmental contexts of decisions, then perhaps it would be fruitful to look for the patterns we need in the decisions themselves.

One advantage of this approach is that it circumvents the levels-of-analysis problem entirely. Decision makers can take their cues from any level of analysis, but this will not fundamentally alter the structure of a decision.

[36] Timothy J. McKeown, "The Limitations of 'Structural' Theories of Commercial Policy"; Benjamin A. Most and Harvey Starr, "International Relations Theory, Foreign Policy Substitutability, and 'Nice' Laws."

[37] The seminal text is Richard C. Snyder, H. W. Bruck, and Burton Sapin, eds., *Foreign Policy Decision-Making.*

[38] All theories are simplifications, and to get the analysis off the ground I will begin with what will seem a particularly unrealistic assumption: that foreign policy decisions can be treated as though they were made by unitary actors. Such decisions generally are the product of group deliberations, of course, and the dynamics of group decision making may be an important complication. See, e.g., Zeev Maoz, *National Choices and International Processes*, pp. 21–25; see also Irving L. Janis, *Groupthink*; Paul 't Hart, *Groupthink in Government*; Jeanne Longley and Dean G. Pruitt, "Groupthink." In the next chapter I will take up

To make a decision, leaders must evaluate their environment in the light of their values and goals, identify a set of options, and make a choice from among those options. This is true whether they concern themselves primarily with strategic, domestic political, governmental, cultural, normative, or other factors; whether or not they react consciously to prior events; and whether or not they think strategically. What we must decide is whether there are any patterns in the way in which decision makers perform the basic tasks of processing information and making choices that can constitute explanations, and that will facilitate anticipation.

THE CASE FOR A THEORY OF FOREIGN POLICY CHANGE

A decision is the output of a process of deliberation. The inputs of the process are the decision maker's goals. The processing consists mainly in trying to decide how best to achieve those goals. To make sense of a decision, then, we need to know something both about a decision maker's goals and about his or her calculations.

What, in general, do we know about what states want? The everyday discourse of International Relations would lead us to believe that we know a great deal. We speak all the time of "the national interest," "power," and "security" as the things states pursue, and we tend to try to explain what states do by invoking them.[39] To a large extent, our comfort with (and our confidence in) concepts such as these is a reflection of the dominance of the Realist paradigm in the postwar North American study of international politics, which is built upon the assumption that when states act, they do so for purposes of either self-aggrandizement or self-preservation. As Robert Gilpin puts it, Realism assumes "the primacy in all political life of power and security in human motivation."[40] A certain version of Realism—what James Mayall calls "soft-line" Realism—

---

this issue and attempt to show that, for the purposes of anticipation, it is not only a manageable complication, but perhaps even a useful one.

[39] The concept of "the national interest" is especially unhelpful because of its pervasive ambiguity. Does the term refer to the interest of all, of most, or of the most important in society? Does it refer to a distinctive interest of the state vis-à-vis societal interests? Does it refer to the interest of the political community as a whole (as understood, for example, by the enlightened) vis-à-vis other states? Is its source to be found within the state, or in the relations of states? Cf. Stephen Krasner, *Defending the National Interest*; Morgenthau, *Politics among Nations*; David A. Welch, "Morality and 'the National Interest'."

[40] Robert G. Gilpin, "The Richness of the Tradition of Political Realism," p. 305; cf. also Gilpin, "The Theory of Hegemonic War," p. 593; Joseph M. Grieco, "Anarchy and the Limits of Cooperation," pp. 487–488.

assumes that states also seek order.[41] Classical or utopian Liberalism stressed the pursuit of welfare.[42]

But whenever one seeks to characterize the central motivations of states in terms of abstract concepts, at least four problems arise. First, the vagueness of these concepts undermines their usefulness. It may well be that, at an abstract level, states generally prefer more power to less, or more security to less, or more welfare to less, but this will not help us explain or predict state behavior, because these preferences underdetermine choice. In many cases—and in perhaps most of the interesting ones—intelligent and well-informed people can reasonably disagree about what course of action these preferences prescribe. Did isolationism safeguard or erode American security in the interwar period? Was the reunification of Germany good, bad, or indifferent, from the perspective of Soviet security, French security, American security—or, for that matter, German security? Will NATO be better off or worse off with the Baltic states as full members? Does NAFTA promote or undermine American welfare? Answering the question "What do states want?" in a vague, abstract way moves them no closer to figuring out how to get it.

Second—and as a corollary to the first point—articulating state goals at a highly abstract level invites tautologous inferences that will undermine any serious attempt to explain or predict behavior in terms of them. The concept of "power" is notorious in this regard. Consider, for example, the following passage by Geoffrey Blainey:

> One generalization about war aims can be offered with confidence. The aims are simply varieties of power. The vanity of nationalism, the will to spread an ideology, the protection of kinsmen in an adjacent land, the desire for more territory or commerce, the avenging of a defeat or insult, the craving for greater national strength or independence, the wish to impress or cement alliances—all these represent power in different wrappings. The conflicting aims of rival nations are always conflicts of power.[43]

Clearly, if all war aims can be characterized as the pursuit of power, then the assertion that "states pursue power" will be vacuous. By the same token, if whatever states do can be construed as attempts to promote

---

[41] James Mayall, *Nationalism and International Society*, p. 15.

[42] For a useful attempt to update and revise Liberalism, with an eye toward offering a true paradigmatic competitor to Realism, see Andrew Moravcsik, "Taking Preferences Seriously." It is possible to argue that at least early formulations of Neoliberal Institutionalism also presumed the centrality of welfare as a motivation. Cf. Robert O. Keohane, *After Hegemony*; Grieco, "Anarchy and the Limits of Cooperation"; Robert O. Keohane, "Neoliberal Institutionalism."

[43] Geoffrey Blainey, *The Causes of War*, p. 150.

"the national interest," or to enhance their security or welfare, then these concepts cannot inform our understanding of state behavior. Tautologies explain nothing.

Third, even if it were true that states generally do have these abstract preferences (i.e., they prefer more power to less; more security to less; more welfare to less, etc.)—and even if we could operationalize them in a meaningful way—this information cannot help us explain or predict behavior unless we also know two other things: (1) how states integrate these preferences and handle trade-offs between them;[44] and (2) which values specific choice problems engage. It may be, for example, that a state's most important foreign policy goal is security from armed attack. But relatively few states ever have to worry about that. Typically, armed forces are insurance policies against unlikely perils. Thus the goal rarely informs foreign policy choices, and it provides little helpful information for anticipating state behavior.[45]

Fourth, and finally, there are no compelling reasons to make strong assumptions about state preferences, and many compelling reasons not to. In this respect, international politics provides an interesting contrast with (say) highly competitive markets, where an assumption about actors' goals—even an inaccurate assumption—can be useful.[46] If we wish to predict production volumes in a highly competitive market for homogeneous goods, for example, it is useful to make two incorrect assumptions: first, that the market is perfectly competitive; and second, that firms are rational profit-maximizers. In a perfectly competitive market, firms are price-takers and maximize profit by producing until the marginal cost of production equals marginal revenue. An economist needs only to estimate the demand function and the factor costs of production to predict production volumes because, if the market is competitive enough, only the firms that just so happen to produce at or near the optimal level (i.e., they behave "as if" they were maximizing profits) will survive to be observed. Their actual goals might have been something quite different: for instance, beating last year's quarterly result, achieving a certain debt-equity ratio, fund-

---

[44] E.g., what does the security-welfare indifference curve look like? Is it the same for all states, or is this a variable? If it varies, what determines how it varies? Certainly the United States and the Soviet Union chose to make the classic "guns vs. butter" trade-off at different points. The USSR consistently spent more on defense (as a proportion of GDP) than did the United States throughout the Cold War.

[45] Joseph Nye writes: "Security is like oxygen—you tend not to notice it until you begin to lose it, but once that occurs there is nothing else that you will think about." Joseph S. Nye, Jr., "The Case for Deep Engagement," p. 91.

[46] The classic treatment is Milton Friedman, "The Methodology of Positive Economics." For further discussion, see Janice Gross Stein and David A. Welch, "Rational and Psychological Approaches to the Study of International Conflict."

ing a dividend, and so forth. But the outcome we wish to predict—production volume—will be roughly the same anyway, simply because poor performers will be selected out of the system. We can get away with an inaccurate simplifying assumption here precisely because a highly competitive market in homogeneous goods structurally constrains actors according to a small number of fixed and knowable parameters. But as I have already discussed, decision problems in international politics are generally ill-structured and are far less tractable analytically. Leaders are often uncertain about the stakes, and their organizational imperatives are clear only when stated at an extremely high level of abstraction ("state survival" or "security," "power," "the national interest," etc.). They must themselves decide what is at issue, and how to go about pursuing their interests. Moreover, they are unlikely to suffer much if they make mistakes. States rarely die or are selected out of the system. It is therefore not the case that states behaving "as if" they pursued a particular goal or set of goals—and only one such set—will survive to be observed.

Whether there are clear and strong patterns to be found in state goals is, in any case, an empirical question. But scholars of International Relations have not systematically explored it. We know that there are no iron laws about state interests—not even that all states at all times seek self-preservation. Counterexamples include Austria in 1937, Denmark in 1940, the USSR in 1991, and Czechoslovakia in 1992. We also know that the goals assumed by Realism, when specified nontautologically, are sometimes only weakly evident even in cases where they ought to be prevalent.[47] But beyond this there is relatively little that we can say.

As an alternative to making assumptions about state goals, we might attempt to generate them by means of an ancillary theory. That is to say, we might attempt to generate hypotheses about the sources of state goals, or the conditions under which states should be expected to pursue some goals rather than others. Answers to the question, "Where do state interests come from?" are implied by virtually every theory of, or approach to, international politics. Structural Realists locate the ultimate sources of a state's interests in a particular conception of human nature—fearful, preoccupied with survival, and predisposed to make strong distinctions between self and other—as it responds to the incentives of the structure of the international system (where "structure" is conceived rather sparely as a simple distribution of power).[48] Constructivists, in contrast, are suspicious of claims about human nature and locate the ultimate sources of state interests in the interactions of states within a "structure" conceived

---

[47] Welch, *Justice and the Genesis of War.*

[48] In addition to Waltz, *Theory of International Politics*, see esp. Jonathan Mercer, "Anarchy and Identity."

in a sociological sense—not merely as a distributional attribute, but as a context of norms and shared meanings.[49] Others locate them in class interests,[50] societal interests,[51] state-society relations,[52] bureaucratic rivalries,[53] belief systems,[54] or interesting combinations of these.[55] In sum, there is no shortage of views on where state interests come from. And each permits a plausible description or reconstruction of the interests at work in specific historical cases. But there is no compelling reason to believe that any one of them can be refined into the powerful predictor of state interests that we would need if we were to rely upon an ancillary theory to generate inputs for a broader theory of state behavior.

Part of the problem here is that relatively few of these approaches are well-suited to generating expectations about state interests at a useful level of specificity. In order to anticipate state behavior, we need to identify states' preferences-over-outcomes for particular stakes (where by "stakes" I mean specific goods at issue in specific interactions between states—e.g., Alsace-Lorraine, access to the Japanese rice market, the credibility of the American nuclear guarantee to Europe). *Interests*, which I take to be synonymous with *goals*, must be articulated in a way that is policy- or situation-specific (e.g., the recovery of Alsace-Lorraine, an open Japanese rice market, a highly credible nuclear guarantee) These in turn can serve *values* (wealth, national honor, security from attack, etc.); but, as we have seen, values are too abstract to employ as a basis for prediction. Only those approaches that permit the identification of preferences-over-outcomes for stakes for the relevant players, and also provide a mechanism for integrating or otherwise translating those into an aggregate state interest, could, in principle, serve as an ancillary theory. This criterion would appear, at a minimum, to eliminate Structural Realist, Constructivist, Marxist, and Statist contenders.

But beyond this, when we examine and attempt to explain states' actual preferences-over-outcomes for particular stakes, we discover enormous variation in their sources, considerable historical contingency, path-dependence, and complex interaction effects. We discover that, while it

[49] Alexander Wendt, "The Agent-Structure Problem in International Relations Theory"; David Dessler, "What's at Stake in the Agent-Structure Debate?"; Wendt, "Anarchy Is What States Make of It"; Wendt, "Collective Identity Formation and the International State"; Wendt, *Social Theory of International Politics*.

[50] Immanuel Wallerstein, "The Rise and Future Demise of the World Capitalist System"; Wallerstein, *The Politics of the World Economy*; Bernard Semmel, ed., *Marxism and the Science of War*.

[51] E.g., James Rosenau, ed., *Domestic Sources of Foreign Policy*.

[52] Peter J. Katzenstein, ed., *Between Power and Plenty*.

[53] Morton H. Halperin, *Bureaucratic Politics and Foreign Policy*.

[54] Steve Chan, "Rationality, Bureaucratic Politics and Belief Systems."

[55] Jack Snyder, *Myths of Empire*.

is commonly possible to provide compelling explanations of why states conceive of their interests in particular ways, doing so typically requires jerry-rigging an explanation out of a hodgepodge body of theory drawn not only from political science, but also from sociology, psychology, and perhaps even anthropology.[56] We also discover that arbitrary factors sometimes play a crucial role in determining why states conceive of their interests in one way rather than another—which in turn can have an important effect on the course of the interactions between states. We do find certain recurrent themes. In particular, we find that conceptions of state interests are often usefully viewed as expressions of group identities shaped by socialization processes. But, as the engineers would say, the signal-to-noise ratio is low.

This has two important implications. First, it means that any particular ancillary theory of interest-formation will have a whopper of a residual-variance problem. It will generate interests tolerably well only in very rare cases and, by implication, will generate either incorrect interests or no determinate interests at all in most cases. Second, it means that a predictive theory of state behavior, for which we need either robust assumptions about state interests or an ancillary theory to generate them, is essentially unworkable. What is to be done?

A possible way out of the difficulty is to seek to base predictions not on explanations of why states behave the way they do in general—i.e., on a theory of state behavior—but on explanations of why they deviate from their prior behavior—i.e., on a theory of foreign policy *change*. In this approach, we take the world as it is, without inquiring as to how it came to be that way, and concentrate merely on looking for patterns that will predict discontinuities. This is akin to reversing figure and ground: we do not look for patterns in what states, in general, do, from which perspective changes in the behavior of individual states represent anomalies to be explained away (or, in the case of some theories, to be ignored); instead, we look for patterns in how states change their behavior, from which perspective what they do in general is irrelevant. This does not, of course, free us of the necessity of determining what states want. A decision-based theory of foreign policy change still requires that we identify goals. But it permits us to treat goals as exogenous inputs. It frees us of having to explain them, and—if things work out right—it makes the empirical task of identifying state goals relatively manageable, because the theory itself will direct us toward indicators that signal the possibility of change in a specific case, and thus the necessity of mobilizing resources to identify with precision the interests that will help us refine our prediction about the change.

---

[56] Kimura and Welch, "Specifying 'Interests.'"

What we really want, then, is not a theory of *international politics*, or a *theory of foreign policy*, but a *theory of foreign policy change*. In the next chapter, I shall attempt to rise to the occasion.[57]

---

[57] Some might object that we already have a theory of foreign policy change, and that we don't need another one. Bruce Bueno de Mesquita and his colleagues, for example, claim a successful point-prediction rate of over 90 percent for what they describe as an expected utility model based upon Black's median voter theorem. (Duncan Black, *Voting in Committees and Elections*; Bruce Bueno de Mesquita, David Newman, and Alvin Rabushka, *Forecasting Political Events*; Samuel S. G. Wu and Bruce Bueno de Mesquita, "Assessing the Dispute in the South China Sea.") This is an impressive rate of accomplishment, if indeed it is accurate—though apparently most of the cases to which the model has been applied are classified, and so we cannot tell.

Bueno de Mesquita's model predicts choice as a function of a contest between interested parties conceived as a decision-making group. It does so on the basis of three variables: the capabilities of each; the preferred outcome of each; and the salience of the issue to each. The model exogenizes all three variables, as well as the identification of relevant parties. The model predicts policy choice as the vector sum of the weighted preferences of the parties.

This representation is intuitively appealing. However, it is not a *theory of foreign policy change*; it is a *model of policy choice*. Models are representations of theories through which we assess the power of theories. Notice that the theory behind Bueno de Mesquita's model is left implicit. Were we to make it explicit, we would best characterize it as a theory of group decision making, not an expected utility theory of choice, because it neither operationalizes nor even requires the concept of expected utility. It is wholly indifferent to the sources or nature of the parties' preferences, their individual processes of decision, or their computational skills. As such it is not a "rational" model at all. This is not to say that it is not a predictive model. With good-quality, exogenously derived inputs, there is no reason why it might not enjoy a high rate of predictive success. For further discussion, see, e.g., Stein and Welch, "Rational and Psychological Approaches."

Notice, too, that if the patterns of behavior I predict in the next chapter hold, they would be reflected in the preferences and intensities of the relevant parties in Bueno de Mesquita's model. But the model itself would mask these patterns from view. Thus the theory I present in chapter 2 is not necessarily incompatible with Bueno de Mesquita's model. It is, instead, orthogonal.

Chapter 2

A THEORY OF FOREIGN POLICY CHANGE

IF THE BEHAVIOR of states changes so often and so radically that events will constantly overtake our attempts to anticipate them, or if the behavior of states changes capriciously, then a theory of foreign policy change will be unworkable. We may be able to finesse the multiple inputs problem, but we cannot get by without having some timely handle on how states match means to ends. Put another way, we can tolerate indeterminacy in goals, but we cannot tolerate indeterminacy both in goals and in calculations. There must be reliable patterns in how states match means to ends for us to anticipate policy changes once we identify what it is that states seek in particular cases.[1] If calculations are as idiosyncratic as interests seem to be, we must admit defeat and accept the fact that international politics will simply always surprise us. What are our grounds for optimism?

---

[1] A truly general theory of foreign policy change, however, must be agnostic as to the *mechanism* of change. Epistemic community explanations of change, for example, posit a precise mechanism: when adherents to an emerging scientific or technical consensus gain positions of influence within government, they can cause policy makers to redefine their conceptions of state interests, and/or to revise their judgments of the consequences of competing policy options. Emanuel Adler and Peter M. Haas, "Conclusion: Epistemic Communities, World Order and the Creation of a Reflective Research Program"; Peter M. Haas, "Introduction: Epistemic Communities and International Policy Coordination"; G. John Ikenberry, "Creating Yesterday's New World Order." It is certainly possible that foreign policy can change as a result of such a process, and there are cases where the descriptive fit is excellent—for example, in the seminal case of the Med Plan; Peter M. Haas, "Do Regimes Matter?" But this is by no means the only—or even a very common—mechanism of foreign policy change. It is easy to identify many cases of foreign policy change where the explanation simply does not apply. Studies comparing the relative explanatory power of epistemic-community explanations and other explanations of change are still relatively rare, but it is clear that the presence of an epistemic community—and its penetration of government—is neither a necessary nor a sufficient condition of policy change; Steven F. Bernstein, *The Compromise of Liberal Environmentalism*. Students of the causes of wars, for example, will have difficulty finding any cases whatsoever in which the notion of an epistemic community helps to explain a decision to wage war. A particular mechanism of foreign policy change does not imply a particular pattern of change, or vice versa.

Building Blocks

There are three bodies of theory that collectively suggest that significant foreign policy changes should be rare, and that when states change their behavior dramatically, they will do so for what are formally (if not substantively) similar reasons. These are organization theory; cognitive and motivational psychology; and prospect theory. Let us examine each in turn.

Organization Theory

Governments are complex organizations, and while relatively small numbers of people may be involved in making important foreign policy decisions, they do so in an institutional setting that influences what they know, how they frame foreign policy problems, and what they believe about their options. There is much greater stability in this institutional setting than there is in the international environment. This contributes to stability in what leaders believe about the world, and in how they deal with it. Moreover, the institutional setting itself imposes costs on policy change. No one pays costs happily, so all things considered, and everything else being equal, organizational considerations should contribute to policy inertia.

Now, none of this is to say that foreign policy decisions can be readily explained with reference solely to the interests and power of departments or bureaucrats. After decades of "bureaucratic politics" explanations of foreign policy making, there is little evidence to suggest that state behavior in general can be understood merely as a bureaucratic epiphenomenon.[2] But it does help to explain why there is often a considerable lag between changes in the international environment and decision makers' responses to them, and why decision makers will typically feel pressure not to deviate radically from the status quo. It helps us understand, in other words, why inertia is the normal condition and default expectation in international politics. Organizational structure, culture, and procedure are all relevant here.

At any given time, the institutions of government that play a role in shaping foreign policy are fixed in number, relate to each other in specific ways, have specific flow charts, and employ a specific set of strategies in pursuit of their organizational tasks. The number, structure, and strategies of organizations can and do change over time, of course, but resource constraints, transaction costs, internal politics, and the domestic environ-

---

[2] For more detailed discussion, see, e.g., Edward Rhodes, "Do Bureaucratic Politics Matter?"; Eric Stern and Bertjan Verbeek, "Whither the Study of Governmental Politics in Foreign Policymaking?"

ment in which organizations operate—in particular, the public legitimation of their activity—all generate pressures that dampen the pace, nature,
and extent of change.[3] So also does organizational history. The costs of
change increase when standards of procedure, assignment of tasks, and
allocation of authority become the subject of normative agreement. Hannan and Freeman note that normative agreement constrains adaptation
in at least two ways: first, by providing legitimate justifications beyond
self-interest for those who oppose it; and second, by precluding serious
consideration of certain responses to threats and opportunities in the environment. Few research universities, for example, consider adapting to declining enrollments by scrapping their undergraduate programs. This option simply challenges central organizational norms.[4] By the same token,
few states blessed with an absence of plausible threats of invasion—Canada, New Zealand, or Switzerland, for example—would consider disarm-
ing completely, because this would violate fundamental norms about the
functions of sovereign states.

Inertial pressures on organizational culture—that is to say, the formal
and informal rules of procedure, behavioral norms, tasks, rituals, jargon,
perceptions, shared memories, and shared beliefs that predominate and
shape activity within organizations—further contribute to the stability of
the organizational setting of policy.[5] To some extent, these inertial pressures seem to be a function of selection biases in recruitment and processes
of socialization.[6] Organizations, accordingly, tend to perceive and approach problems in similar ways over fairly long periods of time and have
difficulty adjusting their perceptions and approaches quickly in the light
of changing circumstances.

The day-to-day functioning of organizations contributes to stability in
two ways. First, most functions of organizations are heavily scripted. People charged with carrying out tasks rely heavily upon routines (standard
operating procedures, or SOPs). Routines are, of course, indispensable.
No organization could function without them. Nor are routines as rigid
as some people believe. Organizations can, and do, alter their routines

---

[3] Michael T. Hannan and John Freeman, "The Population Ecology of Organizations,"
p. 957.

[4] Michael T. Hannan and John Freeman, *Organizational Ecology*, p. 68. For further discussion, see generally pp. 66–90.

[5] The concept of organizational culture is admittedly rather vague, and some would argue
that this renders it problematic analytically. For discussion and a postmodern critique, see
Joanne Martin, *Cultures in Organizations*.

[6] See, e.g., Stephen T. Hosmer, *Constraints on U.S. Strategy in Third World Conflicts*,
pp. 14–15; Peyton V. Lyon and David Leyton-Brown, "Image and Policy Preference." Of
course, generational change is one mechanism by which organizational culture *can* evolve—
so it would be a mistake to think that recruitment and socialization prevent change entirely.

(one is tempted to say "routinely") when they find it necessary to do so. For these reasons, organizational routines do not lend themselves to simple "explanations" of foreign policy behavior.[7] But the fact that organizations are heavily scripted means that they privilege certain sources of information and process information in certain ways. It also means that changes in the ways in which they acquire or process information will be costly. Reasonably enough, organizations will not alter routines simply to realize uncertain, possibly transient marginal gains in efficiency or effectiveness. Indeed, the scripts themselves make it unlikely that organizations will always be able to know *that* certain changes would marginally improve performance. Second, resource pressures generally make it difficult for organizations to keep up with inputs and with demands. Information flows are often highly constrained, and leaders of organizations are typically but dimly aware not only of the international environment, but also of the activities of subordinates within their own organizations. A common coping mechanism is for organizations to adopt satisficing strategies.[8]

Collectively, these considerations imply that there is likely to be greater stability in the organizations charged with responding to the international environment than there will be in the environment itself.[9] This suggests that the foreign policy community will not be especially adept at anticipating change in the environment; will be slow to perceive it when it happens gradually; will be slow to evaluate its implications; and will be loath to pay the adjustment costs necessary to improve performance more than marginally. As a corollary, organizations are unlikely to recognize quickly, and to correct, systematic biases in the ways in which they collect and process information.

U.S. involvement in Vietnam provides a stark illustration. As I discuss in chapter 4, the primary object of American policy was to contain the spread of communism in Southeast Asia. But only well after the United States found itself deeply committed militarily did it become clear to U.S.

[7] Allison's "Model II," which proposed explaining foreign policy with reference to organizational routines, overstated the rigidity of SOPs and therefore overstated their potential explanatory power. Graham T. Allison, *Essence of Decision*. Perhaps partly for this reason, scholars of international politics did not take up Allison's invitation to pursue it. David A. Welch, "The Organizational Process and Bureaucratic Politics Paradigms."

[8] In contrast to an "optimizing" strategy, which seeks the *best possible* course of action, a satisficing strategy seeks merely the *first acceptable* option. Satisficing is a way of economizing on time, energy, and resources. See, e.g., Kenneth J. Arrow, *The Limits of Organization*; Richard Michael Cyert and James G. March, *A Behavioral Theory of the Firm*; James G. March and Johan P. Olsen, *Ambiguity and Choice in Organizations*; James G. March and Herbert A. Simon, *Organizations*; March and Simon, *Organizations*, 2nd ed.; Herbert A. Simon, "Rationality in Political Behavior"; Simon, *Administrative Behavior*; Simon, *Models of Bounded Rationality*.

[9] For related discussion, see Gary Goertz, *International Norms and Decision Making*.

decision makers that the policy had been premised on a fundamental misunderstanding of the adversary and a misdiagnosis of the threat. Far from
being a mere puppet of the "Sino-Soviet bloc," Ho Chi Minh was a Vietnamese nationalist who was wary of both Moscow and Beijing, who had
neither the capability nor the desire to conquer or subvert neighboring
states, and whose primary domestic appeal lay in his anticolonialism, not
in his profession of Marxism. The American attempt to divide the country
into two states, preserving a democratic South as a bulwark against a
communist North, was foredoomed because it ran against the grain of
Vietnamese nationalism. No partition of any kind, let alone one created
and underwritten by a foreign power, could hope to acquire domestic
legitimacy.[10] How is it that the United States made so many fundamental
diagnostic mistakes and took so long to recognize them? Part of the explanation must be organizational. Vietnam had been a French colony, and
hence responsibility for the region lay with the Europeanists in the Department of State. Many of these officials had little expertise on Southeast
Asia, and little time to acquire it, preoccupied as they were with strictly
European matters.[11] There were people in the intelligence community, the
foreign service, and universities who had a sophisticated understanding
of Vietnamese culture and politics, but for the most part their views were
systematically filtered out of the policy-making process because they chal-
lenged central beliefs and organizing concepts in the culture of the U.S.
foreign policy establishment. Indeed, many of the most knowledgeable
officials were hounded out during the McCarthy era precisely because
their views called into question the existence and threat of monolithic
communism. Thus the American foreign policy establishment was ill-
designed, ill-equipped, and ill-disposed to acquire and process the information necessary to avoid a disastrous policy.[12]

Inertia may also be reinforced by the fact that different organizations
and branches of government often have different priorities and perspectives. Competing pressures on policy from different directions tend to
generate compromises, deviations from which trigger costly struggles and
acrimonious debates. We should expect dramatic policy change only
when decision makers consider it absolutely imperative to confront these
struggles and debates, or when circumstances change so dramatically that
organizations that had previously disagreed on the appropriate direction
for policy can be brought closer to a new consensus. Again, this is not to

---

[10] Joseph Buttinger, *Vietnam: A Dragon Embattled*; Robert S. McNamara, *In Retrospect*;
Neil Sheehan et al., eds., *The Pentagon Papers*.
[11] Chester L. Cooper, *The Lost Crusade*.
[12] George McTurnan Kahin, *Intervention*; Robert S. McNamara et al., *Argument without
End*; Archimedes L. A. Patti, *Why Viet Nam?*

say that we can explain foreign policy change simply in terms of organizational interests; it is merely to say that organizational interests typically represent a drag on change in a way that tends to increase the stability of policy.

British defense policy between the two world wars provides a useful illustration. The end of the First World War represented an abrupt change in the policy-making environment that permitted a consensus within the British government on the necessity of dramatic cuts in defense spending and a reallocation of resources to other sectors. The naval budget, for example, shrank by 70 percent in just three years. In August 1919 the Cabinet instructed the armed services to plan on the assumption that Britain would not be engaged in another major war for at least a decade. This became a rolling planning assumption, and the "Ten Year Rule" guided decisions on appropriations, force structure, and deployment for most of the interwar period. Britain did not formally abandon the Ten Year Rule until 1932 and even then did not begin to reallocate significant resources to the defense sector for several years after that—long after the strategic and political assumptions underlying it had become untenable (see, e.g., figure 2.1). The Ten Year Rule had simply become too convenient. It was the central element of a complex bureaucratic compromise that was difficult to alter given the full range of needs and interests competing for governmental resources. The Ten Year Rule imperiled British security, however, because it inhibited the timely adjustment of defense expenditures to changes in the strategic environment.[13]

Richard Clarke's gripping account of U.S. counterterrorism efforts prior to 9/11 clearly illustrates all of these patterns and dynamics. Despite the growing al-Qaeda threat and the considerable information about it inside the American government, the sheer number of players, their competing interests, their parochial perspectives, their organizational cultures, their routines, imperfections in their information flows, and their competing demands stymied a timely adjustment to a new threat environment, with both tragic and world-historical consequences.[14] Organizational factors may not provide a fully sufficient explanation of this particular policy failure, but they clearly explain a good deal of the inertia behind it.

[13] See, e.g., Paul M. Kennedy, *The Rise and Fall of British Naval Mastery*, pp. 273–286. For other cases and discussion, see Dan Caldwell, "Bureaucratic Foreign Policy-Making"; Morton H. Halperin and Arnold Kanter, eds., *Readings in American Foreign Policy*; Roger Hilsman, *The Politics of Policy Making in Defense and Foreign Affairs*; David C. Kozak and James M. Keagle, eds., *Bureaucratic Politics and National Security*; James H. Lebovic, "Riding Waves or Making Waves?"; Hans Mouritzen, *Bureaucracy as a Source of Foreign Policy Inertia*.

[14] Clarke, *Against All Enemies*, chaps. 4–10.

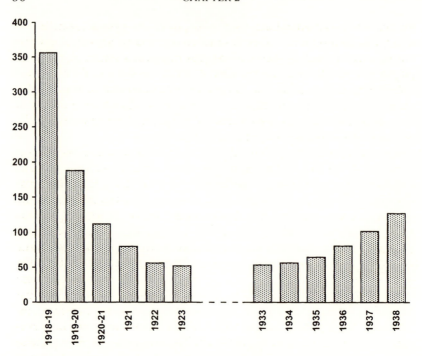

Fig. 2.1. British interwar naval spending (£millions).
Source: Paul M. Kennedy, *The Rise and Fall of British Naval Mastery*.

Cognitive and Motivational Psychology

Cognitive psychologists study how normal, everyday information-processing affects our perceptions, judgments, and choices. Motivational psychologists study how our perceptions, judgments, and choices are influenced by stress, emotion, and the drive to satisfy basic, deep-seated psychological needs.

Neither cognitive nor motivational psychology is terribly satisfying as *theory*. Decades of research have yielded an enormous body of insights into common patterns and tendencies people exhibit, but no coherent set of propositions with clearly specified scope conditions that we can easily take from the laboratory and rigorously apply to help us explain and predict behavior in the real world.[15] Fortunately, my goal here is not to

---

[15] Accordingly, neither cognitive nor motivational psychology has generated a true competitor to rational choice as a general theory of choice. For further discussion, see Richard Ned Lebow and Janice Gross Stein, "Afghanistan, Carter, and Foreign Policy Change"; Stein and Welch, "Rational and Psychological Approaches to the Study of International Conflict." A theory's "scope conditions" are the circumstances under which we should expect it to apply.

fix cognitive and motivational psychology, merely to exploit them. And—also fortunately—these bodies of research do have an important general thrust, notwithstanding their various gaps and tensions: namely, that people do not readily alter their beliefs about the world and do not easily confront their own mistakes. Once they are committed to a particular perspective, judgment, or course of action, it is difficult to get them to change their mind. Perfectly normal human psychology, in other words, contributes, on balance, to policy stability.

Cognitive psychologists have demonstrated that we rely heavily upon our prior beliefs to help us interpret new information and make sense of an ambiguous world. On the whole, this is a good thing. It enables us to conserve our meager cognitive resources, and it allows us to make timely responses to decision problems. But it can also lead us to make significant and systematic errors in judgment. Attribution theory, for example, examines how our "schemata"—i.e., our working sets of beliefs about some aspect of the world—influence how we interpret new information.[16] We tend to interpret information in such a way as to make it fit with our prior convictions. Typically, we do not correct errors in our schemata on the basis of a few pieces of discrepant information, unless the discrepant information is truly overwhelming. Instead, we allow our schemata to corrupt our interpretation of the evidence. Thus when someone we dislike does something indisputably nice, we are more likely to suspect that some dastardly ulterior motive is at work than we are to change our evaluation of his or her character. Similarly, an American president who has an image of an enemy as aggressive, opportunistic, cunning, and committed to the destruction of the United States will tend to interpret everything the enemy does as deliberate and directed toward that goal—even when the behavior fits equally well with the hypothesis that it was motivated by fear, insecurity, or reasons unrelated to the rivalry (for example, domestic politics), and even when it more accurately reflects the enemy's weakness or incompetence.[17]

---

[16] A schema may be a concept of the self (self-schema), other individuals (person schema), groups (role-schema), or sequences of events in the environment (scripts). See, e.g., Harold Kelley, *Causal Schemata and the Attribution Process*; Roger Schank and Robert Abelson, *Scripts, Plans, Goals, and Understanding*; Perry W. Thorndyke and Barbara Hayes-Roth, "The Use of Schemata in the Acquisition and Transfer of Knowledge"; Lynne M. Reder and John R. Anderson, "A Partial Resolution of the Paradox of Inference"; Shelley T. Fiske, "Schema-Based Versus Piecemeal Politics"; Richard R. Lau and David O. Sears, "Social Cognition and Political Cognition"; Stephen G. Walker, "The Impact of Personality Structure and Cognitive Processes upon American Foreign Policy Decisions"; Shelley T. Fiske and Susan E. Taylor, *Social Cognition*, p. 140; Shanto Iyengar, *Is Anyone Responsible?*; Shanto Iyengar and William J. McGuire, *Explorations in Political Psychology*.

[17] For further discussion and historical examples, see, e.g., Raymond L. Garthoff, *Détente and Confrontation*; Garthoff, *Reflections on the Cuban Missile Crisis*; Ole R. Holsti,

It is noteworthy that we create schemata readily, and often on the basis of what is, in fact, relatively little good-quality information (or perhaps no good-quality information at all). But once formed, our schemata resist change. We have, as it were, a double standard of evidence. We require much more evidence to change our beliefs about the world than we require to establish them in the first place.[18]

Of course, change does occur. Our beliefs are not unshakable. From time to time, we will decide that we are mistaken. There is some uncertainty as to whether this is more likely to occur gradually or suddenly. Some evidence suggests that an accumulation of contradictory information from a variety of sources, on a variety of issues, and over an extended period of time is more likely to prompt a change in our schemata than a few isolated instances.[19] As we think about information that is inconsistent with our beliefs, we incorporate into our schemata the conditions under which the schemata do *not* hold, and this permits gradual change and adjustment.[20] This is the *Pride and Prejudice* model. Elizabeth Bennet only gradually changed her opinion of Mr. Darcy on the basis of a large number of relatively minor pieces of information that did not fit with her earlier image (an image that she had formed on the basis of a single initial interaction). On the other hand, historical examples of dramatic changes in leaders' images of the enemy, or judgments about the nature of security threats, often involve acute crises or a small number of intensely frightening events that force leaders to rethink their core beliefs profoundly. It took near brushes with inadvertent nuclear war, for example, to convince John F.

"Cognitive Dynamics and Images of the Enemy"; Holsti, "Cognitive Dynamics and Images of the Enemy: Dulles and Russia"; Richard Ned Lebow and Janice Gross Stein, *We All Lost the Cold War*; Lee Ross and Constance Stillinger, "Barriers to Conflict Resolution."

[18] Lee Ross, Mark R. Lepper, and Michael Hubbard, "Perseverance in Self Perception and Social Perception"; Lau and Sears, "Social Cognition and Political Cognition"; Yaacov Y. I. Vertzberger, *The World in Their Minds*. Some psychological research actually indicates that exposure to discrepant information *strengthens* rather than undermines schemata, because of the process of reasoning we use to explain away apparent inconsistencies. Craig A. Anderson, "Abstract and Concrete Data in the Perseverance of Social Theories"; Craig A. Anderson, Mark R. Lepper, and Lee Ross, "Perseverance of Social Theories"; Jennifer Crocker, "Judgment of Covariation by Social Perceivers"; Edward R. Hirt and Steven J. Sherman, "The Role of Prior Knowledge in Explaining Hypothetical Events"; James A. Kulik, "Confirmatory Attribution and the Perpetuation of Social Beliefs"; Chris S. O'Sullivan and Francis T. Durso, "Effect of Schema-Incongruent Information on Memory for Stereotypical Attributes"; Thomas K. Srull and Robert S. Wyer, "Person Memory and Judgment"; Robert S. Wyer, Jr., and Sallie E. Gordon, "The Recall of Information about Persons and Groups." Note, however, that attribution theorists do not assert that people's schemata necessarily form a coherent whole. We typically tolerate some inconsistent beliefs.

[19] Jennifer Crocker, Darlene B. Hannah, and Renee Weber, "Person Memory and Causal Attributions."

[20] E. T. Higgins and J. A. Bargh, "Social Cognition and Social Perception," p. 386.

Kennedy in 1962, and Ronald Reagan in 1984, that the greatest threat to peace lay not in insufficiently strongly practiced deterrence of the Soviet Union, but in misperception, misunderstanding, and failures to communicate.[21] But whether the change be gradual or sudden, it appears that we change important schemata only when we have no other way of accounting for an overwhelming body of evidence that we regard as both important and reliable.[22] It is difficult for us to recognize that our beliefs about the world are wrong, that we misunderstand the intentions and actions of others, that we have misconstrued the nature of the problems we face, and that changes in the environment warrant changes in our own behavior.[23]

Motivational psychology, which grew out of the Freudian tradition, explains errors in judgment rather differently. It focuses on the satisfaction of basic needs—chiefly, the need to avoid fear, shame, and guilt; the need for self-esteem; the need for social approval; the need for achievement; and the need for effective control. Motivational psychologists argue that these needs bias information processing and result in some of the same kinds of errors that cognitive psychologists describe. However, unlike cognitive biases, which are ubiquitous because they arise out of inher-

---

[21] James G. Blight, *The Shattered Crystal Ball*; Beth A. Fischer, *The Reagan Reversal*.

[22] Markus and Zajonc discuss the importance of the diagnosticity of incongruent evidence in "The Cognitive Perspective in Social Psychology."

[23] There are further points worth making for the sake of completeness, though they are unnecessary for the elaboration of the theory at hand. For example, we are likely to change our beliefs about others only when we cannot explain away their behavior in terms of situational factors. In such a case, we are forced to consider the possibility that we have misjudged their disposition. Crocker, Hannah, and Weber, "Person Memory and Causal Attributions," p. 65. See also Edward E. Jones and Richard E. Nisbett, "The Actor and Observer"; Harold H. Kelley, "Attribution Theory in Social Psychology"; Lee Ross, "The Intuitive Psychologist and His Shortcomings"; Lee Ross and Craig R. Anderson, "Shortcomings in the Attribution Process."

Belief change also appears to be a function of cognitive complexity, or the intricacy of the cognitive rules we use to process information, although the relationships here are somewhat unclear. Cognitive complexity refers to the structure or the organization of cognition, rather than to the content of thought. It appears that complexity can have rather contradictory effects on schema change. On the one hand, the more complex one's cognitive system, the more capable one is of making new or subtle distinctions when confronted with new information. Peter Suedfeld and A. Dennis Rank, "Revolutionary Leaders"; Peter Suedfeld and Philip Tetlock, "Integrative Complexity of Communication in International Crisis"; Philip E. Tetlock, "Integrative Complexity of American and Soviet Foreign Policy Rhetorics." Experts with highly complex cognitive schemata are more sensitive to new information than novices with low cognitive complexity, whose schemata are likely to be fixed and rigid. Pamela J. Conover and Stanley Feldman, "How People Organize the Political World." On the other hand, because experts have more relevant information, they can more easily incorporate inconsistent information as exceptions and special cases. Incongruent data can therefore have less impact on their schemata than they would have on those of novices. Higgins and Bargh, "Social Cognition and Social Perception."

ent limitations in the human capacity for information processing, motivated biases are either individual-specific ("push" models) or situation-
specific ("pull" models).[24]

Push models explain biases in information processing in terms of individual personality structures and the various ways in which they mediate
deep-seated needs. For example, when we have alternative sources of information available, we are inclined to privilege the sources that lead us to
relatively desirable conclusions.[25] Motivational factors may also influence
whether we attribute the actions of others to situational or dispositional
factors. We are far more likely to interpret undesirable actions by people
we dislike as reflecting their basic dispositions, and to interpret undesirable actions by people we like as reflecting circumstantial pressures or
constraints.[26] Push models go a long way toward helping us make sense
of Woodrow Wilson's monumental errors in judgment at the end-game
of his presidency. Alexander and Juliette George, for example, argue that
his inability to compromise, refusal to brook opposition, insistence on
always having his own way, and susceptibility to flattery and sycophancy
were all manifestations of a deeper insecurity that had its roots in his
childhood relationship to an overbearing father.[27]

Pull models emphasize situations and the needs, fears, and anxieties
they arouse in us. A pull model of motivation might emphasize the ways
in which stress—generated, perhaps, by time pressure, fear of loss, and
reluctance to assume responsibility for bad decisions—might lead a decision maker to conduct an inadequate search for information and options,
to make biased estimates of probability, to commit prematurely to a particular course of action, and to resist information indicating that his or
her decision may have been a poor one.[28] Pull models go some way toward
helping us make sense of Kaiser Wilhelm's ghastly mistakes. The kaiser
had his insecurities, too—probably having more to do with his withered
arm and his neurasthenia than with any childhood trauma—but, unlike

---

[24] Katharine Blick Hoyenga and Kermit T. Hoyenga, *Motivational Explanations of Behavior*, pp. 21–63.

[25] Arie W. Kruglanski, "Lay Epistemologic-Process and Contents"; Kruglanski, *Basic
Processes in Social Cognition*; Julius Kuhl, "Motivation and Information Processing";
Joel O. Raynor and Dean B. McFarlin, "Motivation and the Self-System"; Abraham Tesser,
"Some Effects of Self-Evaluation Maintenance on Cognition and Action"; Yaacov Trope
and Zvi Ginossar, "On the Use of Statistical and Nonstatistical Knowledge"; Henri Zukier,
"The Paradigmatic and Narrative Modes in Goal-Guided Inference."

[26] Dennis T. Regan, Ellen Straus, and Russell H. Fazio, "Liking and the Attribution
Process."

[27] Alexander L. George and Juliette L. George, *Woodrow Wilson and Colonel House*.

[28] Irving L. Janis, *Crucial Decisions*; Janis, *Groupthink*; Irving L. Janis and Leon Mann,
Decision Making.

Wilson, the kaiser simply could not handle the heat. He buckled, and ultimately broke, under pressure.[29]

Although there is a great deal that we do not know about cognitive and motivational factors in decision making, and although it is extremely hard to know how well what we *do* know travels from the laboratory to the real world, what we do know justifies the presumption that decision makers' beliefs about the world, and their convictions that their existing policies are the appropriate ones (whatever their goals may be), are likely to be more robust and more durable than an unbiased evaluation of the evidence would warrant. Since there is no such thing as an unbiased evaluation of the evidence, how we process information about the world is likely to lead us to react slowly, if at all, to changing circumstances. For policy makers, this will translate into policy inertia.

Prospect Theory

A third body of theory that helps to justify the expectation of inertia is prospect theory, a behavioral alternative to rational choice theory derived from the empirical observation of the actual choices subjects make when presented with various problems in the laboratory, typically hypothetical ones. While rational choice will tell us how we *ought* to make decisions, prospect theory describes and accounts for discrepancies between the normative ideal and people's actual choice behavior.[30] While prospect theory does not specifically employ or presuppose cognitive or motivational concepts, the behavior it describes is consistent with much of what I just related.

Among the crucial findings of prospect theory is that people assess the alternatives presented to them not by asking, "What are the net assets I can expect to realize under each choice?" (i.e., by comparing expected values), but instead by asking, "How will each choice leave me with respect to a reference point defining what I consider to be an acceptable outcome?"[31] For most people, a crucial consideration when choosing

[29] Ole R. Holsti, "The 1914 Case"; Holsti, *Crisis, Escalation, War*, pp. 7–49, 123–142; Richard Ned Lebow, *Between Peace and War*, pp. 119–147; Barbara W. Tuchman, *The Guns of August*.

[30] Daniel Kahneman, Paul Slovic, and Amos Tversky, eds., *Judgment under Uncertainty*; Kahneman and Tversky, "Prospect Theory"; George A. Quattrone and Amos Tversky, "Contrasting Rational and Psychological Analyses of Political Choice"; Tversky and Kahneman, "Advances in Prospect Theory"; Tversky and Kahneman, "The Framing of Decisions and the Psychology of Choice"; Tversky and Kahneman, "Rational Choice and the Framing of Decisions"; Jack S. Levy, "Prospect Theory and the Cognitive-Rational Debate."

[31] Prospect theory postulates both an editing phase and an evaluation phase. Editing prospects involves performing a number of tasks to simplify evaluation: for example, rounding up extremely high probabilities to certainty; rounding down extremely low probabilities to

among alternatives is whether they stand to lose or gain relative to this reference point. Thus choices are *reference dependent*. People generally consider losses more painful than gains pleasurable; hence they will tend to accept poor gambles in order to avoid certain losses, but they will tend to shun good gambles for large gains in favor of smaller sure gains.[32] People tend, in other words, to be *loss-averse, risk-acceptant when facing prospects of loss*, and *risk-averse when facing prospects of gain*.

Prospect theory does not itself predict what reference point people will choose as a benchmark against which to assess prospective gains and losses, and there is at present no theory that will predict this for us. Indeed, the question of how people choose reference points is not one that scholars have spent much time exploring. Nevertheless, several things appear to bias people in favor of the status quo. One of these is the "endowment effect": people regularly demand more to give up something than they would be willing to pay for it in the first place. Since foregone gains are less painful than perceived losses, people's expectations therefore tend to converge on the status quo over the long run.[33] In addition, people eventually normalize (i.e., adjust their reference points) for gains or losses, reinforcing the status quo bias—though (not surprisingly) they typically do so much more quickly for gains.[34]

Prospect theory has not yet attained the level of development necessary to undergird a general theory of choice—and, by extension, a general theory of state behavior in the realm of international politics. There are several reasons for this. First, just as with cognitive and motivational theories, there are reasons to wonder how well prospect theory travels from

---

zero; eliminating dominated choices; or simplifying multistage prospects. Here I make use only of prospect theory's insights about evaluation. For further discussion, see Kahneman and Tversky, "Prospect Theory."

[32] For example, in a choice involving prospects of monetary gains, Kahneman and Tversky's subjects preferred a sure gain of $3,000 to an 80 percent chance of winning $4,000 (and a 20 percent chance of winning nothing) by a four-to-one margin. The expected value of the preferred alternative was $3,000 × 1.0 = $3,000; the expected value of the second alternative was $4,000 × 0.8 = $3,200. The same problem framed in terms of losses illustrated dramatically different preferences. By a margin of more than eleven to one, respondents preferred an 80 percent chance to lose $4,000 (and a 20 percent chance to lose nothing) to a sure loss of $3,000. They therefore chose the alternative with the lower expected value (\$−3,200 vs. \$−3,000). Ibid., p. 26. This example nicely illustrates the claim that people are risk-acceptant with respect to losses and risk-averse with respect to gains.

[33] Daniel Kahneman, Jack L. Knetsch, and Richard H. Thaler, "The Endowment Effect, Loss Aversion, and the Status Quo Bias"; Jack L. Knetsch, "The Endowment Effect and Evidence of Nonreversible Indifference Curves"; Jack L. Knetsch and J. A. Sinden, "Willingness to Pay and Compensation Demanded"; Richard Thaler, "Toward a Positive Theory of Consumer Choice."

[34] There are exceptions to this, as my discussion of Alsace-Lorraine illustrates below.

the laboratory to the real world.[35] The chief problem is that the experimental choice situations behavioral decision theorists crafted to explore and document deviations from rational norms were highly structured. Subjects knew both the objective payoffs and objective probabilities of the alternatives among which they were asked to choose.[36] But in the real world of international politics (and in almost all of the interesting, everyday choices people face), the decision makers themselves must estimate the costs, benefits, and probabilities associated with the various options before them. Often the information necessary to do this is simply not available, or they are unaware of it. To the extent that they attempt to make these estimates at all, they do so impressionistically, or they invoke a variety of idiosyncratic considerations to do so. Second, the value function prospect theory postulates is not well defined and appears not to be well behaved at the extremes. Accordingly, it has not yet yielded to the kind of formal mathematical representation that would permit straightforward modeling of choice situations and strategic interactions.[37] Nevertheless, in the few studies that exist directly comparing post-hoc explanations of foreign policy choices, prospect theory appears to provide at least as good a fit with the evidence as does rational choice, and sometimes the fit is dramatically better. This suggests that its central insights are relevant to, and useful for, foreign policy analysis.[38]

[35] See esp. William A. Boettcher III, "Context, Methods, Numbers, and Words." For excellent critical discussion of the strengths and weaknesses of prospect theory as a basis for explaining foreign policy behavior, see Jack S. Levy, "Loss Aversion, Framing, and Bargaining"; Levy, "Prospect Theory, Rational Choice, and International Relations." See also William A. Boettcher III, "The Prospects for Prospect Theory," p. 334.

[36] Note, however, that prospect theory has survived a variety of challenges to its internal validity. For further discussion, see Mark J. Machina, "Decision-Making in the Presence of Risk"; John W. Payne, James R. Bettman, and Eric J. Johnson, "Behavioral Decision Research"; Colin F. Camerer, "Individual Decision Making"; Levy, "Prospect Theory, Rational Choice, and International Relations."

[37] See Amos Tversky and Peter Wakker, "Risk Attitudes and Decision Weights."

[38] See, e.g., Barbara Farnham, ed., *Avoiding Losses/Taking Risks*; Janice Gross Stein and Louis W. Pauly, eds., *Choosing to Co-Operate*; Jeffrey Taliaferro, "Cognitive Realism." For critical discussion, see Eldar Shafir, "Prospect Theory and Political Analysis."

Prospect theory tends to aggravate rational choice theorists. Some challenge its internal validity; others challenge its external validity; still others concede that its findings are valid but maintain that they can be subsumed under rational choice theory—for example, by building in risk propensities, weighting utility functions, or refining the constraints under which people make choices; see, e.g., Levy, "Prospect Theory, Rational Choice, and International Relations." I purposefully avoid contrasting my theory of foreign policy change with "rational choice" theory because the term is inherently vague, and at the end of the day nothing hangs upon the distinction but semantics. In its weakest form, "rationality" implies only that people have clear preferences and reasons (good or bad) for doing what they do. In its strongest form, it is very demanding: it requires that people make true expected-utility calculations on the basis of the best possible information; Simon, "Rationality in Political

Organizational, psychological, and behavioral considerations can—and do—interact synergistically. A particular set of schemata about communism, the Soviet Union, the People's Republic of China, and the Viet Minh pervaded the organizational culture of the American foreign policy establishment in the late 1950s and early 1960s. These beliefs were difficult to shake and powerfully affected how American leaders interpreted ambiguous information about the complex and fluid political, strategic, and diplomatic situation in Southeast Asia. American policy in Vietnam was also a classic case of an escalating commitment to a losing course of action, which fits both with the risk propensities predicted by prospect theory and with the motivational need for self-justification that inclines people to try to maintain the illusion that they have not erred.[39] In 1914 the organizational culture of the German Foreign Ministry, which encouraged German ambassadors in European capitals to omit or downplay in their reports any evidence indicating errors in the fundamental premises of German foreign policy, exacerbated the motivated biases of the German leadership and forestalled timely changes in German policy that might well have prevented a general European war.[40] While it is difficult to specify all of the expected interactions of organizational, psychological, and behavioral decision-theoretic considerations, the aggregate effect of their interactions ought to be to reinforce inertia. In the normal course of events, they should enhance the stability of foreign policy. When foreign

---

Behavior." In its purest form, variations in risk propensities are not allowed (extremely risk-averse or risk-acceptant people will not make the choices that have the best prospect of maximizing their net assets). In some of its many modifications, variations in risk propensities are not only allowed but welcomed (after all, "utility" might include one's taste for, or aversion to, gambling). It may well be, therefore, that my theory of foreign policy change is perfectly consistent with some understanding of rational choice. But whether the label fits is to me a matter of complete indifference. The value of the theory depends upon its performance, not upon the assignment of labels.

That said, it seems difficult to argue that prospect theory can be subsumed under rational choice, when among its chief findings is that people routinely violate core axioms of rational choice, such as the transitivity and invariance of preferences. It is true, of course, that for many choices people face—perhaps even the majority of choices—the choice predicted by prospect theory and the choice prescribed by virtually any variant of rational choice will be one and the same. Who will buy grapes at $3 per pound when the same grapes may be had next door for $2 per pound? Nevertheless, I find it useful and convenient to draw explicitly upon prospect theory—and to avoid a debate about whether my theory is consistent with rational choice—because it directs us to ask questions about the choices leaders face (for example, about reference points and frames) that empirical studies have demonstrated are clearly relevant to decision making, whether or not they may be subsumed by rational choice.

[39] Glen Whyte, "Escalating Commitment in Individual and Group Decision Making"; Whyte, "Escalating Commitment to a Course of Action."

[40] Lebow, *Between Peace and War*, pp. 119–147; Tuchman, *The Guns of August*.

policy changes, these various factors should contribute to the momentum of the new policy. Collectively, they imply that the ship of state should more closely resemble a loaded supertanker than an America's Cup yacht. It will be slow and cumbersome. It will not nimbly adjust to the shifting winds and seas. But when it turns, all of the other boats will notice.

A Loss-Aversion Theory of Foreign Policy Change

If we have good reasons for expecting that foreign policy change will be rare, and if we can specify with some precision the conditions under which we should expect it, then we will be halfway to a useful theory to help us anticipate foreign policy change. To get the rest of the way, we merely need to know what signs of change to look for.

What are the conditions under which we should expect foreign policy change? We can specify these conditions as a set of corollaries from the default expectation of inertia and leverage the same bodies of theory that undergird it. This yields the following three propositions:

1. Since interorganizational dynamics combine with structural, cultural, and procedural considerations to reinforce policy stability, then, all other things being equal, we should observe greater policy stability in states that are more highly bureaucratized; in which larger numbers of organizations weigh in on foreign policy making; and where competing domestic interests have relatively greater opportunity to exert pressures on governments (i.e., more points of access, and more opportunities to have their voices heard). Thus, *foreign policy change should be less frequent in highly bureaucratic states with democratic regimes than in less bureaucratic states with autocratic regimes* (Hypothesis 1).

2. A decision to undertake a significant policy change often implies a recognition that existing policy is somehow flawed.[41] Policy makers must come to believe that certain premises of their policy are wrong—e.g., that it was founded upon mistaken beliefs about the interests, calculations, or dispositions of others—or that their chosen means are ineffective. In either case, foreign policy change requires policy makers to admit error, take responsibility, or embrace risk. Cognitive and motivational psychology suggest that these are difficult tasks that normal people shun if at all possible.[42] Avoiding them is possible only

---

[41] The exception, of course, would be a response to a significant change in the environment, such as someone *else's* dramatic policy change.

[42] They are somewhat more likely if the errors may be attributed to the deception of others than to one's own incapacities. The classic case, of course, is Kaiser Wilhelm's at-

so long as the status quo seems reasonably tolerable. Thus, all other things being equal, *foreign policy change will be most likely when policy fails either repeatedly or catastrophically, or when leaders become convinced that it will imminently do so* (Hypothesis 2).

3. Prospect theory provides strong evidence that people are more sensitive to losses than to equivalent gains; that they will shun risks in the domain of gains; and that they will accept risks to avoid losses. All foreign policy change is risky: even though it may offer the prospect of gain, it can also set in train events that may entail serious costs. It is difficult for decision makers to know in advance—let alone control for—all of the consequences of their actions, and thus the choice behavior described by prospect theory should lead us to expect leaders to shun foreign policy change in the absence of compelling reasons to pursue it.

It is conceivable, of course, that the perception of a significant opportunity for gain might provide such a compelling reason. Prospect theory would not predict, for example, that people will prefer a sure gain of $10 to a 50 percent chance of winning $1 million. Prospect theory provides no reason to believe that states will avoid opportunities for gain. But it does suggest that, *all other things being equal, leaders are more likely to pay the inherent costs of (and embrace the inherent risks in) foreign policy change to avoid losses than to realize gains of equivalent magnitude* (Hypothesis 3). As a corollary, we may hypothesize that *only prospects of disproportionate gain are likely to motivate foreign policy change.*

If the above hypotheses hold, then foreign policy change is most likely when decision makers perceive that their current policies are incurring painful costs; that a failure to change policy is virtually certain to result in further painful costs; and that at least one option open to them holds forth the possibility of an acceptable outcome, even if that acceptable outcome is not highly likely. In addition, the thresholds for change should be lower for autocratic regimes and relatively nonbureaucratic states than for democratic regimes and highly bureaucratic states.

For those who like to think more formally about such things, we can, for the sake of clarity—though at the risk of conveying a false sense of precision—state and explore the theory's axioms and assumptions, and represent its cumulative expectations graphically. This will at least help make clear the logic of the theory. In a moment I will confront the inescapable vaguenesses and ambiguities that a more formal presentation obscures.

---

tempt to attribute the escalation of the First World War not to his own errors, but to the deliberate machinations of the British. Immanuel Geiss, ed., *July 1914*, pp. 293–295.

Axioms
   1. All state action is intentional.
   2. Decision makers can rank preferences in any given frame (gains or losses).

Assumptions
   1. The default policy expectation at time t_n is the policy at t_{n-1}.
   2. States may be treated as unitary actors.
   3. States assess gains and losses with respect to a reference point.
   4. States are risk-averse in the domain of gains, and risk-acceptant in the domain of losses.
   5. States are insensitive to small prospects of gain or loss.
   6. Democratic and highly bureaucratic states are less sensitive to small prospects of gain or loss than are autocratic or relatively non-bureaucratic states.

I draw these axioms and assumptions from the three bodies of theory I discussed earlier in this chapter, but it is important to note that this theory is not a strict application of any of them to the international politics domain. Hence, even strong empirical support for the theory will not necessarily constitute empirical support for any of those bodies of theory.

I deliberately avoid a strict application for several reasons. First, none of these bodies of theory directly and specifically addresses the problem of explaining or predicting choices in the domain of international politics. Second, attempts to apply any of the three to the international politics domain in a way that would permit a rigorous "test" (if we could, in fact, decide what such a test would look like) would require methods unsuited to the other two. Third, there are obvious differences between the domains in which these bodies of theory evolved and the world of international politics that would call into question the validity of any strict application. For example, prospect theory and cognitive and motivational psychology are all theories of *individual* choice or judgment, which may or may not be rigorously applied to group decision-making situations in such a way as to generate valid tests of these theories.[43] Fourth, and finally, these theories may not yield determinate expectations about international political behavior because of inherent limitations in their scope conditions. Prospect theory, for example, is a theory of decision under *risk*, whereas international-political decisions take place under conditions of *uncertainty*.[44] These axioms and assumptions are informed by these bod-

---

[43] See, e.g., Boettcher, "Context, Methods, Numbers, and Words"; but cf. the discussion below.

[44] Conventionally, a risky choice is one between alternatives with known probabilities; a choice made under uncertainty is one between alternatives of unknown probability.

ies of theory but do not collectively constitute a derivation from them. The theory stands or falls on its own merits.

With that said, these axioms and assumptions warrant some comment. The first axiom is necessary (and unobjectionable) because concepts such as "gain" and "loss" would be meaningless if behavior were directed toward no particular goal. However, the first axiom does not, all by itself, imply that decision makers are "rational."[45] Rational choice requires, at a minimum, that decision makers have consistent, transitive, and invariant preferences. In other words, if someone prefers A to B, and B to C, then she is irrational unless she also prefers A to C. If we present her with a choice between A and B once and elicit a preference for A, then she is irrational if we present her with the same choice under precisely the same circumstances and elicit a preference for B. There is ample evidence, however, that changes in frame can induce preference reversals. For some choices between A and B, presenting them in the language of *gains likely to be realized*, and a second time in the language of *losses likely to be avoided*, will elicit a change in preference between the two, even though the actual probabilities and payoffs remain unchanged.[46] Hence in the second axiom I require simply that decision makers can rank preferences *within* any particular frame (gains or losses).

The six assumptions are necessary to generate the expectations of likelihood stated in the three hypotheses. The first assumption simply initializes the concept of inertia and motivates the theory as a theory of change. The second assumption is an operational convenience that I acknowledge to be unrealistic, since group preferences are not simply aggregations of individual preferences, nor is group risk-taking a simple aggregation of individuals' risk propensities.[47] Nevertheless, despite the difficulties of transforming individual attributes into group attributes, it is not nonsensical to speak of a group's preferences and risk-taking propensities. In fact, they can even be modeled (for example, as a vector sum).[48] Moreover, while policy choices are outputs of group deliberations, there is no compelling reason *not* to anthropomorphize groups, since they merely replicate at a higher level of analysis the struggles and deliberations that go on within the minds of individual decision makers attempting to decide

---

[45] William H. Riker, "The Political Psychology of Rational Choice Theory"; Simon, "Rationality in Political Behavior."

[46] Kahneman and Tversky, "Prospect Theory"; Paul Slovic and Sarah Lichtenstein, "Preference Reversals"; Amos Tversky and Richard H. Thaler, "Preference Reversals"; Richard H. Thaler, *The Winner's Curse.*

[47] 't Hart, *Groupthink in Government*; Shafir, "Prospect Theory and Political Analysis." But cf. Glen Whyte, "Groupthink Reconsidered"; Whyte, "Escalating Commitment in Individual and Group Decision Making."

[48] See, e.g., Bueno de Mesquita, Newman, and Rabushka, *Forecasting Political Events.*

what options they favor themselves. Third, in most foreign policy decision-making groups, there is one individual (typically a president or a prime minister nowadays) who has a final say, and upon whose shoulders rests ultimate responsibility for the decision. Often it is possible to have a sense of the relative degree of autonomy or influence that person will have on the foreign policy decision-making process, and often it is possible to know which other decision makers are likely to be particularly influential with that person. This information can help guide analysts toward the appropriate cues.[49] Finally, policy changes are typically preceded by statements from officials, diplomats, other representatives, and government organs that can provide a sense of the overall preferences and risk-taking propensities of the decision-making group as a whole. Unless such statements are deliberately distorted for strategic purposes, the more univocal they are, the better they indicate clear preferences and risk-taking propensities. The more confused or ambiguous they are, the clearer the indication that policy change is not imminent.

The third and fourth assumptions are drawn directly from the reference-dependence and loss-aversion postulates of prospect theory. They undergird the expectation that foreign policy change is more likely (all other things being equal) when leaders perceive themselves to be in the domain of losses. The fifth assumption is not, strictly speaking, compatible either with prospect theory or with expected utility theory, both of which would lead us to expect policy change when decision makers can thereby secure a small gain or avoid a small loss.[50] Instead, it reflects the organizational and psychological constraints operating on policy making, which contribute to inertia by desensitizing decision makers to small changes in incentives in the decision-making environment. The sixth as-

---

[49] Provided that it is possible to identify either a reference point that informs group decision making or a decision maker whose reference point can serve as a proxy for that of the group as a whole, the only question that then arises is whether the same risk behavior observed in individuals also characterizes that of groups. There is considerable evidence that it does. Indeed, the group setting may enhance loss-aversion, risk-acceptance in the domain of losses, and risk-aversion in the domain of gains. Timothy McGuire, Sara Kiesler, and Jane Siegal, "Group and Computer-Mediated Discussion Effects in Risky Decision Making"; Avi Fiegenbaum and Howard Thomas, "Attitudes toward Risk and the Risk/Return Paradox"; John Schaubroek and Elaine David, "Prospect Theory Predictions When Escalation Is Not the Only Chance to Recover Sunk Costs"; Taliaferro, "Cognitive Realism," pp. 64–70. Cf. Tatsuya Kameda and James Davis, "The Function of the Reference Point in Individual and Group Risk Taking." Thus there is little reason to fear that group dynamics will cancel out expected patterns of behavior at the individual level, and some reason to believe that they will amplify them. As we have seen, group settings also may be expected, on balance, to enhance policy inertia, and reduce sensitivity to small changes in incentives. Thus the fact that decision making commonly takes place in groups is an advantage because it increases the prima facie plausibility of all three of the hypothesized relationships.

[50] See note 38 above.

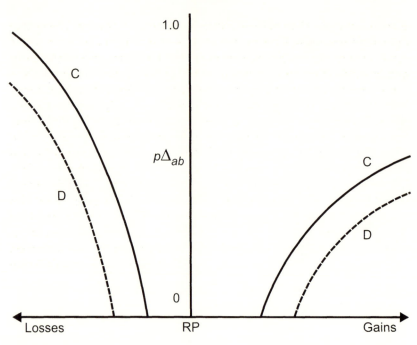

Fig. 2.2. Hypothetical probability curves

sumption motivates the expectation that the contribution of organizational constraints to policy inertia varies according to state and regime
type, resulting in different sensitivity thresholds.

To visualize the hypothesized expectations, imagine a state trying to
decide whether to stick with the status quo policy (call it policy a) or
switch to some other policy (b). We can, if we wish, think of the likelihood
of this change as a probability ($p\Delta_{ab}$), as measured by the y-axis in figure
2.2. This probability varies on two dimensions. First, it depends upon the
extent to which leaders believe they might avoid or recoup losses (if they
are dissatisfied with the status quo) or realize gains (if they are satisfied
with it). Second, it depends upon regime and state characteristics. In figure
2.2, the x-axis is not a continuous scale, but rather a heuristic, measuring
the perceived attractiveness of making the switch from A to B. The further
the distance from the Reference Point (RP), the more attractive the switch,
all other things being equal. To the left of RP, decision makers perceive
themselves to be operating in the domain of losses. The further left they
understand themselves to be, all other things being equal, the more painful
they understand the status quo to be, and the more attractive any best
alternative option will look, even if, when evaluated on its merits, the best
alternative option may be a bad gamble. To the right of RP, decision mak-

ers perceive themselves to be operating in the domain of gains. The further right they understand themselves to be—again, all other things being equal—the more they believe they might be able to improve on the status quo (provided that the expected marginal utility of changing from a to b is positive; bad gambles cannot be attractive in a gains frame). C represents the curve for authoritarian regimes or relatively nonbureaucratic states; D represents the curve for democratic regimes or highly bureaucratic states. The shapes of the curves reflect diminishing sensitivity to changes in value.[51] The intercepts reflect organizationally and psychologically induced insensitivities to small losses or gains. Notice that for a fully informed rational actor operating free of constraints, $p\Delta_{ab}$ would be equal to 1.0 for all values on the x-axis in the domain of gains. It would also be equal to 1.0 for all values on the x-axis in the domain of losses provided the expected marginal utility of making the change were positive; otherwise, as at RP itself, it would equal zero. For the proverbial fully informed and unconstrained "rational actor," in other words, there would be no curves in figure 2.2, merely straight horizontal lines.

DEVILS IN THE DETAILS

The elegance and simplicity of the theory are unlikely to fool the worldly and the wise into thinking that it would be simple to test or to apply, and it is time to start asking some hard questions about these issues. I want to suggest that neither testing nor applying the theory would be simple, but that we can make use of it, and assess its worth, within certain limits.

Operationalizing Concepts

To test these hypotheses, and to apply the theory in practice, we would need to be able to identify the following things:

1. The decision maker's operative reference point.[52]

2. The decision maker's subjective assessment of the status quo vis-à-vis the reference point (i.e., whether the status quo is satisfactory, or whether the decision maker views the status quo in a gains frame or a loss frame).

3. The favored alternative option, if there is one, or some logically possible alternative (or set of alternatives) if there is not.

[51] Amos Tversky and Daniel Kahneman, "Loss Aversion in Riskless Choice," pp. 1048–1050.

[52] Bear in mind that we are working with the simplifying assumption that a decision-making group may be treated as a single unitary decision maker.

4. The perceived riskiness of the alternative(s).

5. The decision maker's behavior (i.e., whether the policy changes or does not change).

6. Regime characteristics (democratic/authoritarian) and state characteristics (bureaucratic/nonbureaucratic).

Let us look at each in turn.

Decision makers sometimes make quite clear through their declarations, statements, and communications what they consider to be an acceptable state of affairs. Thus the available public record frequently suffices for identifying reference points in real time. Documents, memoirs, testimonies, and historical scholarship provide additional evidence of reference points in past events.[53] In some cases, however, there may be room for legitimate disagreement about the operative reference point. For example, a decision-making group may fail to attain closure on foreign policy goals, or even on the acceptability of the status quo. In such a case, research on group decision making suggests that it is often helpful to treat the operative reference point of the leader or of a dominant member of the group as a proxy.[54] In other cases, states may have strategic reasons for wishing to mask their reference points (leaders may feel, for example, that other states are bound to resist them, and that they will jeopardize their chances of success by indicating too clearly what it is that they seek). In 1962, for example, Nikita Khrushchev clearly felt that his chances of repairing the *real* "missile gap" favoring the United States, and of safeguarding Cuba against American attack, would be endangered were he to express his anxieties on both scores too publicly. The historical record provides ample information about Khrushchev's operative reference point; but for analysts to have identified it accurately at the time would have required very careful and impressive detective work indeed. The signal-to-noise ratio was low, and Khrushchev took great pains to mask his fears and objectives.[55]

When the operative reference point deviates from the status quo, it may reflect *aspirations* or *expectations*.[56] In some cases, the aspirations or ex-

---

[53] See, e.g., Farnham, ed., *Avoiding Losses/Taking Risks*; Stein and Pauly, eds., *Choosing to Co-Operate*. For further discussion of the strengths and weaknesses of various sources of evidence for estimating decision-making inputs and parameters, see esp. James G. Blight, Bruce J. Allyn, and David A. Welch, *Cuba on the Brink*, pp. 6–7; Welch, *Justice and the Genesis of War*, pp. 37–39.

[54] Vertzberger, *The World in Their Minds*, pp. 192–259.

[55] The contemporaneous record did provide adequate information for identifying Khrushchev's reference point, but the interpretation of the available evidence was neither straightforward nor obvious. For further discussion, see generally Blight and Welch, eds., *Intelligence and the Cuban Missile Crisis*.

[56] I have already mentioned many of the considerations that can incline decision makers toward treating the status quo as a reference point, including the endowment effect, general-

pectations will concern simple levels of security or material welfare. In others—especially in cases involving certain kinds of stakes, such as control of territory, the exercise of rights and privileges, or spheres of authority—they may find their source and expression in cultural, ethnic/national, normative, legal, or moral commitments. Identifying these commitments may be particularly helpful for fixing operative reference points in international politics because these are among the stakes most likely to lead to international conflict.[57] These commitments also engage a particularly powerful moral-psychological passion that amplifies risk-seeking in the domain of losses: namely, the justice motive. When people perceive a discrepancy between their benefits and what they consider to be their entitlements, they generally feel a unique sense of outrage that increases the likelihood that they will engage in reckless behavior.[58] Subjective conceptions of entitlement are especially helpful clues for two additional reasons. First, they help explain differences between states of affairs that leaders consider *acceptable*, and states of affairs that would simply be *advantageous*, which in turn helps us to understand why leaders of states do not always pursue goals that would enhance their welfare or capability. For example, from the perspective of the British "national interest" classically understood, it made little sense that Britain would be intransigent over the status of the Falkland/Malvinas Islands and accommodating over the status of Hong Kong. The latter was clearly more valu-

---

ized loss aversion, and differential rates of normalization for losses and for gains. Of course, if the status quo always served as the reference point, I would have no theory to test, because decision makers would never consider themselves in the domain of losses or gains.

[57] Kalevi J. Holsti, *Peace and War*.

[58] Welch, *Justice and the Genesis of War*, pp. 18–32. The justice motive should not be confused with self-interest, although there is no necessary contradiction between them. There is evidence that people may value "morally acceptable results" much as they value any other good—in which case, someone pursuing justice as they perceive it at great material cost may nonetheless be said to be acting out of self-interest. Norman Frolich and Joe Oppenheimer, "Beyond Economic Man." In addition, someone who perceives a discrepancy between entitlements and benefits may also suffer a material penalty, such that correcting the injustice would ipso facto increase material welfare. But the justice motive cannot be reduced simply to an aversion to loss and an appetite for gain because the two differ phenomenologically (i.e., the sense of injustice triggers a unique emotional response that increases the stridency of demands, amplifies intransigence, reduces sensitivity to threats and value trade-offs, increases the willingness to run risks, and increases the likelihood of violent behavior). Dale T. Miller and Neil Vidmar, "The Social Psychology of Punishment Reactions." They also differ prescriptively (i.e., the desire to do justice and to see justice done leads to a different net pattern of behavior than we would observe if people simply attempted to avoid losses or secure gains). Daniel Kahneman, Jack L. Knetsch, and Richard H. Thaler, "Fairness and the Assumptions of Economics." And they differ extensively (i.e., the sense of injustice extends only to those benefits that people actually conceive as entitlements). For further discussion, see Melvin J. Lerner, "The Justice Motive in Human Relations."

able to Britain than the former on every conceivable material dimension. By the same token, France would have been vastly better off materially had it annexed the Rhineland and the Ruhr when it had the chance to do so after the First World War. The prize was there for the taking. But instead, France simply insisted that they be demilitarized. What explains British and French behavior is the difference between territory each considered *its own by right* and territory each considered *another's by right*.[59] Second, subjective conceptions of entitlement can explain interesting apparent anomalies in patterns of normalization. For example, behavioral decision theory would lead us to expect states to normalize quickly for territorial gains, and only slowly for territorial losses. But Germany never normalized for the gain of Alsace-Lorraine in 1871 and quickly normalized for its loss in 1918. France, on the other hand, never normalized for the loss and quickly normalized for the gain. The difference may be explained simply by the fact that France—but not Germany—felt a sense of moral entitlement to Alsace-Lorraine.

The same information that enables us to identify decision makers' reference points may enable us to determine their subjective assessments of the status quo, although the added complication of estimating the magnitude of the gap between the two may certainly be an operational challenge, perhaps often an insuperable one. There was no doubt that France believed the territorial status quo unacceptable from 1871 to 1918, but what was the metric? Quantitatively speaking, there was none.[60] Saddam Hussein also clearly seems to have understood the status quo to be unacceptable in July 1990, but in a complicated variety of ways, some of which lend themselves to numerical estimates of magnitude, and some of which do not. Kuwait's refusal to curtail its oil production certainly depressed world oil prices below the level Saddam sought, and we can estimate the magnitude of that gap numerically. Kuwait was also pumping oil from a field that straddled its border with Iraq, which Saddam also considered unacceptable, but the magnitude of that gap is trickier to estimate. We would have to know how much oil Kuwait was pumping from that particular field, how much Saddam felt Kuwait was entitled to pump, and

[59] People do not consider everything that they might like to have to be theirs as a matter of right, and they often consider to be theirs as a matter of right things that are utterly useless. Even if perceived entitlements are utterly useless, people tend to be categorical about them and will tolerate nothing short of their full satisfaction. In contrast, people are much more willing to trade off goods that they do not consider entitlements, or to forebear pursuing them if doing so requires great effort or cost. Welch, *Justice and the Genesis of War*, p. 21.

[60] For a helpful discussion of the challenges of interpreting insights about risk-aversion from prospect theory in the international domain, especially in the absence of meaningful metrics, see Barry O'Neill, "Risk Aversion in International Relations Theory."

whether Saddam had some acceptable rate in mind that Kuwait was exceeding (it may be, of course, that Saddam considered *any* Kuwaiti pumping unacceptable). Saddam also clearly wanted territorial concessions from Kuwait. At a minimum, it seems, he wanted physical control of two strategic islands that commanded the approaches to the Shatt al-'Arab waterway.[61] But he also asserted a longstanding claim to *all* of Kuwait. To make matters even more complicated, it is hard to know exactly what subset of his maximal demands, if any, he would have considered satisfactory at the time. All things considered, it seems difficult to know how to attach a meaningful number to the size of the gap Saddam perceived between the July 1990 status quo and what he considered to be an acceptable state of affairs.[62]

Once we identify reference points, we can normally determine quite easily whether decision makers are operating within a gains frame or a loss frame. But sometimes we can do no better than gauge magnitudes of perceived or prospective gains and losses qualitatively. It would not be surprising if the best we can do, in many interesting cases, is to decide whether decision makers feel that the status quo represents or will lead to a minor loss, a significant loss, a major loss, or a catastrophic loss. These are, after all, the kinds of terms decision makers would normally use to characterize magnitudes themselves. It may be that their language is the best indicator we have, then, because often it is only via their choices of nouns and adjectives that decision makers provide us with explicit reports of such assessments. But these are not always precise indicators. Words are vague; different people use the same words somewhat differently; decision makers are prone to overstatement when attempting to justify themselves, and to understatement when attempting not to reveal too much information about their goals. One must always treat self-reports with circumspection. It would not be surprising if the best we can do is to reflect upon them in combination with other (also imperfect) indicators: for example—when decision makers perceive themselves to be in the domain of losses—the resources they devote to achieving their objectives; the costs they appear willing to pay to achieve them; how much time they devote to the issue in question; its position on their foreign policy agenda; and the degree of material pain and suffering, or social and political stress, for which the gap appears to be responsible.

A particularly useful indicator of the salience of a perceived gap between the status quo and the operative reference point—one, moreover, that would seem to apply *only* to decision makers who perceive the status

---

[61] Bubiyan (683 km²) and Warba (37 km²).

[62] For further discussion, see Judith Miller and Laurie Mylroie, *Saddam Hussein and the Crisis in the Gulf*; Stein, "Deterrence and Compellence in the Gulf, 1990–91."

quo in a loss frame—would be looming "liminal" events. It is natural for people, individually and collectively, to think in terms of stages of life and passages between them. Thus, for example, cultures and religions typically ritualize and celebrate transitions from childhood to adulthood, from presexuality to sexuality, from the unmarried to the married state, and so on. In international politics, we similarly think in terms of periods, eras, and epochs. In some cases, the transitions between stages are meaningful markers—real processes or events of obvious moment. Puberty, for example, is what divides presexuality and sexuality. Yet sometimes liminal events are utterly arbitrary. The millennium is a case in point. The calendar is a human invention, and we might have chosen to mark time in any number of different ways. There was no natural or objective sense in which January 1, 2000, was a special day in the life of the world. It was just like any other day, except for the fact that we denoted it with a round number that just so happened to be an arbitrary artifact of the way in which we mark time. And yet our fears of what it might portend, and our sense of its real importance as a transition from one stage of history to another, were very real, and very human.[63]

The tendency to think in terms of discrete eras and liminal transitions means that decision makers will sometimes fix their minds on specific dates or events as decision points or deadlines. When they do so, this will have the effect of amplifying the salience of any grievances they might have. They may become more strident as a deadline approaches. They may be willing to take greater risks. They may get carried away by symbolism or emotion. History books are full of leaders who set explicit limits to their patience. And so we should pay particularly close attention to whether decision makers define their goals open-endedly, understanding them as things they would merely like to achieve in the indefinite future, or boundedly, with a firm timetable for their satisfaction in mind. If indications suggest the latter, it seems plausible to expect that the likelihood of policy change will increase as a deadline approaches.[64]

What about identifying alternatives? In certain circumstances, this task is trivially easy. Sometimes the current policy and a single alternative exhaust the universe of possibilities. This is often the case when we can characterize policies at a very high level of abstraction. Sometimes the only available alternative to continuing a costly, unsuccessful war, for example, is to seek peace. But in many interesting cases, decision makers will be in a position to consider more than one possible alternative (e.g.,

---

[63] See, e.g., Mark Kingwell, *Dreams of Millennium*.

[64] I suggest that this indicator would seem to apply only to decision makers who perceive the status quo to be in the domain of losses quite simply because it seems unlikely that decision makers operating in a gains frame will be impatient to do worse.

seeking peace or going nuclear), or it may be necessary to evaluate more refined characterizations of a single broad alternative to attain purchase on the likelihood of change (e.g., within the broader category of seeking peace, surrendering unconditionally vs. seeking a negotiated armistice). When more than one alternative is available or conceivable, how do we know what they are?

This task is relatively tractable in historical cases, where the paper trail typically provides many clues as to particular options a decision-making group may have been considering. But it is considerably more difficult in real time. Without well-placed informants in the highest circles of decision making, it is sometimes difficult to know exactly which options are in play, and what decision makers think about them. Still, when we do not have inside information, or useful leaks, the preparation for various contingencies can provide at least some clue as to which alternatives are on the table.[65] In some cases, in the course of voicing their fears, anxieties, desires, and complaints, leaders will tip their hands as to a course of action they might take. Analysts must combine the available testimonial evidence with cautious inferences from behavior and circumstance and must be particularly careful, where evidence and inference prove inconclusive, not to allow their own propensities, beliefs, or presuppositions to fill in the gaps.[66] Obviously, this can be a real minefield.[67]

[65] Note, however, that contingency planning does not provide a sure guide to intentions. On this issue, cf. David A. Welch and James G. Blight, "The Eleventh Hour of the Cuban Missile Crisis"; James G. Hershberg, "Before 'the Missiles of October.' "

[66] Strategic analysis during the Cold War, for instance, was hampered by the willingness of Westerners, even in the absence of evidence, to credit the erroneous view that the Soviet Union harbored designs on Western Europe. David Holloway, *Stalin and the Bomb*; Zubok and Pleshakov, *Inside the Kremlin's Cold War*. A seizure of Berlin, or a rapid drive to the Rhine, seemed in virtually every Cold War encounter to be the Soviets' most favored alternative. Clearly, this is a particular danger for analysts who rely upon the notion of an "operational code." Nathan Leites, *The Operational Code of the Politburo*.

[67] Unfortunately, there is no way of deducing the set of policy options decision makers will consider, or their preferences among them. There is experimental evidence that preferences are constructed by agents, and that they are reference- and context-dependent; Tversky and Thaler, "Preference Reversals"; Amos Tversky and Itamar Simonson, "Context-Dependent Preferences." In my own work on decision making in crisis and war, I have found ample evidence that option sets are generated on the fly, often as a result of the creativity, genius, or perhaps even foolishness of individual decision makers—to some extent constrained by what the organizations charged with formulating and carrying out the options consider feasible. See, e.g., David A. Welch, "Crisis Decision-Making Reconsidered"; James G. Blight and David A. Welch, *On the Brink*; Welch, "The Organizational Process and Bureaucratic Politics Paradigms"; Welch, "The Politics and Psychology of Restraint." Nevertheless—and this is a point that bears on the thorny issue of operationalizing the concept of foreign policy change, which I tackle below—practitioners and analysts alike generally distinguish between a number of broad categories of behavior, and interesting and important foreign policy changes typically involve a shift from one to another: for example,

If simply identifying alternatives can be tricky, gauging their perceived riskiness is much harder still. We are unlikely to be able to do better, in most cases, than to arrive at fairly vague, impressionistic estimates. In part this is because decision makers are notoriously bad risk-estimators themselves. Sometimes they underestimate risks because of wishful thinking, or to avoid postdecisional stress.[68] Sometimes they misjudge risks because they do not do their homework. Sometimes they simply are not smart enough or have blinders on. In any case, they rarely attach numbers to their estimates of risk, which may leave us (the analysts) with no better handle on the matter than the decision makers' own rather vague characterizations and subtle behavioral cues (such as the degree of nervous excitability they exhibit, signs of panic or desperation, or—in cases where they do *not* perceive significant risks—an untoward calm or sang-froid). This is far from perfectly satisfactory.

Still, sometimes we can get a good sense of a decision maker's estimates of risk, and sometimes we can evaluate their accuracy. It is clear, for example, that Nikita Khrushchev badly underestimated the likelihood that the United States would discover his attempt to deploy strategic nuclear missiles to Cuba before they could be made operational, and also that he badly underestimated the risk that President Kennedy, should he discover it, would react strongly. It is conceivable that Khrushchev's overly optimistic estimates reflected wishful thinking or motivated biases. To some extent they also reflected ignorance of military logistics, of the capabilities of American intelligence, and of the American political context. They certainly reflected Khrushchev's failure to make use of what expertise he had in the diplomatic, military, and intelligence communities (though even if he had engaged this expertise more fully, he might have been little better off, given the palpable incompetence of his soldiers and spies).[69] It is possi-

---

from diplomacy to force; from force to diplomacy; from unilateralism to cooperation; from confrontation to conciliation; from deterrence to reassurance. We generally think of these pairs of categories as opposites. We also typically regard shifts from one category of behavior to another as important, for no better (or worse) reason than some conform with the norms of civilized behavior in international society and others do not. Threat perception, for example, appears in part to be a function of the degree to which the actions of others conform to or violate such norms. Raymond Cohen, *Threat Perception in International Crisis*. Commonly, information will exist indicating that decision makers are at least considering options within certain of these categories. Therefore, while it is not possible to predict option sets through deduction, it is often possible to anticipate the categories of behavior into which the various options that decision makers are considering in any given case fall. In short, we can anticipate that foreign policy will change by means of a loss-aversion theory, so long as we can identify an enticing alternative, but we must treat as an empirical question which category of behavior decision makers are contemplating in any given case.

[68] These would be examples of motivated biases.

[69] Aleksandr Fursenko and Timothy Naftali, "Soviet Intelligence and the Cuban Missile Crisis."

ble for an analyst to recognize inaccuracies in estimates if he or she has greater knowledge of—or access to information about—the relevant issues. We can now say a fair bit about Khrushchev's errors, because we know much more than he did.

But there is always the danger, especially when attempting to forecast, of projecting onto decision makers one's own subjective judgments, which may be little or no better than their own. The rather Jesuitical character of debates about strategic nuclear weapons policy during the Cold War, for example, illustrates how analysts can think themselves into circles. American devotees of deterrence strategies often presumed that the Soviets would calculate risks precisely as they did themselves, which led them to favor particular force structures and doctrines over others, and inclined them to favor or oppose particular arms control proposals. In those instances where we have good-quality evidence and testimony about Soviet perceptions of these issues, we discover that Americans and Soviets often understood risk in completely different ways, a fact that not surprisingly greatly complicated arms control negotiations.[70] This leaves us at something of a loss when trying to decide whether (and if so, to what extent) Americans and Soviets misjudged the risks of nuclear war in a serious nuclear crisis. Americans expected Soviets would behave as Americans expected Americans would behave. Soviets expected Americans would behave as Soviets expected Soviets would behave. Presumably, each would have behaved in accordance with their self-understandings, and each would have surprised the other. Would that have made a nuclear crisis more risky, less risky, or exactly as risky as each imagined? It is very hard to say.

Of course, there may be circumstances in which decision makers acknowledge the riskiness of their choices and provide grounds for assessing degrees of risk. Thus decision makers' subjective estimates of risk may provide a useful starting point. Consider President Kennedy's alleged statement during the Cuban missile crisis that he believed the odds that the Soviet Union would be willing to go all the way to nuclear war were "somewhere between one out of three and even."[71] This is a rare and notable attempt by a decision maker to assign a numerical probability to an estimate of risk. Note that Kennedy assigned a range of probabilities; that the range was quite wide; and that the assignment was impressionistic. There was no base rate information available on the Soviet propensity to risk full-scale nuclear war, and so the estimate had no empirical validity. But it did communicate Kennedy's fear that the Soviet Union would hang tough if he refused to be flexible. Given his horror of nuclear war, even a

---

[70] Svetlana Savranskaya and David A. Welch, eds., *SALT II and the Growth of Mistrust*.
[71] Theodore C. Sorensen, *Kennedy*, p. 705.

subjective estimate of one chance in three was enough for Kennedy to rule out complete inflexibility in his quest to reestablish the predeployment status quo, and so he chose a less risky option: demanding the removal of Soviet nuclear missiles from Cuba, and offering in return secretly to withdraw American nuclear missiles from Turkey.[72]

While any attempt to assign numerical values to Kennedy's subjective estimates of the costs, benefits, and probabilities attaching to the various options he was considering would be difficult to justify, there is enough information about his (and his closest advisors') assessment of the options to explain his policy choices as reflecting a willingness to gamble to restore an acceptable status quo, but an unwillingness to press his enormous strategic and conventional military advantages over the Soviet Union to their fullest extent (as his more hawkish advisors pleaded with him to do) to secure an even greater gain, because he believed that this carried an unacceptable risk of disaster.[73] It would not be surprising if this is as close as we can get to a useful characterization of a decision maker's evaluation of risk.

The fifth assessment looks as though it ought to be straightforward. Unfortunately, it is not. What, exactly, *is* a foreign policy change, and how do you know one when you see one? States tweak their policies all the time. In the course of any negotiation, for example, states may add demands or conditions, drop others, modify still others, seek to include something previously excluded, or exclude something previously included. There is a sense in which we might want to say that the U.S. decision to drop its demand that Canada scrap protections for cultural industries during bilateral free trade negotiations in the 1980s represented a foreign policy change.[74] On the other hand, we might not. We might want to say that this was merely an adjustment in a bargaining position—a tactical maneuver en route to a larger goal, namely, redefining, opening up, and stabilizing the world's largest trading relationship. The decision to pursue free trade with Canada certainly was a much more dramatic foreign policy change for the United States than was the decision to drop objections to cultural protection. And the decision to pursue free trade with the United States was an even more dramatic foreign policy change for Canada than it was for the United States, given the gross asymmetry in the two countries' bilateral trade dependence. Arguably, this was the

---

[72] Note that this was not the *least* risky option available. Kennedy might have tried to find some way to accommodate to Soviet missiles in Cuba; he might have tried a purely diplomatic démarche; or he might have pursued more aggressively a public trade of American missiles in Turkey for Soviet missiles in Cuba. For further discussion, see, e.g., Mark J. White, *The Cuban Missile Crisis.*

[73] Welch and Blight, "The Eleventh Hour of the Cuban Missile Crisis."

[74] William A. Dymond, "Cultural Issues," p. 114.

most important foreign policy change in recent Canadian history. Some might even go so far as to say that it was the most important foreign policy change in *all* of Canadian history, since it profoundly redefined Canada's relationship with its southern neighbor and qualified—some would say "compromised" or "eroded"—Canadian sovereignty.[75]

Exactly what kind of changes can a general, abstract, parsimonious theory help us anticipate? I would certainly want a theory of foreign policy change to enable us to anticipate and help explain something such as Canada's decision to pursue free trade with the United States. By any standard, this was a dramatic shift in policy. Other kinds of changes that I would want the theory to help us anticipate and explain would include (for example) a decision to go to war; a decision to surrender or terminate a war; a change in alliance; a decision to go nuclear; a decision to disarm; a decision to attempt a serious experiment in international integration; a decision to terminate a major integration arrangement; or a decision to negotiate a solution to a longstanding nonnegotiated dispute. These are the kinds of decisions that command headlines and attention, make other states sit up and take notice, generally call for some kind of response or adjustment, and dramatically change a threat environment or an opportunity structure. They are all, in short dramatic foreign policy changes.[76]

It would be nice if the theory could help us anticipate and explain something like the U.S. decision to negotiate free trade with Canada. This was a less monumental change for Washington than it was for Ottawa, but nevertheless it had what most observers would describe as important consequences. I do not know whether the theory would capture this change, but it would clearly speak in its favor if it did. I strongly doubt, however,

---

[75] Maude Barlow, *Parcel of Rogues*; David Orchard, *The Fight for Canada*.

[76] See also my discussion in n. 67 above. Note that the theory thus subsumes or supplants certain other theories with narrower scope conditions—for example, theories of international cooperation, which seek to explain only one type of behavior, albeit in a variety of domains. See, e.g., Joseph M. Grieco, *Cooperation among Nations*; Lisa Martin, *Coercive Cooperation*; Kenneth A. Oye, ed., *Cooperation under Anarchy*. Such theories seek to identify the conditions under which, and the reasons why, states will or will not cooperate with each other. I suspect that explaining international cooperation per se is impossible because of the variety and indeterminacy of state goals. Different states—even the same states, at different times—will have very different reasons for cooperating (or refusing to cooperate) with other states. The evident intractability of the debate about cooperation would appear to justify this skepticism. See, e.g., David A. Baldwin, ed., *Neorealism and Neoliberalism*. But we do not necessarily have to explain cooperation per se in order to explain or to predict the phenomena that truly interest us: namely, *changes* in state policies from confrontation, exceptionalism, or self-reliance to cooperation, or vice versa. Whatever the status quo may be, it is the ability to understand and anticipate discontinuity that is most valuable to us. While we may be unable to explain in general terms why cooperation is the exception or the norm in any given case, we may nevertheless be able to explain in general terms decisions to deviate from the norm.

whether any theory could successfully capture the U.S. decision to drop its objections to cultural protection. The change simply was not important enough in the grand scheme of things. Minor tactical adjustments in diplomacy and negotiation are like the hundreds and thousands of small-magnitude earth tremors we simply never feel. We cannot predict them, but neither do we have a compelling reason to try. The major earthquakes are the important ones.

Recognizing, therefore, that the theory is really a theory of major foreign policy change, we will have to live with a somewhat subjective and imprecise standard for distinguishing change from no change. To some extent, unavoidably, foreign policy change is in the eye of the beholder. But at least we can console ourselves with the expectation that the theory ought to be able to perform better in helping us understand and anticipate the kinds of events we care more about, even though, in the ideal world, it would help us understand and anticipate less dramatic changes as well. As an added consolation, we can take cheer from the fact that when the theory successfully anticipates change, it will, as a bonus, also successfully anticipate the precise nature of the change when the most attractive alternative policy is obvious.[77]

Finally, there is the question of regime and state characteristics. We need some way of distinguishing democratic regimes from authoritarian ones, and highly bureaucratic states from relatively nonbureaucratic states. The raging debate about who counts as a democracy in the democratic peace debate might give us pause here.[78]

Intuitively, it makes sense to say that there are degrees of democracy. At one extreme are multiparty constitutional democracies with regular competitive elections, robust mechanisms of public accountability, multiple points of access for domestic interests, and strong norms of deference to the public will. Exactly what lies at the other extreme is precisely what proponents and critics of the democratic peace debate disagree about; but a loose criterion would let us call "democratic" a country in which people elect their governments at least once in a while, even if a single party dominates and the governing elite rules in relative isolation from domestic pressures or constraints (for example, Mexico under the PRI).

It is even harder to decide how "bureaucratic" a state may be. This is because the adjective "bureaucratic" can mean one or both of at least two somewhat independent things: first, the sheer complexity of the govern-

---

[77] When two or more alternatives are equally attractive, the theory will not choose among them. However, considerations extraneous to the theory may give the analyst a handle on which is most likely. See, e.g., my discussion of the role of analogies in chapters 4 and 6.

[78] Joanne S. Gowa, *Ballots and Bullets*; John M. Owen IV, *Liberal Peace, Liberal War*; Russett, *Grasping the Democratic Peace*.

mental apparatus (the number of ministries, departments, offices, or bureaus; their internal complexity; the number of channels within and between units of government; and the number of civil servants employed by the state); and, second, the extent to which they exhibit stereotypically "bureaucratic" behavior: the rigidity of their procedures, the amount of paper they produce, the red tape involved in making and implementing policy, and the amount of resistance policy entrepreneurs within the bureaucracy encounter from other offices and officials. It seems intuitive to suggest that these two things correlate, but there are interesting cases where they do not. Nazi Germany, for example, was a highly bureaucratic state on the first criterion, but not on the second. The German bureaucracy was massive, but it was also pliant. Hitler and his minions managed to neutralize virtually all resistance to their directives within every ministry and to govern almost as though unencumbered by any machinery of government at all.

There is, unfortunately, no generally accepted metric for degrees of bureaucratization. There are, however, various measures for degrees of democratization, of which those found in the Polity project are rapidly becoming canonical.[79] The Polity project data set scores countries annually for both democratic and autocratic political characteristics, reporting an overall composite democratization score on the POLITY variable (ranging from −10 for highly autocratic states to +10 for highly democratic states). Fortuitously, the Polity data set also scores countries for "Executive Constraints" (on the XCONST variable), which is an imperfect but not wholly unsatisfactory proxy for degrees of bureaucratization. As the project directors describe it, the XCONST variable refers operationally to "the extent of institutionalized constraints on the decision-making powers of chief executives, whether individuals or collectivities":

> Such limitations may be imposed by any "accountability groups." In Western democracies these are usually legislatures. Other kinds of accountability groups are the ruling party in a one-party state; councils of nobles or powerful advisors in monarchies; the military in coup-prone polities; and in many states a strong, independent judiciary. The concern is therefore with the checks and balances between the various parts of the decision-making process.[80]

---

[79] See generally the *Polity IV Project*, Integrated Network for Societal Conflict Research (INSCR) Program, Center for International Development and Conflict Management (CIDCM), University of Maryland, College Park; http://www.cidcm.umd.edu/inscr/polity.

[80] *Polity IV Project: Dataset Users' Manual*, p. 23; available online at http://www.cidcm.umd.edu/inscr/polity.

XCONST scores range from 1 ("Unlimited Authority," denoting an absence of "regular limitations on the executive's actions") to 7 ("Executive Parity or Subordination," meaning that "[a]ccountability groups have effective authority equal to or greater than the executive in most areas of activity").[81] This is an imperfect proxy for bureaucratization as I have described it, since bureaucracy represents a specific kind of constraint on executive action. Not all accountability groups are bureaucrats, governmental agencies, ministries, or departments, and bureaucrats, agencies, ministries, and departments may not always operate as accountability groups. Moreover, whereas degree of democratization and degree of bureaucratization are conceptually independent, the Polity project uses XCONST as an input for POLITY. But bureaucracy does constrain the executive in a highly bureaucratic state, and so intuitively we should expect some correlation with the XCONST variable notwithstanding. As we shall see later in the case studies, the Polity project's XCONST scores map fairly well—with but one exception—on the informal judgments of degrees of bureaucratization that country specialists might reasonably make.

Scope Conditions

So much for operationalizing concepts. What are the circumstances under which we should expect the theory to apply, and what are the circumstances under which we should *not* expect the theory to apply?

To some extent this is a theory about run-of-the-mill decision makers running run-of-the-mill states. It is designed to help us explain and anticipate major foreign policy changes initiated by people who exhibit "typical" risk propensities. On the face of it, it would seem hard to explain the behavior of opportunists, adventurers, risk-seekers, megalomaniacs, or madmen by means of a *loss-aversion* theory of foreign policy change. Hitler, for example, would seem to lie outside the theory's scope conditions. So also (some might argue) would Mao, Khrushchev, Kim Il Sung, and Saddam Hussein. If so, the theory would seem to fail us in most of the interesting cases of the twentieth century. Does it? If so, is it a debilitating limitation?

If the theory could not help us in the vast majority of cases where we would need it most, then clearly it would not be worth very much. The acid test of a theory is certainly its performance. One might simply reply that we should wait and see. But this is not an especially satisfying response, since before we invest the time and effort in evaluating the theory, we want to have good prima facie reasons for thinking that the effort will be worthwhile. Should we, in fact, expect the theory to fail precisely when we need it most?

[81] Ibid., pp. 23–24.

One question we can ask is: what proportion of the foreign policy changes that we truly care about are the result of opportunism, adventurousness, risk-seeking, megalomania, or madness? It would be unrealistic, I think, to presume that the answer is "none." I am suspicious of attempts to defend a theory by bringing the problematic cases inside the tent, as one might do by trying to argue, for example, that since from Hitler's perspective anything short of a racially pure Germany dominating a large Eastern European hinterland was unacceptable, and since he understood himself throughout the 1930s to be operating in the domain of losses, his decision to accept various poor gambles to try to reach his reference point and avoid what he saw as further painful costs to the German nation is exactly what the theory would predict. What is wrong here is not that this is a bad characterization of Hitler's train of thought, so far as it goes. Hitler certainly made it clear often enough in the prewar period that he did, in fact, seek a racially pure Germany dominating an Eastern European hinterland. Time and again he stressed Germany's urgent need for *lebensraum* and described as dire the consequences of failing to secure it.[82] What is wrong is that this characterization attempts to sweep under the rug the plain fact that Hitler wanted war, found the prospect thrilling, enjoyed taking risks, and clearly derived a great deal of satisfaction from conquest and domination. He *was* adventurous, opportunistic, risk-seeking, megalomaniacal, and mad.[83] He was not typical of Kahneman and Tversky's subjects, and I see no point in pretending otherwise. Since figure 2.2 does not even remotely accurately represent Hitler's risk propensity for war, he falls outside the theory's scope conditions.

Kim Il Sung seems to fall broadly into the Hitler category, too. Records from Soviet archives paint a fairly clear picture of Kim as an opportunistic risk-seeker who managed to manipulate his Soviet and Chinese patrons into letting him run rampant on the Korean peninsula.[84] Khrushchev, Mao, and Saddam are more complex cases.[85] One could have an interesting argument about exactly how risk-seeking and opportunistic they were. My own inclination would be to say that Khrushchev's and Mao's

---

[82] See, e.g., Adolf Hitler, *Mein Kampf*, pp. 288–289, 601, 947; Hans Staudinger, *The Inner Nazi*, pp. 31–52; H. R. Trevor-Roper, "The Mind of Adolf Hitler."

[83] In November 1937, for example, Hitler told Germany's military and civilian leaders, "The aim of German policy was to make secure and preserve the racial community and to enlarge it. It was therefore a question of space. . . . Germany's problems could only be solved by means of force and this was never without attendant risks." Minutes of the Conference in the Reich Chancellery, Berlin, 5 November 1937 ("Hossbach Memorandum"), in Auswärtiges Amt, *Documents on German Foreign Policy*, pp. 29, 34.

[84] Kathryn Weathersby, "Korea, 1949–50"; Weathersby, "New Russian Documents on the Korean War," esp. pp. 30–39; Evgueni Bajanov, "Assessing the Politics of the Korean War, 1949–51."

[85] Philip Short, *Mao*; Ross Terrill, *Mao*; Miller and Mylroie, *Saddam Hussein and the Crisis in the Gulf*; Elaine Sciolino, *The Outlaw State*.

risk propensities were fairly typical of the average person's. Khrushchev
was famous for his bluster, bravado, and penchant for the bold stroke,
and when his colleagues finally forced him from power in 1964, reckless
foreign adventurism was among the charges they laid at his feet. But what
we now know about his motives and calculations in cases such as the
Berlin and Cuban missile crises strongly suggests that he was driven more
by fear than by opportunity, more by insecurity than by aggressiveness,
and that, when push came to shove, he was very cautious about pressing
his luck too far.[86] Mao, too—though he sometimes talked an erratic
game[87]—seems in retrospect to have been very status quo–oriented in foreign affairs, and inclined to act boldly only in response to what he perceived to be serious provocations.[88] Saddam seems to fall somewhere between Hitler and Kim, on the one hand, and Khrushchev and Mao, on
the other, though closer to the latter. Jerrold Post, who has assembled
the most elaborate publicly available psychological profile of Saddam,
characterizes him as a "malignant narcissist" with a grossly inflated sense
of self and grandiose ambitions. Concerned with his survival and power
above all else, Saddam was ruthless and amoral, but profoundly instru-
mentally rational. He fairly easily reversed course whenever he sensed a
threat to his position. He did not pick fights he did not think he could
win, though his errors in judgment and perception often misled him on
this score. While willing to take risks, he was not a notable risk-seeker.[89]
His decision to attack Iran in 1980 was something of an opportunistic
gamble, but his invasion of Kuwait in 1990 was probably more the product of desperation and outrage.[90] All things considered, Saddam seems to
fall within the theory's scope conditions, though he poignantly illustrates
the importance of carefully reconstructing leaders' subjective world views
so as to understand properly how *they* understand the choices they face.

Risk propensities do seem to vary, as these examples all illustrate. The
theory is likely to capture the behavior of some leaders more readily than

[86] Aleksandr Fursenko and Timothy Naftali, '*One Hell of a Gamble*'; Nikita S. Khrushchev, *Khrushchev Remembers*; Sergei Khrushchev, *Nikita Khrushchev and the Creation of
a Superpower*; William Taubman, *Khrushchev*; William J. Tompson, *Khrushchev*; Zubok
and Pleshakov, *Inside the Kremlin's Cold War*.

[87] According to Andrei Gromyko, for example, Mao proposed luring the United States
into a nuclear showdown during the second Quemoy-Matsu crisis in 1958. Andrei Gromyko, *Memories*, pp. 251–252.

[88] E.g., in the Korean and Sino-Indian wars. See, e.g., Alexandre Y. Mansourov, "Stalin,
Mao, Kim, and China's Decision to Enter the Korean War, September 16–October 15,
1950"; Yaacov Vertzberger, *Misperceptions in Foreign Policymaking*; Lebow, *Between
Peace and War*, chap. 6.

[89] Jerrold M. Post, "Saddam Hussein of Iraq."

[90] Majid Khadduri, *The Gulf War*; Stephen C. Pelletiere, *The Iran-Iraq War*; Pollack, *The
Threatening Storm*, pp. 30–34; Stein, "Deterrence and Compellence in the Gulf."

others. But while opportunistic aggressors, risk-seekers, megalomaniacs, and madmen have certainly been responsible for some of the more dramatic events in recent history, it is doubtful whether they are really very common after all. I do not see why we should allow Hitler and Kim to undermine our initial optimism about the potential of the project at hand. Most leaders of states are fairly ordinary human beings. "I've met and worked with a good many people whose names are in the history books or in the headlines," former Secretary of State Dean Rusk once said, "[and] I have never met a demigod or a superman. I have only seen relatively ordinary men and women groping to deal with the problems with which they are faced."[91]

Even though it would be a mistake in a technical sense to apply the theory to the behavior of a Hitler or a Kim—since they do not exhibit the risk profile the theory presumes and thereby fall outside its scope conditions—nevertheless, occasionally the theory will anticipate (if not explain) their behavior. It may still, in short, be useful, even when misapplied, much as a wrench can sometimes drive a nail in the absence of a hammer. Here it is useful to distinguish between two different kinds of errors: false positives and false negatives. A false positive would occur when the theory wrongly indicates a dramatic change. A false negative would occur when the theory wrongly indicates continuity. A false positive is unlikely when we attempt to anticipate the behavior of an opportunistic aggressor who indeed understands himself to be operating within the domain of losses. In fact, a dramatic change is all the more likely when an opportunistic aggressor, rather than a run-of-the-mill decision maker, understands the status quo in a loss frame. The theory might not *explain* Hitler's behavior particularly well, since he was a psychotic who sought war for its own sake.[92] But the theory might still have correctly predicted that Hitler would attempt various bold démarches, and ultimately unleash war on Poland, since he did indeed understand the status quo as painfully costly. Where the theory is likely to fail, when inappropriately applied to an opportunistic aggressor or a madman, is in predicting no change—for example, when he or she understands the status quo in a gains frame and when a run-of-the-mill decision maker would not be tempted by the alternatives. Thus false negatives are more likely than false positives when the theory is stretched to cases that lie outside its appropriate scope conditions.

Two further points are in order. First, one can argue that the spread of liberal democratic norms, and the global reach of modern media and telecommunications, have made it harder for opportunistic aggressors

---

[91] Blight and Welch, *On the Brink*, p. 183.
[92] Cf. Alan Bullock, *Hitler*; Fritz Redlick, *Hitler*; Robert G. L. Waite, "Adolf Hitler's Anti-Semitism."

and madmen to capture interesting states. The heyday of the tyrant and the psychotic dictator may be passing. When someone as dispositionally autocratic as Vladimir Putin can become president of Russia only by toeing what for Russia is an essentially democratic line, times have changed. When someone as marginally fascist as Austrian Freedom Party leader Jörg Haider can effectively be hounded from the center stage of Austrian politics by an outraged international community simply because he offered tepid words of praise for Nazis, it is clear that the world is not prepared to risk any more Hitlers. If present trends continue, Hitlers and Kims should simply be less and less common.

Second, even in a world populated in part by Hitlers and Kims, their presence merely requires that scholars and policy makers seeking to apply the theory begin by asking a prior question that they ought always to ask in any case: "Is this the kind of person, or is this the kind of state, to which the theory is meant to apply?" The answer may from time to time be "no," in which case it would be appropriate to tackle the tasks of explanation and forecasting with somewhat different tools. But we have no reason to think that the answer will be "no" so often as to shrink the theory's scope conditions beyond all usefulness.

Testing

Finally, there is the question of "testing" the theory. Since my hypotheses are all framed in terms of conditional likelihoods, there are those who would argue that in the best of all possible worlds I would tease some strength-of-association measures out of a large-n study. This is not in the cards. First, there is no data set to test. Second, given the various difficulties in operationalizing the relevant concepts I discuss above, there would be a significant mismatch between the degree of precision of which quantitative techniques are capable and the confidence we could have in the data.[93] Third, data sets do not let us pry into dynamics. They merely give us a series of arbitrary snapshots of the world. A large-n statistical study, in short, would be unlikely to yield a satisfying test even if we could conduct it.

What I propose to do instead is something both more and less ambitious: I propose to *test drive* the theory, using a set of detailed case studies to put it through its paces, assessing its design, comfort, and handling.

---

[93] Coding unmeasurable variables requires detailed, subtle, painstaking historical interpretation, which is controversial at the best of times. Cf. Huth and Russett, "What Makes Deterrence Work?"; Lebow and Stein, "Rational Deterrence Theory"; Huth and Russett, "Testing Deterrence Theory"; Lebow and Stein, *When Does Deterrence Succeed and How Do We Know?*; Lebow and Stein, "Deterrence."

This is less ambitious than a rigorous effort to conduct a large-*n* test because it involves looking at far fewer historical events, but it is more ambitious because it requires detailed process-tracing. Process-tracing requires the analyst to grapple with complexities and fluidities. It reveals path dependencies. It raises questions about the relative plausibility of counterfactual inferences. It requires a much closer degree of intimacy with events. Codes in data sets abstract away from all of this and prevent us from getting at endogeneities. Recall that decision makers are constantly reacting to, drawing lessons about, and taking inspiration from history and experience in ways that strongly affect their own later choices. To understand *patterns* in foreign policy change requires a method that permits an understanding of the *dynamics* of change, and static snapshots of the world are not particularly good at this.

Looking closely at a small number of cases over a fairly long period of time also has the virtue of helping us better understand how analysts attempting to use the theory to anticipate change in real time would actually go about doing so. Put another way, it enables us to demonstrate technique. The theory has some fairly clear practical implications for intelligence assessment and for judging ripeness, which I discuss more explicitly in the conclusion, and the importance of these implications will be clearer if I can show both that the theory works fairly well and how one might exploit it.

Obviously, our confidence in conditional likelihood claims rises the more we can show them to hold. The more cases, the better. Our confidence in them also rises the more we can plausibly argue that the patterns we find are the results of the mechanisms and dynamics that actually generate our expectations, rather than the spurious results of something else entirely. Wherever possible, in short, we should try to control for other factors. This is the point of disciplining case study research by means of the "structured, focused comparison."[94] The idea here is to compare events that differ as little as possible from each other except on the crucial dimensions whose importance we are trying to gauge. In the next three chapters, I look at sets of cases structured and focused in various ways, to probe my three hypotheses from a variety of angles.

In chapter 3, I ask why Argentina resorted to arms to try to resolve its longstanding territorial dispute with Britain over the Falkland/Malvinas Islands, while Japan stuck with diplomacy in its attempt to recover the Northern Territories from Russia. In most material respects, these two disputes are essentially similar. Argentina and Japan both sought to "recover" a set of relatively small islands of negligible economic or strategic

---

[94] George, "Case Studies and Theory Development"; George and McKeown, "Case Studies and Theories of Organizational Decision Making."

value from countries that had previously seized them and expelled most of the inhabitants. In both cases, Argentina and Japan asserted claims against a militarily superior, nuclear-armed Great Power. Neither the instrumental value of the stakes nor the geopolitical context would appear to help us understand why we observe a dramatic policy change in the one case, but not in the other. Can our three hypotheses help us make sense of the difference instead?

Chapter 4 compares a series of decision points within a single case over an extended period of time. Why did the United States abruptly commit its own armed forces to battle in Vietnam in 1965? Having done so, why did it stay the course for so long? Why, in 1973, did the United States suddenly withdraw? We have here two interesting, dramatic policy changes, flanking a long period of policy stability. In most respects (though not all, of course; history is never so congenial as to provide perfect controls), the stakes and the political context did not change. Throughout, the United States had essentially the same goals, faced essentially the same adversaries, and operated under essentially the same constraints. The case has the added virtue of enabling us to see how earlier periods of policy stability, and earlier episodes of dramatic policy change, can be important endogenous factors for later periods of stability or later episodes of change.

Chapter 5 looks at Canada's twentieth-century flirtations with free trade. Three times Canadian prime ministers seriously entertained the idea of abandoning economic nationalism in favor of bringing the U.S. and Canadian economies closer together. The first two times—in 1911 and 1948—Canada got cold feet. In 1988 it did not. What explains Canada's unwillingness to change its policy twice, but its eagerness to do so the third time? I look at this case in part because I just finished saying that it is precisely the kind of change that I would like the theory to be able to help us anticipate. But I do so primarily because I am keen to see whether the theory works as well in the economic domain as it does in the security domain. Chapters 3 and 4 are largely about the use of force. This is a case in which the actual or potential use of force plays no role. Are similar patterns evident here? If not, does the case give us any clues as to why not?

While these sets of cases enable us to probe my three hypotheses, they do not, of course, add up to fully persuasive "tests." Among other things, there simply are not enough cases with enough variation on all of the relevant dimensions to give us a handle on all of the hypothesized relationships, let alone to decide which hypotheses are stronger and which are weaker. But in any case, fully satisfactory tests are impossible here because laboratory conditions do not apply. International political reality is neither static nor appropriately controllable, and the phenomenon of interest here—foreign policy change—resists simple observation and measurement. But these cases do give the theory a good workout and enable me to demonstrate technique. In the conclusion, I will step back and reflect on the performance of the theory as a whole, taking care to note both its strengths and weaknesses, and both its potential and its limitations.

Chapter 3

USELESS ISLANDS DISPUTES

NATURE RARELY blesses students of international politics with good-quality experimental controls, but a notable exception—relatively speaking—may be found in the contrast between Argentina's attempt to resolve by force of arms its longstanding territorial dispute with Britain over the Falkland/Malvinas Islands,[1] and Japan's reluctance to do anything but lobby to resolve its not-quite-so-longstanding territorial dispute with the Soviet Union (and its successor state, Russia) over what the Japanese call the "Northern Territories" and what the Russians call the "Southern Kurils."[2] The first was an unambiguously dramatic change in policy—a sudden shift from pure diplomacy to coercive diplomacy, as it were. On the morning of April 2, 1982, in "Operation Rosario," 2,800 Argentine soldiers—more than half again the entire British population of the Falkland Islands—swarmed ashore, overwhelmed the British defenders, ran up the Argentine flag, and expelled the governor. It was a bold, decisive stroke designed to force an end once and for all to the territorial dispute and to "recover" the Malvinas for Argentina.

Japan did no such thing to force an end to its dispute with Russia. From the 1950s to the present, Japan has patiently and steadily pursued a purely diplomatic solution. Especially interesting is the period from 1990 to 1995, when Japan's hopes rose dramatically in the wake of the collapse of the Soviet Union. Moscow was ceding territory extensively at the time, and in the course of becoming Russia once again, the USSR shrank by more than 5.4 million km^2 (almost 25 percent). A few small islands did not seem like much extra, and officials in Tokyo became positively giddy with expectation. But Japan made no threats of any kind. It brandished no sticks. It did nothing fundamentally different from what it had been doing for more than forty years: it lobbied. Japan lobbied a little harder than usual for a while, but it never abandoned lobbying.

---

[1] For the sake of neutrality, I will use "Falklands" or "Falkland Islands" when speaking about or with respect to Britain or the British perspective; "Malvinas" when speaking about or with respect to Argentina or the Argentine perspective; and "Falklands/Malvinas" in all other cases.

[2] Likewise, I will use the phrase "Northern Territories" when speaking about or with respect to Japan or the Japanese perspective; "Southern Kurils" when speaking about or with respect to the USSR/Russia or the Soviet/Russian perspective; and "Northern Territories/Southern Kurils" in all other cases.

In most interesting respects other than this, the two cases are remarkably similar. Argentina and Japan both understood what they claimed as unredeemed national territory opportunistically seized by force of arms in the distant past. In both cases, most of the original inhabitants were driven out. Neither country allowed its claim to lapse, and both actively and patiently sought a negotiated solution. Both countries were dealing from a position of relative weakness, attempting to wrest concessions from a nuclear-armed Great Power. And in both cases the stakes over which they contended were essentially worthless materially. There are differences between the cases, of course, and I do not mean to overdo the similarities, but some of the differences render only more puzzling the difference in behavior we observe. Britain and Argentina, for instance, enjoyed generally cordial and mutually beneficial relations. Their dispute over the Falklands/Malvinas was the sole sore point in their relationship. Japan and Russia, on the other hand, have a long history of antipathy and conflict. And yet, remarkably, the friendlier dyad went to war.

I will begin with the Falklands/Malvinas. I will provide some brief background, and then attempt to lay bare the motives and calculations that led to the fateful decision of the Argentine military Junta to force an end to their sovereignty dispute, paying particular attention to their reference point, their assessments of their alternatives, and the organizational constraints under which they operated. I will argue that the theory fits the Argentine case superbly. I will then do the same for the Northern Territories/Southern Kurils dispute, concentrating on the period 1990–95, when it is most plausible to suggest that Japanese leaders might have tried to do something dramatically different. My conclusion will be that the theory works fairly well in this case, though a fully satisfactory explanation of both cases, and of the differences between them, may require appeal to extraneous considerations. In the final part of the chapter, I will consider these and address their implications for the theory. Along the way I will anticipate and respond to some likely objections.

Las Islas Malvinas

Samuel Johnson once described "Falkland's Island" (*sic*) as "a bleak and gloomy solitude, an island thrown aside from human use, stormy in winter and barren in summer; an island which not even the southern savages have dignified with habitation; where a garrison must be kept in a state that contemplates with envy the exiles of Siberia; of which the expense will be perpetual and the use only occasional; and which, if fortune smiles upon our labours, may become a nest of smugglers in peace, and in war the refuge of future buccaneers."[3] The Malvinas, as Argentina calls them, are actually a group of islands, not one—two major, and more than two hundred minor—and Argentina claims sovereignty over them on the ground that in 1833 Britain violated the colonial title Argentina inherited from Spain when the Royal Navy landed and kicked out most of the Spanish-speaking inhabitants.[4] Britain bases its counterclaim largely on the Islanders' right of self-determination. The overwhelming majority of "Kelpers," as they call themselves, are of British descent, have British manners and customs, speak English, and wish to remain British.[5]

The United Nations jumped into the fray in 1965, calling upon the two countries to negotiate a settlement. London was happy to oblige. The islands had no strategic or economic value and were expensive to administer. Moreover, the welfare of the Islanders clearly seemed to depend upon closer ties to the Argentine mainland. Without much difficulty, the two countries negotiated a Memorandum of Understanding in August 1968, the crucial passage of which read as follows:

> The Government of the United Kingdom as part of . . . a final settlement will recognise Argentina's sovereignty over the islands from a date to be agreed. This date will be agreed as soon as possible after (i) the two governments have resolved the present divergence between them as to the criteria according to which the United Kingdom Government shall consider whether the interests of the Islanders would be secured by the safeguards and guarantees to be offered by the Argentine Government, and (ii) the Government

[3] "Thoughts on the Late Transactions respecting Falkland's Islands," quoted in Paul Eddy et al., *The Falklands War*, p. 38.

[4] A common British reply is that the Falkland Islands have been British longer than Argentina has been Argentine, since an independent, unified Argentina dates only from about 1860. This is something of a debating trick, and at various times British officials have privately admitted the injustice of the British seizure in 1833. In 1910, for example, Gaston de Bernhardt, a member of the British Foreign Office's research department, prepared a memorandum on the sovereignty dispute that prompted the head of the American department to remark, "[I]t is difficult to avoid the conclusion that the Argentine government's attitude is not altogether unjustified and that our action has been somewhat high-handed." In 1946 a Foreign Office paper bluntly described the occupation as "an act of unjustifiable aggression." Ibid., pp. 40–41. The index of Foreign Office files at the Public Record Office has an entry for 1940 labeled "Proposed offer by HMG [His Majesty's Government] to reunite [sic] Falkland Islands with Argentina and acceptance of lease," tacitly admitting that the islands were once Argentine. FO 93 14/4 (A 4514/2382/2, Public Record Office, London, embargoed until 2016).

[5] The details of the dispute are quite complicated, involving in addition decolonization and acquisitive prescription. Notably, Britain asserts only the Islanders' right of *internal* self-determination, not *external* self-determination. The best discussions may be found in Lowell S. Gustafson, *The Sovereignty Dispute over the Falkland (Malvinas) Islands*; and Fritz L. Hoffmann and Olga Mingo Hoffmann, *Sovereignty Dispute*.

of the United Kingdom are then satisfied that those interests are so secured.[6]

The rub was the word "interests." If this were to be the controlling consideration, the Islanders realized, their fate would be sealed. Enlisting the help of a handful of Conservative members of parliament, the Islanders set up the Falkland Islands Emergency Committee (later simply the Falkland Islands Committee) to find some way to thwart the Foreign Office's plans to deliver them to Argentina. Under the leadership of Hunter Christie, a barrister and former foreign service officer in Buenos Aires who was well known for his hard line on the Falklands question, the Falkland Islands Emergency Committee led a brilliant campaign, engineering an uproar in Parliament that forced the government to pledge that the *wishes*, not the *interests*, of the islanders would be "an absolute condition" for any deal.[7] Thenceforward the Islanders would be able to block any transfer of sovereignty merely by expressing a preference for the status quo. And this is precisely what they proceeded to do.

Unable to outflank the Kelpers, the Foreign Office sought instead to convince them of the merits of a transfer of sovereignty by letting Argentina demonstrate the good things to come. As Under Secretary for Dependent Territories David Scott put it, Britain would not tolerate the rape of the Falkland Islands but would actively encourage their seduction.[8] To that end, the two countries concluded the Communications Agreement of 1971, which brought the Islanders regular air service to the mainland, exotic goods such as fresh fruit, and tourists. But the Kelpers were unseducible. Much as they enjoyed the benefits of the Communications Agreement, they steadfastly opposed a transfer of sovereignty. "The Archangel Gabriel could not have talked Mr Hunter Christie and his colleagues out of their deep suspicion of, and antagonism towards, Argentina," complained maverick Labour M.P. Tam Dalyell. "They were intransigent. Foreign Office men who wanted the representatives of the Falkland islanders to be reasonable and accommodating towards Argentina were near despair. There was no hope of a meeting of minds. They were more British than the British."[9]

In 1973 Juan Perón returned to the Argentine presidency, triggering a nationalistic outburst fueled in part by frustration over the lack of progress on the Malvinas issue. In April negotiations came to a virtual standstill. Once again the United Nations stepped in, urging the parties to resume

[6] The Rt. Hon. Lord Franks, Chairman, *Falkland Islands Review*, p. 6 [hereafter Franks Report].

[7] Clive Ellerby, "The Role of the Falkland Lobby."

[8] Max Hastings and Simon Jenkins, *The Battle for the Falklands*, p. 23.

[9] Tam Dalyell, *One Man's Falklands . . .* , p. 10.

talks.[10] But with Argentina continuing to insist on a transfer of sovereignty, and the Kelpers adamantly against it, there was no room for progress.

Toward the end of 1975, the Argentine ambassador to the United Nations, Carlos Ortiz de Rozas, formally expressed his frustration with what Argentina interpreted as Britain's failure to negotiate seriously and ominously stated that Argentina's patience was beginning to wear thin.[11] Britain did not help matters by dispatching Lord Shackleton to the islands to assess their economic potential, a move that Argentina interpreted as a unilateral repudiation of further negotiations.[12] In 1976 a diplomatic row triggered by the standoff led to a withdrawal of ambassadors.[13]

The Argentine military coup of 1976 further lessened the Kelpers' interest in Argentine sovereignty and increased bilateral tensions.[14] For the next three years, there was complete stalemate. The new Conservative government of Prime Minister Margaret Thatcher decided in 1979 to reconsider its options. The Foreign and Commonwealth Office presented the new minister of state, Nicholas Ridley, with three broad policy alternatives:

1. "Fortress Falklands," i.e., breaking off negotiations and preparing to defend the islands.
2. Relinquishing the islands, offering to resettle the inhabitants (an option the Foreign Office considered "politically and morally indefensible").
3. Continuing with the negotiations in search of a settlement with Argentina.[15]

The Foreign Office settled on the third option, favoring a policy called "leaseback," which had apparently been considered as early as 1940.[16] The idea would be to concede sovereignty to Argentina in return for a long lease on the Hong Kong model. Ridley visited the islands in November 1980 to try to sell the idea to the Kelpers but failed.[17]

---

[10] Resolution 3160 (December 1973).

[11] Hoffmann and Hoffmann, *Sovereignty Dispute*, p. 127.

[12] Lord Shackleton, *Economic Survey of the Falkland Islands*. For a distillation of Shackleton's 400-page report, see Lord Shackleton, R. J. Storey, and R. Johnson, "Prospects of the Falkland Islands."

[13] Hoffmann and Hoffmann, *Sovereignty Dispute*, pp. 127–128. The two countries restored ambassadorial relations in 1979.

[14] Franks Report, p. 75. On the nature of the military regime, see Charles Maechling, Jr., "The Argentine Pariah."

[15] Franks Report, p. 20. Foreign Minister Lord Carrington sent a revised list of options to Thatcher and the other members of the Defence Committee in a minute on 20 September 1979. They were: (1) Fortress Falklands; (2) protracted negotiations with no concession on sovereignty; and (3) substantive negotiations on sovereignty. Ibid., pp. 20–21.

[16] See the Foreign Office file cited in n. 4 above.

[17] Franks Report, p. 23.

Nevertheless, the Foreign Office refused to break off negotiations and continued to insist that Britain truly did desire to arrange a formal transfer of sovereignty. This line encouraged Argentine hopes and expectations and reinforced Argentine leaders' already powerful belief in the justice of their claim. Why, after all, would the British maintain that they wished to find a way to transfer sovereignty if the islands were not rightfully Argentina's? But as time wore on with no tangible progress, Argentine frustrations grew.[18]

In December 1981 a Junta came to power that would simply run out of patience. Its three members were President and Commander-in-Chief of the Army General Leopoldo F. Galtieri, Commander-in-Chief of the Navy Admiral Jorge Isaac Anaya (pronounced "Anasha"), and Commander-in-Chief of the Air Force Brigadier Basilio Lami Dozo. Anaya was the driving force on the issue. His lifelong ambition was to recover the Malvinas for Argentina.[19] He supported Galtieri's bid for the presidency only on condition that Argentina recover the Malvinas no later than January 1983, the 150th anniversary of the British seizure of the islands. Galtieri and Lami Dozo shared Anaya's goal, though Lami Dozo—the junior member of the Junta—was by nature more cautious. All three agreed, however, that if push came to shove, they would use military force in support of diplomacy to achieve their objective by their self-imposed deadline.

Soon after the Junta took power, military contingency planning began in earnest.[20] The Junta began to send signals that its patience was running out but of course was careful not to communicate its willingness to use force *too* clearly, lest the British respond by beefing up their meager military capability in the region (the sum total of which was a handful of Royal Marines stationed at Port Stanley, and the lightly armed ice-patrol

---

[18] I draw much of the following material from interviews I conducted in Buenos Aires with senior Argentine officials, some of whom requested anonymity, either in general or with respect to specific points. Where possible, I will identify interviewees.

[19] Anaya interview, 30 August 1995; see also Michael Charlton, *The Little Platoon*, p. 116; Jorge I. Anaya, "Malvinas." U.S. Secretary of State Alexander Haig remarked on the intensity of Anaya's passion during his peace mission in April 1982: "My son is ready to die for the Malvinas," Anaya told Haig, "and it is my family's point of view that we would be proud to know his blood had mingled with this sacred soil." Alexander M. Haig, Jr., *Caveat*, p. 288.

[20] The navy took the lead, and planning began seriously in January 1982, when the Junta approved National Strategy Directive 1/82: "The Military Committee, faced with the evident and repeated lack of progress in the negotiations with Great Britain to obtain recognition of our sovereignty over the Malvinas, Georgias and South Sandwich Islands; convinced that the prolongation of this situation affects national honour, the full exercise of sovereignty and the exploration of resources; has *resolved* to analyse the possibility of the use of military power to obtain the political objective. This resolution must be kept in strict secrecy and should be circulated only to the heads of the respective military departments." Lawrence Freedman and Virginia Gamba-Stonehouse, *Signals of War*, pp. 12–13.

vessel HMS *Endurance*, scheduled to be withdrawn within a matter of months under the terms of the Thatcher government's 1981 defense review). Accordingly, an influential journalist known to have close ties with the Junta, Jesús Iglesias Rouco, warned in two newspaper articles in early 1982 that Argentina would shortly present Britain with a series of "firm and clear" conditions for continuing negotiations, with a strict deadline for a resolution. He hinted, but did not say outright, that Argentina might use military means to recover the islands if Britain proved to be intransigent.[21] On January 27 the Ministry of Foreign Affairs delivered a *bout de papier* to the British ambassador calling for negotiations concluding "within a reasonable period of time and without procrastination" in the recognition of Argentine sovereignty.

Britain agreed to talks in New York, with the proviso that there could be no preconditions on the outcome. These got nowhere because the scene of action quickly shifted to South Georgia, one of the "Falkland Islands Dependencies" seven hundred miles southeast of Port Stanley over which, along with the South Sandwich Islands, Argentina also claimed sovereignty (see figure 3.1).[22] Constantino Davidoff, an Argentine scrap-metal dealer under contract to a Scottish firm to salvage an abandoned whaling station, arrived at Leith Harbour on March 18 aboard the Argentine naval transport *Bahía Buen Suceso* without reporting for entry to the British Antarctic Survey station at Grytviken as his contract required. This was the second time in four months that Davidoff had failed to observe the necessary formalities on South Georgia, and this, coupled with the fact that his transports maintained radio silence while in transit on both occasions, inclined British authorities to suspect that he was up to no good.[23] Britain demanded that he withdraw.

---

[21] *La Prensa* (Buenos Aires), 24 January and 7 February 1982.

[22] Throughout, whenever I refer to the Argentine claim to the "Malvinas," I mean to imply also the Argentine claims to the Dependencies.

[23] There is reason to believe that these suspicions may have been well founded. The Argentine Navy began planning "Project Alpha" in September 1981, by which Argentine marines would infiltrate Davidoff's team of workers and establish a permanent presence on the island. The idea was to repeat a similar operation that took place in the South Sandwich Islands in 1976, when Argentina had covertly established a "scientific station" on Southern Thule, prompting nothing more than a British protest. In February 1982 Argentine Foreign Minister Nicanor Costa Méndez recommended that Project Alpha be postponed, so as not to complicate the impending negotiations in New York. The Junta agreed. Anaya interview, 29 August 1995; Galtieri interview, 29 August 1995; Lami Dozo interview, 30 August 1995. A well-placed Argentine official I interviewed who asked not to be identified on this point nevertheless expressed his conviction that Davidoff's team included marines with orders to carry out the principal elements of Project Alpha. This source insisted, however, that all three members of the Junta were unaware of this.

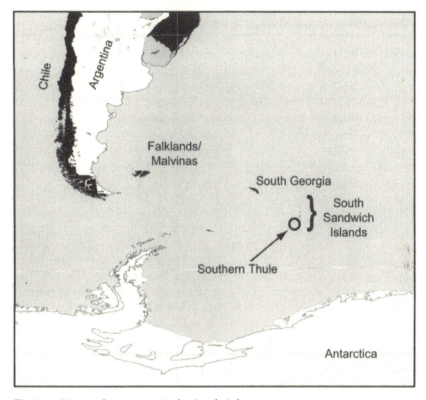

Fig. 3.1. Disputed territories in the South Atlantic

The two countries' foreign ministries tried to contain the incident and agreed that *Bahía Buen Suceso* would leave the island. It did so on March 22. However, the British assumed that Davidoff's entire party would be aboard, and issued a public statement to that effect later that evening. When it became clear that this was not the case, the British press played the event as an "invasion," and Thatcher ordered *Endurance* to South Georgia to evict the remaining Argentine personnel. The Junta, suspicious of Britain's unexpectedly vehement reaction to what they saw as an innocuous salvage mission, determined not to permit such a humiliation and ordered a second ship in the vicinity, the ice patrol vessel *Bahía Paraíso*, to land a party of marines at Leith to protect Davidoff's men.

Still looking for a way to contain the crisis, Argentine Foreign Minister Nicanor Costa Méndez proposed that the British authorities at Grytviken issue "White Cards" to the Argentines on South Georgia. White Cards had served as travel documents for Argentines in the Malvinas since the Communications Agreement of 1971. Not being passports, they cleverly finessed the sovereignty issue. Falklands Governor Rex Hunt, however, insisted that White Cards were not valid on South Georgia because the Communications Agreement applied only to the Falkland Islands proper, not to the Dependencies. He persuaded his government to demand that the Argentines at Leith have their passports stamped if they wished to remain.

The Junta would not stand for this. If Argentina acquiesced in Britain's demand that Davidoff's team present their passports, they would, in effect, be acknowledging British sovereignty over South Georgia and, by extension (so they believed), over all of the disputed territories, including the Malvinas proper. In Anaya's view, "This was aggression on the part of Britain against the territory of Argentina."[24]

On the evening of March 26, the Junta decided to occupy the Malvinas. The idea was to seize and disarm the British garrison without shedding any British blood, expel the governor, and then withdraw, placing the islands under temporary international administration while Britain and Argentina finalized an agreement recognizing formal Argentine sovereignty and safeguarding the "interests" of the Islanders. The Junta believed that a bloodless touch-and-go operation would signal Argentina's resolve and give the necessary impetus to stalled diplomacy. They did not expect that it would trigger international outrage or a British military response. On this, of course, they were mistaken.[25]

The Junta felt that if they were to act, they had to act quickly. They believed they had a narrow, and closing, window of opportunity. *Endurance* was in the vicinity of South Georgia, with a detachment of marines from Stanley. Argentine intelligence reported—wrongly, it seems—that a British nuclear submarine had already left Gibraltar for the South Atlantic.[26] The

---

[24] Interview, 29 August 1995. As Lami Dozo put it, "Britain's escalation of the dispute—especially its demand about the passports—came as a complete surprise. . . . [T]here was unanimous agreement that we could not permit that." Interview, 30 August 1995.

[25] The reasons for their mistake are fascinating and instructive, but I do not have space to elucidate them fully here. I refer readers interested in this issue to Welch, "Culture and Emotion as Obstacles to Good Judgment."

[26] Freedman and Gamba-Stonehouse examine Argentine perceptions of British mobilization in considerable detail and find no plausible basis for any such intelligence report, noting that no British submarines left for the South Atlantic until April 1 (HMS *Spartan* from Gibraltar, and HMS *Splendid* from Faslane). *Signals of War*, pp. 73–77. Their account stresses a more general fear in Argentina that Britain was mobilizing reinforcements of various kinds. In my interviews, the Junta singled out their concerns about nuclear submarines and were adamant that they had reliable intelligence of a British nuclear submarine being dispatched to the South Atlantic on March 25.

The 1982 recollections of Admiral Harry Train, USN, Supreme Allied Commander Atlantic, only further confuse the issue. "When the BBC announced, I believe it was March 17th, that HMS *Superb* had sailed from Gibraltar, Anaya felt, as he told me, that this was his last opportunity to carry out his life's ambition to retake the Malvinas Islands for Argentina. He said, when this nuclear-powered submarine arrived on the scene, it would not be possible

Falklands were virtually undefended, but only briefly.[27] Military preparations were not quite complete. The Junta had not expected to have to play the military card for several months, if at all. The earliest they could mount the operation was April 1, and this was the date agreed upon during the Junta's March 26 meeting. Weather would subsequently delay the landing until April 2.

Assessing the Fit

How well do the three hypotheses fit the Argentine case? Recall from chapter 2 that we need to be able to determine the following things:

1. The decision maker's operative reference point.

2. The decision maker's subjective assessment of the status quo vis-à-vis the reference point (i.e., whether the status quo is satisfactory, or whether the decision maker views the status quo in a gains frame or a loss frame).

3. The favored alternative option, if there is one, or some logically possible alternative (or set of alternatives) if there is not.

4. The perceived riskiness of the alternative(s).

5. The decision maker's behavior (i.e., whether the policy changes or does not change).

6. Regime characteristics (democratic/authoritarian) and state characteristics (bureaucratic/nonbureaucratic).

Let us look at each in turn.

It is plain that the operative reference point for Argentine leaders throughout the period was an Argentina that included the Malvinas. At

---

to execute the surface operations that would be required to place Argentine troops ashore at Port Stanley. The window of opportunity was limited by the steaming time it would take HMS *Superb* to get from Gibraltar to the vicinity of the Falklands." Quoted in Charlton, *The Little Platoon*, p. 116. The BBC has no record of such a report on March 17; the first was on March 29.

[27] As Rear Admiral Carlos Büsser put it, "Argentina . . . had a very short period in which to act, and during that period Great Britain could *not* act. *After* that the position would be absolutely the opposite. The British *could* act, and Argentina would not be in any position to stop the scrap workers being removed from the Georgias. . . . The overall situation, at the time, was set up in the following terms. British forces are heading south. Either we continue negotiations, which would not solve the problem but would give the British ships time to arrive. Or we could send our claim the the UN Security Council, but there the British had a veto and the prospect was dim. Third was the military solution which would *force* Britain to negotiate. The basic idea was to recover the islands with a small force, and leave a small force there. As we did. Of all these alternatives, only the military option offered the promise of a solution." Quoted in Charlton, *The Little Platoon*, pp. 114–115. Dr. Alberto De Vita, a close associate of the Junta, confirmed Büsser's account of the Junta's representation of their options in an interview I conducted on 28 August 1995.

all times, the status quo—disputed sovereignty, de facto British control of the islands—was, for Argentine decision makers, unsatisfactory. For almost 150 years, Argentines had felt a palpable and painful sense of loss.

Now, it is important to note that, contrary to Argentine mythology, this palpable and painful sense of loss was not constant. It varied considerably. As one would expect, in 1833 the Buenos Aires government of Juan Manuel de Rosas reacted with outrage and a sense of violation when the British seized the islands. But for much of the nineteenth century and the first half of the twentieth, Argentina was engaged in a difficult process of political consolidation and nation building, trying to stake out governable turf in what amounted to a postcolonial frontier free-for-all. Not surprisingly, it dwelt on other things. The Malvinas claim never lapsed, but it lay dormant. Only after World War II did it become prominent. Only in the 1960s did it begin to preoccupy Argentine leaders. Only in the 1970s did the issue become acute. What explains its dormancy, resurrection, and ultimate urgency?

Much of the answer has to do with the fact that Argentina was, and remains, one of the most ethnically diverse countries in Latin America. In the early going, it had a serious identity crisis. Political consolidation required cultivating a sense of one-ness, of *Argentine* nationhood. This was as much of a challenge as it was a political priority. But Argentine elites found the perfect tool for the job: irredentism.[28]

A good way to cultivate a sense of identity, or of an in-group, is to create a sense of grievance against out-groups. Irredentism works particularly well, because people invest their sense of national identity in territory and develop a powerful emotional attachment to it. If one can be persuaded that others have appropriated territory that is rightfully one's own, the emotional sense of moral outrage that accompanies the conviction acts as a kind of patriotic glue. The genius of Argentine political elites was to target a particularly impressionable audience: children. They deliberately played up irredentism in the textbooks precisely so as to socialize Argentine children as nationalists.[29]

Argentine textbooks have stressed different irredentist claims of various degrees of merit at various times. Almost all of Argentina's neighbors, at one time or another, have played the role of Nemesis. Only in the postwar period did the Malvinas become prominent. This is because more important claims withered on the vine as Argentina's land frontiers stabilized and normalized. The big prizes—Uruguay, for example, which Argentine leaders in the nineteenth century had considered an integral part

---

[28] By any standard, they succeeded brilliantly. Argentine nationalism is universally acknowledged to be a particularly virulent strain.

[29] Carlos Escudé, *Education, Political Culture, and Foreign Policy.*

of the nation they sought to build—was clearly lost forever. Only the Malvinas dispute with Britain and the Beagle Channel islands dispute with Chile remained, and by the late 1970s the handwriting was clearly on the wall with respect to the latter.[30] Argentine leaders had powerful reasons to hope and expect, however, that the Malvinas would ultimately come home, and in contrast to the Beagle Channel islands case, where even strident Argentine leaders harbored doubts about the legitimacy of Argentina's claim, virtually no one in Argentina doubted that *las Islas Malvinas son Argentinas*.[31] The UN's repeated calls to negotiate a solution reinforced the Argentine view that there was a grievous historical wrong to correct. Britain's initial willingness to negotiate confirmed this belief. Britain's later intransigence, and apparent bad faith, added insult to the injury. And on top of it all loomed the utterly arbitrary, yet psychologically potent, sesquicentennial of the British occupation.

The Junta that came to power in December 1981 was the first to cut its teeth on the textbooks that gave the Malvinas issue prominence. They were the first forced to admit to themselves the hopelessness of the Argentine claim to the Beagle Channel islands. They expected to be at the helm during the all-important 150th anniversary in January 1983. It was Anaya's "life's ambition" to recover the islands for Argentina, and he and his colleagues perceived a narrow window of opportunity to do so. It is no great surprise that this regime in particular felt the loss, and the urgency to redeem it, more acutely than any Argentine government before or since.

All Argentine governments, of course—including the Galtieri regime—preferred a negotiated solution to a military one. Despite the fact that Argentina had been ruled by the military for six years (and for all but three of the previous sixteen), Argentina was not a militaristic society and had not gone to war for more than a century.[32] Its people were literate, cosmopolitan, and urbane. Its social and political fabric was torn by the military's Dirty War against leftists and suspected leftist sympathizers. Its economy was in tatters.[33] The country was hardly in condition for war. But the preferred alternative to a negotiated solution was nevertheless a

---

[30] The International Court of Justice ruled in favor of Chile's claim in 1977. Only after the pope supported Chile's claim, however, did Argentina finally throw in the towel, formally acknowledging Chilean sovereignty in 1984.

[31] This was the refrain of a popular schoolyard chant. For further discussion of the intensity of Argentine feeling on the issue, see generally Welch, *Justice and the Genesis of War*, pp. 171–172, and citations therein.

[32] The last major war in which Argentina participated was the War of the Triple Alliance against Paraguay, 1865–1870. Juan Perón did declare war against Germany in 1945, to secure Argentina's admission to the United Nations, but this was essentially pro forma.

[33] In 1981 inflation in Argentina reached 130 percent; the peso fell to one-fifth of its value against the dollar; the gross national product dropped 6 percent; manufacturing output dropped 22.9 percent; real wages fell 19.2 percent; and 500,000 people out of a total work

solution by force. Argentine leaders had simply run out of other ideas. They had tried inducement, persuasion, third-party pressure (primarily through the United Nations), and veiled threats. Nothing had worked. They had not the slightest evidence of progress to show for their efforts. From the Junta's perspective, Argentina had been patient, solicitous, and restrained. As events unfolded on South Georgia, and as the Junta's suspicions grew that Britain was using the incident to justify a harder line and a "Fortress Falklands" policy, they felt that they faced a starker and starker choice between playing the military card and throwing in the hand.[34]

In fact, the military option had been on the table for some time, and at various points Argentine governments may even have flirted with it. Jimmy Burns reports that in 1942 the Argentine government apparently asked the military academy in Buenos Aires to study the feasibility of an invasion of the islands.[35] Anaya himself had been involved in the preparation of military plans in the late 1960s.[36] In December 1966 an Argentine submarine apparently conducted elaborate reconnaissance of East Falkland.[37] Max Hastings and Simon Jenkins suggest that the Videla regime may have considered an invasion after the 1976 coup, and again after Argentina's World Cup victory in 1978, only to be deterred by British submarine strength.[38] The Franks Report claims that Argentina stepped up its military activities in the region in 1977, and that Britain responded with naval deployments so as to "be able to respond flexibly to limited acts of aggression."[39] The possibility of military action seems never to have been very far from the minds of Argentine leaders. But only in 1982 did it begin to look like Argentina's last hope.

How risky did the military option seem to be? Here the story is somewhat complex and counterintuitive. Argentine leaders had to ask them-

---

force of just under 8 million were unemployed. *Economist*, 10 April 1982, p. 22; Jimmy Burns, *The Land That Lost Its Heroes*, p. 29.

[34] Exactly why Britain would need to engineer an incident on South Georgia to justify an increased military presence in the South Atlantic is something the Junta seems never to have explained. But the intense sincerity of the Junta's belief after the fact that they had fallen into a trap brilliantly laid and sprung by Mrs. Thatcher to serve some nefarious geopolitical end was apparent to me in my interviews. The case is presented in detail in Alberto A. De Vita, *Malvinas 82*.

[35] Burns, *The Land That Lost Its Heroes*, p. 3.

[36] "Plan Goa," named in honor of India's seizure of the Portuguese colony by the same name. The plan involved a surprise landing and apparently involved removing the existing population and resettling the islands with Argentines—a mirror image of the British operation in 1833. Hastings and Jenkins, *The Battle for the Falklands*, p. 31.

[37] Burns, *The Land That Lost Its Heroes*, pp. 3–5.

[38] Hastings and Jenkins, *The Battle for the Falklands*, p. 32.

[39] These deployments were shrouded in secrecy, however, and the Franks Commission "found no evidence that the Argentine Government ever came to know" of them. Franks Report, p. 18.

selves four questions: (1) What were the odds that Argentine forces could successfully seize the islands? (2) What were the odds that the British would attempt to retake them? (3) What were the odds of the British successfully retaking them if they tried? (4) How costly would the likely international political fallout be? An ideal observer might answer these questions as follows:

1. Given its overwhelming local conventional military superiority, Argentina would have little difficulty seizing the islands. Argentina would enjoy complete air superiority, and in the absence of a significant British naval presence (for example, in the form of nuclear-powered hunter-killer submarines), Argentine ships would not be seriously threatened. The small garrison of Royal Marines at Port Stanley would be unable to put up more than a token resistance.

2. Margaret Thatcher was highly unlikely to allow an Argentine invasion to stand. If she could not secure a return to the status quo ante by diplomatic means, she would be very likely to attempt to retake the islands by force (a) to redeem what she perceived to be the legitimate rights of the Islanders and of Britain itself, (b) to avoid rewarding aggression, (c) to avoid the stigma of weakness or appeasement, (d) to maintain the credibility of British commitments, and (e) to avoid encouraging others with claims against British possessions.[40]

3. Without resort to nuclear weapons, a successful British campaign to recapture the islands would be difficult. Using nuclear weapons against a nonnuclear opponent would be unthinkable given the strength of the international taboo, which Britain had fully internalized in any case. Britain could not count upon local air superiority, not having an air base within tactical range of the Falklands, and having limited carrier-borne air capability.[41] Naval superiority would be assured, which would prevent Argentine relief or reinforcement; but Britain could not expect to come close to putting ashore troops

---

[40] I examine these concerns and possible others in greater detail elsewhere; see particularly *Justice and the Genesis of War*, pp. 177–184, and "Culture and Emotion." I list them above in the order of my estimation of their importance. I discount strategic or economic motives (see below).

It is apparent from Thatcher's negotiating stance immediately before the landing of British troops in mid-May that she would have settled for international administration of the islands—with Argentine representation—so long as no transfer of sovereignty took place against the wishes of the Islanders, and so long as existing laws and customs remained in place pending any final negotiated settlement. This was not quite the status quo ante, but it would have avoided war and protected the rights of the Islanders indefinitely, even as it would inevitably have been perceived internationally as rewarding aggression to some extent.

[41] During the actual battle, Argentina outnumbered Britain in high-performance aircraft by a four-to-one ratio.

in the three-to-one ratio military planners typically use as a rule of thumb for a successful assault against prepared defenses.[42] In addition, the logistics of supplying and sustaining an invasion force almost seven thousand miles from home would be daunting. Britain would enjoy advantages in intelligence, training, leadership, and equipment that would partially offset numerical and logistical problems. But all in all it would be hard for Thatcher to be very optimistic about recapturing the islands militarily—particularly at a cost in blood and treasure proportionate to the tiny population whose rights she sought to redeem. This would not necessarily mean, however, that she would not try.

4. Argentina would likely weather intense international criticism for militarizing the dispute. Few would sympathize with the Argentine claim that one cannot commit aggression against one's own territory. The United States would ultimately side with Britain, given the closeness of their historical, cultural, linguistic, political, and military ties. Argentina could count on no significant Great Power support. Some countries in Latin America would pay lip service to the justice of Argentina's cause, but Argentina's stock was low, owing to the brutality of the military regime and its support of American policy in Central America. Thus the international political costs were almost certain to be significant.

All things considered, the military option should therefore have appeared rather risky. Argentina either would be forced to yield, militarily or diplomatically, or would hold the islands only at great cost.

The Junta saw things somewhat differently. They were considerably more sanguine. Their answers to these same four questions were as follows:

1. Seizing the islands would present no difficulties, for the reasons given above. Seizing them without shedding British blood added somewhat to the challenge, since the Junta could not control what its commandoes would do in the heat of battle, nor prevent British forces from bloodying themselves through friendly fire. But British casualties would certainly be light at worst, given how few soldiers were defending Port Stanley.

2. The British were unlikely to attempt to retake the islands because of their physical distance from British bases, because Thatcher would be unwilling to make the necessary effort and pay the necessary political price internationally to redeem the demands made upon

---

[42] In fact, the defeated Argentine defenders actually outnumbered the victorious British attackers by more than two to one. For the British and Argentine orders of battle, see Martin Middlebrook, *Operation Corporate*, pp. 395–409.

her by a mere 1,800 people of British descent, and because Thatcher would consider Britain's future relationship with Argentina more important than fulfilling the demands of the Islanders.[43] If for any reason she were inclined to attempt a military response, the United States would restrain her and encourage her to negotiate a final diplomatic settlement because of (a) Argentina's support for American policy in Central America, (b) Argentina's value to the United States as a bulwark against communism in the Southern Cone, (c) the Monroe Doctrine, and (d) Washington's desire not to be seen supporting a European colonial power against a Latin American country.[44]

3. If for some reason Thatcher did attempt to retake the islands by force, she was certainly no more likely to succeed than to fail, for all of the reasons given above.[45]

4. There would, of course, be some international criticism of the Argentine operation, but this would be muted. Most countries would

[43] There is reason to believe that the Junta discounted the risk of a military response in part because they had internalized sexist stereotypes. U.S. Secretary of State Alexander Haig recalls Galtieri insisting that "That woman wouldn't dare" fight to recover the islands. Haig, *Caveat*, p. 280.

[44] Interviews; cf. also David Lewis Feldman, "The U.S. Role in the Malvinas Crisis, 1982." In reaching this estimate, the Junta relied heavily upon the judgment of Costa Méndez. Anaya recalls, "Costa Méndez's view was that, from [Suez in] 1956, Britain's behavior was always to deal, but not on the basis of force. Rhodesia was the most recent example. There, Britain had abandoned 600,000 British subjects. The sum of perceptions led to the conclusion that Britain would not respond with force.... When we met on March 26, Costa Méndez explained the situation and said British actions required military action in order to get them to negotiate seriously. We respected his intellect and his achievements.... He had a great deal of experience. He advised us to take military action. How could we doubt his judgment?" Interview, 29 August 1995.

[45] To this day, the Junta insist that the British effort to recapture the islands *would* have failed, were it not for God and the United States. According to Anaya, an Argentine submarine managed to get one of the two British aircraft carriers (HMS *Invincible*, by far the more capable of the two) in its sights, but its torpedoes misfired. If *Invincible* had been sunk or damaged, the British Task Force might well have had to withdraw. This prompted Anaya to quip: "God must be English." Interview, 29 August 1995.
The United States made available to Britain its facilities on Ascension Island, satellite and other intelligence, and improved versions of the *Sidewinder* air-to-air missile that enabled the relatively small number of British Harrier jets to fend off furious Argentine air attacks. The Junta saw the U.S. willingness to let Britain use its facilities on Ascension as a particularly egregious violation of its purported neutrality. However, Washington had no choice in the matter. Ascension was a British possession, and the terms of the American lease required allowing the British military to make use of it in case of "emergency."
There is some inconsistency in the Junta's assessments of the likely success of a British effort to retake the islands. Lami Dozo reports: "We believed it was possible to seize the islands, but not to hold them, because the U.S. would be supporting Britain militarily." Interview, 30 August 1995. In interviews, Anaya and Galtieri expressed a clear conviction that the United States would remain neutral.

sympathize with Argentina's claim, because it was just, and would not perceive it as aggression, because one cannot commit aggression against one's own territory. Moreover, Argentina was acting in accordance with the internationally sanctioned principle of decolonization. Argentina had already demonstrated its patience and good faith, while Britain had acted in bad faith. Britain, in fact, was the aggressor, as was evident from its demand that Argentines at Leith have their passports stamped, and as was also evident in the dispatch of *Endurance* to evict them if they did not. Finally, by immediately turning over the islands to international administration pending a final negotiated solution with Britain, Argentina would defuse the objection that it was forcibly acquiring territory.[46]

This analysis, of course, made the operation seem far less risky and is evidence of extremely poor judgment on the Junta's part, since it proved incorrect in most important respects. It is possible, of course, that the Junta underestimated the risks of the operation because of wishful thinking or other motivational considerations. As I discussed in the previous chapter, this would have been perfectly normal. There is no way to know for certain how much weight to put on a motivational-psychology explanation of the Junta's misjudgment, but as I have argued elsewhere, their judgments were evidently sincere and can be traced in part to a unique and insular world view.[47]

In authorizing a military operation, the Junta was, of course, abandoning a *purely* diplomatic approach to the problem. But the Junta understood it as a "spur" or "adjunct" to diplomacy and therefore saw it as an additional or supplementary means to their end. In their own minds, they were not abandoning diplomacy wholesale. Nevertheless, it is plain that they themselves acknowledged that this was a dramatic and momentous departure from past practice, and that they were taking a fateful step. They agreed that they would proceed only if they were all on board, and the atmosphere on March 26 was appropriately solemn.[48] By any standard the decision represented a dramatic policy change, and the Junta understood it as such.

---

[46] Of course, the Junta did not stick to its script on this last point—or I should say, Galtieri failed to do so. When news broke on April 3 that Argentine forces had seized Port Stanley, there were spontaneous wild celebrations in the streets of Buenos Aires. Galtieri let his reception as *Libertador de Las Islas Malvinas* go to his head and declared from the balcony of the Casa Rosada that Argentina would never withdraw from the Malvinas. Anaya and Lami Dozo, standing behind him, looked at each other, dumbfounded. Confidential interview.

[47] Welch, "Culture and Emotion."

[48] Lami Dozo interview, 30 August 1995.

What can be said about Argentina's regime and state characteristics? The military regime was clearly authoritarian, and the state was not particularly bureaucratic. Domestic and governmental interests had little opportunity to shape Argentine policy. Opponents of the regime, of course, were persecuted, and the ministries were staffed with generally pliant officials. The Junta made its decision to occupy the Malvinas without consulting broadly within the country as a whole, or even within the government. They did consult to some extent, as is evident in their reliance upon Costa Méndez's judgment of Britain's likely reaction to the occupation; but there was no sense in which competing interests struggled to shape Argentine policy or canceled each other out. The one noteworthy exception to this characterization concerns consultation within the military. *After* the occupation, each of the members of the Junta sought and took guidance from senior officers within their respective branches. This seems to have represented a constraint on the Junta's flexibility—or so it seemed to Alexander Haig, at any rate, who expressed his frustration in trying to negotiate a settlement by noting that "If Galtieri did not hold the power of decision, neither did the junta. On every decision, the government apparently had to secure the unanimous consent of every corps commander in the army and of their equivalents in the navy and air force. Progress was made by syllables and centimeters and then vetoed by men who had never been part of the negotiations."[49] The Junta, in short, may have felt its hands were tied after the occupation by the strength of opposition to compromise within their various constituencies.[50] There is no evidence, however, that the decision-making process leading up to the invasion was similarly diffuse. By all accounts the Junta made its fateful decision to occupy the islands largely by itself. Indeed, senior officers charged with various crucial tasks in the occupation were only informed of the mission three days after the decision had been made.[51] The Polity project scores for the Galtieri regime seem entirely appropriate: −8 on the POLITY variable (highly autocratic), and 1 on the XCONST variable ("unlimited authority").[52]

How, then, do the three hypotheses stand up? The first holds that foreign policy change should be less frequent in highly bureaucratic states with democratic regimes than in less bureaucratic states with autocratic regimes. We can certainly say that Argentine leaders were relatively unfet-

---

[49] Haig, *Caveat*, p. 289. Cf. also *Times* of London, 5 May 1982, p. 10.

[50] Either that, or the Junta used subordinates as excuses for their own inflexibility.

[51] On March 29; Freedman and Gamba-Stonehouse, *Signals of War*, p. 109.

[52] Argentina's Polity IV Project codings vary considerably for the period in which the United Nations took an interest in the status of the Falklands/Malvinas prior to the war: −1 and 3 for POLITY and XCONST, respectively, for 1965; −9 and 1 for 1966–1972; 6 and 5 for 1973–1975; −9 and 1 for 1976–1980; and −8 and 1 for 1981–1982. See figure 6.1 below.

tered by regime or state characteristics. As a counterfactual thought experiment, we might try to decide whether Argentina would have played
the military card as readily if it had been a more highly bureaucratic democracy. It is notoriously difficult to handle a nontrivial counterfactual
such as this rigorously, and a clear answer to this question would be difficult to justify no matter what it turned out to be.[53] In the Argentine case,
however, it would be hard to argue that a more highly bureaucratic democracy would have been more willing to play the military card, and it
is fairly easy to argue that it would have been less willing. As I mentioned
earlier, Argentine society is not militaristic and held the military in low
esteem for much of the period in question. Commercial interests, the foreign policy elite, and the professional civil service would all have been at
least somewhat more sensitive to the downside risks of military action
than the Junta appears to have been, and more flexible both on the timing
and terms of a possible agreement with Britain.[54] While Argentines in
general shared the Junta's belief in the justice of the Argentine claim, not
all felt it quite so acutely, or took it so personally, as did Anaya. It is, in
any case, difficult to imagine the chain of events taking place on South
Georgia that provided the trigger for military action if a military Junta
had not been in power to provide a permissive environment for the kind
of adventurism to which the British were reacting. All things considered,
to the extent that the *frequency* of dramatic foreign policy change depends
upon its *ease*, the Argentine case would seem to bear up the first hypothesis. Strictly speaking, however, we should hold any conclusions about frequency in abeyance until we compare other cases.

The second hypothesis holds that foreign policy change will be most
likely when policy fails either repeatedly or catastrophically, or when leaders become convinced that it will imminently do so. This certainly describes
the Junta's attitude toward the purely diplomatic route. By early 1982 the
Junta had clearly decided not only that many years of energetic diplomacy
had failed to move Argentina closer to recovering the islands, but that time
was running out for recovering the islands at all. Given the operative reference point, this permanent loss would indeed have seemed catastrophic.

Finally, the third hypothesis holds that, all other things being equal,
leaders are more likely to pay the inherent costs of (and embrace the inherent risks in) foreign policy change to avoid losses than to realize gains of
equivalent magnitude. Here again we must rely upon a counterfactual
question to arrive at a conclusion: would the Junta have been as willing

[53] See generally Philip E. Tetlock and Aaron Belkin, eds., *Counterfactual Thought Experiments in World Politics.*

[54] Interviews: Oscar Raúl Cardoso, 28 August 1995; Dr. Lucio García del Solar, 30
August 1995.

to take military action to secure the Malvinas if they were operating in a gains frame, rather than a loss frame? From one perspective this is an easy question to answer, and from another it is difficult. If we suppose, for example, that Argentina had no claim to the Malvinas and did not regard them as *terra irredenta*, there is no serious possibility that the Junta would have embarked upon a course of military adventurism to acquire them. No member of the Junta—indeed, no Argentine leader in living memory, civilian or military—could be described as a risk-seeking, opportunistic aggressor. The islands offered nothing that would have tempted any Argentine leader to risk war with a friendly, nuclear-armed Great Power in a context in which Argentina would have had no international sympathizers and would have had to have understood its own actions as aggression against the sovereign territory of another state.

But of course, there *was* no possibility of gains of a magnitude equivalent to the loss Argentines of all stripes felt as a result of the historical injustice they believed they had suffered at the hands of the British. The stakes in this case were wholly symbolic, and their potency was a direct function of, and could not be disentangled from, the loss frame. Moral psychology tells us that people with an aggrieved sense of entitlement are notoriously difficult to buy off. They tend to be categorical in their demands and are generally unwilling to accept compromises or side-payments. Almost by definition there was no possibility of a material gain comparable in absolute magnitude to what Oscar Camilión describes as "metaphysics," "the *essence, or the being, of the state*."[55] To imagine a comparably alluring gain would be to entertain what Richard Ned Lebow calls an analytically intractable "miracle-world" counterfactual.[56]

What we can say, however, is that given the meager material value of the stakes, it is difficult to understand what motivation other than an aggrieved sense of entitlement might have enticed Argentina to embark upon such a reckless course of action. Here, at any rate, the loss frame itself would appear to be a necessary condition of the behavior we observe. And this, of course, is fully consistent with the body of theory undergirding the third hypothesis.

Quibbles and Responses

At this point, readers who remember the Falklands War and the commentary that accompanied it are likely to have one or more of three popular objections. The first is that the war was a war for oil or some other economic benefit. The second is that the war had an ulterior strategic motive.

[55] Quoted in Charlton, *The Little Platoon*, p. 102 (emphasis in the original).
[56] Richard Ned Lebow, "What's So Different about a Counterfactual?"

The third is that the war was simply about keeping the regime in power. These three objections challenge my representations of stakes and motives.

It is difficult to make the case that the Junta had economic stakes in view because the islands are virtually worthless economically. If they had had genuine economic value, Britain would not have been quite so keen to give them up.[57] From time to time people have come to believe that rich oil deposits lie just offshore, but each time they have been sorely disappointed. No exploitable deposits have yet been found.[58] The land itself supports nothing but peat and sheep. The potential tourist trade is limited by the islands' remoteness and infrastructure. The inshore waters are rich in seaweed and krill, but neither commands a lucrative market. The offshore waters abound with fish, but Britain has always been willing to grant Argentine fishermen access as part of a comprehensive settlement.

It seems clear enough, at any rate, that the Junta was not significantly motivated in 1982 by economic concerns. The possibility that there might be viable offshore oil deposits did concern Argentine leaders, but only because successful development of the islands' resources would complicate sovereignty negotiations.[59] The British bluntly told Haig that oil was not the issue, and he was convinced that it was "the last thing on Galtieri's mind."[60] As Douglas Kinney puts it, neither side "was directly

[57] One of the few books claiming that the islands have significant economic value is Alejandro Dabat and Luis Lorenzano, *Argentina*, esp. pp. 45–50, whose argument is thin and unpersuasive. As a Marxist analysis, it must of course advance a materialist explanation of Argentine policy. Not surprisingly, it concludes that "the main objective of the Junta in 'recovering' the Malvinas was to forge a new basis for consensus and to relegitimize the state and the monopoly-finance fractions controlling it" (p. 76).

[58] In 1976 Lord Shackleton suggested that oil production might be economically viable in the region, but he concluded otherwise in 1982. Peter Beck, *The Falkland Islands as an International Problem*, p. 185; Lord Shackleton, *Falkland Islands*. Desire Petroleum, a firm that staked its future on possible oil concessions off the Falklands during a recent bout of enthusiasm, saw its stock price plummet from a high of £495 in 1998 to less than £10 in early 2004 and has never generated any operational revenue.

[59] Peter Calvert writes: "In the case of the Falkland Islands there is no evidence that their economic value as such was of any interest to Argentina until United States speculation that their territorial waters might contain valuable oil reserves appeared to receive some confirmation from the Shackleton Report. The effect of this was to strengthen the determination of the military government that took power in 1976 to resist any attempt to exploit what it saw as part of the Argentine patrimony. It should be said that this was a purely negative sentiment. The military government were not, as far as it can be ascertained, motivated in any way by commercial considerations. . . . For their part, the islanders did not realise (and still have not realised) that the greater the economic development of the islands, the more nationalist sentiment would be generated on the mainland." Calvert, "The Malvinas as a Factor in Argentine Politics," p. 51.

[60] Haig, *Caveat*, p. 268.

motivated in its diplomacy by resource considerations."[61] Opinion is virtually unanimous on this point among close scholars of the conflict. Economic considerations are an almost insignificant part of the Argentine interest in the Malvinas.

The Franks Report raised the possibility that Argentina's strategic interest in the Falklands might have increased as a result of losing the Beagle Channel islands to Chile, and other analysts have echoed this theme from time to time.[62] Particularly notable is the argument of Lawrence Freedman and Virginia Gamba-Stonehouse—certainly the two best-informed and most insightful scholars of the conflict—who suggest that, according to the geopolitical perspective of the Argentine military, the loss of the Beagle Channel islands placed Argentina's entire strategic position in the South Atlantic in jeopardy. With Chile in control of the Beagle Channel islands and Britain in control of the Falklands and Dependencies, these two countries could more easily support each other against Argentina in the event of conflict. Moreover, Argentina's hand in the forthcoming 1991 review of the 1959 Antarctic Treaty would be greatly weakened.[63]

This objection certainly has more prima facie appeal than the first. Curiously, however, strategic rationales of this kind are conspicuously absent from Argentine accounts. Very few of my interviewees (and none in the professional military) even bothered mentioning strategic considerations as a reason for seeking sovereignty. This is especially odd in view of the fact that they would consider a strategic justification perfectly cogent and respectable. Typical are the remarks of Dr. Alberto De Vita, who curtly cut short my inquiries into the strategic value of the islands by insisting that "The Malvinas is an issue of national identity, not a political, military, or strategic issue."[64] Anaya was just as blunt:

The overwhelming motive for the reoccupation of the Malvinas was *justice*—the feeling of the Argentine people. We were submitted to Great Power force. The feeling of the people cannot be killed. In 1989 the only politician who said Argentina could recover the Malvinas was [Carlos] Menem. He said generations will come; blood will flow if it has to; but the Malvinas will be Argentine again. He won. On September 26, 1989, he said something similar at the UN, although he stressed that Argentina will use only political and diplo-

---

[61] Douglas Kinney, *National Interest/National Honor*, p. 87. The only serious evidence suggesting that the Junta had economic considerations in mind is a passing reference in National Strategy Directive 1/82 to "the exploration of resources," which, when viewed in context, seems rather pro forma. See n. 20 above.

[62] Franks Report, p. 75; cf. also Eddy et al., *The Falklands War*, p. 29.

[63] Freedman and Gamba-Stonehouse, *Signals of War*, pp. 4–7.

[64] Interview, 28 August 1995.

matic means to recover the Malvinas. There is a broad national consensus on this. There is a feeling of intolerable injustice.[65]

The notion that strategic considerations were important in Argentine decision making is, as far as I can tell, a purely speculative deduction.[66]

The third objection advances the view popular in the English-speaking press immediately during and after the war—and popular among political scientists to this day—that the Junta's *real* motive in ordering the occupation of the Malvinas was to distract the Argentine public's attention from the nation's dire economic straits and to bolster the public standing of the military regime.[67] This explanation has an enduring appeal because the Junta's behavior is consistent with the behavior we would expect to observe from a regime thus motivated, and because we naturally tend to assume that leaders of states are cynical, self-interested, and consumed by the desire merely to stay in office. There is, however, no serious evidence or testimony to support the diversion hypothesis. Everything we know about the decision-making process leading up to the occupation of the islands points toward a simple irredentist explanation.[68]

But even if the Junta had been motivated by domestic political concerns, or by a desire to compensate for the loss of the Beagle Channel islands, the theory would fit the story just as well. In neither case would the Junta have been restrained from boldness by domestic or governmental pressures; in both cases boldness would have been attractive because of the manifest failure of prior policy; and in both cases the behavior could easily

[65] Interview, 29 August 1995. Anaya went on later to add; "Honor played a role; but it and economic concerns are all subservient to the basic concern with justice. The more interests are involved, the more the injustice hurts."

[66] In any case, there are other reasons to doubt the merits of a strategic rationale. The islands are simply too remote to have any real strategic value. They would be worse than useless in a shooting war with Chile because, as the British know only too well, bases in the islands are difficult to supply, expensive to maintain, and more vulnerable to attack than bases on the Argentine mainland. Very little commercial traffic travels through the area, and there are no targets of any value in southern Argentina that could not be protected more cheaply and more effectively from a mainland base. Moreover, if Chile and Britain wished to gang up on Argentina, it would make little practical difference whether the Beagle Channel islands were in Argentine or Chilean hands.

Rubén Moro claims that the region has strategic value because of the volume of oil shipped around the Cape of Good Hope; *The History of the South Atlantic Conflict*, p. 17. But the Falklands/Malvinas are thousands of miles from the Cape of Good Hope, and no force operating from them could hope to dominate the tip of southern Africa. It is, in any case, difficult to imagine why either Britain or Argentina would want to interdict oil traffic to Europe or North America.

[67] Jack S. Levy and Lily I. Vakili, "Diversionary Action by Authoritarian Regimes." See also n. 33 above.

[68] See, e.g., *Justice and the Genesis of War*, pp. 164–169; and Welch, "Culture and Emotion."

be understood as a desperate gamble to try to avoid what appeared to be a certain painful loss. The theory would fail to fit only the putative economic motivation, since Argentina had suffered no significant economic penalty as a result of 150 years of British occupation of the Malvinas. If economic motives had been in play, the Junta would clearly have been gambling to secure uncertain future gains.

In sum, then, it would appear that the theory does, in fact, fit Argentine policy toward the Falklands/Malvinas very well. What we have here is a dramatic example of an authoritarian, relatively nonbureaucratic regime embarking upon what it acknowledged to be—and which was, by any standard—a dramatic foreign policy change to avoid a painful loss in the face of the demonstrable failure of prior policy. Why do we see no similarly dramatic change in Japanese policy on the Northern Territories/ Southern Kurils dispute, despite its similarly spectacular failure?

THE NORTHERN TERRITORIES

On August 8, 1945, Stalin abrogated his neutrality treaty with Japan, declared war, and pounced upon the Japanese half of Sakhalin Island and the chain of islands extending south from Kamchatka to Hokkaido.[69] This opportunistic land grab in the waning days of the Second World War has always stuck in Japan's craw. In fact, Russia and Japan are still technically at war. The chief reason for this is that Japan insists, as a precondition for signing a formal peace treaty, that Moscow return some of the captured islands.

The islands in question are the southernmost of the Kurile (or "Kuril") chain: Etorofu, Kunashiri, Shikotan, and the Habomai Islets. Together, they amount to a mere 5,000 square kilometers of territory, or less than 2 percent of the Japanese total (see table 3.1). Actually, the Japanese deny

TABLE 3.1
The Northern Territories/Southern Kurils—Land Area

	Area (km²)	As Proportion of Japanese Total
Etorofu	3,139	0.84%
Kunashiri	1,500	0.40%
Shikotan	254	0.07%
Habomai Islets	101	0.03%
Total	4,994	1.33%

[69] David Rees, *The Soviet Seizure of the Kuriles.*

that these are "Kurile" islands at all, for reasons I shall get to shortly. The key point for the moment is that Japan wants them back—very badly.

The question is: Why? By any measure, the material value of these islands does not warrant the time, effort, political capital, and opportunity cost successive Japanese governments have paid trying to get them back.[70] Their economic value is marginal. They have no petroleum potential; the larger two are forested and contain modest mineral deposits, but these would be costly and difficult to exploit given the islands' physical geography and nonexistent infrastructure;[71] and while they command an impressive maritime exclusive economic zone (EEZ), which includes spawning grounds for a variety of commercially viable fish species,[72] sovereignty is in no sense a necessary condition for Japan's benefitting from it. Russian patrols have generally been unable to prevent Japanese boats from catching what they wish,[73] and Soviet and Russian officials have always expressed a willingness to grant the Japanese access if only they would drop their insistence on sovereignty.[74] If Japan were primarily interested in sovereignty so as to reap the benefit of maritime resources, it is in any case difficult to understand why Japan does not insist either upon the return of the *entire* Kurile chain, which commands a much larger and much more

---

[70] For a more detailed analysis, see Kimura and Welch, "Specifying 'Interests,' " from which I draw portions of the following text.

[71] Tsuneo Akaha and Takashi Murakami, "Soviet/Russian-Japanese Economic Relations," pp. 168–169. In 1990 the economist Kenichi Ohmae estimated that the cost of bringing the islands' infrastructure up to Japanese standards would be approximately ¥60,000 per taxpayer. "Calmer Waters: Ambitious Plans May Transform Contested Islands." No senior official I interviewed at the Ministry of Foreign Affairs or the Japan Defense Agency in July 1994 claimed that recovery of the islands is important because of the timber or mineral resources they contain.

[72] The Northern Territories/Southern Kurils' EEZ totals 196,000 km². The seabed may also contain exploitable deposits of titanium, magnetite, nickel, copper, chromium, vanadium, and niobium, if anyone ever figures out how to mine them. Akaha and Murakami, "Soviet/Russian-Japanese Economic Relations," pp. 168–169.

[73] William F. Nimmo, *Japan and Russia*, p. 130.

[74] Andrew Mack and Martin O'Hare, "Moscow-Tokyo and the Northern Territories Dispute"; Gerald Segal, *Normalizing Soviet-Japanese Relations*; Takahiko Tanaka, *Nisso Kokko Kaifuku no Shiteki Kenkyu*; see also Gerald Segal, "Moscow Adopts a New Realistic Line on Japan." In the late 1990s the Japanese government changed tactics and actively pursued functional cooperation agreements with Russia as steps toward a full, comprehensive settlement. These included, for example, a Framework Agreement on Japanese fishing vessels in the waters of the disputed islands; Japan, Ministry of Foreign Affairs, *Diplomatic Blue Book 1999*. However, Japan consistently maintains that its ultimate goal is a comprehensive settlement "based on the Tokyo Declaration" (ibid.) of October 1993, which calls for "negotiations towards an early conclusion of a peace treaty through the solution of [the territorial] issue on the basis of historical and legal facts"—code-speak, from the Japanese perspective, for reversion. Japan, Ministry of Foreign Affairs, *Tokyo Declaration on Japan-Russia Relations (Provisional Translation)*.

attractive EEZ than do the Northern Territories/Southern Kurils alone, or, alternatively, Shikotan and the Habomais, whose EEZ is larger and richer than that of the two bigger islands, and whose status the Soviets indicated they would be quite willing to negotiate as far back as 1956.[75]

Japanese leaders may not have pressed for the entire Kurile chain in part because they knew that the Soviets considered it vital for their security during the Cold War.[76] This was especially true during the 1970s and 1980s, when the Barents Sea and the Sea of Okhotsk served as the two "bastions" protecting Soviet submarine-launched ballistic missile (SLBM) submarines from American anti–submarine warfare (ASW) operations.[77] But the Soviets had little strategic reason not to offer up Shikotan and the Habomais, which lay on the Pacific side of the Kuriles, and which would have added essentially nothing to Japanese or American military capabilities. Soviet submarines would have been marginally more vulnerable during the Cold War if the Southern Kurils had been in enemy hands, since American submarines would have found it that much easier to move into and out of the Sea of Okhotsk.[78] But since the end of the Cold War, the Japanese military has downgraded its estimate of the islands' strategic value,[79] and analysts generally now agree that strategic interests do not explain the consistency, intensity, or substance of Japan's grievance. If anything, to the extent that it has aggravated Moscow, the persistence of the Japanese claim has actually jeopardized Japanese security. As William Nimmo puts it, "A realistic analysis of the value of the islands—economically, militarily, politically, strategically, and diplomatically—reveals that neither acquisition nor release of the territory would materially affect the fortunes of Russia or Japan."[80]

The real value of the islands to Japan is symbolic. Japan's national identity is invested in the Northern Territories much the same way Argen-

---

[75] Akaha and Murakami, "Soviet/Russian-Japanese Economic Relations," p. 169.

[76] The best analysis of the strategic value of the islands is Geoffrey Jukes, *Russia's Military and the Northern Territories Issue*. See also Michael MccGwire, "The Rationale for the Development of Soviet Seapower"; Rajan Menon and Daniel Abele, "Security Dimensions of Soviet Territorial Disputes with China and Japan"; Mike M. Mochizuki, "The Soviet/Russian Factor in Japanese Security Policy"; Alexei Zagorskii, "Russian Security Policy toward the Asia-Pacific Region"; Nimmo, *Japan and Russia*, p. 118; Brian Cloughley, "Bring the Boys Home from the Kuriles, Too"; Edward W. Desmond, "The Screen of Steel."

[77] The Soviet strategic nuclear deterrent rested primarily upon vulnerable land-based intercontinental ballistic missiles (ICBMs), and only marginally upon manned aircraft. From the Soviet perspective, relatively invulnerable SLBMs provided a crucial guarantee of second-strike capability.

[78] Interviews with senior Japan Self-Defense Forces (JSDF) officers and Japan Defense Agency (JDA) officials, July 1994.

[79] E.g., "A Gentle Breeze of Change Blows through Japanese Defence," *Jane's Defence Weekly*, 15 July 1995, pp. 20–21.

[80] Nimmo, *Japan and Russia*, p. 177.

tina's is invested in the Malvinas. Without acknowledged sovereignty over the Northern Territories, the Japanese feel that Japan is simply not complete. On this point there is virtually no dissent. Every February 7, the country celebrates Northern Territories Day. Nearly one hundred organizations are devoted to lobbying for their return.[81] A leader who managed to secure it would reap an immediate and lasting political reward.[82] A leader who expressed doubt about the claim would commit political suicide because "abandoning the claim would trigger an explosion among the Japanese people."[83]

Seen in this light, the recovery of the islands is a *moral* imperative of sufficient power and cogency to justify the remarkable priority the issue has enjoyed in Japanese foreign policy.[84] In part, the moral imperative flows from what the Japanese perceive as the simple injustice of the Soviet occupation and annexation, which consists both in the opportunism and in the violation of what Japan considers its title to the islands under international law. Some also feel the injustice of Moscow's unequal treatment of Japan. After all, the USSR made territorial concessions both to North Korea in 1984 and to the People's Republic of China in 1986,[85] and Russia yielded millions of square kilometers of what was very valuable territory indeed to the newly independent states of the former Soviet Union. Many Japanese also see the Russian occupation of the islands as "an increasingly intolerable reminder of the war and defeat which the Japanese would like to forget."[86] And underneath it all is the long history of enmity and hostility between the two countries that antedates, but became acute during, the Russo-Japanese War of 1904–05. "[T]he real issue," as David Sanger puts it, "has been a century-long clash of national egos."[87]

That the symbolic value of the islands drives Japanese policy was evident to me from interviews I conducted in 1994 with senior Ministry of Foreign Affairs (MOFA) and Japan Defense Agency (JDA) officials—none of whom, alas, spoke for attribution, since the issue was very much on the front burner at the time. The number of interviews I conducted (six) was not large enough to permit strong conclusions about elite opinion,

[81] Miyuki Mineshiga, "In the Way."

[82] In 1992, when Japanese hopes ran high that Russia might acknowledge Japan's claim at the Munich summit, the Tokyo correspondent of the *Economist* wrote: "If Mr. Yeltsin can be persuaded to agree at least in principle to Japan's sovereignty over the islands, [Prime Minister Kiichi] Miyazawa will not only return home in triumph, but he will be able to write his ticket for as many terms in office as he wants." "Alternatively, Harakiri," p. 36.

[83] Interview, senior Foreign Ministry official, July 1994.

[84] E.g., Kenichi Ito, "Japan and the Soviet Union," p. 40.

[85] Ibid., p 43; Mack and O'Hare, "Moscow-Tokyo and the Northern Territories Dispute," p. 386. Cf. also Segal, *Normalizing Soviet-Japanese Relations.*

[86] Wolf Mendl, "Japan and the Soviet Union," p. 198.

[87] David E. Sanger, "In Russia and Japan, Once Again, National Egos Block Cooperation."

but it was a good sample of the total number of officials at this level. I asked each interviewee four topical questions and followed up with hot-pursuit questions within each topic that varied from interview to interview. My goal was to elicit both official and personal responses. In some cases (although not in all), there were interesting differences between the two. The topical questions I put to these officials were as follows: (1) How would you characterize Russo-Japanese relations now? (2) Has there been any progress on the territorial issue? (3) What progress (if any) do you expect in the near future? (4) How would you describe the nature of Japan's interest in securing the return of the islands? Questions 1–3 were primarily ice-breakers; question 4 elicited the truly interesting responses and, in fact, occupied most of the discussions. In table 3.2 I summarize the responses, which clearly indicate that these officials understood the Japanese claim primarily in moral, legal, and symbolic terms. For the most part, they discounted the islands' instrumental value.

As interesting as the substance of the responses was the demeanor of my interviewees. They all responded to questions 1–3 entirely matter-of-factly. Four out of six, however, came unglued when the discussion of question 4 ventured beyond the instrumental value of the islands.[88] They became flustered when I asked in hot pursuit whether Japan's interests might not be better served by abandoning the claim entirely and acknowledging Russian sovereignty. The question left them at a temporary loss for words, evidently because they simply regarded the proposition as unthinkable. Upon recovering, they experienced great difficulty articulating their objections to it because the importance of reversion seemed to them to be obvious on its face. In all four cases, the substantive answer they eventually articulated appealed to the moral, legal, and symbolic importance of reversion. "The territorial issue is special—very emotional," said one. "The issue will not go away. It is about who we are." What I witnessed, in short, was precisely the same moral-psychological dynamic that was at work among Argentine leaders: a sincere and powerful sense of aggrieved entitlement that triggered a strident emotional response.

Perhaps not surprisingly, given the intensity of Japanese feeling on the issue, securing the return of the Northern Territories has overwhelmed all other considerations in bilateral relations with the Soviet Union and Russia for more than forty years. Commentators describe it as a "religion" that became "a substitute for Japan's entire policy toward Russia."[89] When the Soviet Union collapsed, securing the return of the islands took

---

[88] One of the six—a senior military officer—spoke single-mindedly of strategic issues. The sixth was skeptical of the claim and did not personally regard the recovery of the islands as important to Japan.

[89] "Boris, about Our Islands," p. 30; Tsuyoshi Hasegawa, "Rocks and Roles."

TABLE 3.2

Summary of responses to Question 4: "How would you describe the nature of Japan's interest in securing the return of the islands?"

	Number of Mentions—MOFA Officials (n = 3)						Number of Mentions—JDA Officials (n = 3)					
	Unimportant		Somewhat Important		Very Important		Unimportant		Somewhat Important		Very Important	
	M	P	M	P	M	P	M	P	M	P	M	P
Economic value of the islands	3	3					2					
Strategic value of the islands	2	2	1	1				1	1	1	2	1
Prestige				1								
Honor				1								
Bringing WWII to a conclusion					1	1						
Credibility of Japanese diplomacy		1										
Popular will					1	1						
Righting injustice/illegality of Soviet occupation					3	3					1	1
Fair treatment of Japan by Russia					1	1						
Entitlement					3	3					1	1
Rights of displaced inhabitants			1					1				
Territorial integrity/sovereignty of Japan					2	2					2	2
Emotion						1						1

Note: M = Ministry view; P = Personal view

priority in Japanese foreign policy over contributing to political and economic stability in Russia or facilitating the smooth integration of Russia into multilateral economic and security arrangements.[90] Japanese leaders felt sufficiently strongly about the issue to take uncharacteristically tough positions on it at G-7 summits, and to break ranks with other G-7 countries on the provision of aid to Russia.[91] Richard deVillafranca notes with some puzzlement that "Taxpayers in all the other G-7 countries seem to understand the provision of aid to Russia in national security, not historical terms, despite the fact that Russia's predecessor may have inflicted economic and human hardships on them on a scale far exceeding the seizure of four islands."[92] The recovery of the islands remains Japan's number one foreign policy goal, although the stridency of Japanese policy has muted in recent years, partly for tactical reasons, and partly because of the press of other issues.

Japan has paid a considerable price for its stubbornness. First, and most directly, the issue has strained Russo-Japanese relations. When Japanese hopes and expectations rose in the wake of the Soviet Union's collapse, several acutely embarrassing diplomatic incidents inflamed hostility on both sides.[93] Mikhail Gorbachev tripped over the issue on his visit to Tokyo in 1991 (the first by any Soviet leader), triggering a wave of anti-Soviet feeling when he failed to make any concessions on the territorial issue because the Japanese government invited him on the sole condition that he discuss it.[94] His successor, Boris Yeltsin, twice canceled trips to Japan—once on just three days' notice—so as to avoid having to discuss

[90] Official Japanese statements do not clearly indicate this priority, suggesting instead that these are simultaneous goals. See, e.g., Japan, Ministry of Foreign Affairs, *Japan's Policy on the Russian Federation*: "The basic objectives of Japan's policy on Russia are to make the utmost efforts to resolve the Northern Territories issue, thereby concluding a peace treaty and fully normalizing relations with Russia, and to provide appropriate assistance for the reform efforts of Russia in coordination with the international community."

[91] Japan first attempted to internationalize the dispute at the 1990 Houston summit and was particularly assertive in this regard at Munich in 1992. "Yeltsin's Yoke." See also "Carrots for Gorbachev"; "Stuck on the Rocks."

[92] Richard deVillafranca, "Japan and the Northern Territories Dispute," p. 623.

[93] The Soviets themselves encouraged these hopes in 1988 by acknowledging publicly for the first time that there was an issue to discuss, and by floating several informal trial balloons—including demilitarization of the islands, special cooperative arrangements, UN trusteeship, and a resurrection of the 1956 formula whereby Shikotan and the Habomais would revert to Japan immediately in exchange for long-term negotiations over the status of Kunashiri and Etorofu (the so-called two-island formula). Formally, however, the Soviets displayed less flexibility. See Brian Bridges, "Japan," esp. p. 57; Gerald Segal, "Gorbachev in Japan"; and "Four Bones of Contention."

[94] Nimmo, *Japan and Russia*, p. xxv. Many commentators considered this "the one real diplomatic fiasco of his career." Alexei Zagorsky, "Kuriles Stumbling Block."

it, both times causing a bilateral uproar.[95] Most importantly, the ongoing dispute has reinforced anti-Japanese sentiment in Russia and anti-Russian sentiment in Japan. These mutual antipathies color virtually every dimension of the bilateral relationship and make it difficult for the two countries to do business.

Japan has also paid a price in its relations with its G-7 partners, whom it irritated by refusing to maintain solidarity on aid to Russia and by insisting upon G-7 backing for its territorial claim at a time when Western countries were seeking to defuse issues that would tend to undercut Yeltsin at home.[96] By choosing to call in its G-7 chips on an issue over which the group had no real influence, Japan clearly squandered political capital. The United States was particularly vexed, since Russo-Japanese tensions also implicated the U.S.-Japanese security relationship, which remains the cornerstone of American security policy in the region to this day.[97]

Third, Japanese policy on the territorial dispute undermined the credibility of Japanese diplomacy. Recognizing that Moscow viewed Japan as vital to the reconstruction of the post-Soviet economy,[98] Japanese leaders proffered economic carrots to secure territorial concessions. Japan could credibly hold out the promise of increased official aid and credits.[99] But increased trade and private-sector investment was another matter entirely because these were things over which Japanese officials had little control. Undeterred, beginning in 1988, Japanese officials attempted at virtually every opportunity to convince their Soviet and Russian counterparts that progress on the territorial issue would open the floodgates of Japanese trade and investment, and they suggested that stagnant levels of trade and investment could be traced directly to Soviet/Russian intransigence.[100] Japanese trade and investment certainly failed to meet Russian hopes and expectations, particularly in the Far East; but the primary reasons for this were declining energy prices, the lack of infrastructure, and political instability in Russia.[101] Japanese businessmen are wary of Russia for rea-

---

[95] Serge Schmemann, "Yeltsin Cancels a Visit to Japan as Dispute over Islands Simmers"; "Off Again."

[96] See, e.g., Yoji Takagi, "Getting on Track."

[97] Harry Gelman, *Russo-Japanese Relations and the Future of the U.S.-Japanese Alliance.*

[98] Segal, "Moscow Adopts a New Realistic Line on Japan"; Mette Skak, "Post-Soviet Foreign Policy," pp. 165–166.

[99] See, e.g., deVillafranca, "Japan and the Northern Territories Dispute," p. 622: "In a remarkable statement to NHK News just after the cancellation of Yeltsin's trip, Foreign Minister [Michio] Watanabe revealed that Tokyo had told Moscow in advance that a Russian reconfirmation of the 1956 Declaration [see n. 93 above] and an agreement to discuss the future of Etorofu and Kunashiri would have been enough to unleash 'full-scale' Japanese assistance, hitherto withheld until the full resolution of the territorial dispute."

[100] Interview, senior MOFA official, July 1994. Cf. Bridges, "Japan," esp. pp. 57–58.

[101] "The Rising Sun in Russia's Sky."

sons other than the territorial dispute. As table 3.3 indicates, Japan proved neither more nor less willing than its other G-7 partners to trade with post-Soviet Russia. And while Japan appears to have been the least willing member of the G-7 to invest in Russia (see table 3.4), its levels of investment in Eastern Europe as a whole were conspicuously lower than those of its G-7 partners, suggesting that the territorial dispute was not the primary cause of Japanese restraint.[102] Thus it seems that Japan's attempt to wield private-sector carrots was a bluff, and Japanese officials have privately voiced their concern that both the attempt and the fact that it was a bluff have hurt Japanese diplomacy by encouraging those in Russia who argue that Japan does not take Russia seriously, and who feel that Japan has attempted to take advantage of Russia during a painful period of economic and political adjustment.[103]

Fourth, and finally, Japan's global role and reputation suffered significantly. The end of the Cold War gave Japan an opportunity to cultivate a new image and a new role as a regional leader in the quest for stable economic and security regimes. Far-sighted analysts foresaw the possibility of Japan reestablishing its Great Power status, if not in military terms, at least as a global "civilian power."[104] This would have required that Japan anticipate long-term macrogeopolitical trends and pursue a broad-based multilateralist agenda designed to integrate the former Soviet Union into emerging cooperative arrangements and to devalue the currency of military force. But Japan failed to do this, remaining "bogged down in the niggling details of an old and insignificant territorial dispute."[105] As Tsuyoshi Hasegawa put it, the "ultimate victim" of the Northern Territories dispute was Japanese foreign policy, which "could not respond adequately to the profound changes in the Soviet Union and which proved unable, because of these failures, to fulfill global responsibility commensurate with Japan's international influence."[106] The *New York Times* was less delicate: "[T]he broader and more troubling question was why Russia and Japan—two countries with every incentive to mend relations—could allow a minor territorial dispute [to] grow to such damaging proportions. In both countries, the triumph of nationalist sentiments over rational foreign policy suggested immaturity and insecurity."[107]

---

[102] United Nations Conference on Trade and Development Division on Transnational Corporations and Investments, *World Investment Report 1994*.

[103] Interviews, MOFA, July 1994.

[104] Yoichi Funabashi, "Japan and the New World Order."

[105] Segal, *Normalizing Soviet-Japanese Relations*, p. 38.

[106] Tsuyoshi Hasegawa, "The Gorbachev-Kaifu Summit," p. 78. Cf. also Robert M. Orr, Jr., "Japan Pursues Hard Line on the Northern Territories Issue": "[F]ocusing on the fate of relatively inconsequential tiny dots in the Pacific seems to call into question, once again, [Japan's] capacity for leadership in the post-Cold War order."

[107] Serge Schmemann, "Little Isles, Big Fight."

Table 3.3
Japan's Relative Trade Performance with USSR/Russia

Exports to G-7 Countries (Millions of US Dollars)

	1985	1986	1987	1988	1989	1990	1991	1992	1993	1994	Slope	Rank[b]
Canada[c]	21	19	26	114	99	140	185	218[a]	273[c]	184	0.03166	1
UK[c]	851	936	1,319	1,178	1,237	1,453	1,444	1,077	1,121[a]	3,640	0.00226	2
US	402	551	427	592	713	1,062	832	465	1,679[a]	3,694	0.00212	3
Japan	1,307	1,807	2,152	2,520	2,718	3,064	3,016	2,184	1,713[a]	2,165	0.00154	4
Italy	2,738	2,111	2,588	2,850	3,273	3,775	4,100	1,881[d]	3,519[a]	2,729	0.00116	5
Germany[f]	4,264	3,889	3,678	3,558	4,061	6,680	8,018	3,887	5,890[a]	5,296	0.00099	6
France	2,267	2,400	2,317	2,548	2,383	3,063	2,778	1,210[d]	2,367[a]	1,234	-0.00214	7

Imports from G-7 Countries (Millions of US Dollars)

	1985	1986	1987	1988	1989	1990	1991	1992	1993	1994	Slope	Rank[b]
UK[c]	756	871	887	1,009	1,227	1,165	687	887	907[a]	889	0.00085	1
US	2,665	1,372	1,628	3,033	4,698	3,396	3,935	2,307	3,264[a]	2,029	0.00063	2
Germany[f]	3,963	4,752	4,817	5,904	6,763	13,038	12,179	3,999	7,565[a]	5,520	0.00029	3
Italy	1,697	1,795	2,428	2,323	2,842	2,921	2,656	1,303[d]	1,889[a]	1,489	-0.00096	4
Japan	3,049	3,496	2,845	3,444	3,376	2,819	2,329	1,187	1,659[a]	1,088	-0.00280	5
Canada[c]	1,280	970	666	1,025	639	1,061	1,411	1,169[a]	277[c]	180	-0.00345	6
France	2,070	1,677	1,928	2,132	1,893	1,645	1,604	744[d]	1,620[a]	984	-0.00495	7

Sources: For 1994, International Monetary Fund, *Direction of Trade Statistics Quarterly* (June 1995); for 1992–1993, International Monetary Fund, *Direction of Trade Statistics Yearbook, 1994* (Washington, DC: IMF, 1995); for 1985–1991, International Monetary Fund, *Direction of Trade Statistics Yearbook, 1992* (Washington, DC: IMF, 1993).

Notes: [a] Derived from partner data. N.B. All data based on partner data prior to 1994 except Canada.
[b] Secular rate of increase (from Slope).
[c] Estimated by other methods.
[d] Estimated by other methods including partner data.
[e] Trade is for former USSR in 1992 for Canada and the UK. For all other countries, 1992 figures and later are trade with Russia. Prior to 1992, all figures are for USSR.
[f] Figures prior to 1990 are for West Germany only.
N.B. Trade statistics are calculated to take into account insurance and freight costs for imports as per IMF practice. Partner data have been adjusted up 10% for imports and down 10% for exports in comparison to partner country figures.

TABLE 3.4
Joint Ventures in Russia by Foreign Partner (as of April 23, 1992)

Country	Joint Ventures	Total Capital (Millions of Rubles)
United States	398	11,034
Germany	373	781
Italy	198	1,038
United Kingdom	122	228
France	90	501
Canada	71	328
Japan	43	138

Source: *Foreign Direct Investment in the States of the Former USSR* (Washington, DC: World Bank, 1992), table 24.

Back to the Theory

There is no doubt that Japanese leaders understand the status quo as a loss and have done so for half a century. Their operative reference point has been a Japan that includes sovereignty over the Northern Territories. It is interesting to note, however, that this particular conception of what would be a satisfactory state of affairs appears to be somewhat arbitrary and is the product of historical contingencies. For the purpose of giving us some insight into reference-point formation, it is perhaps worth spending a few moments examining why this is so. To that end, we need to look briefly at the history of the claim.

Territorial issues first arose between Russia and Japan in the nineteenth century, as Russians and Japanese explored and settled Sakhalin and the Kuriles. In the Treaty of Shimoda (1855), the two countries established an international boundary between the islands of Etorofu and Urup (i.e., the boundary that Japan seeks to reestablish today). However, they were unable to determine the fate of Sakhalin, which they jointly controlled, for another twenty years, when Russia acquired title in the Treaty of St. Petersburg (1875) in return for ceding the Kurile chain to Japan. At the end of the Russo-Japanese War, under the terms of the Treaty of Portsmouth (1905), Japan recovered the southern half of Sakhalin. Thus, upon the outbreak of the Second World War, Japan was the acknowledged rightful owner of the *entire* Kurile chain, as well as southern Sakhalin (see figure 3.2).

In the San Francisco Peace Treaty (1951), Japan renounced "all right, title and claim to the Kurile Islands, and to the portion of Sakhalin and

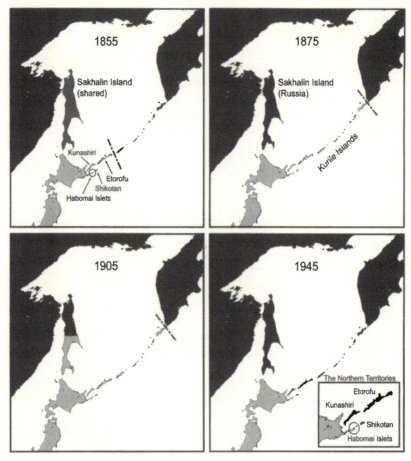

Fig. 3.2. Russo-Japanese borders since 1855

the islands adjacent to it over which Japan acquired sovereignty [by] the Treaty of Portsmouth on September 5, 1905."[108] This treaty formally brought an end to the state of war between Japan and the United States, but not to the state of war between Japan and the Soviet Union, as the USSR was not a signatory. The Japanese insist that by the phrase "the Kurile Islands" they meant the islands to the north of Etorofu and did not mean to include the Northern Territories. Russia insists otherwise. There is room for debate on this point. In San Francisco, Japanese Prime Minister Shigeru Yoshida sought explicitly to include a provision for a later negotiation to establish *which* islands Japan would give up, indicat-

[108] Nimmo, *Japan and Russia*, p. 41.

ing his intention not to relinquish all (or, at least, not to do so readily). But U.S. Special Envoy John Foster Dulles prevailed upon him not to insist upon this, on the ground that it would delay, complicate, and possibly prevent the conclusion of a peace treaty. One might argue that Yoshida's compliance constituted a surrender of Japan's title to the Northern Territories/Southern Kurils. But even if this were Yoshida's intention (or the implication of his action), Japan continues to claim that the Soviet Union cannot rightfully be said to have gained title to the disputed islands under the terms of a treaty it did not sign.

Things got more interesting in 1955–56, when Japan and the Soviet Union sat down to try to negotiate a formal peace. Each side began with maximal demands. Japan sought sovereignty over *all* the Kuriles (including Shikotan and the Habomais), plus southern Sakhalin. The Soviet Union sought exactly the same thing and also demanded that Japan abrogate its security treaty with the United States. Eventually, the negotiators on each side reached a compromise: Japan would insist only upon the return of Shikotan and the Habomais, and the Soviet Union would drop its objection to the U.S.-Japan Security Treaty. Japanese Foreign Minister Mamoru Shigemitsu demurred, initially insisting also upon the return of Etorofu and Kunashiri. But the Soviets would not agree, and in 1956 the Japanese government was about to settle *only* for Shikotan and the Habomais when Dulles threatened to annex Okinawa if Japan did not also insist upon the two larger islands.[109]

Given the Soviet Union's clearly opportunistic declaration of war in 1945, it would seem intuitive to expect Japan to feel a strong claim to the status quo ante bellum.[110] But in view of the fact that Japan was prepared to settle for only Shikotan and the Habomais in 1956, it is puzzling that Japan is not willing to settle for this today. Why insist now upon Etorofu and Kunashiri as well?

The Japanese answer is that no treaty has ever acknowledged any other country's sovereignty over these particular islands.[111] This is true enough and would seem to go some way toward solving the puzzle. But things are not quite so simple as that. In view of the relatively late exploration and settlement of these islands, it would be a mistake to think of them as comparably important to the Japanese sense of identity as (say) the four home islands of Honshu, Shikoku, Kyushu, or Hokkaido. Moreover, the

---

[109] Ibid., pp. 46–48; Marc Gallicchio, "The Kuriles Controversy," esp. pp. 95–99; but cf. deVillafranca, "Japan and the Northern Territories Dispute." Dulles claimed that he was merely attempting to strengthen Japan's bargaining position; it would appear, however, that his chief purpose was to prevent a rapprochement between Japan and Russia.

[110] Kahneman, Knetsch, and Thaler, "The Endowment Effect, Loss Aversion, and the Status Quo Bias."

[111] See, e.g., Ito, "Japan and the Soviet Union," p. 40.

fact that no country but Japan had ever before enjoyed sovereignty over the islands does not explain why Japan would have been willing to relinquish the larger two in 1956.

The solution to the puzzle lies in domestic politics. Since 1945, all Japanese political parties, including the Socialists, have officially called for the return of the *entire* Kurile chain— except for the Liberal Democratic Party (LDP), which was the ruling party in 1956 when Dulles prevailed upon Yoshida to insist upon what has since become known as the "four-island formula."[112] The LDP called merely for the return of the Northern Territories. The LDP ruled Japan without interruption until 1993, and so its claim was the official claim for thirty-seven years. Two generations of citizens and officials were socialized politically during this period, and the four-island formula gradually came to shape and to dominate popular and elite expectations. Since 1993 non-LDP coalition governments have maintained the four-island claim unaltered, notwithstanding the historical platforms of their various member parties.

While the four-island formula was therefore itself the result of a historical accident (Dulles's 1956 interference in Japanese-Soviet diplomacy), well-understood socialization processes can explain how the sense of entitlement has crystallized around it.[113] Over the course of more than forty years, Japan has internalized and normalized the claim, and but for a few voices on the margins of Japanese politics, no one today doubts its legitimacy. There is no question now of Japan insisting upon more, nor of settling for less. Not surprisingly, given the arbitrary influences that shaped the claim, the legal and historical justifications offered on behalf of it have been a matter of debate.[114] But this is entirely beside the point. What matters is why Japan has come to regard the claim in its current form as legitimate.

Despite the evident importance the Japanese attach to recovering the islands, and despite the various costs they have incurred in the process, Japan has never abandoned a relatively gentle form of diplomacy to try to get them back. There is no evidence whatsoever that Japanese leaders ever considered—and they certainly never threatened—military action. For that matter, Japan never threatened to try to obstruct Russia's participation in the G-8, to block its accession to the World Trade Organization

---

[112] Mack and O'Hare, "Moscow-Tokyo and the Northern Territories Dispute," p. 387.

[113] For further discussion of socialization and its application to international relations theory, see G. John Ikenberry and Charles Kupchan, "Socialization and Hegemonic Power." Cf. also Robert N. Bellah, "Legitimation Processes in Politics and Religion"; Anna Emilia Berti, "The Development of Political Understanding in Children between 6–15 Years Old." The relevant moral psychology dates back to David Hume, "Treatise of Human Nature."

[114] See, e.g., Keith A. Call, "Southern Kurils or Northern Territories?"; Glen W. Price, "Legal Analysis of the Kurile Island Dispute"; Gregory Clark, "Japanese Emotionalism Surfaces in the Northern Territories Issue."

(WTO),[115] or to impose economic, diplomatic, cultural, academic, or athletic sanctions. Tokyo repeatedly proffered carrots, mostly in the form of promises on trade, aid, and investment, but never once brandished a stick. The tempo and tone of Japanese policy on the issue heightened in the early 1990s when a window of opportunity seemed to open for a final resolution. But since being disappointed in its sense of expectation, Japan has settled once again into a policy of patiently but firmly reminding Russia of its claim, urging negotiations, and working the edges of the issue by pursuing limited functional agreements on such things as fishing and visitation rights.[116] We see no dramatic change in Japanese policy throughout the entire period. Why not?

It is no great surprise that the Japanese have never considered an overt use of force to resolve the dispute. Japan has no stomach for military options. The country has profoundly embraced the antimilitarism expressed in Article 9 of its constitution, which most Japanese consider the very cornerstone of their democracy:

> Aspiring sincerely to an international peace based on justice and order, the Japanese people forever renounce war as a sovereign right of the nation and the threat or use of force as means of settling international disputes.
>
> In order to accomplish the aim of the preceding paragraph, land, sea, and air forces, as well as other war potential, will never be maintained. The right of belligerency of the state will not be recognized.[117]

Antimilitarism is so entrenched domestically that public and official sensitivities almost derailed, and severely curtailed, Japanese participation in peacekeeping operations when Tokyo first considered the idea in the early 1990s.[118] Japan has played a more active peacekeeping role since then, and

---

[115] Russia currently has observer status but is not a full member.

[116] See, e.g., Japan, Ministry of Foreign Affairs, *Japan's Policy on the Russian Federation*.

[117] http://www.ilrg.com/nations/jp/const-jp.html. Notwithstanding the apparent plain meaning of this article, Japan does maintain a competent standing military of approximately 200,000 highly trained and well-equipped soldiers and has justified doing so by invoking its inherent right of self-defense, for which these are logically necessary means. But they are strictly configured for self-defense; colonized bureaucratically by civilian ministries such as Finance, Foreign Affairs, and Economy, Trade and Industry; and kept firmly under civilian control. They are also deeply unpopular domestically. On ideational and institutional checks on militarism in Japan, see, e.g., Thomas U. Berger, "From Sword to Chrysanthemum"; Peter J. Katzenstein, *Cultural Norms and National Security*, pp. 99–130; Peter J. Katzenstein and Nobuo Okawara, "Japan's National Security"; Katzenstein and Okawara, *Japan's National Security*, pp. 21–56; Susumu Yamakage, "Japan's National Security and Asia-Pacific's Regional Institutions in the Post-Cold War Era," esp. pp. 278–279. On Japanese military capabilities, see Norman D. Levin, Mark A. Lorell, and Arthur J. Alexander, *The Wary Warriors*.

[118] See, e.g., *The United States and Japan in 1994*, pp. 57–62; Katzenstein and Okawara, "Japan's National Security," pp. 109–111.

Japanese forces were even deployed to Iraq in support of the American occupation, but domestic suspicions continue to run high.[119]

Japanese leaders are also acutely aware of international sensitivities about the use of Japanese military force. Whereas Argentine leaders might have been able to convince themselves that the international community would look with equanimity—perhaps even with muted approval—upon a limited use of force to occupy what they assumed most other countries agreed was Argentine territory, Japanese leaders, with the memory of Japanese militarism fresh in their minds, would have had no doubt that others would put the worst possible spin on an analogous move.

Even if Japan had not been constitutionally indisposed toward the military option, there were other strikes against it as well, particularly during the Cold War. Given the United States's intimate role in Japanese security, a Japanese military operation to recover the islands would have carried with it a significant risk of direct conflict between the superpowers. It would probably also have failed. As late as 1988 the JDA estimated that there were forty MiG-23 interceptors and ten thousand troops stationed on the islands.[120] Moreover, while the Royal Navy might have seemed a remote threat to the Argentine Junta in 1982, no Japanese leader could have failed to appreciate the size, strength, and proximity of the Soviet Far Eastern fleet, which could have sailed in force from Vladivostok and Petropavlovsk to relieve the islands in a matter of days. In a purely conventional conflict today, of course, Japan almost certainly could overrun and hold the islands against a determined Russian attempt to retake them, since most of the Russian troops and aircraft have been withdrawn, and since the Far Eastern fleet has fallen into disrepair. But Japan has no more stomach for the idea today than it did ten or twenty years ago.

More plausible was a strategy of nonmilitary coercion: the threat or use of economic, diplomatic, and moral sanctions (cultural, academic, athletic, and the like). It is an open question whether any of these stood any reasonable chance of success. Since Japan was not among the largest underwriters of Russia's economic reconstruction and integration into Western-dominated trade, finance, and governance regimes, there were limits on the amount of pain Japan could inflict by withdrawing resources. And while an attempt to cut off relations or restrict official and civil-society interactions certainly would have been irritating to Russia, it is hard to imagine these being painful enough to induce pliancy on what the Russians sincerely, if somewhat delusionally, consider a vital high-politics issue. Japan's best sticks were its abilities to derail effective Rus-

---

[119] Peter Feaver, Takako Hikotani, and Shaun Narine, "Civilian Control and Civil-Military Gaps in the United States, Japan, and China," pp. 34–37.

[120] Mack and O'Hare, "Moscow-Tokyo and the Northern Territories Dispute," p. 391.

sian participation in the G-8, to try to block IMF credits, or to delay Russian accession to the WTO. Again, it is an open question how effective these sticks might have been. But a country in search of a stick would no doubt have seriously entertained these options, and the lack of evidence suggesting that Japan ever did so is quite striking.

A policy of obstruction would have been risky. Japan's partners in the G-7 were irritated enough as it was merely by Japan's attempts to have them back it up in its demand for serious negotiations on a final settlement. Crossing them on a matter that they considered vital to the stability and security of the post–Cold War world would have been orders of magnitude more irritating. Tokyo would have been in for some heavy weather indeed. Shifting to a policy of nonmilitary threats would therefore have been quite risky. All things considered, Japanese leaders appear to have been dealt a very weak hand on the issue, and it is perhaps not surprising that they chose to stick with a policy of prodding and lobbying.

Can Japan's regime or state characteristics explain the constancy of Japanese policy? Perhaps to some extent. Japan is certainly democratic, if in an old-boy-network kind of way that gives the government a relatively free hand to conduct the nation's business as long as it doles out the expected patronage. The LDP can usually count upon power because it has found a formula for governing that co-opts virtually all potentially threatening domestic interests. The machinery of government is highly bureaucratic: it is large, complex, and operates in a highly scripted way.[121] A Japanese leader who wished to entertain a bold departure on the Northern Territories issue would certainly have felt the constraints of a jittery and uncertain public and civil service. The Japanese do not like to rock the boat, and Japanese leaders know this. On the other hand, Japanese leaders would enjoy greater deference from the press and from other opinion makers than would leaders in many other countries if they did choose to change course on the Northern Territories issue—so long as they neither entertained a military option nor considered relinquishing the claim. Regime and state characters, in other words, were not obviously an insurmountable obstacle to a somewhat tougher-minded line.

The first hypothesis, then—that foreign policy change should be less frequent in highly bureaucratic states with democratic regimes than in less bureaucratic states with autocratic regimes—fits here much as it fits the Argentine case. We observe dramatic foreign policy change by the authoritarian nonbureaucratic state, but not by the democratic bureaucratic state. Of course, there is far too much else going on in both cases

---

[121] Japan's Polity IV Project codings for the entire period since 1952 are +10 on the POLITY variable (highly democratic) and 7 on the XCONST variable (executive parity or subordination). See figure 6.1.

to allow us to put too much weight on regime and state characteristics alone to explain this particular difference. Japan's unwillingness to contemplate even moderately bolder strategies has a great deal to do with factors utterly extrinsic to the theory, such as its experience in World War II, its dependence upon the United States for security, and its internalized antimilitarism. But it is probably no coincidence, either, that postwar democratic Japan has been notably less reckless in its foreign policy than prewar authoritarian Japan. Indeed, that was the whole point of uprooting militarism and planting democracy in its place.[122]

What of the second hypothesis—that foreign policy change will be most likely when policy fails either repeatedly or catastrophically, or when leaders become convinced that it will imminently do so? Japanese policy on the Northern Territories has certainly failed repeatedly. Tokyo is not appreciably closer to its goal today than it was in 1956. But it is important to note that there is no sense of catastrophe, either among Japanese officials or among the Japanese people as a whole. The unredeemed Northern Territories are a fixed feature of the diplomatic landscape. They are a constant irritant, but one the Japanese have managed to live with. There is no looming deadline, real or imagined. There is not now, nor has there ever been, a sense that if the issue is not soon resolved, the game will be up. As one of my interlocutors in the Ministry of Foreign Affairs correctly put it, though perhaps meaning something else entirely: "This issue will not go away."[123]

We might be tempted to say that the third hypothesis meets approximately the same fate here as it did with the Malvinas case. If Japanese leaders were operating in a gains frame, it is difficult to imagine that they would bother making an issue of the Northern Territories at all. The stakes are simply too meager. The fact that the Japanese do not assert a claim to all of the territory Stalin seized at the end of World War II strongly suggests that the possibility of significant material gain is not, in fact, much of an inducement. That would be a prize worth having. It is interesting to speculate on what non-LDP governments might have done if they had had an opportunity, even if only periodically, to hold the reins on the issue prior to 1993; but the counterfactual provides a poor thought-test of this particular hypothesis, because presumably their con-

---

[122] John W. Dower, *Embracing Defeat.*

[123] Only one official I interviewed expressed a contrary fear. "There is a risk that the issue will die out with generational change. People's concern is changing slowly, but steadily. The number of people with direct physical experience of the Soviet occupation—having family members killed; being forced from their homes—is declining. This is one reason why the issue is urgent." Notice that his fear is not simply that Japan will fail to recover the islands, but that the Japanese people will cease to care.

ception of an acceptable status quo would have required a return of all of the territory Stalin seized, as their platforms demanded. Thus they would still have been operating in a loss frame; only the reference point would have differed. Still, Japanese leaders have taken surprisingly few risks, and there is little reason to imagine that non-LDP leaders would have been more risk-acceptant. They, too, would have had difficulty finding attractive alternatives, and presumably they would also have accommodated themselves to the open-endedness of the dispute. As I explain in the conclusion, these considerations make it difficult to know how well the Northern Territories case fits the expectations of Hypothesis 3.

CRUCIAL DIFFERENCES

Despite the many similarities between these two cases, there are crucial differences worth flagging, even at the price of some repetition, for they invite further reflection on the underlying dynamics of foreign policy change that are the root concern of this book. I would like to dwell for a moment on three.

The Presence or Absence of a Deadline

Argentine leaders felt an acute sense of urgency to resolve the Malvinas issue. January 1983 was a crucial "liminal date." The deadline was arbitrary but nonetheless seemed real. A firm determination to recover the islands by that date shaped Argentine calculations and decisions as the issue came to a head in 1982. The fact that the issue did come to a head in 1982 in the first place was, of course, largely a function of this self-imposed artificial deadline.

In contrast, Japanese leaders have thus far never fixed a deadline for a resolution of the Northern Territories issue. Curiously, although 1995 was the fiftieth anniversary of the seizure of the islands, and while this anniversary loomed precisely during the period of heightened expectation that followed the collapse of the Soviet Union, it never took on the quality of a deadline the way the 150th anniversary of the British seizure of the Malvinas did in the minds of Argentine leaders.

This difference is not, of course, something that could be predicted or accounted for by the theory. I know of no good way to account for it. But it clearly seems to be an important difference, and it confirms that the perception of a deadline is an exogenous datum worth noting when attempting to gauge the intensity and urgency of a sense of loss.

Perceptions of the Feasibility of Alternative Options

Faced with the demonstrable failure of their preferred means of attempting to solve their respective problems, Argentine leaders seized on their preferred alternative—military action in support of diplomacy—whereas Japanese leaders did not even have a preferred alternative (though a policy of nonmilitary sanctions was at least imaginable in principle). Japanese leaders—correctly, in my view—were aware that they had been dealt a weak hand and had no difficulty understanding that nothing stood any better chance of success than perseverance in an admittedly unproductive approach. They were under no illusions about the utility of military force or a threat-based strategy. They did not succumb to wishful thinking and did not misjudge or misperceive opportunities and constraints because of cognitive or motivated biases. One can ask hard questions about whether the game has been worth the candle; that is to say, one can wonder whether the various diplomatic and political costs Japan has paid in its relations with Russia, with its G-7 partners, and in its foreign policy as a whole justify the attempt to recover a handful of useless islands. But since their value to the Japanese is symbolic rather than instrumental, there is a sense in which it is not the place of an outsider even to ask the question. Given that they want the islands back, and given that they have every right to try to persuade Russia to return them, they are certainly to be complimented for having no illusions about the efficacy of the various alternative means open to them.

Argentine leaders, in contrast, suffered from severe delusions. Although they did understand the military option to be risky, and although they did confront the possibility that they might be isolated diplomatically and trigger a British military response, by any standard they grossly underestimated these dangers. They did so primarily because they erred in assuming that others would understand, and sympathize with, their own perspective on the issue, and because they overestimated the weight others would put on the importance of maintaining good relations with Argentina. There was unmistakable myopia and hubris in Argentine decision making for which the Junta paid dearly.

Again, there is nothing in the theory that would help us anticipate or explain myopia or a pathological sense of national self-importance, but the contrast between the two cases does point to the operational value of attempting to determine just how sensitive leaders are to alternative perspectives on the dilemmas they face, and to the interests and concerns of other relevant parties. Argentina miscalculated, as I have argued elsewhere, because culture and emotion got in the way.[124] The Northern Territories issue may have been emotional for the Japanese (and no doubt still

---

[124] Welch, "Culture and Emotion."

is), but throughout the period in question the Japanese foreign policy establishment has had a nuanced and realistic appreciation of various international concerns and perspectives on the problem.

International-Society Constraints

Compared to Japanese leaders, Argentine leaders were relatively unconstrained, both institutionally and normatively. I have already discussed this difference with respect to domestic political and governmental constraints in the course of evaluating fits with Hypothesis 1. But there is an additional asymmetry in constraints having to do with international norms and institutions that seems worth flagging as well.

Throughout the period in question, Japan was a security client of the United States, a member of the G-7, and a central player in virtually every part of the complex apparatus of postwar global governance. Moreover, it was a defeated power with a militarist past acutely aware of regional sensitivities to Japanese assertiveness and unilateralism. Argentina, on the other hand, lived on the frontier. Its regime was something of an international pariah. It lived in a rough, macho neighborhood where unilateralism was a mark of masculinity. It did not feel the constraints of a superpower patron or a robust collective-security arrangement. And, not having experienced war for more than a hundred years, it had not fully internalized strengthening taboos against the use of force to solve international disputes that were taking hold in security communities elsewhere.[125]

These differences appear to have played a role, if somewhat ineffably, in leaders' assessments of the likely costs and benefits of their alternatives. They help us understand, for instance, why Japanese leaders saw no good alternatives for solving the Northern Territories issue, and why Argentine leaders thought they did see a way out of their predicament with the Malvinas. The theory, in other words, indirectly picks up international normative and institutional constraints along the way, registering their effects in leaders' formulations of options and calculations. But it is worth considering whether they should be broken out more explicitly. There may be some validity to the more general claim that dramatic foreign policy change is less likely among states that operate in a more profoundly social and more deeply multilateral context. While I have not put myself in a position to judge this particular proposition in this book, it is certainly worth bearing in mind as a supplementary consideration—or perhaps even as part of an alternative explanation of foreign policy change.

Collectively, these three differences help take much of the mystery out of the striking contrast in behavior we observe in these two cases. They also help us see how a loss-aversion theory of foreign policy change might

---

[125] See generally Emanuel Adler and Michael Barnett, *Security Communities*.

have led us to expect a dramatic change in Argentine behavior sometime in 1982, if we were looking for the appropriate cues,[126] and how it would not have led us to expect a dramatic change in Japanese behavior, even during the heady days immediately following the collapse of the Soviet Union when Tokyo thought a breakthrough might at last be at hand. These cases are therefore encouraging. But they are far from definitive. And so we move on, rejigging controls, to see whether the patterns the theory leads us to expect are also evident elsewhere. Next stop: Vietnam.

---

[126] Contrast the discussion on this point in the Franks Report and in Freedman and Gamba-Stonehouse, *Signals of War*, pp. 84–90.

Chapter 4

AMERICAN BOYS IN AN ASIAN WAR

IN THE PREVIOUS CHAPTER, I attempted to assess the performance of the theory in a comparison of two independent cases. While the comparison was not a wholly static one—it was necessary to delve into the histories of both, if briefly, to understand the events, or lack of events, at crucial moments—I did not dwell on longitudinal endogeneities. How well does the theory work in the security domain within a single case exhibiting more than one dramatic policy change? Do path dependencies play a role? If so, what can we learn from them?

In this chapter, I explore these questions by looking at American policy in the Vietnam War. This case commends itself to the purpose for several reasons. First, the Vietnam War is one of the most-studied events of modern times, and, at least as far as the American side is concerned, we have a rich body of testimony, documentation, and interpretation upon which to draw. Second, it was an event that spanned two decades and was the product of a long prior history, providing ample longitudinal purchase. Third, it took place in a remarkably stable geopolitical context (the Cold War) that minimized confounding events. Finally, it contains well-defined, easily identified turning points that render analytically tractable a complicated event that might otherwise overwhelm us with detail.

I will begin with the briefest possible background and then proceed to identify significant changes in American policy. I will argue that there were two: President Lyndon Baines Johnson's[1] 1965 decision to escalate the war, committing American forces to large-scale combat roles, and President Richard Nixon's 1973 decision to withdraw. I will then reflect on how well the history of the American commitment to Vietnam fits the expectations of the theory, although I hope to do so less formulaically than I did in the previous chapter, so as not to belabor the argument. I will conclude that the fit is indeed very good, all things considered, but also that the case points up some additional gaps and weaknesses in the theory. In the conclusion to the book as a whole I will reflect on these, taking in the broad sweep of all of my cases.

[1] Hereafter LBJ.

Background

Many Americans inside and outside the government understood the Vietnam War as an interstate war in which the United States sought to help
one country—the Republic of Vietnam, or simply "South Vietnam"—
defend itself against a communist neighbor, the Democratic Republic of
Vietnam, or "North Vietnam." It seems that relatively few Vietnamese
understood it this way. Most saw it as a civil war in which the United
States had interfered to prevent the unification of the country.[2] For them,
it was a war of self-determination, or of "national liberation" in its original non-Marxist sense, a function of a nationalism that was "nearly xeno-
phobic in intensity."[3]

The Vietnamese are ethnically and linguistically distinct, but for much
of their recorded early history they were ruled by their more powerful
Chinese neighbors. Fighting the Chinese in a dozen or more uprisings
from 39 to 939 c.e. contributed significantly to the development of a
distinctively Vietnamese national consciousness and prevented cultural
assimilation.[4] Vietnam became an independent state in 939 and remained
so, with one interruption, until 1883. In the tenth, eleventh, and thir-
teenth centuries, Vietnam thwarted a series of invasions from the north,
dealing the Mongol leader Kublai Khan two of his rare defeats, in 1284
and 1287. Early in the fifteenth century, the Chinese finally succeeded in
reimposing their rule, but only for twenty years.[5] For almost four centuries after that, feudal and dynastic civil wars, particularly between the
Nguyen and Trung families, kept Vietnam divided. Only in 1802 did Vietnam finally unify politically. But in language, culture, and national feeling,
the country had been one for almost two thousand years.

France conquered and colonized Indochina in 1883, making a conscious but futile effort to destroy the unity of the country by dividing it

---

[2] For background and discussion, see, e.g., Buttinger, *Vietnam*; Cooper, *The Lost Cru-
sade*; Patti, *Why Viet Nam?*; Stanley Karnow, *Vietnam*; Bernard B. Fall, *The Two Viet-
Nams*; George C. Herring, *America's Longest War*; Kahin, *Intervention*; Philippe Franchini,
Les Guerres D'Indochine. Important recent books include McNamara, *In Retrospect*; Fre-
drik Logevall, *Choosing War*; McNamara et al., *Argument without End*; David E. Kaiser,
American Tragedy. Good short histories include Joseph Buttinger, *A Dragon Defiant*; and
Anthony Short, *The Origins of the Vietnam War*.

[3] Karnow, *Vietnam*, p. 182.

[4] In 39 c.e., the Lady Trung Trac and her sister led a revolt against Chinese rule. Beaten,
the two committed suicide by throwing themselves into a river, earning themselves immor-
tality as national heroines. To this day the Vietnamese worship them as Joans of Arc. Early
uprisings were led by and for the Vietnamese elite, but later insurrections enjoyed widespread popular support because of the peasants' resentment over the hardships of Chinese
rule. Joseph Buttinger, *Smaller Dragon*, pp. 107–108.

[5] Ibid., pp. 130, 152.

into three parts: Tongking, Annam, and Cochinchina. The French never enjoyed a sustained period of peaceful rule because Vietnamese nationalism was too potent a force to put down. The Japanese displaced France during World War II, but in 1945 Vietnam declared independence under Ho Chi Minh. Neither France nor the United States recognized the declaration, and France reimposed its rule.[6]

While not philosophically opposed to decolonization or Vietnamese independence as such, American policy makers understood support for France as a price to be paid for stability in Europe. In addition, Ho Chi Minh was an avowed communist, and there was no enthusiasm in Washington for a communist Vietnam. When General Vo Nguyen Giap finally dealt the French a decisive defeat in the battle of Dienbienphu (1954), the United States had no choice but to accept Vietnamese independence. The only questions were: Who would rule in Vietnam? And how many Vietnams would there be? From Washington's perspective, there clearly had to be at least two, because the communists were firmly in control in the North. What was needed, in the dominant (Korean) trope of the day, was an offsetting noncommunist regime in the South.

Under the terms of the 1954 Geneva peace settlement, Laos, Cambodia, and Vietnam all gained independence, and Vietnam was temporarily partitioned into a communist North and a noncommunist South along a cease-fire line at the 17th parallel pending reunification through free elections to be held no later than July 20, 1956.[7] The southern regime of President Ngo Dinh Diem refused to hold elections, however, ostensibly on the ground that they could not be fair, but conscious also that they could not be won. The United States agreed and committed itself to the defense of an independent southern republic. But the Diem regime— unwilling to undertake much-needed economic and political reforms— proved unpopular and unstable and by the early 1960s was seriously threatened by a communist insurgency supported by the North. Diem himself fell in a 1963 coup, which Washington tacitly blessed.[8] But his many successors proved no more popular, stable, or effective, and things went from bad to worse.

The essence of the difficulty was twofold. First, viable, well-organized, and popular noncommunist nationalist movements were hard to find in

[6] Between 1950 and 1954, Washington supplied France with $2.6 billion in military equipment, effectively underwriting 80 percent of the cost of the French military effort in the region. Cooper, *The Lost Crusade*, p. 62.

[7] See the Geneva Cease-fire Accord, "Agreements on the Cessation of Hostilities in Viet-Nam, Cambodia, and Laos, July 20, 1954," U.S. Senate, Committee on Foreign Relations, *Background Information Relating to Southeast Asia and Vietnam*, pp. 67–96; and the Final Declaration of the Geneva Conference, ibid., pp. 97–99.

[8] On the Diem coup, see Kaiser, *American Tragedy*, pp. 248–283.

Vietnam, for complex historical reasons.[9] Second, relatively few Vietnamese nationalists of any stripe looked favorably on dividing the country in two. Those willing to cooperate with American attempts to shore up an independent South Vietnam suffered from the taint of collaboration with a foreign power seeking to thwart reunification. These noncommunist nationalists delegitimized themselves by appearing to be puppets of neocolonialism. Too late, the United States discovered that its own activism was the kiss of death to any regime it supported, and a vital source of strength to those it opposed, merely by virtue of the fact that it was a foreign power meddling in Vietnam's affairs.[10]

Certainly Ho and his colleagues were unwilling to tolerate a division indefinitely. At first they tried to charm, flatter, prod, and cajole Diem into holding the promised elections. They made sweet promises to guarantee the safety and property of southern capitalists and were eager not to be the first to resort to force.[11] But their patience—which in any case was strictly tactical—had limits. At the Third Congress of the Lao Dong (Workers Party) in September 1960, the Hanoi leadership formally endorsed a policy of overthrowing Diem by force and "liberating" the South.[12]

---

[9] In essence, noncommunist nationalist movements had been crushed or flushed by the French, or co-opted by the communists. In any case, they appealed primarily to the elite, not to the masses, and they were comparatively poorly organized. For detailed discussion and analysis, see particularly Buttinger, *Vietnam*, passim.

Relatively few supporters of the communists were true believers; communism was a foreign ideology with limited appeal to a largely illiterate agrarian populace. But the communists' attempt to pitch themselves as the party of national independence and social reform was nonetheless largely successful.

There is an ongoing scholarly debate about whether Ho Chi Minh was himself more of a nationalist or a communist. The question is somewhat difficult to answer because although Ho wrote many pamphlets, he kept no diaries, wrote no memoirs, and never related his experiences to a biographer. Informed opinion is divided. Many observers maintain that Ho's turn toward communism was tactical: see, e.g., Jules Archer, *Ho Chi Minh*, p. 20; William J. Duiker, *Ho Chi Minh*; David Halberstam, *Ho*; Karnow, *Vietnam*, p. 122; Patti, *Why Viet Nam?*, p. 373; Jean Sainteny, *Ho Chi Minh and His Vietnam*, p. 20. Ruth Fischer, a former German Communist leader who knew Ho in Moscow in the 1920s, insists that "His main interest was . . . the struggle for the independence of his country." Quoted in Reinhold Neumann-Hoditz, *Portrait of Ho Chi Minh*, p. 79. Others insist that communism was as important to him as nationalism; e.g., Jean Lacouture, *Ho Chi Minh*, pp. 223–242. The view that Ho was a communist first and nationalist second—or even no nationalist at all—was widely held in the United States during the 1950s and early 1960s but has few adherents today.

[10] This theme is extensively developed in Timothy J. Lomperis, *The War Everyone Lost— and Won*.

[11] The Diem regime was the first to use force in the struggle for the South, in 1956; in response, the communists turned to insurgency in 1957. Buttinger, *Vietnam*, vol. 2, p. 982.

[12] Ibid., p. 980.

The vehicle for this task was the National Front for the Liberation of the South (or the National Liberation Front), formed on December 20, 1960. The NLF was a political umbrella group that included noncommunist nationalists opposed to the southern regime, but that the communist party controlled. Diem took to deriding it as the *Viet Cong San*, or "Vietnamese communists," and in American parlance "Viet Cong," "Viet-Cong, "Vietcong," and "VC" all came to denote, rather ambiguously and somewhat inaccurately, the NLF and/or its military arm, the People's Liberation Armed Forces (PLAF).[13]

The PLAF drew largely from a South Vietnamese pool of manpower, but the North provided encouragement, supplies, leadership, training, and indoctrination. Before long it controlled much of the southern countryside. What most impressed the South's American patrons was the PLAF's staying power. "The ability of the Viet-Cong continuously to rebuild their units and to make good their losses is one of the mysteries of this guerrilla war," Ambassador Maxwell Taylor noted in a 1964 briefing:

> We are aware of the recruiting methods by which local boys are induced or compelled to join the Viet-Cong ranks and have some general appreciation of the amount of infiltration of personnel from the outside. Yet taking both of these sources into account, we still find no plausible explanation of the continued strength of the Viet-Cong if our data on Viet-Cong losses are even approximately correct. Not only do the Viet-Cong units have the recuperative powers of the phoenix, but they have an amazing ability to maintain morale. Only in rare cases have we found evidences of bad morale among Viet-Cong prisoners or recorded in captured Viet-Cong documents.[14]

What Taylor did not appreciate was the depth of the current of nationalist feeling upon which the insurgents were able to draw. The communist lines often fell on deaf ears, but appeals to Vietnamese nationalism proved highly effective.[15]

Why did decision makers in Washington feel compelled to try to shore up a noncommunist South? Why not let the elections go forward, watch Ho win, and be done with it? The American people, after all, had little knowledge of Southeast Asia, and took little interest in it, until after the main lines of American policy had been set. There was neither active public resistance to nor significant public pressure for any particular course

---

[13] Not to be confused with the People's Army of Vietnam, or PAVN, which was the armed forces of the North. I am indebted to Robert Brigham for clarifying these points.

[14] Paper Prepared by the Ambassador in Vietnam (Taylor), Subject: "The Current Situation in South Viet-Nam—November, 1964," *Foreign Relations of the United States* [hereafter *FRUS*] 1964–1968, vol. 1: Vietnam, 1964, Doc. 426.

[15] William Darryl Henderson, *Why the Vietcong Fought*, esp. pp. 48–60, 121.

of action—merely a quiescent approval of whatever the White House was doing.[16] The American people did not begin to raise serious questions about U.S. policy in Vietnam until the reality of combat, brought into the nation's living rooms through the miracle of television, began to have an effect. Washington was therefore left free to conduct the nation's business in Southeast Asia as it saw fit. For its part, the Congress left the matter entirely to the executive branch.[17] America became involved in Vietnam as the direct consequence of the concerns of the Truman, Eisenhower, Kennedy, and Johnson administrations. What were they?

To understand American policy, it is important to note that no administration assigned Indochina a very high priority until the mid-1960s. Berlin, Korea, Quemoy and Matsu, Suez, Hungary, Cuba, Berlin again, A-bombs, H-bombs, bomber gaps, missile gaps, and the task of holding together the Atlantic alliance preoccupied makers of America's foreign policy at least until 1964.[18] The result was that crucial decisions on Indochina were made on the basis of comparatively scant attention from those at the highest levels of authority, who, in the absence of a detailed knowledge of the specific circumstances of the area, hastily applied a wide range of cognitive short-cuts in an attempt to make sense of the situation.[19] These short-cuts included the relatively uncritical invocation of historical analogies (Munich, Korea, the "loss" of China) and assumptions devoid of nuance about both the nature of the problem and the nature of the opposition. The bulk of the attention the Vietnam situation received came from lower-level civil servants in the State Department, many of whom (including some of the most knowledgeable) fell victim to McCarthyism at a crucial stage in the development of America's Indochina policy.[20] Those that survived repeatedly found their recommendations overruled by the European hands whose top priority was to keep relations with France in good repair.[21]

---

[16] See, e.g., Karnow, *Vietnam*, pp. 374, 414; and Logevall, *Choosing War*, passim.

[17] See, e.g., David Halberstam, *The Best and the Brightest*, p. 146.

[18] See, e.g., Cooper, *The Lost Crusade*, p. 164.

[19] President Kennedy, for example, appears to have had a sense of the seriousness of the Vietnam problem only after reading a January 1961 memorandum from Major General Edward G. Lansdale. Kahin, *Intervention*, p. 129. Lyndon Johnson claimed, "My first exposure to the details of the problem of Vietnam came forty-eight hours after I had taken the oath of office." Lyndon B. Johnson, *The Vantage Point*, p. 46. But cf. n. 39 below.

[20] Cf. McNamara, *In Retrospect*, p. 33.

[21] Not all Americans entirely misunderstood the developing situation in Vietnam. William Bullitt, for example, wrote perceptively in 1947 that "Not one in a hundred Annamites is a Communist; but all decent Annamites want independence; and just as General de Gaulle was followed by millions of Frenchmen who disagreed with his political views, because he was the symbol of resistance to Hitler, so today Ho Chi Minh, the Communist leader of the Annamite fight for independence, is followed by millions of Annamites who disagree with

The State Department's Office of Intelligence and Research was not entirely convinced that Ho was a communist worth worrying about. It found no hard evidence in the fall of 1948 that he took his orders from Moscow.[22] But American policy proceeded on the assumption that he did. The mere fact that Ho Chi Minh professed communism led Secretary of State Dean Acheson to a disastrous misjudgment:

> In light Ho's known background, no other assumption possible but that he outright Commie so long as (1) he fails unequivocally repudiate Moscow connections and Commie doctrine and (2) remains personally singled out for praise by internatl Commie press and receives its support. Moreover, US not impressed by nationalist character red flag with yellow stars. Question whether Ho as much nationalist as Commie is irrelevant. All Stalinists in colonial areas are nationalists.[23]

Acheson would later make clear that he meant something even stronger: that Ho wasn't a nationalist at all. "The recognition by the Kremlin of Ho Chi Minh's Communist movement in Indochina comes as a surprise," he declared in 1950. "The Soviet acknowledgement of this movement should remove any illusions as to the 'nationalist' nature of Ho Chi Minh's aims and reveals Ho in his true colors as the mortal enemy of native independence in Indochina."[24]

Acheson's misunderstanding was the product of a monolithic view of communism. On this view, the goals of communism and self-determination seemed logically incompatible, since all communists were thought to owe a higher allegiance to Moscow. International communism was therefore just another form of imperialism and enslavement; a true Vietnamese patriot, by definition, would be anticommunist. In fact, Ho was never a puppet either of China or of the Soviet Union. His skill at playing Moscow and Beijing off against each other while remaining on relatively good terms with both was among the most remarkable features of his career.[25] But Acheson's misperception, which served as the basis of Amer-

---

his political views because he is the symbol of resistance to France." Bullitt, "The Saddest War."

[22] Sheehan et al., *The Pentagon Papers*, p. 9.

[23] Telegram, Acheson to Consulate in Hanoi, 20 May 1949; ibid., p. 79. Cf. also Acheson's telegram to Division Chief Abbot Low Moffat in Saigon, 5 December 1946: "Keep in mind Ho's clear record as agent international communism, absence evidence recantation Moscow affiliations, confused political situation France and support Ho receiving French Communist Party." Gareth Porter, ed., *Vietnam*, p. 54.

[24] *Department of State Bulletin*, vol. 22, no. 554 (13 February 1950), p. 244.

[25] See Lacouture, *Ho Chi Minh*, pp. 243–260; R. B. Smith, *An International History of the Vietnam War*, vol. 2, pp. 35–53; Odd Arne Westad et al., "77 Conversations between Chinese and Foreign Leaders on the Wars in Indochina, 1964–1977."

ican policy in the region, made possible the irony that both sides in the Vietnam War honestly saw themselves as the true champions of Vietnamese self-determination against the forces of imperialist domination.

It is easy in retrospect to condemn American policy for proceeding on the basis of a naïve understanding of international communism, but it should not be forgotten that in the late 1940s and through the 1950s, communism *did* appear to be monolithic—indeed, communists were insisting that it *was* monolithic—and it preached a doctrine of implacable hostility to capitalism that few could calmly ignore. Americans could be forgiven for misjudging the nature of the opposition they faced in Vietnam when the Lao Dong itself was proclaiming that "the final objective of the international communist movement remains as always the overthrow of imperialism as a whole, the abolition of all regimes of oppression and exploitation in human society, and the building up of socialism and communism in every country of the world."[26] Against the background of America's immediate historical experiences, the smug and chilling millennialism of communist rhetoric led quite naturally to an obsession with containment. This may well have been an overreaction, but it was an honest one. As John Kenneth Galbraith put it, the United states simply "went into the war in Vietnam in response to a view of the world which was then deeply graven as official truth and which has turned out to be sharply in conflict with circumstance."[27]

Beginning with NSC 48/2, which President Truman approved on December 30, 1949—right after the fall of China—the United States committed itself to blocking communist expansion in Asia and justified that commitment on primarily strategic grounds.[28] A detailed analysis of U.S. strategic interests in the region appeared in a 1952 National Security

[26] 9th Plenum of the VNWP Central Committee, December 1963; communiqué issued 20 January 1964; in Smith, *An International History of the Vietnam War*, p. 219. It should not be forgotten that the South Vietnamese did everything in their power to represent their struggle in exactly this light, which only reinforced the American perception. For example, in 1961 Diem appealed to President Kennedy for more aid in the following terms: "Mr. President, my people and I are mindful of the great assistance which the United States has given us. Your help has not been lightly received, for the Vietnamese are proud people, and we are determined to do our part in the defense of the free world. . . . But Viet-Nam is not a great power and the forces of international communism now arrayed against us are more than we can meet with the resources at hand. We must have further assistance from the United States if we are to win the war now being waged against us." Quoted in Johnson, *The Vantage Point*, p. 56. Was it an accident that Diem sent this message on December 7?

[27] John Kenneth Galbraith, *How to Get Out of Vietnam*, p. 13. See also Larry Berman, *Planning a Tragedy*, esp. pp. 130–135; Ernest Henry Gruening and Herbert Wilton Beaser, *Vietnam Folly*; and Ralph K. White, *Nobody Wanted War*.

[28] *Pentagon Papers*, p. 10. See also NSC Staff Study on Objectives, Policies and Courses of Action in Asia (Annex to NSC 48/4), 17 May 1951; in Porter, ed., *Vietnam*, pp. 105–108.

Council paper titled "United States Objectives and Courses of Action With Respect to Southeast Asia":

> Communist domination, by whatever means, of all Southeast Asia would seriously endanger in the short term, and critically endanger in the longer term, United States security interests.
>
>   a. The loss of any of the countries of Southeast Asia to communist aggression would have critical psychological, political and economic consequences. In the absence of effective and timely counteraction, the loss of any single country would probably lead to relatively swift submission to or an alignment with communism by the remaining countries of this group. Furthermore, an alignment with communism of the rest of Southeast Asia and India, and in the longer term, of the Middle East (with the probable exceptions of at least Pakistan and Turkey) would in all probability progressively follow: Such widespread alignment would endanger the stability and security of Europe.
>
>   b. Communist control of all of Southeast Asia would render the U.S. position in the Pacific offshore island chain precarious and would seriously jeopardize fundamental U.S. security interests in the Far East.
>
>   c. Southeast Asia, especially Malaya and Indonesia, is the principal world source of natural rubber and tin, and a producer of petroleum and other strategically important commodities. The rice exports of Burma and Thailand are critically important to Malaya, Ceylon and Hong Kong and are of considerable significance to Japan and India, all important areas of free Asia.
>
>   d. The loss of Southeast Asia, especially of Malaya and Indonesia, could result in such economic and political pressures in Japan as to make it extremely difficult to prevent Japan's eventual accommodation to communism.[29]

It was easier to take a stand in Indochina sooner, American decision makers believed, than to be forced to take a stand somewhere else later, most likely on less favorable terms. Such was the apparent lesson of the Rhineland, *Anschluss*, and Munich.[30] The dominant idiom for this would later

---

[29] *Pentagon Papers*, pp. 28–29.

[30] "Under the conditions of today, the imposition on Southeast Asia of the political system of Communist Russia and its Chinese Communist ally, by whatever means, would be a grave threat to the whole free community. The United States feels that that possibility should not be passively accepted but should be met by united action. This might involve serious risks. But these risks are far less than those that will face us a few years from now if we dare not be resolute today." Address by Dulles, New York City, 29 March 1954; in Porter, ed., *Vietnam*, p. 135.

become "the domino theory," inspired by President Eisenhower's remark at an April 1954 press conference: "You have a row of dominoes set up, you knock over the first one, and what will happen to the last one is the certainty that it will go over very quickly."[31]

The domino theory was pithy, but pat and poorly specified.[32] Almost every important American decision maker expressed doubts about it at one point or another, but almost everyone harbored a lingering fear that it might basically be correct.[33] This fear persisted, if in somewhat muted form, even after the CIA's Board of National Estimates debunked the notion in a 1964 paper known throughout the intelligence community as the "Death of the Domino Theory Memo."[34] But by that point American decision makers felt that they had staked American credibility on the survival of an independent, noncommunist South Vietnam, and as fears of falling dominoes ebbed, concerns about credibility flowed.[35]

---

[31] Jeffrey Kimball, *Nixon's Vietnam War*, p. 17, quoting *Public Papers of the Presidents of the United States: Dwight D. Eisenhower, 1954*, pp. 382–383. On the origin of the domino metaphor and its cognates—the finger in the dike, the chain reaction, the first rotten apple in a barrel, etc.—see ibid., p. 381, n. 7.

[32] See., e.g., Robert Jervis, "Domino Beliefs and Strategic Behavior."

[33] Dulles himself—an early enthusiast—insisted in May 1954 that the rest of Southeast Asia could be held even if Indochina fell. But the key, he believed, was to internationalize the effort. Hence the creation of the Southeast Asia Treaty Organization, or SEATO. *New York Times*, 12 May 1954, pp. 1, 6. Johnson seems to have been a fairly strong adherent, invoking it repeatedly: e.g., Michael R. Beschloss, *Taking Charge*, pp. 213–214, 248–249, 264. Secretary of Defense Robert McNamara admits to having believed it in the early 1960s and insists most of his associates did as well; e.g., McNamara, *In Retrospect*, pp. 32, 62, 106–107. Richard Nixon was a domino man, too: Memorandum of Conversation with Australian Prime Minister John Gorton, April 1, 1969, *FRUS 1969–1976*, vol. 1, Doc. 17; Kimball, *Nixon's Vietnam War*, pp. 88–89; H. R. Haldeman, *The Haldeman Diaries*, p. 96. Of all the Vietnam era presidents, Kennedy appears to have been the most skeptical; Kaiser, *American Tragedy*, p. 101. But even Kennedy professed faith in the domino theory from time to time. As a young Senator in 1956, for instance, Kennedy said: "Vietnam represents the cornerstone of the Free World in Southeast Asia, the keystone to the arch, the finger in the dike. Burma, Thailand, India, Japan, the Philippines and obviously Laos and Cambodia are among those whose whole security would be threatened if the red tide of Communism overflowed into Vietnam. . . ." Speech at Gettysburg College, April 1959; quoted in Johnson, *The Vantage Point*, p. 51. Cf. also his NBC interview with David Brinkley, 9 September 1963, http://www.presidency.ucsb.edu/site/docs/pppus.php?admin=035&year=1963&id=349.

[34] Kai Bird, *The Color of Truth*, p. 285. The paper concluded, "We do not believe that the loss of South Vietnam and Laos would be followed by the rapid, successive communization of the other states of the Far East. . . . With the possible exception of Cambodia, it is likely that no nation in the area would quickly succumb to Communism as a result of the fall of Laos and South Vietnam." Memorandum From the Board of National Estimates to the Director of Central Intelligence (McCone), June 9, 1964, *FRUS 1964–1968*, vol. 1, Doc. 209. http://www.state.gov/www/about_state/history/vol_i/181_225.html.

[35] On the importance of credibility as a motive, see, e.g., Logevall, *Choosing War*, pp. 388–389. The "Death of the Domino Theory" memo (ibid.) did cite the threat failure posed to U.S. credibility.

As early as 1950, credibility had an effect on American policy. Dulles wrote: "[T]here is a civil war [in Indochina] in which we have, for better or worse, involved our prestige. Since that is so, we must help the government we back. Its defeat, coming after the reverses suffered by the Nationalist Government of China, would have further serious repercussions on the whole situation in Asia and the Pacific. It would make even more people in the East feel that friendship with the United States is a liability rather than an asset."[36] Initially, dominoes and credibility were linked. To the extent that America's allies in the region doubted America's commitments, they might be more inclined to "accommodate" to communism, and the dominoes would fall. But later, American policy makers would worry less about credibility in the region and more about credibility globally. Unless the United States kept its word to South Vietnam, so the argument went, NATO and the Soviet Union would begin doubting American resolve, undermining deterrence in central Europe.

A third factor undergirding American support for South Vietnam was a profound moral disgust of what Dulles frequently called "godless Communism," and a sincere desire to promote the freedom of the people of South Vietnam. Maxwell Taylor described as "the basic objective" of American policy "that some fifteen [sic] million South Vietnamese be free from aggression and able to choose their own government and their own way of life."[37] That if given the choice those people would overwhelmingly elect a communist government was, of course, something of an embarrassing paradox resolved in a paternalistic way. The South Vietnamese had to be educated and socialized as pro-Western, freedom-loving liberals through a process of "nation building" and "Winning Hearts and Minds" (known by its strangely appropriate acronym, WHAM). A period of tutelage was unavoidable. But there was a sincere, abiding faith in Washington that, if given the chance to taste the fruits of genuine freedom, the people of South Vietnam would never willingly opt for communist enslavement.

These three chief concerns, then—preventing the dominoes from falling, buttressing American credibility, and defending the freedom of the South Vietnamese people—permeated American policy from start to finish. Their proportions varied over time, but inside the Beltway they made for a strong amalgam. American policy was the product both of *realpolitik* and idealism, of self-interest and altruism. Eisenhower's characterization was typical:

Strategically South Vietnam's capture by the Communists would bring their power several hundred miles into a hitherto free region.

---

[36] John Foster Dulles, *War or Peace*, p. 231.
[37] Maxwell D. Taylor, *Responsibility and Response*, p. 22.

The remaining countries in Southeast Asia would be menaced by a great flanking movement. The freedom of twelve [*sic*] million people would be lost immediately and that of one hundred fifty million others in adjacent lands would be seriously endangered. The loss of South Vietnam would set in motion a crumbling process that could, as it progressed, have grave consequences for us and for freedom. . . . We reach the inescapable conclusion that our own national interests demand some help from us in sustaining in Vietnam the morale, the economic progress, and the military strength necessary to its continued existence in freedom.[38]

Since communism had to be stopped, Ho had to be stopped. But that did not mean that the Americans were the best ones to do it, and in recognizing this, American policy makers demonstrated admirable sensitivity.[39] It was far better for the Vietnamese themselves to hold the line against communism than for Americans to do it for them. "In the final analysis," President Kennedy declared, "it is their war. They are the ones who have to win it or lose it. We can help them, we can give them equipment, we can send our men out there as advisers, but they have to win it—the people of Viet-Nam—against the Communists."[40] Echoing Kennedy's view, Johnson insisted in his 1964 campaign that "we are not about to send American boys nine or ten thousand miles away from home to do what Asian boys ought to be doing for themselves."[41] But when it became clear that

[38] Speech at Gettysburg College, April 1959; quoted in Johnson, *The Vantage Point*, p. 51.

[39] In his report to President Kennedy after his mission to Saigon in 1961, Vice President Johnson noted that "American combat troop involvement is not only not required, it is not desirable. Possibly Americans fail to appreciate fully the subtlety that recently-colonial peoples would not look with favor upon governments which invited or accepted the return this soon of Western troops." Memorandum, "Mission to Southeast Asia, India and Pakistan," 23 May 1961; *Pentagon Papers*, p. 133. A few years later, Johnson might have done well to remember his own recommendation that "We should make clear, in private, that barring an unmistakable and massive invasion of South Viet Nam from without we have no intention of employing combat U.S. forces in Viet Nam or using even naval or air-support which is but the first step in that direction. If the Vietnamese government backed by a three-year liberal aid program cannot do this job, then we had better remember the experience of the French who wound up with several hundred thousand men in Vietnam and were still unable to do it. And all this, without engaging a single Chinese or Russian. Before we take any such plunge we had better be sure we are prepared to become bogged down chasing irregulars and guerrillas over the rice fields and jungles of Southeast Asia while our principal enemies China and the Soviet Union stand outside the fray and husband their strength." Report by the Vice President, *FRUS 1961–1963*, vol. 1, Doc. 60. http://www.state.gov/www/about_state/history/vol_i_1961/f.html.

[40] Interview with Walter Cronkite, CBS, 2 September 1963; United States Senate, Committee on Foreign Relations, *Background Information Relating to Southeast Asia and Vietnam*, p. 129.

[41] Karnow, *Vietnam*, p. 395.

the Republic of South Vietnam could not stem the communist tide, Johnson faced a difficult choice between sending American boys to try to do what Asian boys had failed to do, or suffering the consequences of their failure. He chose the former.

TURNING POINTS

From 1945 to 1954, American policy toward Vietnam had been simple and consistent: support France. Dienbienphu forced a change because France withdrew. This is a straightforward example of a policy change made necessary by a change in external circumstance. Such things are important, of course, but they are not difficult to understand, and they are not particularly interesting theoretically. I propose to put this policy change aside and simply note that American policy makers chose to try to maintain a divided Vietnam rather than acquiesce in its unification under communist rule. I think it is fair to say that this was the option most consistent with the remaining salient concern that had been behind American support for France in the first place (alliance politics no longer being relevant): the desire not to allow Vietnam to fall to communism largely to prevent dominoes from falling.

From 1954 to 1973 the United States did its best to shore up an independent, noncommunist South Vietnam, refusing to go along with the provisions of the Geneva Accords, which, in any case, it had not signed. Only in 1973 did the United States give up on this goal. The Paris Peace Agreement allowed American leaders to wash their hands of the whole matter. Of course, they managed to pretend that it had not. The agreement bought a "decent interval" of two years in which Washington could indulge the pretense that it had honored its commitment to Saigon before communist forces swooped down and forcibly unified the country in 1975. But in 1973 the United States essentially gave up on South Vietnam. Thus 1973 must also stand as a significant policy change.

Were there any other significant changes in U.S. policy between 1954 and 1973? Few would quibble that Lyndon Johnson's 1965 decision to "Americanize" the war—that is, to commit American forces to direct combat and to authorize nonretaliatory aerial combat missions against North Vietnamese targets—was an important change. This did not represent a change in U.S. *goals*, for the whole point of the exercise was to shore up South Vietnam. But it did represent a dramatic change in the *means* by which the United States proposed to do this. For years, Kennedy, Johnson, and other senior American officials had gone out of their way to insist that Americanizing the war was neither necessary nor desirable: Asian boys could and should do the job themselves.

When the change came, it came quickly and decisively. On February 13, 1965, LBJ approved regular, sustained bombing of North Vietnam and enemy-held areas of South Vietnam. On February 19 the United States carried out the first air attack against the PLAF in which no South Vietnamese aircraft were involved. On March 2 Operation "Rolling Thunder" began with the first nonretaliatory air attack on North Vietnam. On March 8 the first marines splashed ashore at Danang.[42] Once they began coming, American troops poured into Vietnam as quickly as the country's limited infrastructure could accommodate them.[43]

Now, there are two qualifications I must make at this point. First, American troops had actually been fighting in Vietnam for some time—unofficially. The Geneva Accords had limited the number of U.S. military advisers in Vietnam to 685, and while Eisenhower felt no compunction ignoring Geneva's political provisions, he scrupulously observed this particular limit. Kennedy did not. Under Kennedy, the number of U.S. military "advisers" in Vietnam rose to more than 16,000, many of whom saw action either as helicopter pilots or as leaders of ARVN combat missions.[44] This fact rendered somewhat disingenuous Kennedy's last public comment on the war: "The most important program, of course, is our national security, but I don't want the United States to have to put troops there."[45] They already were. Second, although LBJ authorized independent American combat operations, deployments of active ground combat units, and new kinds and levels of air missions, he bent over backwards to try to represent these as more of the same rather than as something different. "Look, get this straight," Special Assistant for National Security McGeorge (Mac) Bundy told his brother, Deputy Secretary of State William P. Bundy, "the President does not want this depicted as a change in policy."[46]

But the massive influx of U.S. forces in 1965, the sudden change in the intensity and kind of combat operations, the fact that the U.S. military

---

[42] Logevall, *Choosing War*, pp. 362–363.

[43] Kaiser, *American Tragedy*, p. 311.

[44] Kahin, *Intervention*, p. 129.

[45] News conference, 14 November 1963; quoted in McNamara, *In Retrospect*, p. 86.

[46] Logevall, *Choosing War*, p. 331. National Security Action Memorandum No. 328 formalized the spin campaign: "The President desires that with respect to the actions in paragraphs 5 through 7, premature publicity be avoided by all possible precautions. The actions themselves should be taken as rapidly as practicable, but in ways that should minimize any appearance of sudden changes in policy, and official statements on these troop movements will be made only with the direct approval of the Secretary of Defense, in consultation with the Secretary of State. The President's desire is that these movements and changes should be understood as being gradual and wholly consistent with existing policy." 6 April 1965, *FRUS 1964–68*, vol. 2, Doc. 242. http://www.state.gov/www/about_state/history/vol_ii/241_260.html.

began fighting a war *as* the U.S. military rather than merely as advisers to the ARVN, and the predictably dramatic spike in U.S. casualties (see figures 4.1–4.3)[47] all confirm Secretary of Defense Robert S. McNamara's contention that this was a "revolutionary change in U.S. policy."[48] There is little doubt that LBJ understood it as such.[49] So also did the American people. As George Herring would later remark, "despite the administration's disclaimers, the February decisions marked an important watershed in the war."[50]

Were there any other significant policy changes between 1965 and 1973? The next most likely candidate is Richard Nixon's "five-point strategy" for peace, which he promoted upon coming to office in early 1969. The elements of Nixon's strategy, as he later described it, were the following:

1. "Vietnamization" (trying to get the ARVN to shoulder more of the military burden)
2. "Pacification" of the South Vietnamese countryside through stepped up counterinsurgency operations
3. "Diplomatic isolation" of North Vietnam, largely by means of a cautious détente with the Soviet Union and an opening to the People's Republic of China
4. "Peace negotiations" in Paris
5. "Gradual withdrawal" of American troops[51]

Jeffrey Kimball prefers to call this the "Nixinger strategy" since Henry Kissinger had an important hand in it, and he characterizes it rather differently: as a combination of "big military plays, Vietnamization, pacification, clever negotiating ploys, Soviet linkage, the China card, and counterattacks against domestic opponents."[52] But however one characterizes it, and whatever one chooses to call it, Nixon, at least, represented it as something dramatically different. Was it?

Nixon's strategy was certainly different in some respects, but one can have an interesting philosophical debate about whether it was "an important watershed." On the one hand, as figure 4.1 shows, U.S. deployments in Vietnam peaked in early 1969 and declined fairly steadily there-

---

[47] Figure 4.2 shows monthly U.S. combat fatalities, which occasionally varied quite dramatically from month to month. Figure 4.3 therefore shows instead rolling nine-month averages, which provide a clearer indication of the changes in combat intensity and the relevant inflection points.

[48] McNamara, *In Retrospect*, p. 109.

[49] Logevall, *Choosing War*, p. 375.

[50] Herring, *America's Longest War*, p. 129.

[51] Richard M. Nixon, *No More Vietnams*, pp. 104–107.

[52] Kimball, *Nixon's Vietnam War*, p. 99.

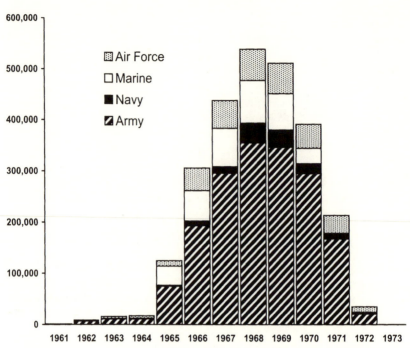

Fig. 4.1. U.S. troop deployment levels in Vietnam (troops ashore as of September)
Source: Compiled from U.S. Department of Defense, *Deployment of U.S. Military Personnel by Country*. http://web1.whs.osd.mil/mmid/military/history/hst0961.xls. . .hst0973.xls.

after. So also did American fatalities, though changes in the weather and the dance of competing offensives generated spikes and lulls (see figures 4.2 and 4.3). Nixon also clearly shifted the military emphasis from the ground to the air, dropping unprecedented levels of ordnance on enemy targets not only in Vietnam, but in Laos and Cambodia as well. As was the case in 1965, these represented changes in means, not in goals.[53] But unlike the Argentine Junta in 1982—which clearly did something dramatically and importantly different in pursuit of old goals—Nixon's policy represented more of a change in degree than in kind. McNamara himself had suggested the essence of "Vietnamization" in October 1967,[54] and throughout the war the United States had done what it could to get the ARVN to carry more weight. Pacification differed only marginally from

[53] Ibid., p. 86.
[54] George C. Herring, *LBJ and Vietnam*, p. 58.

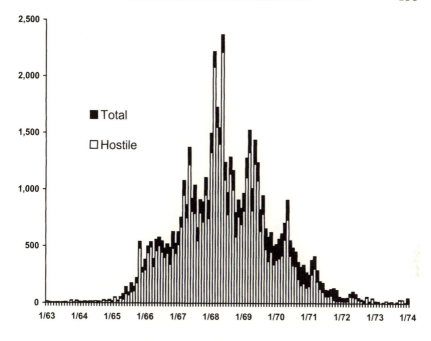

Fig. 4.2. Monthly U.S. combat troop fatalities
Source: Compiled from U.S. National Archives and Records Administration State-Level Casualty Lists for the Vietnam Conflict. http://www.archives.gov/research_room/research_topics/vietnam_war_casualty_lists/as_alphabetical.html.

earlier styles of counterinsurgency. The Johnson administration had been trying to get peace talks going for years. Of the five elements of Nixon's "new strategy," only his overtures to the Soviet Union and China and his shift in emphasis from ground war to air war represented departures from past practice, and the latter was a change in proportion rather than in kind.

This is one of those cases where it is impossible to be formulaic. Nixon's Vietnam strategy falls somewhere in that gray zone between "more of the same" and "something radically different," and it must inevitably be a judgment call exactly where to put it. My call is that it falls much closer to the former. For several years after he came into office, Nixon merely made tactical adjustments to LBJ's Vietnam policy. Only late in his first term did he decisively resolve to wind up the war and finally withdraw. The only unambiguous dramatic change in Nixon's Vietnam policy, in other words, came in 1973. I propose to concentrate on the two unambiguous changes here.

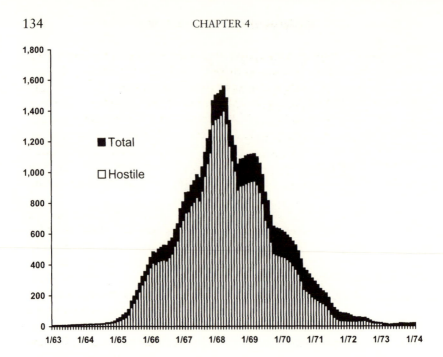

Fig. 4.3. U.S. combat troop fatalities (rolling nine-month averages)
Source: Calculated from source, fig. 4.2.

THE JOHNSON ESCALATION

LBJ became president on November 22, 1963, under unhappy circumstances. Initially, he did little to rock the boat. The first detailed statement of his Vietnam policy, issued just four days after he took the oath of office—National Security Action Memorandum (NSAM) 273—reiterated Kennedy's central objective: "to assist the people and Government of [South Vietnam] to win their contest against the externally directed and supported Communist conspiracy."[55] The means would remain the same, too: training and support, but no overt application of U.S. military force. But as the post-Diem chaos deepened in South Vietnam, things began to look as though they were coming to a head. McNamara traveled to Saigon and reported on December 20 that "[t]he situation is very disturbing." He warned that "current trends, unless reversed in the next 2–3 months, will lead to neutralization at best or more likely to a Communist-con-

[55] NSAM 273, November 26, 1963, Lyndon Baines Johnson Library and Museum. http://www.lbjlib.utexas.edu/johnson/archives.hom/NSAMs/nsam273.asp.

trolled state."[56] It did not take LBJ long to figure out that he would soon face a painful choice. "[T]here's one of three things you can do," he told John S. Knight, chairman of the board of the *Miami Herald*, on February 3: "One is run and let the dominoes start falling over. And God Almighty, what they said about us leaving China would just be warming up compared to what they'd say now. . . . You can run, or you can fight, as we are doing, or you can sit down and agree to neutralize all of it. But nobody is going to neutralize North Vietnam, so that's totally impractical. And so it really boils down to one or two decisions—getting out or getting in."[57]

South Vietnam had a little more staying power than McNamara thought, but things were not going well. On May 15, 1964, the CIA warned that "[t]he over-all situation in South Vietnam remains extremely fragile. Although there has been some improvement in GVN [Government of (South) Vietnam]/ARVN performance, sustained Viet Cong pressure continues to erode GVN authority throughout the country, undercut US/GVN programs and depress South Vietnamese morale. We do not see any signs that these trends are yet 'bottoming out.' . . . [I]f the tide of deterioration has not been arrested by the end of the year, the anti-Communist position in South Vietnam is likely to become untenable."[58] The military, for its part, was itching to carry the war to the North.[59] LBJ demurred, seemingly for three reasons. First, he was genuinely uncertain about what he should do.[60] Second, he understood the momentousness of his choice and felt that he ought to have the mandate of an electoral victory before making it.[61] Third—and not least importantly—he realized that delaying a decision until after the election gave him the best shot at winning the presidency, since both withdrawal and escalation could hurt him at the polls. He wanted neither to lose South Vietnam nor to "start a war before November."[62] He wanted to hold tight. "I just can't believe

[56] Memorandum to the President, December 21, 1963, *FRUS*, 1961–1963, vol. 4, pp. 732–735.

[57] Beschloss, *Taking Charge*, pp. 213–214.

[58] Memorandum prepared by the Directorate of Intelligence, Central Intelligence Agency, May 15, 1964, *FRUS*, 1964–1968, vol. 1, Doc. 159. http://www.state.gov/www/about_state/history/vol_i/146_180.html.

[59] E.g., Memorandum From the Joint Chiefs of Staff to the Secretary of Defense (McNamara), JCSM-174-64, Washington, March 2, 1964, FRUS 1964–1968, vol. 1, Doc. 66. http://www.state.gov/www/about_state/history/vol_i/28_69.html.

[60] See, e.g., LBJ's comments to McNamara, quoted in Beschloss, *Taking Charge*, pp. 248–249.

[61] On March 4, 1964, LBJ told McGeorge Bundy, "I'm just an inherited—I'm a trustee. I've got to win an election. Or Nixon or somebody else has. And then you can make a decision." Ibid., p. 267.

[62] Quoted in Kaiser, *American Tragedy*, p. 304.

that we can't take fifteen thousand [U.S.] advisers and two hundred thousand [ARVN] people and maintain the status quo for six months," he told Mac Bundy in March.[63]

Seeking to exploit the electorate's unease with Republican candidate Barry Goldwater's unabashed belligerence, LBJ set about laying the foundations for his own political demise. It was a classic case of myopia—of short-term gain for long-term pain. On the one hand, he painted himself as the peace candidate—the one who could keep America out of Vietnam. "Some others are eager to enlarge the conflict," he said in a speech before the American Bar Association in August, in a thinly veiled reference to his opponent. "They call upon us to supply American boys to do the job that Asian boys should do. . . . Such action would offer no solution at all to the real problem of Vietnam." Reiterating past policy, LBJ stated flatly that "The South Vietnamese have the basic responsibility for the defense of their own freedom."[64] Such words would come back to haunt him because at the same time he and his advisers were preparing the ground for taking over the war if necessary.

On August 2, 1964, the destroyer U.S.S. *Maddox*, conducting a DeSoto intelligence patrol just outside Vietnamese territorial waters in the Tonkin Gulf, skirmished with three North Vietnamese patrol boats, seriously damaging one. The North Vietnamese were apparently responding to shore raids conducted by South Vietnamese forces and supported by the U.S. Navy as part of OPLAN [Operational Plan] 34A, a clandestine hit-and-run sabotage program along the coast. According to North Vietnamese officials, an overzealous local commander ordered the attack, and a countermand order arrived too late to prevent it.[65] Two nights later the *Maddox* and another ship, the U.S.S. *Turner Joy*, reacting to ambiguous radio intercepts and sonar readings, reported a second attack that now seems clearly never to have taken place.[66] But despite mounting evidence of an honest mistake, the White House cried unprovoked aggression and asked Congress to grant the president authority to respond to North Vietnamese attacks. On August 7 the Gulf of Tonkin Resolution passed in the House of Representatives unanimously and the Senate with only two dissenting votes, effectively giving LBJ carte blanche to deal with Vietnam as he saw fit.

As summer turned to fall, the Johnson team got down to brass tacks. The election would soon be over; Johnson seemed increasingly certain to win; and the situation in Vietnam seemed increasingly untenable. The moment of decision would soon be at hand. The problem was that the relevant

---

[63] Quoted in Beschloss, *Taking Charge*, p. 263.
[64] McNamara, *In Retrospect*, p. 147.
[65] McNamara et al., *Argument without End*, pp. 203–204.
[66] Edwin E. Moïse, *Tonkin Gulf and the Escalation of the Vietnam War*, pp. 203–207.

players could see only bad options. Before long it became clear to all that the task was to find the least unattractive alternative.

The most important players in the process were Robert McNamara, Secretary of State Dean Rusk, McGeorge Bundy, and LBJ himself—the group that Fredrik Logevall calls the "inner war cabinet," or the "Awesome Foursome." "To a large extent," Logevall writes, "these four men made the Vietnam policy, made it with input from various assistant secretaries, to be sure, and from the Joint Chiefs of Staff and the various members of the National Security Council, and, especially, from ambassador to Saigon General Maxwell Taylor, but with decisive power preserved for themselves."[67] What were their respective takes on the problem?

McNamara was at the time a strong believer in the domino theory.[68] He believed that if the United States withdrew from Vietnam, Malaysia and Thailand would "go fast."[69] He believed that South Vietnam could never be neutralized, since unification under communist rule would likely follow in short order.[70] Thus the only acceptable course was to expand the U.S. effort. However, McNamara was beginning to feel, and soon became acutely aware, that the war could not be "won" militarily. The United States might be able to destroy Vietnam, but there was no way to defeat the NLF insurgency in the South, or choke it off at the source, without a massive escalation of the kind likely to lead to horrific casualties and provoke Chinese intervention. Taking over some of the military effort from the ARVN and carrying the war to the North might, however, have some chance of accomplishing one or both of two things, McNamara felt: first, it might convince Moscow to pressure Hanoi into softening its line; and second, it might impress America's friends and foes alike that the United States would live up to its commitments, contributing to deterrence elsewhere. McNamara, in short, believed that Americanization was the only option that held out any hope of preventing dominoes from falling, and of maintaining U.S. credibility.[71] He would later flail both himself and his colleagues for not thinking more critically about the crucial assumptions and cavalier style of this line of reasoning. Commenting on his consultations in Saigon in the spring of 1964, in which the proposal by the Joint Chiefs of Staff to wage an air campaign against the North figured prominently, McNamara noted that

[t]he risk of Chinese escalation and the possibility that air attacks would neither break the will nor decisively reduce the ability of the

---

[67] Logevall, *Choosing War*, p. 387.

[68] McNamara, *In Retrospect*, p. 32.

[69] Logevall, *Choosing War*, p. 317.

[70] See, e.g., McNamara, *In Retrospect*, p. 62.

[71] Ibid., pp. 106–107; Logevall, *Choosing War*, p. 368.

North to continue supporting the insurgency in the South were recognized. But, because no better alternative appeared to exist, the majority of the group meeting in Saigon favored such attacks! This was the sort of desperate energy that would drive much of our Vietnam policy in the years ahead. Data and analysis showed that air attacks would not work, but there was such determination to do something, anything, to stop the Communists that discouraging reports were often ignored.[72]

Rusk was a somewhat enigmatic figure in the process. Having served as General Joseph W. ("Vinegar Joe") Stilwell's deputy chief of staff for the China-Burma-India theater in World War II, and then as assistant secretary of state for Far Eastern affairs during the Korean War, Rusk had more relevant knowledge and experience of Asia than any of Johnson's senior advisers. But though well informed, his view of the situation lacked nuance. He saw it quite simply as an acid test of American credibility. "The integrity of the U.S. commitment is the principal pillar of peace throughout the world," Rusk told LBJ. "If that commitment becomes unreliable, the communist world would draw conclusions that would lead to our ruin and almost certainly to a catastrophic war. So long as the South Vietnamese are prepared to fight for themselves, we cannot abandon them without disaster to peace and to our interests throughout the world."[73] If the United States did not stand up to communist aggression in Vietnam, Rusk believed, the credibility of the American commitment to Berlin—the fulcrum of European security—would erode because it was all "part of the same struggle."[74] Rusk was therefore a stalwart defender of the war in Vietnam once the decision to Americanize had been made. Yet he had been wary of provoking China in Korea and was likewise wary of provoking China in Vietnam. And—most interestingly—Rusk was the

---

[72] McNamara, *In Retrospect*, p. 114. George Kahin argues that while McNamara stressed dominoes and credibility in the spring of 1964, things had changed a year later. "Partly because the administration had publicly endowed the struggle in Vietnam with enormous importance—through its apocalyptic rhetoric as well as its actions—the American involvement had become the focus of such a glaringly intense spotlight of worldwide attention that Johnson's advisers now placed much greater emphasis on how the United States looked in its efforts to manage events in this increasingly prominent part of the world. And both the president and his advisers often seemed to have difficulty in distinguishing between their personal prestige and that of the United States." Kahin, *Intervention*, p. 312. David Kaiser faults McNamara for being, in effect, too much of a representative of his department, and too loyal a subordinate to his president. Kaiser understands McNamara as fundamentally "implementing other men's plans, in pursuit of other men's objectives." Kaiser, *American Tragedy*, p. 462.

[73] McNamara, *In Retrospect*, p. 195.

[74] Quoted in Herring, *America's Longest War*, p. 115; cf. also Kaiser, *American Tragedy*, p. 461.

only official of consequence who argued for the status quo in January 1965. At a time when LBJ and the rest of his team were becoming increasingly convinced that they faced a choice between "getting in" and "getting out," Rusk was the only one who favored "muddling through."[75]

Bundy is in many ways the most interesting of LBJ's advisers. Young, intellectual, self-confident, supremely articulate, and anything but simplistic, Bundy could hold a complicated problem up to the light, spin it around, and convince himself—and others—that he had grasped the whole and knew precisely what to do. It was thus with Vietnam. He certainly shared Rusk's concerns about American credibility.[76] But he later insisted that he was not at all concerned with falling dominoes. He also claimed that he was concerned with "the existence of what I thought a clear obligation to the people of South Vietnam," though he hastened to add that he thought of this as a political obligation rather than a moral one.[77] Bundy was not aware of the extent to which American policy makers alone thought credibility was at stake in Vietnam, nor did he fully appreciate at the time the punishment the North Vietnamese and the NLF were willing to take to drive the Americans out and topple the southern regime. But he was acutely aware that the United States had no good options. Unlike Rusk, he believed that the status quo was untenable; he understood why cutting and running was a nonstarter politically; and he knew that the war could not be won. What he hoped—and it was merely a hope, not really an expectation—was that by fighting a war in Vietnam, the United States might give the South the time it needed to shore itself up through social and economic reform. Bundy, in short, wanted to fight a war to buy some time.[78]

Johnson himself was, of course, the most important figure, and also the most inscrutable. The consummate politician, he generally played his cards close to his chest. He had the uncanny ability to know exactly what to say to someone and how to say it, which makes it difficult to know when he meant what he said and when he said things for ulterior purposes. It also makes it difficult to know exactly when he decided to do what. To this day, for example, there is debate about when Johnson finally made up his mind to Americanize the war.[79] When he did make up his mind, however, he rarely brooked opposition. He would normally bring

[75] McNamara, *In Retrospect*, p. 148. For background and further discussion, see esp. Thomas J. Schoenbaum, *Waging Peace and War*; Dean Rusk, *As I Saw It*.

[76] See, e.g., his February 1965 memo, quoted below.

[77] Personal correspondence, 22 April 1990.

[78] The best discussion is Bird, *The Color of Truth*, pp. 270–349. See also James G. Blight's review, "Red, White and Blue Blood."

[79] Cf., e.g., McNamara, *In Retrospect*, p. 145; Kaiser, *American Tragedy*, p. 411; George C. Herring, "Review of David Kaiser, *American Tragedy*."

the full force of his imposing personality to bear on dissidents and the recalcitrant. If he could not persuade through force of argument, he would resort to sheer physical intimidation. Once the commitment had been made, he demanded unwavering support from his subordinates.[80]

How did LBJ understand the situation, as far as we can tell? On the one hand, he had a prescient understanding of the difficulties he faced if he escalated the war. He sensed the danger of quagmire. "It's damned easy to get in a war," he told Mac Bundy in May 1964, "but it's gonna be awfully hard to ever extricate yourself if you get in."[81] In response to John Knight's comment on February 3 that "Long-range over there, the odds are certainly against us," Johnson replied: "Yes, there is no question about that. Anytime you got that many people against you that far from your home base, it's bad."[82] And yet a powerful mixture of motives pushed Johnson toward escalating the American commitment. He seems to have believed strongly in the domino theory.[83] He powerfully felt that American credibility was at stake, fearing that the very security of the United States hung in the balance in Vietnam.[84] He probably believed, at some level, in South Vietnamese self-determination.[85] He certainly felt that hanging tough in Vietnam was a price he had to pay to conservatives to get his domestic program through Congress.[86] If Fredrik Logevall is right, he may also have understood Vietnam as a test of his manhood.[87] His complex of concerns, both conscious and subconscious, are evident in a remarkable statement he made to Doris Kearns after leaving office:

[80] For a good general discussion, see Robert Dallek, *Flawed Giant*.

[81] Beschloss, *Taking Charge*, p. 372. See also n. 39 above.

[82] Ibid., p. 214.

[83] See, e.g., ibid., pp. 213–214, 248–249, 264.

[84] Johnson told Doris Kearns in 1970: "You see, I was as sure as any man could be that once we showed how weak we were, Moscow and Peking would move in a flash to exploit our weakness. They might move independently or they might move together. But move they would—whether through nuclear blackmail, through subversion, with regular armed forces or in some other manner. As nearly as anyone can be certain of anything, I knew they couldn't resist the opportunity to expand their control over the vacuum of power we would leave behind us. And so would begin World War III." Quoted in Doris Kearns, *Lyndon Johnson and the American Dream*, p. 253. In a more graphic statement, Johnson told Kearns: "If you let a bully come into your front yard one day, the next day he'll be up on your porch and the day after that he'll rape your wife in your own bed." Ibid., p. 258.

[85] United States Senate, Committee on Foreign Relations, *Background Information Relating to Southeast Asia and Vietnam*, pp. 157, 161.

[86] Bird, *The Color of Truth*, p. 337; Lloyd C. Gardner, "Review of David Kaiser, *American Tragedy*."

[87] "What he really feared was the personal humiliation that he believed would come with failure in Vietnam. He saw the war as a test of his own manliness." Logevall, *Choosing War*, p. 393. See also Logevall, "Vietnam and the Question of What Might Have Been," p. 46.

[E]verything I knew about history told me that if I got out of Vietnam and let Ho Chi Minh run through the streets of Saigon, then I'd be doing exactly what Chamberlain did in World War II. I'd be giving a big fat reward to aggression. And I knew that if we let Communist aggression succeed in taking over South Vietnam, there would follow in this country an endless national debate—a mean and destructive debate—that would shatter my Presidency, kill my administration, and damage our democracy. I knew that Harry Truman and Dean Acheson had lost their effectiveness from the day that the Communists took over in China. I believed that the loss of China had played a large role in the rise of Joe McCarthy. And I knew that all these problems, taken together, were chickenshit compared with what might happen if we lost Vietnam. . . . Losing the Great Society was a terrible thought, but not so terrible as the thought of being responsible for America's losing a war to the Communists. Nothing could possibly be worse than that.[88]

"Lyndon Johnson is not going down as the president who lost Vietnam," LBJ reportedly told David Nes in November 1963; "Don't you forget that."[89]

The question, of course, was: what to do? Johnson was clearly unwilling to withdraw and let Vietnam go. Nor did he look favorably upon the neutralization option, since he equated this with a communist takeover *tout court*.[90] He was acutely concerned to avoid another Korea, as indeed were all of his civilian advisers at the time, a fact that placed limits on the kind of war he would be willing to fight and would surely have eroded his optimism about the utility of military options.[91] None of the options looked attractive, but the military option seemed the best of a bad lot.

There were other significant players in the process also. Two particularly tragic figures were Undersecretary of State George Ball and Bill Bundy. Ball is a tragic figure because, of all of the players, he had the most clear-eyed view of the situation, and yet he lost every major argument. On October 5 Ball drafted a remarkable memorandum to Rusk, McNa-

[88] Quoted in Kearns, *Lyndon Johnson and the American Dream*, pp. 252–253, 259–260.

[89] Logevall, *Choosing War*, p. 77, quoting a telephone interview.

[90] Ibid., pp. 91, 183.

[91] Bird, *The Color of Truth*, p. 272. The only civilian member of the Johnson administration willing to consider sending U.S. troops north of the 17th parallel was Walt Rostow, who succeeded Mac Bundy as national security advisor in 1966. Kahin, *Intervention*, pp. 338–341.

A standard critique of Johnson's policy maintains that he squandered an opportunity for victory in Vietnam by forcing the U.S. military to fight with one arm tied behind its back. See, e.g., Harry G. Summers, *On Strategy*. This argument is persuasively rebutted by Col. Herbert Schandler's analysis in McNamara et al., *Argument without End*, pp. 313–371.

mara, and Mac Bundy assessing the pros and cons of four options: (1) continuing the present course of action; (2) taking over the war; (3) mounting an air offensive against the North; and (4) working for a political settlement. Ball picked apart the first three effortlessly, leaving the fourth by process of elimination. But his superiors found Ball's memo easy to ignore. As the administration's acknowledged in-house devil's advocate, Ball's job was to make arguments for others to reject. Moreover, neither he nor anyone else could guarantee that diplomacy would actually do the trick, and so his argument by process of elimination lacked punch. It had no hope of persuading the president since LBJ did not see the memorandum until February 1965, by which time events were already in train.[92]

Ball's memo did have an effect on Bill Bundy, however, who saw as clearly as anyone that the war in Vietnam was truly a civil war rather than an international war, harbored serious doubts about the domino theory as "at least oversimplified,"[93] and recognized that the United States had no good options, only bad ones.[94] Bundy drafted a withdrawal memo in November 1964 but backed off when McNamara and Rusk told him it "won't wash."[95] He would never again make the case for walking away and embraced bombing instead. He realized bombing might not have a decisive effect but thought it offered "at least a faint hope of really improving the situation," whereas the alternative of sticking with the status quo could "only lead to a disastrous defeat."[96] Before long, Bundy would loyally and energetically support the full Americanization program.

The military, for its part, consistently advocated the use of force. Almost from the very beginning of Johnson's presidency, the Joint Chiefs of Staff lobbied for taking the fight to the North, first with air power, and later with ground troops (crossing the 17th parallel, if necessary, to disrupt sanctuaries and supply depots).[97] When Johnson finally agreed to commit American forces to the fight in the South, the military lobbied for progressively larger deployments and progressively greater combat latitude.

The Chiefs combined optimism about the utility of force with a powerful belief both in the domino theory and in the importance of maintaining

[92] For the text of the memorandum, see George W. Ball, "Top Secret." For Ball's recollection of the drafting and discussion of the memorandum, see Ball, *The Past Has Another Pattern*, pp. 380–384. For detailed discussion, see Logevall, *Choosing War*, pp. 242–251.

[93] Kaiser, *American Tragedy*, p. 357.

[94] Overreaching his erudition, Bundy wrote in November 1964 that all U.S. options were in the "Hobson class." Logevall, *Choosing War*, p. 247. A "Hobson's choice" is a choice between the one thing offered or nothing at all.

[95] Bird, *The Color of Truth*, pp. 293–295.

[96] Herring, *America's Longest War*, p. 128.

[97] Jeffrey Record, *The Wrong War*.

the credibility of American commitments.[98] Short of authorizing actions he felt carried a significant risk of provoking Chinese intervention, Johnson proved generally accommodating, but he occasionally evinced both exasperation and unease. "Every time I get a military recommendation it calls for large-scale bombing," LBJ complained to Taylor in a December 1964 cable. "I have never felt that this war will be won from the air. . . . What is much more needed and would be more effective is . . . appropriate military strength on the ground. . . . I am ready to look with great favor on that kind of increased American effort."[99]

With the election in the bag, things began to happen quickly. On November 2 LBJ set up a working group to review Vietnam policy alternatives beginning from scratch. Under the chairmanship of Bill Bundy, the group met every day for two weeks, beginning on November 3 (election day), initially focusing on three options: (1) a negotiated settlement on any basis obtainable; (2) a sharp increase in military pressure on North Vietnam; and (3) an in-between course of increased military pressure but open channels for negotiation.[100] In its deliberation, the group reflected on the importance of South Vietnam to the United States. It backed gingerly away from a simplistic understanding of the domino theory and treated the issue of credibility with rather more nuance than most had done up to that point. Nevertheless, the group framed the problem starkly as one of attempting to avoid an uncertain but possibly catastrophic loss. The analysis is worth quoting at some length:

> The political situation remains critical and extremely fragile. The security situation in the countryside has continued to deteriorate.
>
> It is possible that the new government in Saigon can improve South Vietnamese esprit and effectiveness, though on the basis of current indications this appears unlikely. It is also possible that GVN determination and authority could virtually give way suddenly in the near future, though the chances seem better than even that the new GVN

---

[98] See, e.g., the Chiefs' memorandum of 2 March 1964 asserting "the overriding importance to the security interests of the United States of preventing the loss of South Vietnam." McNamara, *In Retrospect*, p. 111. McNamara also reports the Chiefs' view that the loss of South Vietnam would have a disastrous effect on the faith and resolve of other noncommunist nations, and that South Vietnam was "the military keystone." Ibid., p. 161n.

[99] Quoted in ibid., p. 165. Yet when the military proposed exactly that, LBJ would agonize before approving their requests. See, e.g., McNamara's discussion of LBJ's response to Gen. William Westmoreland's demands for more troops on 7 June 1965; ibid., pp. 186–206. As the war escalated and dragged on, LBJ rode herd on the military as no president had ever done before, micromanaging missions and targets to minimize the risks of provoking the Chinese and (so he naïvely hoped) to send the North the signals he believed they needed to see to come to the bargaining table and settle on terms he could accept.

[100] Ibid., pp. 159–161.

can hang on for this period and thus afford a platform upon which its armed forces, with US assistance, can prosecute the war and attempt to turn the tide. Even under the best of circumstances, however, reversal of present military trends will be extremely difficult.

A. *US Objectives and the Present Basis of US Action.* Behind our policy in South Vietnam and Laos have been three factors, all closely related to our over-all policy of resisting Communist expansion:

1. The general principle of helping countries that try to defend their own freedom against Communist subversion and attack.

2. The specific consequences of Communist control of South Vietnam and Laos on the security of other nations in Asia.

3. The implications worldwide of South Vietnam, and, to a lesser extent, Laos as test cases of Communist wars of national liberation.
. . .

C. *Consequences of Communist Control of South Vietnam.*

1. *In Southeast Asia.* The so-called domino theory is over-simplified. It might apply if, but only if, Communist China entered Southeast Asia in force and/or the US was forced out of South Vietnam in circumstances of military defeat. Nonetheless, Communist control of South Vietnam would almost immediately make Laos extremely hard to hold, have Cambodia bending sharply to the Communist side, place great pressure on Thailand (a country which has an historic tendency to make peace with the side that seems to be winning), and embolden Indonesia to increase its pressure on Malaysia. We could do more in Thailand and with the British in Malaysia to reinforce the defense of these countries, but the initial shock wave would be great.

2. *In Asia Generally.* The effects in Asia generally would depend heavily on the circumstances in which South Vietnam was lost and on whether the loss did in fact greatly weaken or lead to the early loss of other areas in Southeast Asia. Nationalist China (shaken already by the Chicom [communist Chinese] nuclear explosion and the UN membership crisis), South Korea, and the Philippines would need maximum reassurance. While Japan's faith in our military posture and determination might not be shaken, the growing feeling that Communist China must somehow be lived with might well be accentuated. India and Iran appear to be the Asian problem cases outside the Far East. A US defeat could lead to serious repercussions in these countries. There is a great deal we could still do to reassure these countries, but the picture of a defense line clearly breached could have serious effects and could easily, over time, tend to unravel the whole Pacific and South Asian defense structures.

3. *In the World at Large*. Within NATO (except for Greece and Turkey to some degree), the loss of South Vietnam probably would not shake the faith and resolve to face the threat of Communist aggression or confidence in us for major help. This is so provided we carried out any military actions in Southeast Asia without taking forces from NATO and without generating a wave of isolationism in the US. In other areas of the world, either the nature of the Communist threat or the degree of US commitment or both are so radically different than in Southeast Asia that it is difficult to assess the impact. The question would be whether the US was in fact able to go on with its present policies.

4. *Summary*. There are enough ifs in the above analysis so that it cannot be concluded that the loss of South Vietnam would soon have the totally crippling effect in Southeast Asia and Asia generally that the loss of Berlin would have in Europe; but it could be that bad, driving us to the progressive loss of other areas or to taking a stand at some point where there would almost certainly be major conflict and perhaps the great risk of nuclear war.[101]

On December 1, 1964, the working group issued its report to the president, dropping the option of negotiating a settlement on any basis obtainable. Instead it presented three: (1) "Continuing the present course indefinitely with little hope of avoiding defeat"; (2) initiating a sharp bombing campaign against North Vietnamese targets with aim of forcing Hanoi to cease its support for the PAVN and/or begin negotiations; and (3) initiating a graduated bombing campaign that would have a similar objective but run fewer risks. LBJ instructed Taylor to give Saigon one last chance to get its act together, conditionally approving a two-phase bombing plan as an incentive for South Vietnamese leaders (reconnaissance flights against infiltration routes in Laos and reprisal strikes against North Vietnam for attacks on U.S. targets, followed by an air campaign against the North).[102]

South Vietnam did not, in fact, get its act together, and the situation became desperate. It was in this context that Mac Bundy and Bob McNamara wrote Johnson the famous "Fork in the Road" memorandum toward the end of January 1965:

---

[101] Paper Prepared by the National Security Council Working Group, Washington, November 21, 1964, *FRUS 1964–1968*, vol. 1, Doc. 418. http://www.state.gov/www/about_state/history/vol_i/393_440.html.

[102] See the discussion in McNamara, *In Retrospect*, pp. 161–163. Taylor responded that "we are presently on a losing track and must risk a change" because "to take no positive action now is to accept defeat in the fairly near future." Ibid., p. 166.

What we want to say to you is that both of us are now pretty well convinced that our current policy can lead only to disastrous defeat. What we are doing now, essentially, is to wait and hope for a stable government. . . . *We see two alternatives.* The *first* is to use our military power in the Far East and to force a change in Communist policy. The *second* is to deploy all our resources along a track of negotiation, aimed at salvaging what little can be preserved with no major addition to our present military risks. Bob and I tend to favor the first course. . . .

You should know that Dean Rusk does not agree with us. He does not quarrel with our assertion that things are going very badly and that the situation is unraveling. He does not assert that this deterioration can be stopped. What he does say is that the consequences of both escalation and withdrawal are so bad that we simply must find a way of making our present policy work. This would be good if it were possible. Bob and I do not think that it is.[103]

Johnson dispatched Bundy to Saigon for an on-the-spot inspection. Logevall writes: "What he encountered was a South Vietnam teetering on the brink of social and political disintegration."[104] On the third day of his visit, the PAVN launched a mortar attack upon an ARVN military headquarters and U.S. air base near Pleiku in the central highlands, killing 8 American servicemen and wounding 128 others. Bundy recommended, and Johnson authorized, an immediate retaliatory air strike against North Vietnam. An important threshold had been crossed. Bundy's flippant remark a few weeks later that "Pleikus are streetcars"—i.e., one comes along every once in a while if you want to get on—has led many to conclude that the Johnson administration was merely looking for an excuse to escalate.[105] But Bundy did not believe that the United States *needed* an excuse: the facts on the ground, he believed, fully justified a new kind and level of commitment, and he later regretted having made the remark because it distracted attention from this fundamental point.[106]

Upon his return, Bundy reported:

The situation in Vietnam is deteriorating and without new U.S. action defeat appears inevitable—probably not in a matter of weeks or perhaps even months, but within the next year or so. There is still time to turn it around, but not much.

The stakes in Vietnam are extremely high. . . . The international prestige of the United States, and a substantial part of our influence,

---

[103] Ibid., pp. 167–168; Logevall, *Choosing War*, p. 317.
[104] Logevall, *Choosing War*, p. 320.
[105] Townsend Hoopes, *The Limits of Intervention*, p. 30.
[106] In conversation, January 1989.

are directly at risk in Vietnam. There is no way of unloading the burden on the Vietnamese themselves, and there is no way of negotiating ourselves out of Vietnam which offers any serious promise at present. . . . [A]ny negotiated withdrawal today would mean surrender on the installment plan.[107]

Bundy argued that "[t]here is one grave weakness in our posture in Vietnam which is within our power to fix—and that is a widespread belief that we do not have the will and force and patience and determination to take the necessary action and stay the course." He noted that, "At its very best the struggle in Vietnam will be long," and he insisted that it was "important that this fundamental fact be made clear and our understanding of it be made clear to our own people and to the people of Vietnam."[108]

Within days, Johnson authorized a graduated bombing campaign against North Vietnam. Within a few months he would authorize a massive introduction of U.S. combat troops to do the job he had earlier insisted Asian boys should do for themselves. At no time did he make clear to the American people that "at its very best the struggle in Vietnam will be long"—nor would he even acknowledge that he had embarked upon a new course. But without question, American policy had taken a decisive and momentous turn. It had done so because the earlier policy, followed consistently for ten years, appeared to be on the verge of failing catastrophically. The course of action LBJ and his advisers chose was not one about which they were genuinely optimistic or enthusiastic. All acknowledged its dangers and limits. Many knew, or at least suspected, that it might at most buy some time. No one would have described it as a good gamble. And, most importantly, no one saw in it an opportunity for *gain*. LBJ changed course not because he thought he had an opportunity to *win*, but because he desperately hoped he might thereby *not lose*.

NIXINGER AND THE ENDGAME

Johnson accomplished his goal of not losing. During his presidency, the Saigon regime survived. It exercised control over only part of its territory, but at least it survived. It even enjoyed a degree of political stability under strongman Nguyen Van Thieu reminiscent of Diem's better days. But it was clear to all that South Vietnam survived because the United States was propping it up. It was not politically viable on its own. More than

---

[107] Memorandum From the President's Special Assistant for National Security Affairs (Bundy) to President Johnson, *FRUS 1964–1968*, vol. 2, Doc. 84. http://www.state.gov/www/about_state/history/vol_ii/81_86.html.
[108] Ibid.

three years of sustained bombing and energetic counterinsurgency efforts failed to bring the war discernibly closer to what the United States considered a satisfactory conclusion: namely, an independent South Vietnam free from "external" interference.

On the ground, the United States never did better than fight to a stalemate. Hamlets it took during the day reverted to the enemy during the night. Fighters it killed, and arms it captured, were replaced the next day. The United States enjoyed only one significant military victory during the Johnson presidency, and it was, ironically, its worst political defeat. On January 30, 1968, during the Tet holiday, while many ARVN troops were on leave, the PAVN launched an all-out, no-holds-barred, coordinated attack on U.S. and ARVN targets throughout South Vietnam, infiltrated South Vietnamese cities, attacked government installations, and even succeeded in penetrating the American Embassy grounds in Saigon. It caught the Americans and South Vietnamese largely by surprise and enjoyed some temporary successes (holding the city of Hue, for example, long enough to commit atrocities on a truly Stalinesque scale).[109] In so doing, it spent itself as a military force and gave the Americans and their Saigon clients a welcome breather. But not long after the predictable rally-'round-the-flag effect wore off Stateside, the American people began to question their leaders' consistently overly optimistic public pronouncements on the progress of the war. If things were going as well as the White House and the Pentagon insisted, why were PAVN fighters running through downtown Saigon on the *CBS Evening News*?

Bombing accomplished nothing, in large part because there was nothing to bomb. Vietnam was an underdeveloped agrarian society fighting a low-tech guerrilla war. There was no developed industrial or transportation infrastructure to disrupt. There were no large-scale military formations to attack. The most tempting targets—dikes holding back floodwaters around Hanoi, port facilities in Haiphong—were largely off limits because attacking them would kill large numbers of innocent civilians or risk sinking Soviet ships. So American planes attacked roads, makeshift bridges, and jungle tracks instead—things the Vietnamese could repair or circumvent in a matter of hours. The military never lost faith in the efficacy of the air war, but McNamara and Bundy did.[110]

---

[109] Alje Vennema, *The Viet Cong Massacre at Hue*; Don Oberdorfer, *Tet!*; Eric M. Hammel, *Fire in the Streets*; James J. Wirtz, *The Tet Offensive*; Marc Jason Gilbert and William P. Head, *The Tet Offensive*; George W. Smith, *The Siege at Hue*.

[110] United States Senate, *Hearings before the Preparedness Investigating Subcommittee of the U.S. Senate Armed Services Committee*. McNamara's successor as secretary of defense, Clark Clifford, entered office a stay-the-course man on March 1, 1968, but within weeks he came to favor disengagement. Clifford, "A Vietnam Reappraisal: The Personal History of One Man's View and How It Evolved." Mac Bundy's successor, Walt Rostow, entered office in 1966 a hawk and remained one to the end of his days.

The one thing LBJ hoped bombing might accomplish was to convince Hanoi that the costs of pursuing the war outweighed the gains. He would bomb for a while, then pause, hoping that the North Vietnamese would seize the window of opportunity to come to the negotiating table without exploiting it to rush more men and matériel down the Ho Chi Minh trail. An endless series of feelers, peace initiatives, and abortive mediations accomplished little.[111] But in October 1968 Johnson ordered a total bombing halt, and the North Vietnamese and the Americans finally agreed to meet in Paris for preliminary peace talks.

It was at this point that Richard Nixon began to take over the conduct of the war. He was not yet president, but that did not stop him. Fearful that productive peace talks in Paris might hand Democratic presidential candidate Hubert Humphrey the 1968 election, the Nixon campaign engaged "The Dragon Lady," Anna Chennault, to act as a back channel to Thieu. Nixon's message was simple: a Republican administration would be a better friend to South Vietnam than a Democratic one, and Thieu had it within his power to boost Nixon's chances. All he had to do was refuse to cooperate in Paris. A clear violation of American laws against conducting private foreign policies, the gambit nevertheless worked.[112] Thieu refused to cooperate, and the Paris peace talks got nowhere.[113]

If Jeffrey Kimball is right that "in 1969, 1970, 1971, or 1972, Nixon could have negotiated the same settlement he got in 1973," then Nixon's disruption of the Paris peace talks was truly tragic.[114] Strictly in terms of substance, this is easy to imagine. As Lloyd Gardner notes, Nixon had been sharply critical of LBJ's offer to withdraw American troops six months after a ceasefire in 1966, arguing that a commitment of that kind would have left him without options if the war resumed. But the Paris Peace Agreement of January 27, 1973, provided a much earlier cut off date even than that. Moreover, it sanctioned the existence of two governments in South Vietnam and permitted North Vietnamese troops to stay in the South to protect territory they controlled.[115] It provided just enough of a fig leaf to cover an American withdrawal, and just enough of a decent interval before the final collapse of the Saigon regime, to permit the United

---

[111] The best discussion is McNamara et al., *Argument without End*.

[112] Kimball, *Nixon's Vietnam War*, pp. 56–61; Christopher Hitchens, "The Case against Henry Kissinger, Part One," pp. 37–42.

[113] It is, of course, an open question whether they would have gotten anywhere even if the Nixon campaign had not interfered. The very fact that the talks were proceeding, however, would have boosted Humphrey's candidacy.

[114] Jeffrey Kimball, "Review of Fredrik Logevall, *Choosing War: The Lost Chance for Peace and the Escalation of War in Vietnam*." See also Hitchens, "The Case against Henry Kissinger, Part One."

[115] Gardner, "Review of Jeffrey P. Kimball, *Nixon's Vietnam War*."

States to claim that it had met its commitments. If these terms had satisfied Nixon in 1969, almost certainly they would have satisfied Hanoi as well.

Whether circumstances were ripe for an agreement is another matter altogether. The answer to this question depends in large part upon what Nixon and Kissinger thought they could accomplish that Johnson could not, and exactly how they thought they could accomplish it. And it is really these two alone with whom we need concern ourselves here. They were the key players, generally neither seeking nor paying much heed to the advice of others. They held the reins as closely as they possibly could. Kissinger did his best to keep Secretary of State William Rogers on the sidelines; Secretary of Defense Melvin Laird did not seek to play a forward role. In most essential respects, Nixon and Kissinger understood the stakes in Vietnam the same way, had the same goals, and commonly favored the same means. When they did not, they managed to find common ground or at least to paper over any real disagreements.[116] They did, to some extent, fight for the limelight and the glory. Nixon usually won, being president. But the tensions between them, while of psychological interest, are not really of historical interest, and with respect to Vietnam at least, Kimball is fully justified in referring to them jointly as "Nixinger."[117]

Until Nixon and Kissinger lost faith in their own abilities to succeed where LBJ had failed, they were unlikely to settle for the decent-interval solution. The record makes clear that it took more than two and a half years of frustration to shake Nixon's confidence, and somewhat longer to shake Kissinger's. In the meantime, even if they had had the opportunity to secure the agreement they ultimately settled for in 1973, it is hard to argue that they would have seized it. Circumstances may have seemed ripe for throwing in the towel in 1973, but neither Nixon nor Kissinger seems to have understood the circumstances to be ripe much earlier than that.

Of course, neither Nixon nor Kissinger ever described the endgame to Vietnam as "throwing in the towel." They have variously described it as an American victory, "peace with honor," and outright defeat. This last

---

[116] Kissinger, for example, appears to have had more doubts about the prospects of Vietnamization than did Nixon, though these differences were not readily apparent to the public. Kissinger, *The White House Years*, pp. 1480–1482.

[117] For background and insight into these two complex figures, see, e.g., Richard M. Nixon, *Six Crises*; Bruce Mazlish, *In Search of Nixon*; Tad Szulc, *The Illusion of Peace*; William Shawcross, *Sideshow*; John Ehrlichman, *Witness to Power*; Dan Caldwell, *Henry Kissinger*; Seymour M. Hersh, *The Price of Power*; Harvey Starr, *Henry Kissinger*; Stephen E. Ambrose, *Nixon*; Richard C. Thornton, *The Nixon-Kissinger Years*; Walter Isaacson, *Kissinger*; Joan Hoff-Wilson, *Nixon Reconsidered*; Vamik D. Volkan, Norman Itzkowitz, and Andrew W. Dod, *Richard Nixon*; William Bundy, *The Tangled Web*; Melvin Small, *The Presidency of Richard Nixon*; Anthony Summers, *Arrogance of Power*.

characterization, of course, refers not to the conclusion of the Paris Peace Agreement, but to the failure of the United States Congress to fund the levels of economic and military support for Saigon *after* the American withdrawal that they claim would have staved off total collapse in 1975.[118] Whether wishful thinking or simple delusion, this is characteristic scape-goating and spin-doctoring. And therein lies one of the great difficulties of attempting to get under the hood of Nixon's Vietnam policy. The principals' own accounts are simply unreliable (Kimball characterizes them as "incomplete, disingenuous, and self-serving.")[119] In addition, we do not yet have access to quite the same wealth of declassified materials now available for the Johnson years.

Probably the most useful source of insight is H. R. Haldeman's diary, which provides almost a daily blow-by-blow insider's account, and which is especially good at communicating several important things not ordinarily obvious from memoirs and documents: the fragile egos, short fuses, and petty paranoias of key players (especially "P" and "K," Haldeman's shorthand for "the president" and "Kissinger"); the sniping, infighting, and jockeying for glory; and—perhaps most importantly of all—the constant barrage of demands on the time and attention of the president and his advisers, which of course made impossible the careful deliberations that would lie behind important decisions in the ideal world, that put a premium on reaction, and that limit the possibilities for proaction.[120] It is against the background of the Haldeman diaries that the principals' retrospective accounts appear most strongly fictional. What Nixon and Kissinger would later describe as a well-thought-out, methodical, profoundly strategic approach to the Vietnam problem was largely, in fact, something that they made up as they went along.

Historians of the Nixon period are fortunate, too, to have at their disposal Jeffrey Kimball's remarkable book, *Nixon's Vietnam War*. Kimball has beaten the bushes for any and all relevant information, and he tells what surely must stand for many years as the definitive story. His deeply psychological interpretation of the Nixinger policy is not easily falsified,

---

[118] "Our defeat in Vietnam sparked a rash of totalitarian conquests around the world as we retreated into a five-year, self-imposed exile. In crisis after crisis in Africa, the Mideast, and Central America, critics of American involvement abroad brandished 'another Vietnam' like a scepter, an all-purpose argument-stopper for any situation where it was being asserted that the United States should do something rather than nothing." Nixon, *No More Vietnams*, p. 13.

[119] Kimball, *Nixon's Vietnam War*, p. xiii. See also Jeffrey Kimball, "Debunking Nixon's Myths of Vietnam." Nixon and Kissinger provide detailed discussions in various places: e.g., Henry A. Kissinger, "The Viet Nam Negotiations"; Richard M. Nixon, *Peace in Vietnam*; Kissinger, *American Foreign Policy*; Kissinger, *White House Years*; Kissinger, *Years of Upheaval*; Nixon, *No More Vietnams*; Nixon, *RN*.

[120] Haldeman, *The Haldeman Diaries*.

of course, and it will not appeal to all readers. But the analysis is empirically rich, and I have found it extremely insightful. I shall make liberal use of it here.

How did Nixon understand the problem in Vietnam? For decades, he had been an outspoken proponent of the domino theory. In December 1953, for example, Nixon had said: "If Indochina falls, Thailand is put in an almost impossible position. The same is true of Malaya with its rubber and tin. The same is true of Indonesia. If this whole part of Southeast Asia goes under Communist domination or Communist influence, Japan, who trades and must trade with this area in order to exist, must inevitably be oriented toward the Communist regime."[121] Nixon stuck to this line throughout. "Our primary interest in Vietnam was to prevent the fall of Indochina to the Communists," he wrote in 1985. "We wanted to prevent the loss of Vietnam because we believed it would lead to the fall of the rest of Southeast Asia."[122] In fact, Nixon asserted, ultimately the dominoes *did* fall, thanks to the pusillanimity of Congress. "For six years after Vietnam, the new isolationists chanted 'No more Vietnams' as the dominoes fell one by one: Laos, Cambodia, and Mozambique in 1975; Angola in 1976; Ethiopia in 1977; South Yemen in 1978; Nicaragua in 1979."[123] This was an odd statement for Nixon to make. Mozambique, Angola, Ethiopia, South Yemen, and Nicaragua are nowhere near Southeast Asia. Nor is there reason to think that events in any of these countries but Cambodia had even the slightest connection to Vietnam.[124] But Nixon either believed it or sought rhetorical advantage from the claim.

More than just dominoes were at stake in Nixon's view, however. So also was the prestige, credibility, and ultimately the security of the United States (considerations that certainly weighed heavily on Kissinger's mind, given his profoundly *realpolitik* approach to the world).[125] "Abandoning the South Vietnamese people . . . would threaten our longer term hopes for peace in the world," Nixon proclaimed. "A great nation cannot renege on its pledges. A great nation must be worthy of trust."[126] And—to give Nixon some credit for moral sensibility—as a long-standing, dedicated, philosophical anticommunist, he seems to have had some qualms, too, about abandoning the South Vietnamese people to what he no doubt sin-

---

[121] Kimball, *Nixon's Vietnam War*, p. 17.

[122] Nixon, *No More Vietnams*, p. 29.

[123] Ibid., p. 212.

[124] Laos had been a Vietnamese puppet state, for all intents and purposes, for many years. Left-wing insurgencies elsewhere had fully sufficient indigenous roots.

[125] See, e.g., Henry Kissinger, *Diplomacy*; Kissinger, *Nuclear Weapons and Foreign Policy*; Kissinger, *A World Restored*; Michael Joseph Smith, *Realist Thought from Weber to Kissinger*.

[126] Nixon, *Peace in Vietnam*, p. 3. Cf. also Herring, *America's Longest War*, p. 223.

cerely understood to be a fate worse than death under totalitarian communist rule.[127]

Nixon, therefore, operated on the basis of a fairly typical complex of concerns. Not surprisingly, during the Johnson years he wholeheartedly endorsed the administration's goal of securing a stable, independent South Vietnam.[128] He also endorsed the use of military force to achieve that end. But he was highly critical of Johnson's apparent enthusiasm for negotiations, and he thought LBJ too indecisive, insufficiently aggressive, too enamored of ground troops, and too timid in the use of air and naval power.[129]

By 1968, however, Nixon had realized that there was no prospect of military victory. On March 29 he told his speechwriters Richard Whalen, Raymond Price, and Patrick Buchanan: "I've come to the conclusion that there's no way to win the war. But we can't say that, of course. In fact, we have to seem to say the opposite, just to keep some degree of bargaining leverage."[130] From the very beginning of his presidency, in other words, he clearly saw that the only way out of Vietnam was via the bargaining table. But to get an acceptable outcome, Nixon believed that he had to convince Hanoi that the United States could not be defeated and would not go away unsatisfied. To do this, he had to convince them that he would pay any price, and bear any burden, to secure a "peace with honor" that preserved the Saigon regime. He would use diplomatic and military pressure "to persuade Hanoi itself that the war is not worth the cost."[131] He would convince Hanoi directly, and he would convince Moscow to try to convince Hanoi as well.

How did he plan to do this? Essentially, by frightening everybody. He would use both psychological and physical warfare. He would rant and

---

[127] "The United States intervened in the Vietnam War to prevent North Vietnam from imposing its totalitarian government on South Vietnam through military conquest, both because a Communist victory would lead to massive human suffering for the people of Vietnam and because it would damage American strategic interests and pose a threat to our allies and friends in other non-Communist nations." Nixon, *No More Vietnams*, p. 46.

[128] Missing the ironies, Nixon stated in 1969 that "In determining what choices would be acceptable, we have to understand our essential objective: We seek the opportunity for the South Vietnamese people to determine their own political future without outside interference. Let me put it plainly: What the United States wants for South Vietnam is not the important thing. What North Vietnam wants for South Vietnam is not the important thing. What is important is what the people of South Vietnam want for themselves." Nixon, *Peace in Vietnam*, p. 4. Unless, of course, the people of South Vietnam wanted to join the North. "[A]ny settlement," Nixon wrote in the *New York Times*, ". . . must provide for the territorial and political integrity of South Vietnam" (8 October 1968).

[129] Kimball, *Nixon's Vietnam War*, pp. 29–30.

[130] Ibid., p. 52. Cf. also Nixon, *RN*, p. 349.

[131] "Viet 3rd Redraft," in Richard J. Whalen, *Catch the Falling Flag*, pp. 284–286.

rave, both literally and through the metaphor of aerial bombardment. He would make Moscow and Hanoi think that he was obsessed. He would make them wonder whether he had lost all sense of proportion. He would make them fear that he might even use nuclear weapons. Taking a page from Machiavelli, he would make them think, in short, that he was mad.[132]

There were two problems with Nixon's approach. First, while he would *pretend* to be willing to pay any price to achieve his goals, his opponents *actually were* willing to pay any price to achieve theirs. Second, Nixon had the misfortune to preside over a democracy growing weary and increasingly critical of the struggle. This encouraged the North Vietnamese to hang tough, on the one hand, and impressed upon Nixon the importance of winding up the war as quickly as possible, on the other. The war, he believed, was harming the United States domestically, economically, culturally, and morally.[133] Vietnam was the nation's number one priority, and Nixon's as well.[134] He felt that he did not have unlimited time to get the job done. As Haldeman put it: "From the start of his Presidency, Nixon focused primarily on Vietnam, recognizing that it was his overriding major challenge. On one hand, he was determined to reach a conclusion of the war on a basis of 'peace with honor' and not a 'cop out' that would result in abandoning South Vietnam and a collapse of South East Asia along the lines of the 'domino theory.' On the other hand, he knew the domestic dissatisfaction with the ongoing 'impossible war' would inevitably increase daily and become more and more unmanageable."[135] Assuaging his domestic audience inevitably stood in tension with his

---

[132] Niccolò Machiavelli, *Discourses on Livy*, book 3, chap. 2, "That It Is a Very Wise Thing to Simulate Craziness at The Right Time" (pp. 213–214). Much of Kimball's discussion in *Nixon's Vietnam War* is intended to bring to the fore just how central this "madman theory" of coercive diplomacy was to Nixon's whole approach. The logic behind the madman theory is most commonly associated with Thomas Schelling, who wrote famously of the "rationality of irrationality" and of the utility of the "threat that leaves something to chance" in his classic works *The Strategy of Conflict* and *Arms and Influence*. Kimball argues, however, that Nixon arrived at the notion independently, via practice rather than theory, primarily by watching Eisenhower's handling of the Korean War. He also notes important differences in nuance between Nixon's and Kissinger's understandings of the diplomatic usefulness of risk-taking. See Kimball, *Nixon's Vietnam War*, pp. 76–86.

[133] Kimball, *Nixon's Vietnam War*, p. 44. Haldeman's diary demonstrates the intensity of Nixon's almost pastoral concern about the nation's morals. On April 19, 1969, for example, Haldeman wrote: : "P well recognizes K's thesis that a really strong overt act on part of P is essential to galvanize people into overcoming slothfulness and detachment arising from general moral decay." Haldeman, *The Haldeman Diaries*, p. 52.

[134] See, e.g., Haldeman's diary entry for March 25, 1969: "P opened with 35 minute oration on the office, emphasized priorities, first, settle the war; second, establish law and order; third, stop inflation and settle the economy." *The Haldeman Diaries*, p. 43.

[135] Ibid., p. 96.

tough international message. In a press conference on June 19, 1969, for example, Nixon said that he hoped to have all U.S. soldiers out of Vietnam before the end of 1970, announced that there would be more withdrawals in the summer, stated that he wasn't "wedded" to the Thieu regime, and said that he did not oppose a cease-fire. "All this shook K pretty badly," Haldeman noted.[136]

Nixon thought he could do it. He believed he could succeed where Johnson had failed. As Haldeman reports, "He had fully expected that an acceptable, if not totally satisfactory, solution would be achieved through negotiation within the first six months."[137] Haldeman's diary entries are striking on this point. Nixon consistently underestimated the amount of time it would take to bring the war to a successful conclusion. "P stated flatly that war will be over by next year," Haldeman recorded in his diary entry for March 20, 1969.[138] On April 15 Nixon "hoped we would have it over in a few months."[139] On September 27 he "Pointed out in Vietnam the enemy misjudges two things, the time (P still has three years and three months) and the man (he won't be first President to lose a war). Emphasized importance of the next 60 days (first said 30)."[140] For October 8 Haldeman records Nixon saying, "Main problem is Vietnam, and we've bought nine months, but can't expect to get any more time. Kept doves at bay this long, now have to take them on, first [Vice President Spiro] Agnew etc., then later the P. Problem is that this does make it his war."[141] On April 23, 1970, Haldeman wrote, "He still feels he can get it wound up this year if we keep enough pressure on and don't crumble at home. K agrees."[142]

Nixon continued the slow, steady withdrawal of American ground troops and continued to pound Indochina from the air, but as his timeta-

---

[136] Ibid., p. 65. David Kaiser picks up this tension in his review of Kimball: "Both at the time and in their memoirs, Nixon and Kissinger always liked to believe they were in control of events and would eventually bring them to a satisfactory conclusion. Yet what I found most fascinating about Kimball's lengthy narrative is the extent to which, again and again, they found themselves constrained by the very factors—public opinion, student demonstrations, international pressure, and the Congress—which they prided themselves upon ignoring. Nowhere was this truer than in November 1969, when Nixon, while proclaiming publicly that the moratorium on demonstrations would have no effect upon him, shelved plans for drastic escalation against the North because he feared the effect that it might have." David Kaiser, "Review of Jeffrey P. Kimball, *Nixon's Vietnam War*."

[137] Haldeman, *The Haldeman Diaries*, p. 96.

[138] Ibid., p. 42.

[139] Ibid., p. 50.

[140] Ibid., p. 90.

[141] Ibid., p. 96. Up to this point, Nixon had been attempting to frame the conflict publicly as Johnson's war, which he was going to wind up.

[142] Ibid., pp. 153–154.

ble for a negotiated solution kept receding from view like a mirage on a hot desert highway, the 1972 elections began to loom larger on the horizon, and Nixon and Kissinger began to think of the Vietnam war in a more expressly electoral frame. On December 15, 1970, for example, Haldeman records: "K came in and the discussion covered some of the general thinking about Vietnam and the P's big peace plan for next year, which K later told me he does not favor. He thinks that any pullout next year would be a serious mistake because the adverse reaction to it could set in well before the '72 elections. He favors, instead, a continued winding down and then a pullout right at the fall of '72 so that if any bad results follow they will be too late to affect the election."[143] On May 26, 1971, Haldeman wrote: "Then [Nixon] got to talking about election issues, and made the ironic point that of all the major issues, the only one that is a sure thing for us is Vietnam. That all the rest are in doubt, but we know precisely what we're going to do and where we're going to be on Vietnam."[144] "The P emphasized that all foreign policy initiatives are going to have to be completed by July 1972," Haldeman wrote two days later, "because after that there will be a Democratic nominee and they'll insist that he be taken along on any trips and brought in on any discussions. The ideal scenario still would be to get the Vietnam thing settled this summer."[145] The closer the election drew, the more Nixon understood Vietnam as an electoral issue.[146]

It is hard to know how to explain Nixon's optimism about his ability to conclude the war successfully. He faced essentially the same set of pressures and constraints that LBJ faced. If anything, they were more severe. He had no instruments at his disposal that LBJ did not also have. He essentially did nothing more than tweak LBJ's policy. And yet he appears sincerely to have believed that with his shoulder to the wheel in place of Johnson's, the enemy would fold. Eventually, however, reality sank in. Kimball writes: "When he entered office, he, as had previous presidents, intended to 'win' in South Vietnam—that is, preserve it as a non-Communist, procapitalist, pro-Western political entity, thereby also preserving the credibility of American power. Only later, when he understood that

---

[143] Ibid., p. 221. See also Haldeman's entry for December 19, 1970, p. 223, where Nixon seems convinced by this logic but still feels a need for some peace initiative in 1971.

[144] Ibid., p. 293.

[145] Ibid., pp. 293–294. Indeed, Kimball argues that Nixon shaped his withdrawal timetable in 1972 in part to defuse the issue before Democratic National Convention. Kimball, *Nixon's Vietnam War*, p. 301.

[146] E.g., October 26, 1972: "He makes the point that only great events can change things in the campaign now, and Vietnam is the only great event happening. We've got to be sure that if it changes anything, it changes it our way." Haldeman, *The Haldeman Diaries*, p. 524.

his original strategy was failing, did he and Kissinger accept the decent-interval solution."[147]

In the late summer of 1971, Nixon appears to have had his first serious crisis of confidence. It lingered for several months. "He talked a little about Vietnam and the point that he was sorry that we hadn't been able to actually end the war directly," Haldeman recorded in his entry for September 19, "but made the point that there really was no way to end it—it was doomed always just to trickle out the way it is, and that's now become clear."[148] This rattled Kissinger, whose faith was stronger. "Henry's concerned that the P's looking for a way to bug out and he thinks that would be a disaster now," Haldeman wrote on New Year's Day. "His instinct is that the North Vietnamese are ready to give, so we'd be totally wrong to show any nervousness."[149] But by the following spring, Nixon had bucked up his courage again—at least for a few more months—as Haldeman's diary clearly shows.[150]

The United States never did negotiate an agreement that would preserve a secure, independent South Vietnam. Eventually, it gave up trying. To some extent, the need seemed to fade. With both U.S.-Soviet and U.S.-Chinese relations on the upswing, thanks to Nixon's and Kissinger's energetic and creative Great Power diplomacy, and with Sino-Soviet relations in tatters, Vietnam lost a good deal of its salience as the front line of the Cold War. Congress and the American people were certainly running out of patience and simply wanted the whole thing to go away. Troop withdrawals were continuing, and Nixon felt it necessary to have them continue. At some point the United States would run out of ground troops in Vietnam anyway.

By August and September, Nixon had stopped thinking of the election as a firm deadline for being out, since he was running well ahead in the polls, but everyone recognized that it was still time to wrap things up.

---

[147] Kimball, *Nixon's Vietnam War*, p. xii.

[148] Haldeman, *The Haldeman Diaries*, p. 356.

[149] Ibid., p. 391.

[150] See, e.g., April 4, 1972: "Got into several political discussions, the P's concerned that we've got to get moving on the attack, that we should have someone attacking [Democratic presidential candidate Edmund] Muskie as a defeatist, because he's saying that we shouldn't react to the Vietnam attack by the enemy. [On March 30, 1972, the PLAF launched a massive, coordinated invasion of South Vietnam.] We shouldn't let him build that lie about just getting out of Vietnam. That shows no concern for the POW's or protection for the 70,000 GI's that are there. He made the point that the P has the responsibility for these people and that our continued withdrawal can only go on if South Vietnam is able to hold." Ibid., p. 435. Cf. also May 4, 1972: "He said that he had been thinking it over, and that he'd decided that we can't lose the war. We're going to hit hard and we're going to move in. The [Moscow] Summit is not important in this context, and that going to the Summit and paying the price of losing in Vietnam would not be satisfactory." Ibid., p. 454.

Nixon merely wanted to wrap things up in such a way, and at such a time, that he could make it all look good.[151] There was one important false start. In September 1972 Kissinger agreed for the first time to North Vietnamese language by which the NLF and its Provisional Revolutionary Government would have equal standing with Thieu's government in a postwar South Vietnam, in effect letting go of America's primary war aim.[152] On October 22 the United States and North Vietnam reached an agreement on that basis. The war looked as though it might be over.

Kissinger quickly ran into trouble selling the agreement to Thieu, and Nixon got cold feet. Worried about credibility, giving the impression of having betrayed a friend, and displeasing his hawks, he went back to the North Vietnamese and demanded a number of minor modifications that would enable him to put a better spin on things.[153] "As far as I was concerned, almost everything involving a Vietnam settlement was negotiable," Nixon later wrote, "except two things: I would not agree to anything that did not include the return of all our POWs [prisoners of war] and an accounting for our missing in action; and I would not agree to any terms that required or amounted to our overthrow of President Thieu."[154] He had to ensure that the wording and practical provisions of the agreement did not obviously portend Thieu's imminent demise.

Hanoi sensed a renege and resisted. Nixon's response was to launch the most intensive bombing campaign of the war: Operation Linebacker II, or the "Christmas bombing," in which American aircraft pounded North Vietnamese targets virtually around the clock from December 18 to 29, with a break for Christmas day itself. Kimball writes:

> In its purpose, Linebacker II was aimed less at punishing Hanoi into making concessions and more at providing Saigon with incentives to cooperate. By hurting North Vietnam's war-making ability in a relatively brief but massive campaign, it would give Thieu a lease on life; in its boldness, it would signal Saigon—and Hanoi—that Wash-

---

[151] Kimball, *Nixon's Vietnam War*, p. 328. Kimball writes: "Nixon's thinking at this time about the timing of a settlement was almost entirely conditioned by political calculations, which included assessments of a long list of interconnected possibilities and necessities: the adverse impact of a settlement on perceptions of American global credibility; the possibility that Hanoi might publicly reveal the prospective terms of an agreement if he refused to meet the timetable; the necessity of concluding an agreement far enough in advance of the election so that it did not appear to be a political ploy, but if an agreement were not reached, to take the negotiations as close to the date of the election as possible in order not to appear to be the obstacle to a settlement; the necessity of avoiding the appearance of selling out; and the possibility that Thieu might publicly announce his opposition to American terms" (p. 336).

[152] Kaiser, "Review of Jeffrey P. Kimball, *Nixon's Vietnam War*."

[153] Kimball, *Nixon's Vietnam War*, p. 348.

[154] Nixon, *RN*, p. 348.

ington might intervene with airpower in the civil war that lay ahead. But Linebacker II was also motivated by psychological processes and political considerations: as a forceful, symbolic closure to the American war, it would fulfil the promise Nixon had made to himself that he would not go out of Vietnam whimpering: and it had the potential of convincing Hawks that he had been tough, compelling the enemy to accept an agreement that was in reality an ambiguous compromise, but which he touted as a clear-cut victory for his skillful management of war and diplomacy.[155]

James Reston called it "war by tantrum."[156] At home and abroad, people were appalled. Kissinger met once again with his North Vietnamese counterpart in Paris, Le Duc Tho. They tinkered with the wording of the October agreement, split the difference on a few minor issues, and called it a day. Nixon told Thieu to put on a game face and make the most of it, and that was that.

Haldeman recorded the following in his diary for January 23:

We had the Cabinet meeting at 8:45. The P opened by saying that this was basically a pro forma meeting. We're doing it for the purpose of the eyes of the world and the nation so that they will think that we have consulted with the Cabinet, but we can't really get into anything now because we can't release the agreement until tomorrow. Then he read the official statement that he will read on TV tonight, said all our conditions have been completely met. The P said the GVN and Thieu are totally onboard and will issue statements to that effect. There will be heavy fighting between now and the cease-fire [on the 27th], and after the cease-fire there will be inevitable violations, which is why the supervisory body is so important. He said we have a cease-fire for Vietnam, possibly in Laos and Cambodia. We have peace with honor, the POW's are back, the supervised cease-fire, and the right of South Vietnam to determine their own future. It's been long, painful, and difficult for all of us. This is not Johnson's war, or Kennedy's war. They did start it and they did handle it badly, but the United States was involved. We have now achieved our goals—peace for Vietnam, the right of the South Vietnamese to determine their future without an imposed Communist government. The fact that we have stood firm as a country was responsible and has had a decisive effect on the world. If the United States did not prove to be responsible in Vietnam, if this had ended in defeat and surrender, the Chinese and the Russians would have no interest in talking to us. Europe wouldn't consider us a reliable ally, in spite of their

---

[155] Kimball, *Nixon's Vietnam War*, p. 364.
[156] Ibid., p. 366.

bitching about the war. We must understand, for the United States
to keep the peace and save freedom, we have to be responsible, and
that's what this peace is about. It was not a Republican achievement.
He has as much contempt for the Republicans who would cut and
run as he does for the Democrats. Thank God for those who stood
with us, like the hard hats. He got fairly emotional at the end, but
did a darn good job at the Cabinet meeting, although he worried
Henry a little about some of the areas he went into.[157]

Thus began the spin-doctoring. "What Nixon had won in his four years
of war," Kimball writes, "was a decent interval. It was not a decent interval for Thieu, whose government would be driven from power within two
years, but it was a long enough interval to permit Nixon and Kissinger to
claim that they had provided Thieu with a chance to survive—if, however,
Congress would continue supporting him, if only the American people
possessed the will to continue bombing."[158]

As to Nixon's claim of victory, Kimball simply notes that it "is not
supported by this negotiating record, a record he tried to obscure with
his December 1972 bombing campaign and his postagreement public relations spin on the war."[159]

How Do the Hypotheses Fare?

I do not wish to belabor an already lengthy chapter with an overly technical discussion of how the Vietnam case fits the theory at hand, so I will
conclude by making a select few points that will help focus attention on
issues on which I believe the story in any case largely speaks for itself. My
conclusion is that the case largely confirms my hypotheses, but that it also
points up some interesting gaps and limitations of the theory.

The first point to note is that U.S. policy in Vietnam clearly exhibited
punctuated equilibria. A few brief periods of dramatic change separated
long periods of inertia. From the end of World War II to 1954, the United
States simply supported France. When France withdrew in defeat after
Dienbienphu, the United States had no choice but to do something dramatically different (an uninteresting example of a dramatic change forced
by circumstance, not willfully chosen). From 1954 to 1973 the United
States sought to maintain a divided Vietnam with a friendly, pro-Western
capitalist state south of the 17th parallel. Until 1965 it sought to do so
strictly through economic and military aid (though late in the Kennedy

[157] Haldeman, *The Haldeman Diaries*, p. 572.
[158] Kimball, *Nixon's Vietnam War*, p. 370.
[159] Ibid., p. xiii.

presidency, military aid and advice sometimes took a form tantamount to outright belligerence). In the face of the imminent collapse of the southern regime, LBJ chose to escalate the conflict, introducing massive numbers of American troops to fight on behalf of—no longer solely in support of—South Vietnamese forces, and authorizing an intensive air campaign. In 1969 Nixon began to withdraw ground troops but escalated the air campaign both horizontally (i.e., geographically) and vertically (i.e., in intensity). Johnson and Nixon shared the hope that American military power would awe Hanoi into agreeing to a settlement that would preserve an independent, noncommunist south. Late in 1972 Nixon gave up on this goal, securing in 1973 an agreement that would permit the United States to withdraw from Vietnam on terms that it could represent as "victory" or "peace with honor," but which in fact virtually everyone understood as giving Washington a face-saving decent interval before the North swooped down upon the South and forcibly reunified the country. The case therefore fits the theory's default expectation of inertia and its claim that dramatic change will be rare.

The long periods of inertia we see in U.S. Vietnam policy were no doubt functions in part of state and regime characteristics. The machinery of government in the United States is notoriously complex, and domestic interests of all kinds have an unusually large number of points of access to decision makers, the most important of whom are acutely aware of their answerability to the voting public. This does not mean that U.S. foreign policy is essentially the product of an open decision-making process, either bureaucratically or democratically, but it does increase the likelihood that the constellation of forces for and against policy change—and, if *for* change, for and against different *options*—will frequently cancel each other out, giving the status quo somewhat more stability than would be the case in a top-down autocratic system.[160] During the French phase, the political concerns of the Europeanists at the State Department and the geostrategic concerns of the Pentagon reinforced the support-France policy up to, but not including, providing nuclear relief for the besieged French garrison at Dienbienphu.[161] During the Kennedy presidency, the disagreements between hawks who wanted to escalate the conflict and the doves who wanted to negotiate a solution reinforced the wait-and-see tendency to stay the course with economic and military support as long as there appeared to be hope for stability in South Vietnam. Once

---

[160] The United States's Polity IV Project codings for the period between Dienbienphu and the reunification of Vietnam (1956–1975) are +10 on the POLITY variable (highly democratic) and 7 on the XCONST variable (executive parity or subordination). See fig. 6.1 below.

[161] These matters are discussed in detail in McGeorge Bundy, *Danger and Survival*, pp. 260–270.

that hope disappeared and the United States threw itself into Vietnam, hawks and doves largely canceled each other out again, and policy stabilized around heavy ground troop commitment in the South (not quite as heavy as the Chiefs wanted, and heavier than the doves wanted), and an intensive air campaign (not as intense, and not as far north of the 17th parallel as the hawks wanted; more intense, and further north of the 17th parallel than the doves wanted).

The second point to note is that American policy was driven at every stage overwhelmingly by the desire to *avoid loss*. While it is trivially easy to pluck from the tens of thousands of pages of documents and memoirs references to the costs of "losing" Vietnam, to the likely "loss" of Southeast Asia, to the "loss" or "damage" that American credibility would suffer if the United States did not hold firm, it is, as far as I have been able to tell, impossible to find any references to what the United States would stand to *gain*. The operative frame throughout was a loss frame. As McNamara put it, "As the likely failure of our training strategy became more apparent . . . we tilted gradually—almost imperceptibly—toward approving the direct application of U.S. military force. We did so because of our increasing fear—and hindsight makes it clear it was an exaggerated fear—of what would happen if we did not."[162]

Now, interestingly, it is not always easy to know exactly what loss decision makers feared at any given time, and in what proportion. The ongoing puzzle over LBJ's motivations makes this clear. Johnson seems to have worried about falling dominoes, credibility, prestige, his domestic program, and (if Logevall is correct), his manhood.[163] For the Johnson administration as a whole, there seems to have been a gradual, ineluctable drift in concern from fear of falling dominoes to credibility. Nixon and Kissinger shared these concerns as well, perhaps in slightly different proportions. Like LBJ (until March 1968, at least), Nixon had his eye on electoral concerns and sought to manage Vietnam in such a way that it would not damage his chances at the polls. Also like LBJ, he probably had deep ego-gratification reasons for not wanting to lose Vietnam. But whatever the exact nature of the reasons *why* it was important not to lose Vietnam, for the most part the operative reference point throughout was, as a practical matter, stable and clear. A divided Vietnam with a noncommunist regime in the South was an acceptable state of affairs. A unified communist Vietnam was not.

This picture changed somewhat toward the end of Nixon's first term. Nixon operated with a more complex set of reference points. In fact, there

---

[162] McNamara, *In Retrospect*, p. 107.

[163] Cf., e.g., Logevall, *Choosing War*, pp. 391–393; McNamara, *In Retrospect*, p. 102; Bird, *The Color of Truth*, p. 337.

is reason to believe that he understood the United States not to be struggling to *prevent* a loss, but to *recoup* a loss suffered many years before. "[The] Power of the United States must be used more effectively, at home and abroad or we go down the drain as a great power," Haldeman records Nixon saying on July 21, 1969: "[We have] already lost the leadership position we held at end of WW II, but can regain it, if fast!"[164] The combination of an improving geopolitical situation, thanks to his Soviet and Chinese policies, and a deteriorating domestic scene—what Nixon understood as the country's economic, cultural, and moral decay caused largely by the war itself—mitigated the prospective pain of losing South Vietnam and focused his mind on geopolitical and domestic reference points. As the context changed, it ripened for throwing in the towel.[165]

Third, when the Johnson administration opted to Americanize the war, they did not see it as a good gamble. They acknowledged that its prospects of success were not especially bright. At best, most of the key players believed that Americanization would buy some time. As Logevall puts it, "The most striking thing about the Johnson administration's decision to move to an escalated war was . . . that it came despite deep pessimism among many senior officials that the new measures would succeed in turning the war around. They were certainly hopeful that pressure on North Vietnam could improve morale in the South and perhaps cause Hanoi to end its support of the insurgency, but the internal record leaves little sense that they actually believed these things would happen."[166] While the Joint Chiefs expressed confidence that they could get the job done if given the right tools and freedom of action, even the Pentagon's top analyst was unsure. Assistant Secretary for International Security Affairs John Mc-Naughton estimated in July 1965 that even with a commitment of 200,000–400,000 or more U.S. troops, the odds that the United States could "win" within three years were no better than even. The most likely outcome, McNaughton thought, was some kind of compromise arrangement that would see communists in a coalition southern government (see table 4.1).[167] But to all but Rusk, who favored muddling through, and

---

[164] Haldeman, *The Haldeman Diaries*, p. 73.

[165] Michael Lind argues: "It was necessary for the United States to escalate the war in the mid-1960s in order to defend the credibility of the United States as a superpower, but it was necessary for the United States to forfeit the war after 1968, in order to preserve the American domestic political consensus in favor of the Cold War on other fronts. Indochina was worth a war, but only a limited war—and not the limited war that the United States actually fought." Lind, *Vietnam, the Necessary War*, p. xv. My only quibble with this claim is that we should insert "U.S. policy makers believed" before each occurrence of "it was necessary" and before "Indochina was worth a war."

[166] Logevall, *Choosing War*, p. 271.

[167] Kahin, *Intervention*, p. 357.

TABLE 4.1
McNaughton's Estimates of Outcome Probabilities

Outcome/Effort Combinations	Probabilities of Success/Inconclusiveness/Collapse		
	By 1966	By 1967	By 1968
"Win" with 200–400,000+ U.S. troops	20/70/10	40/45/15	50/30/20
"Win" with 75,000 U.S. troops	10/70/20	20/50/30	30/30/40
"Compromise" with 200–400,000+ U.S. troops	40/50/10	60/25/15	70/10/20
"Compromise" with 75,000 U.S. troops	20/60/20	30/40/30	40/20/40
"Capitulate and withdraw"	0/0/100	0/0/100	0/0/100

Source: Kahin, Intervention, p. 357 (first cell corrected from 20/70/70).

Ball, who favored cutting a political deal, the alternatives seemed worse. They looked like guaranteed losers.

This leads directly to the fourth point, which is that U.S. policy toward Vietnam did not change dramatically until prior policy had demonstrably failed, and failed at great cost, over a long period of time. The Johnson administration tired of throwing good money after bad and tried to recoup a decade of failed policy by shouldering the military burden itself. Johnson and Nixon continued to throw good money after bad (and good lives, too) for years to come even when it became obvious to all but the most panglossian Pentagonian that the new policy was getting nowhere. This is a classic example of an escalating commitment to a losing course of action, easily explained by the bodies of theory I discuss in chapter 2. Johnson knew his policy was failing but never concluded that it had crashed and burned. Nixon was initially just as unwilling as Johnson to write off the sunk costs of that policy but ultimately did so when the costs became unbearable, when there was no longer any basis even for a remote hope that the policy might ultimately succeed, when changes in the international and domestic environments made writing off the sunk costs appear less unattractive, and when his first term finally came to an end.

Which leads to the fifth point: U.S. presidential elections obviously served as important liminal events. Despite McNamara's disclaimer that Johnson "never indicated to me or to the Joint Chiefs that he wanted us to hold back in Vietnam because of the [1964] election," there is ample evidence that LBJ was desperate to wait until afterward before changing course one way or another. The 1968 election might have served as a fulcrum for a dramatic policy change if the context had been permissive, but it was not. The Democrats were eager for peace talks to get under way beforehand to help them keep the White House, and the Nixon campaign was just as eager to derail them for the obverse reason. But it remains an open question in any case whether circumstances would have been ripe in 1968 for the kind of deal both sides could have agreed to, particularly given the enormous difficulties they had had even reaching an agreement to talk. Once in office, Nixon sought to distinguish his Vietnam policy from Johnson's, and if we were to consider this a dramatic policy change, then the 1968 election would certainly have served as a liminal event. But I have made the argument that Nixon did not dramatically change Johnson's policy—he merely tinkered with it. The 1972 election, on the other hand, very clearly served as a liminal event for a dramatic change. For much of his first term, Nixon treated it as a deadline by which he had to be out of Vietnam, and for at least two years before the election Nixon and Kissinger expressly factored it into their deliberations. Even when the polls took the pressure off in August and September, allowing Nixon to miss his deadline by a couple of months, he still felt the sense of urgency to wrap it up that the looming election had earlier imparted. It stands to reason that, in a country such as the United States that has regular elections for its chief executive, the periods immediately before and after the elections themselves would carry with them a heightened likelihood of dramatic policy change, and the Vietnam case bears out that expectation.

The case does, however, point up a few gaps and weaknesses in the theory. For example, it can be argued (indeed, I would argue myself) that while regime and state characteristics help explain the long periods of inertia in U.S. Vietnam policy, they must also get some credit for spurring dramatic policy change in 1973. Kimball writes that "[d]espite Nixon's brave front, the combined effect of demonstrations, congressional resolutions, and polls was to remind the president that he must end the war sooner rather than later. Because he had not given up on his aim of saving the Saigon regime, he needed to play for time. Thus, he walked a tightrope between having to strengthen Thieu's position and having to withdraw American troops from South Vietnam before the 1972 elections."[168] A unitary, authoritarian regime relatively immune to domestic or governmental pressures would not, of course, have felt the need to change course quite so acutely, or to do so on exactly the same timetable. The first hypothesis may therefore be right that foreign policy change should be less frequent in highly bureaucratic states with democratic regimes, but here

---

[168] Kimball, *Nixon's Vietnam War*, p. 259.

is an apparent counterexample within a longitudinal case that otherwise seems to bear out the claim. Obviously, this must lead us to wonder about whether (and if so, how) we might tinker with the scope conditions of the theory to improve the leverage we get on the likelihood of dramatic foreign policy change from regime and state characteristics. We might, for example, explore the proviso that highly bureaucratic and democratic states are likely to exhibit greater policy stability unless regime preferences and public preferences diverge significantly. This might be right, and it might be useful, but it lacks parsimony, raises a host of thorny questions about operationalization, smacks of theoretical degeneration, and for all I know may be the first step down the slippery slope to an insidious tautology of the kind "X is more likely than Y except when Y is at least as likely as X." I do not propose to solve the problem here; I merely flag it.

Second, while it is clear that in Americanizing the war the Johnson administration took what they understood to be a bad gamble to avoid a certain painful loss, this is a case where an important part of the theoretical explanation for this behavior is unnecessary. Since they believed they faced a choice between an unlikely prospect of an acceptable outcome and a certain prospect of disaster, classical expected-utility theory would explain the escalation just as well as prospect theory does. There are many situations where prospect theory and rational choice theory predict precisely the same behavior, and this would appear to be one of them. This observation is not evidence *against* the theory at hand, but neither does it provide the kind of glorious support for the third hypothesis against a strong alternative that a theory-tester would ideally like to see.

Finally, while I believe the theory helps us make sense of the patterns we observe in U.S. Vietnam policy, and in particular while I believe it helps us to see exactly why dramatic changes were more likely when they occurred than at any other time, the theory itself does not point us toward the specific changes to expect. This is not a weakness of the theory per se, since it is not part of its purpose to do this. Recall that the options actually on the table, or conceivably on the table, are exogenous to the theory itself. Its job is merely to alert us to the conditions under which we should expect dramatic foreign policy change *of some kind* assuming the presence of some plausible option. But, of course, it would be nice if we had some handle on exactly what kind of change to expect.

There are ways to do this. One method, for example, would be to attempt to ascertain the weighted vector sum of the preferences of the relevant players, as do Bruce Bueno de Mesquita and his colleagues.[169] Another would be to assess the relative "winnability" of the options, as do

---

[169] Bueno de Mesquita, Newman, and Rabushka, *Forecasting Political Events*.

David Sylvan and Stephen Majeski.[170] A third way is just to do some old-fashioned historical detective work and make a judgment call. But Yuen Foong Khong has demonstrated that a particularly powerful way to anticipate not only which options the Johnson administration considered, but the relative likelihood of their being chosen, is to look closely at the historical analogies in terms of which the participants in the process deliberated. Khong demonstrates that the Korean War and Munich analogies predisposed the Johnson administration not only toward intervention, but toward a specific *form* of intervention.[171] Khong argues that Ball's memo of October 5, 1964, failed in part because it called into question the applicability of the Korean analogy, and "The two most important believers in the Korean analogy were Lyndon Johnson and Dean Rusk."[172]

Anticipating the precise form a significant policy change will take is a remarkable and powerful ability. There is nothing in the present theory that is hostile to claims about the importance of analogical reasoning. Quite the contrary. The two are, in fact, quite complementary. Keying on historical analogies can help us anticipate which specific changes are likely when change of *some* kind is likely, but historical analogies will not help us anticipate the conditions of the latter. No theory will wash both dishes and windows, and it would not be surprising that we would need more than one to keep the house in order.

U.S. policy in Vietnam, then, provides a good deal of evidence in support of the theory at hand but also points up some of its limitations. At the end of the book, I will attempt to put these in perspective. But first, we will give the theory one final test drive, this time in a domain outside the traditional realm of high politics. To that end, we move from the 17th parallel to the 49th.

---

[170] David Sylvan and Stephen Majeski, "A Methodology for the Study of Historical Counterfactuals."

[171] Khong, *Analogies at War*, p. 11.

[172] Ibid., p. 110.

Chapter 5

FREE TRADE WITH THE UNITED STATES:

TWO FUNERALS AND A WEDDING

INTUITION TELLS US that significant foreign policy changes are more likely to catch us by surprise when they concern "high-politics" issues than when they concern "low-politics" issues. High politics—military security, alliance formation, sovereignty, territoriality, prestige—is a largely competitive realm in which advantages sometimes accrue to states that manage to avoid telegraphing their intentions. In contrast, low politics—trade, investment, the environment, law, culture, health, sports—is a realm in which states occasionally have harmonious interests, and very often have interests that they can realize only cooperatively. In such circumstances, surprise can be counterproductive. Harmony and cooperation are best sustained through stable relationships. Instability and unpredictability threaten the trust upon which successful cooperation often depends.[1] The distinction between high politics and low politics is gradually falling out of favor, as scholars and commentators pay more and more attention to nontraditional threats to the welfare and security of states, individuals, groups, the species, and even the biosphere.[2] But if we remain interested in explaining and anticipating dramatic changes in state behavior, perhaps for the purpose of helping to determine what kinds of international agreements are possible at any given time, we would still do well to ask whether the same set of tools will help us outside the traditional high-politics domain.

Trade policy is in one sense an obvious place to look, and in another it is not. It is an obvious place to look because trade policy is important. In contrast to (for example) the environment, trade has been an issue for centuries and was among the very first subjects of treaties between states. Typically a great deal depends upon the choices states make as between autarky, mercantilism, development-inspired protectionism, free trade, customs union, and integration. The stakes are high not merely for the

---

[1] Such, at any rate, are the insights from the neoliberal institutionalist research agenda inspired by the work of Robert Axelrod and Robert Keohane, among others. Axelrod and Keohane, "Achieving Cooperation under Anarchy"; Axelrod, *The Evolution of Cooperation*; Keohane, *After Hegemony*.

[2] See, e.g., Ken Booth, "Security and Emancipation"; Barry Buzan, Ole Wæver, and Jaap de Wilde, *Security*; Steve Smith, "The Concept of Security in a Globalising World."

states that make the choices, but for other states as well. On the other hand, trade policy is not the "lowest" of low-politics issues. Indeed, on a traditional understanding of mercantilism, trade is just another chessboard on which states compete for power and prestige. Only from a classical liberal perspective does trade appear as a relatively benign positive-sum game, if one fraught with free-rider problems, collective action problems, and problems of market failure.[3]

I suspect that an exhaustive comparison of the advantages and disadvantages of looking at alternative issue domains for a final test drive of the theory at hand—economic, environmental, legal, cultural, and so on—would ultimately prove inconclusive. In choosing trade policy, therefore, I do not mean to make any strong claims about crucial or critical cases. Nor, for that matter, do I mean to draw conclusions across these categories at the end of the day. I merely mean to suggest that the obvious importance of trade policy counts for a good deal when seeking a preliminary judgment on the theory's goodness-of-fit outside the traditional security realm. While policy makers may not be particularly concerned with anticipating dramatic changes in trade policy, they are no doubt very much concerned with determining what trade agreements are achievable at any given time.

The particular case of U.S.-Canadian trade has additional obvious merit. For much of recent history, this has been the largest trading relationship in the world. Moreover, it is one that has undergone a good deal of change over the years, allowing us a degree of purchase on longitudinal questions—questions about path dependencies, endogeneities, and the role of exogenous shocks. Finally, the U.S.-Canadian trade relationship offers us an opportunity to examine change and stability in an asymmetrical dyad from the perspective of the weaker state—Canada, in this case— by way of contrast to our examination of change and stability in an asymmetrical dyad from the perspective of the stronger state, as in the previous chapter. To that end, and in view of space constraints, I will ask in this chapter whether the theory at hand helps explain patterns of continuity and change in Canadian trade policy vis-à-vis the United States, dealing only incidentally and in passing with the view from Washington's side of the border.

OVERVIEW AND BACKGROUND

The intensity of the U.S.-Canadian trade relationship is probably not surprising in view of the history, geography, and demography of North

---

[3] From a Marxist perspective, of course, trade may be understood as a zero-sum—or even a negative sum—game between classes, not states.

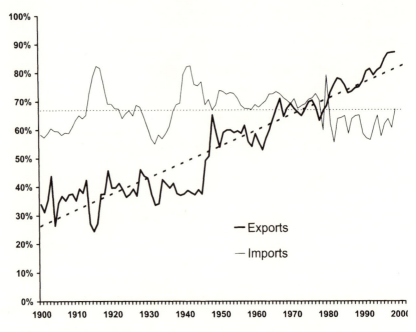

Fig. 5.1. Twentieth-century U.S. share of Canadian trade (by value).
Sources: Canada Year Book; Dominion Bureau of Statistics: Department of Trade and Commerce; Statistics Canada, Canadian International Merchandise Trade tables 0226–001, 002, 009 (with interpolations).

America. The two countries followed similar, if not identical, trajectories of economic development; had similar British colonial origins; and have had similar population profiles over the years. The chief difference between the two countries, of course, is the fact that the United States began life as a sovereign state willfully, suddenly, and as the result of armed insurrection. Canada, in contrast, acquired sovereign autonomy reluctantly, gradually, and in fact has yet fully to sever its formal political ties to the mother country, though at present the remaining ties are merely symbolic.

Despite the two countries' closeness, the United States has not always been Canada's most significant trading partner, and Canada's reliance upon American trade has fluctuated considerably over the years. The most striking feature of Canada's trade, of course, is the long-term trend toward greater and greater concentration and dependence upon the United States. This is true both in relative terms (Canada has increasingly traded with the United States relative to all other trading partners) and in absolute terms (the value of trade with the United States has risen dramatically over the years as a proportion of Canadian gross national product). While reliable figures are difficult to come by for the nineteenth century, and while variations in the ways in which officials have collected and reported

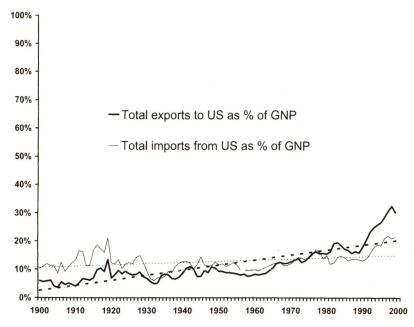

Fig. 5.2. Twentieth-century Canadian trade dependency on the United States (as proportion of GNP)
Sources: Canada Year Book; Dominion Bureau of Statistics: Department of Trade and Commerce; Statistics Canada, Canadian International Merchandise Trade tables 0226–001, 002, 009 (with interpolations); M. C. Urquhart et al., *Gross National Product, Canada, 1870–1926: The Derivation of Estimates* (Kingston, ON: McGill-Queen's University Press, 1993), pp. 11–15; Statistics Canada Catalogue numbers 13-001-XIB, 13-201, 13-531 (National Income and Expenditures Accounts); OECD Statistical Directorate.

trade figures over the course of the twentieth century confound an attempt to be exact in certain respects, the big picture is nevertheless fairly clear. Figures 5.1 through 5.4 capture the essence, and are worth some preliminary comment.

The most striking feature of figure 5.1 is the dramatic secular rise in the importance of the United States as an export market for Canadian goods. Interestingly, Canada has imported goods from the United States in more or less constant proportion over the years, relative to imports from other countries, with the exception of the two world wars, when the exigencies of military production spiked demand (in the case of the Second World War, financed largely by the United States itself). Indeed, the trend for the postwar period alone would be negative: Canada today imports relatively more from countries other than the United States, owing in large part to the rapid economic development of Asia. Canadian exports, however, increasingly go to the United States and are very close to

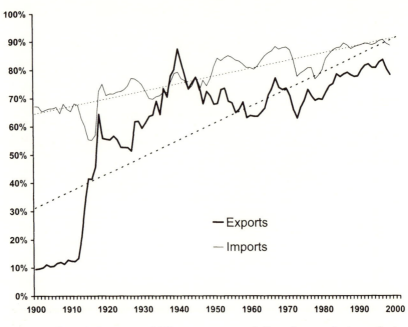

Fig. 5.3. Twentieth-century HVA component of Canadian trade (overall, by value) *Source*: As with fig. 5.1.

an astonishing 90 percent by value today.[4] Such a level of export dependence upon a single market is unprecedented for a large, sophisticated, and diversified economy such as Canada's.

Not only do Canadian exports increasingly go to the United States, but Canada's trade with the United States represents an increasingly large fraction of Canada's national wealth as well. Almost a third of Canada's gross national product now finds its way to American markets, and the long-term trend is both strong and clear (see figure 5.2). Canada's import dependency on the United States is considerably lower (less than 20 percent of GNP), and the trend is far less clear. Recent levels represent a recovery to levels that were normal before the First World War, but much lower during most of the Cold War.

What kinds of goods have Canadians bought and sold abroad? Canada began life as a pure resource "staple" economy, although different resource industries dominated at different periods of time. Before Confederation, fish and fur were among Canada's most important products, over-

---

[4] This figure is somewhat misleading, as the data do not easily distinguish Canadian goods destined for the United States from Canadian goods destined for the rest of the world via American ports, a problem aggravated by the integration of North American railroads and prevailing invoicing practices. By some estimates the true figure is 4–5 percent lower. I am grateful to Alan Alexandroff and John Kirton for pointing this out.

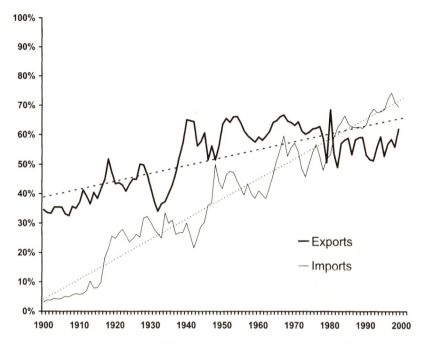

Fig. 5.4. Twentieth-century HVA component of Canadian trade (U.S. only, by value) *Source*: As with fig. 5.1.

taken in the nineteenth century by softwood for pulp and lumber, minerals, grains, and livestock.[5] During the early years, Canada imported virtually all of its manufactured goods. In the latter part of the nineteenth century, however, Canada began to develop its own manufacturing capacity, which saw spectacular growth during World War I. Figure 5.3 reports the proportion of Canadian imports and exports that might be considered "high value-added" (HVA) goods—essentially manufactures and processed raw materials. The high and generally increasing proportion of imports such goods represent is notable, but far more striking is their rising importance on the export side. Though HVA goods peaked as a proportion of Canada's total exports during World War II, both the overall trend and the trend since the 1960s have been strongly positive.

If we look only at the HVA component of Canada's trade with the United States (figure 5.4), we see immediately that, in the early years, finished products counted for relatively little of what Canadians imported from their neighbors to the south. In large part, this simply reflected the fact that British manufactures dominated the Canadian market. Over the years, however, finished goods came to represent an increasing proportion of the American goods sold in Canada. The trend in the proportion of

[5] A good overview is Michael Hart, *A Trading Nation*, pp. 14–44.

HVA goods Americans bought from Canada is far less dramatic, though still unmistakably positive.

Overall, then, the twentieth century was a period of time in which Canada increasingly relied for its welfare upon international trade; increasingly relied upon the United States as an export market; and increasingly traded in high value-added goods. Canada's current reliance upon trade in general, and upon the United States as a trading partner in particular, is nothing short of remarkable.

These trends, however, do not reflect gradual adjustments in policy, nor even changes in policy of the kind one would expect (namely, steady liberalization). Canadian trade policy is best understood as a punctuated equilibrium in which a long period of relatively unfree trade separated two periods of relatively free trade. The high-water mark for trade liberalization in the nineteenth century—the Reciprocity Treaty of 1854, spurred by the British repeal of the Corn Laws—actually predated Canadian Confederation. From 1866 to 1988 the two countries maintained significant, though fluctuating, tariff barriers, relieved only in a limited way by the exigencies of wartime production and by sectoral free-trade agreements, of which the 1965 Auto Pact was the most significant.[6] Only recently have the two countries dramatically liberalized their trade relationship, first in the 1988 Canada-U.S. Free Trade Agreement (FTA), and six years later in the larger North American Free Trade Agreement (NAFTA).

The parties to the 1854 Reciprocity Treaty were the United States and the British North American colonies of New Brunswick, Prince Edward Island, Nova Scotia, Newfoundland, and the United Province of Canada (essentially what is now southern Québec and Ontario). The 1854 agreement provided for reciprocity only in fur, fish, wheat, and lumber, but these were British North America's key products, and the economic effect was tantamount to full free trade. The treaty provided for unilateral abrogation after ten years, and in 1866—almost immediately after the U.S. Civil War—Washington gave notice of termination, partly out of anger for Britain's wartime support of the Southern Confederacy, and partly because domestic economic and political circumstances increasingly favored the forces of protectionism. Many in British North America interpreted this shocking loss of vital market access as a hostile act. Indeed, the U.S. abrogation of the treaty helped keep some of the reluctant partners negotiating Confederation at the bargaining table and thereby contributed to the creation of the Dominion of Canada in 1867.[7]

Canada's first prime minister, Sir John A. Macdonald—a Conservative—immediately set about enlarging and consolidating the new Canadian state, purchasing the Hudson's Bay Company territory, bringing Manitoba into Confederation, crushing a *Métis* uprising in the Red River valley, and seducing British Columbia with the promise of a transcontinental railroad (the Canadian Pacific Railway, or CPR).[8] During these early years, Canadians generally continued to hope for an American change of heart on reciprocity. The Liberal party was especially keen, and Liberal prime ministers were more energetic than Macdonald had been in attempting to rekindle American interest. All such efforts proved fruitless, and some proved humiliating. The prominent Liberal reformer George Brown, founder and editor of the influential Toronto *Globe*, made the most headway and suffered the most embarrassing defeat. Sent to Washington by the first Liberal prime minister, Alexander Mackenzie, Brown actually managed to conclude a draft reciprocity treaty with American officials in Washington in the summer of 1874, but the agreement languished in the Foreign Relations Committee and never made it to the Senate floor for a vote.[9]

By the late 1870s Macdonald and the Conservatives had given up hope. Macdonald ran in the 1878 election on a protectionist platform and won. The following year he brought in "the National Policy," which provided for tariffs as high as 35 percent on refined sugar, woolen clothing, certain iron products, agricultural implements, bricks, carriages, wagons, and railway cars.[10] The point was to kick-start Canadian industrialization, to transform Canada from a resource economy into a modern wealthy society. In Macdonald's view, the National Policy had to be more or less permanent, lest the specter of reciprocity frighten away investors. "There is the danger," Macdonald insisted, "that capitalists who are now with some degree of trembling and hesitancy investing their capital in new enterprise . . . will be turned aside from their purpose if they find us tampering with the integrity of the National Policy."[11]

---

[7] Randall White, *Fur Trade to Free Trade*, pp. 47–55. The original partners to Confederation were the non-American parties to the 1854 Reciprocity Treaty, minus Prince Edward Island and Newfoundland. The new Dominion took the name of Canada, but the former United Province of Canada split at the time into Ontario and Québec. Prince Edward Island joined Confederation in 1873; Newfoundland joined only in 1949.

[8] The most popular and most engaging accounts of these years are Pierre Berton, *The National Dream: The Great Railway, 1871–1881*; Berton, *The National Dream: The Last Spike*.

[9] White, *Fur Trade to Free Trade*, pp. 60–61.

[10] Ibid., pp. 61–66; Bernard Ostry, "Conservatives, Liberals, and Labour in the 1870s"; J. L. Granatstein and Norman Hillmer, *For Better or for Worse*, pp. 16–19.

[11] Quoted in White, *Fur Trade to Free Trade*, p. 64.

The difficulty was that the Canadian market was not big enough to sustain industrialization under the National Policy. The Liberal party continued to pay lip service to unrestricted reciprocity,[12] but Canadian leaders of all stripes looked to enhance access to foreign markets in a way that would compromise neither Canadian industrial development nor Canada's fledgling sovereignty. The two great hopes were the two largest potential markets: Britain and the United States. Britain had long embraced a policy of free trade, which made it difficult for Canada to secure preferential access. The United States, however, maintained high tariffs, and so any Canadian preference could in theory translate into a significant advantage. Thus Canadian leaders were especially keen to seek preferential access to the American market.

Overture after overture met with rebuff. The McKinley Tariff of 1890 raised U.S. rates to unprecedented heights, prompting an outpouring of anger and resentment in Canada. The Liberal party—self-identifying as the party of free trade—took a beating the following year at the hands of Macdonald and the Conservatives, whose more avowedly nationalistic economic platform appealed to voters in what historians generally consider the first intensely anti-American Canadian political campaign.[13] But even the Conservatives kept going back to the well and coming home empty handed. As Secretary of State James G. Blaine said bluntly in 1892, nothing short of full "commercial union" (what today we would call "customs union") discriminating in favor of the United States and against Britain would tempt Washington.[14]

It was the great Liberal prime minister, Sir Wilfrid Laurier, who made the last serious attempt to entice the United States, and who then, in failure, turned decisively toward Britain as Canada's preferred export market. Laurier always thought of himself as a free trader philosophically. "I was a free trader before I came to England," he said during an 1897 speech to the Cobden Club; "I am still more a free trader after having seen what free trade has done for England."[15] But his feelers toward Washington resulted only in higher rates still. The 1897 Dingley Tariff was America's highest yet. "We may as well tell a Yankee to go to Hades and we will go to England," Laurier's trade envoy in Washington wrote in disgust. Exasperated, Laurier pledged "no more pilgrimmages" and promptly instituted a de facto imperial preference.[16]

[12] See, e.g., Richard Clippingdale, *Laurier, His Life and World*, p. 172.

[13] Patricia K. Wood, "Defining 'Canadian'"; see also Granatstein and Hillmer, *For Better or for Worse*, pp. 24–28.

[14] White, *Fur Trade to Free Trade*, pp. 71–75.

[15] Oscar Douglas Skelton, *Life and Letters of Sir Wilfrid Laurier*, vol. 2, pp. 72–73.

[16] White, *Fur Trade to Free Trade*, pp. 75–76, 87. The 1897 tariff had two tiers: a high tariff for all countries with protectionist tariffs against Canada (primarily the United States), and a tariff of up to 25 percent less for countries that admitted Canadian goods at a rate

By the turn of the century, Canada had given up hope of recovering the halcyon years of the 1854 treaty, embarking on an energetic program of nation-building and industrialization behind moderate tariff barriers, looking primarily across the Atlantic for new export opportunities. Only three times during the course of the twentieth century would Canada again seriously entertain the idea of concluding a far-reaching bilateral free trade agreement with the United States. In 1911 and 1948 Canada flirted but drew back. The third time, in 1988, Canada jumped. What were the circumstances that led to these flirtations? What determined their outcome? What do they tell us, individually and collectively, about dramatic foreign policy change? How well do our three hypotheses explain them?

LAURIER AND THE RECIPROCITY AGREEMENT OF 1911

Sir Wilfrid Laurier had the good fortune to preside over rosy economic times, winning four straight majority governments (in 1896, 1900, 1904, and 1908)—an all-time Canadian record. Canada had found an economic formula that worked. Not all sectors of the Canadian economy were equally happy with the status quo; prairie farmers, for instance, repeatedly gave Laurier's Liberals their votes in the hope and expectation that he would someday live up to his avowed free trade principles and open American markets to their products. But with the country doing well, and with the Americans perched atop high tariff walls seemingly forever, Laurier repeatedly dashed their hopes by doing little and getting nothing.

It was the Americans, not the Canadians, who made the initial overture that ultimately led to a reciprocity deal in 1911. The impetus came from certain rapidly growing sectors of the American economy that stood to benefit from lower tariffs (most notably, the politically consequential and well-connected newspaper industry, which increasingly depended upon Canadian sources for newsprint). In President William Howard Taft they found a receptive ear. A Progressive Republican who had regularly summered in Québec, and who therefore had a natural affection for Canada, Taft was concerned that Congress's affinity for high tariffs was hurting the American economy and embarrassing his administration. As an entrée, he exempted Canada from the 1909 Payne-Aldrich Tariff, which, while modestly more liberal than either of the preceding two tariffs, was none-

---

equal to the lowest Canadian tariff (primarily Britain and the Empire). The 1907 tariff introduced a third intermediate tier, which Laurier offered to countries prepared to strike limited reciprocity arrangements. France, Japan, and Italy soon qualified, leaving the United States almost alone at the high tariff rate. Ibid., p. 86.

theless more protectionist than Taft had requested.[17] The following year he put out feelers for a far-reaching bilateral deal. Negotiations opened in Ottawa on November 4. Laurier approached them warily. During his summer tour of the West, he had heard long and loud complaints from Prairie agricultural interests about his inaction on free trade.[18] But manufacturers in his Central Canadian power base were fearful. After a Christmas recess, however, things proceeded rapidly. When the talks resumed in January, Richard Clippingdale writes, it became "clear that the Americans were so anxious to reach agreement that Canada was virtually able to write the terms."[19] The final text provided for reciprocal free trade on farm animals, grain, fruits and vegetables, dairy, fish, salt, and unprocessed lumber; a reduction in tariffs for some food products, agricultural implements, and building materials; and limited reductions in tariffs for certain manufactured goods, such as clocks, engines, and plumbing fixtures. The two countries agreed to implement the accord by means of concurrent legislation, to avoid the two-thirds majority needed in the U.S. Senate for ratification and to finesse the difficulty that Canada did not yet have independent treaty-making authority.

Taft called the agreement "the most important measure of my administration."[20] As Clippingdale puts it: "As if by magic—but actually mainly as a result of American political exigencies—the Canadian government was moving to meet the main demands of the Prairie farmers while leaving the protective tariff on manufactures virtually untouched."[21] Laurier's Minister of Finance, W. S. Fielding, who led the Canadian delegation in Washington, wired his prime minister the good news on January 21: "Negotiations concluded today. . . . [Y]ou will come to the conclusion that we have not made a bad bargain."[22]

The initial reaction in Canada was that it was an excellent bargain indeed—far better than anyone could possibly have hoped. Sir Robert Borden, the Conservative leader of the opposition, confessed to his diary his belief that it would sweep Laurier back into office for a fifth straight time.[23] Laurier himself certainly thought the deal could not be opposed.[24] Joseph Schull captures the euphoria thus:

> There had seemed to be a mood not known between the two countries since the first reciprocity treaty was denounced at the close of

[17] In return, Canada applied its intermediate tariff on some U.S. exports. Clippingdale, *Laurier, His Life and World*, p. 173.

[18] Laurier L. LaPierre, *Sir Wilfrid Laurier and the Romance of Canada*, p. 321.

[19] Clippingdale, *Laurier, His Life and World*, p. 174.

[20] Lawrence Martin, *The Presidents and the Prime Ministers*, p. 69.

[21] Clippingdale, *Laurier, His Life and World*, p. 175.

[22] Joseph Schull, *Laurier*, p. 520.

[23] White, *Fur Trade to Free Trade*, p. 89.

[24] LaPierre, *Sir Wilfrid Laurier and the Romance of Canada*, p. 327.

the Civil War. Red tape had been swept aside, hostilities had been forgotten, and everything had given place to a large-minded, businesslike concern with the best arrangement possible. Fielding and William Paterson, the Minister of Customs, had met with better proposals than they had dared to hope for. What was shaping up, as the coded messages passed back and forth between Ottawa and Washington, promised free or almost free entry to the United States for Canadian grain, meat, cattle, dairy products, lumber, pulpwood, minerals, and fish. American duties would be lowered on a sizeable list of Canadian manufactures, and little or nothing was asked in the way of return. The tariffs protecting Canadian industry were hardly to be touched. The imperial preference was to remain and all the United States was to receive was a general lowering of Canadian tariffs to the levels enjoyed by other countries of the world. The mighty sister was opening her own gates and was not demanding, for once, the key to her neighbour's house.

Everything appeared to be granted that had been asked for by both Canadian parties since the days of John A. Macdonald. Even in the heyday of the National Policy, even during the hottest battles over Commercial Union, no one had denied the hope or the desirability of obtaining the American market for raw materials. The fear had been of the flood of returning manufactures that would close Canadian factories and turn workmen into the streets. With that fear removed, what was there left to fear? What argument was possible against a free flow of trade, against an adjustment that every fact of history and geography made natural, and in which the needs of the smaller partner were still recognized?[25]

Interestingly, it was Taft himself who first seems to have sensed the potential difficulties the agreement would run into in Canada. "The amount of Canadian products we would take," Taft wrote Theodore Roosevelt on January 10 (before the conclusion of the deal), "would produce a current of business between western Canada and the United States that would make Canada only an adjunct of the United States. . . . It would transfer all their important business to Chicago and New York, with the bank credits and everything else, and it would greatly increase the demand of Canada for our manufactures. I see this as an argument made against reciprocity in Canada and I think it is a good one."[26]

Laurier had no such fears. So it was to his great surprise that opposition to the deal began to appear from a variety of quarters. Taft would prove

---

[25] Schull, *Laurier*, p. 519.
[26] Quoted in Martin, *The Presidents and the Prime Ministers*, pp. 71–72.

prophetic. The Conservatives energetically sought to portray the agreement as a threat to Canadian welfare, to Canadian sovereignty, and to the British connection. In the House of Commons, Borden greeted the announcement of the deal on January 26 with multidimensional skepticism, calling it "an arrangement of a most indefinite and unsatisfactory character" that would "in the immediate future dislocate the conditions which the government have pronounced for many years past to be absolutely satisfactory to the people of this country." The draft, Borden complained, "does not sufficiently regard the position of this country as an integral and important nation of the British Empire and does not sufficiently regard the purpose, the object, and scope of the policy to which Liberals and Conservatives alike . . . have been committed with respect to the development of Canada and its status as a nation of the British Empire."[27] Representative Champ Clark of Missouri, the Democratic House Leader, aided Borden's cause by endorsing the agreement in the strongest possible terms: "I am for it," he declared on the floor of the House on February 14, "because I hope to see the day when the American flag will float over every square foot of the British North America possessions clear to the north pole! They are people of our blood. They speak our language. Their institutions are much like ours. . . . I do not have any doubt whatever that the day is not far distant when Great Britain will see all of her North American possessions become a part of this Republic. That is the way things are tending now."[28] Taft did his best to minimize the damage, declaring talk of annexation "bosh."[29] But he undermined his own effort by repeatedly insisting in speech after speech that Canada faced "a parting of the ways," inclining Canadian commentators to wonder just how much bosh Taft considered it. And Clark, who in April would rise to the influential position of Speaker, refused to back down. "You let me run for President on a platform for the annexation of Canada," he is reported to have said, ". . . and let President Taft run against me opposing annexation—and—well, I'd carry every State in the nation."[30] "No human being seriously thought that this was a step toward annexation," Teddy Roosevelt later reflected. "Unfortunately three or four prize idiots of importance, including the Speaker of the House, in-

[27] Parliament of Canada, *House of Commons Debates*, vol. 2, pp. 2499, 2502 (26 January 1911).

[28] Quoted in Martin, *The Presidents and the Prime Ministers*, p. 72.

[29] "The United States has all it can attend to with the territory it is now governing, and to make the possibility of the annexation of Canada to the United States a basis for objection to any steps toward their great economic and commercial union should be treated as one of the jokes of the platform." Speech to New York newspaper editors, 27 April 1911; quoted in ibid., p. 74.

[30] Quoted in H. S. Ferns and Bernard Ostry, *The Age of Mackenzie King*, p. 140.

dulged in some perfectly conventional chatter which, although universally understood here as being a rehearsal of 'letting the eagle scream' on the fourth of July, was apparently accepted seriously in Canada. And poor Taft seemingly cannot learn anything about foreign affairs and made some remarks that were as thoroughly ill-judged as was possible."[31]

Borden was happy to leverage the "parting of the ways" image:

> I think that the people of Canada have indeed come to the parting of the ways, and that the issue of infinite gravity which is presented to them at the present time is whether they will continue in the work of nation building, in which they have been engaged in the last forty years, whether they will maintain their own markets as they have maintained them for the past forty years, whether they will preserve the autonomy of this country as they have preserved it during the past forty years, or whether they will undo the work which the fathers of confederation, and which their sons have been carrying out.[32]

Borden adroitly raised the specter of the United States once again *revoking* reciprocity, as it had done in 1866. Was Canada to pay the enormous adjustment costs of configuring its economy on a continental basis only to have the rug pulled out from underneath once again?[33]

The doubts Borden and others sowed in the minds of Canadian voters gradually took root. Powerful domestic interests hardened in opposition—industry, railways, banks, jingoists, imperialists—either because they feared absorption, detachment from Britain, or were simply "concerned about risking the prosperity that had been achieved with a tariff that worked well."[34]

Laurier seems to have been genuinely puzzled by the growing opposition. But as the debate dragged on, it became clear that he could not proceed with the agreement without first going to the country. The issue was a matter of high national importance. In any case, he felt confident that he could defeat the opposition on the issue. He called an election for September 21.

Laurier ran an energetic campaign, insisting that the agreement contained no threats, only opportunities, and emphatically defended his com-

---

[31] Quoted in Martin, *The Presidents and the Prime Ministers*, pp. 75–76. Ferns and Ostry suggest that annexationist sentiment was actually fairly strong in the Republican Party at the time, reflecting a lingering current of Manifest Destiny, and they imply that Republican disavowals of annexationist sentiment might have been tactical and disingenuous. Ferns and Ostry, *The Age of Mackenzie King*, p. 141.

[32] Canada, *House of Commons Debates, 1910–1911*, p. 3309 (9 February 1911).

[33] Schull, *Laurier*, p. 522.

[34] LaPierre, *Sir Wilfrid Laurier and the Romance of Canada*, p. 327.

mitment to a secure and prosperous Canada. But he was swimming against the tide. Borden campaigned vigorously on the slogan, "No truck or trade with the Yankees." As the election approached, emotions peaked. Celebrities weighed in against the deal. From England, Rudyard Kipling warned that Canada was risking its very "soul."[35] Stephen Leacock insisted that Canada had settled the matter of its future when it had made the choice for Britain. William Van Horne, builder of the CPR, proclaimed himself "out to bust the damn thing."[36] When the dust settled, Laurier and reciprocity stood defeated. While the popular vote was close—51 percent for the Conservatives, 49 for the Liberals—Borden commanded a majority in the House of 134 seats to Laurier's 87.

Analysts largely agree that reciprocity was the decisive issue of the 1911 election, but without detailed voter-attitude survey data it is difficult to speak with high confidence on several important matters.[37] While it is fairly clear that reciprocity was popular with farmers in Alberta and Saskatchewan, who voted strongly Liberal, the Conservatives' success in Québec may have had less to do with opposition to reciprocity than to Laurier's 1910 decision to build a Canadian navy, and to the decision of the prominent Québecois nationalist politician Henri Bourassa to throw in his lot with Borden. Laurier's stunning reversals in Ontario may have reflected antireciprocity sentiment but may also have had a fair bit to do with urbanization, the growth of Toronto's fairly strongly Tory financial community (itself a product of the National Policy), and superior Conservative organization.[38] Race and religion were salient issues to many Canadian voters, and discord within Liberal ranks helped undermine Laurier's attempt to calm irrational fears. Among voters for whom reciprocity was a crucial consideration, it is difficult to disentangle economic calculations from emotionally charged political ones. Most commentators doubt that annexation held any strong appeal among Canadian voters, so it stands

[35] "I do not understand how nine million people can enter into such arrangements as are proposed with ninety million strangers on an open frontier of four thousand miles, and at the same time preserve their national integrity. Ten to one is too heavy odds. No single Canadian would accept such odds in any private matter that was as vital to him personally as this issue is to the nation. It is her own soul that Canada risks to-day. Once that soul is pawned for any consideration, Canada must inevitably conform to the commercial, legal, financial, social and ethical standards which will be the imposed upon her by the sheer admitted weight of the United States." Quoted in Ferns and Ostry, *The Age of Mackenzie King*, p. 141.

[36] Martin, *The Presidents and the Prime Ministers*, pp. 78–79; White, *Fur Trade to Free Trade*, p. 92.

[37] Paul Stevens, ed., *The 1911 General Election*, pp. 181–182; Granatstein and Hillmer, *For Better or for Worse*, pp. 46–53.

[38] See, e.g., Robert Cuff, "The Conservative Party Machine and Election of 1911 in Ontario."

to reason that those who voted Liberal because they favored reciprocity did so because they saw in it significant prospect of economic gain. But those who voted against the Liberals out of opposition to reciprocity could have feared either economic loss, political loss, or some mixture of the two. It is impossible to know, too, how much weight to assign discord within the Liberal party, voters' eagerness for a change after fifteen years of Liberal rule, or the simple fact that Laurier was getting old (on election day, he was two months shy of his seventieth birthday).[39] If J. W. Dafoe is correct in his post-mortem, we must assign a certain weight to plain old-fashioned spite: "Perhaps the determining factor with the man in the street," Dafoe wrote, "was the conviction that at last he was sufficiently prosperous to be able to sacrifice further gain for himself—or for his neighbours—in order to show his resentment of long years of United States hostility and condescension."[40]

What is clear, both from debates in the House of Commons and from speeches on the stump, is that Liberals and Conservatives framed the agreement in strikingly different ways, and struggled mightily to convince voters to embrace their particular frame. The Liberals sought to promote a gains frame, whereby the agreement would expand markets, boost exports, improve Canada's balance of trade, and attract investment capital.[41] The Conservatives sought to promote a loss frame, whereby the agreement would jeopardize Canada's welfare, political and fiscal freedom, natural resources, economic stability, domestic industry, national unity, and imperial connection.[42] The rhetorical tide certainly flowed the Conservatives' way. The strategy of playing on fears of uncertain future losses proved astonishingly effective.[43] As Paul Stevens puts it, "[t]he Conservatives were successful in distorting the issue from the economics of reciprocity to the national and imperial question."[44] The sense of glee

---

[39] An interesting recent econometric analysis that uses census and vote pattern data to infer support for and opposition to reciprocity from voting swings by riding argues that, "Other than pork packers, Canadians were supportive or indifferent to reciprocity in 1911, which suggests that Laurier's defeat in 1911 was not a rejection of open trade relations with the United States." Eugene Beaulieu and J. C. Herbert Emery, "Pork Packers, Reciprocity, and Laurier's Defeat in the 1911 Canadian General Election," p. 1085. Among other things, this analysis assumes, problematically, that prospective economic gains and losses were both obvious by sector and uniquely salient to voters.

[40] Quoted in White, *Fur Trade to Free Trade*, p. 90. Dafoe was a Laurier Liberal, Reciprocity supporter, and editor of the *Winnipeg Free Press*.

[41] E.g., Canada, *House of Commons Debates, 1910–1911*; speeches by D. B. Neely, pp. 3567–3568, 3576, 3579; Hugh Guthrie, pp. 3651, 3653.

[42] Ibid.; speeches by Borden, pp. 3303, 3308, 3532; George Foster, pp. 3550, 3552, 3553, 3545–3546, 3561, 3563; Martin Burrell, pp. 3582–3583, 3586.

[43] Schull, *Laurier*, pp. 523–525.

[44] Stevens, ed., *The 1911 General Election*, p. 5.

that had pervaded the Liberal benches in January turned to gloom as the election approached. The sense of gloom that had pervaded the Tory benches turned to glee. Borden's initial fear that reciprocity was a sure winner for Laurier proved stunningly wrong.

No one was more surprised than Laurier. To him, reciprocity *was* a sure winner—not only for him, but for Canada. As Skelton put it:

> Neither Sir Wilfrid nor any member of his cabinet had had any fear or doubt of the outcome. The government had achieved what every previous administration had tried in vain to win. It had reached the goal which had been the professed aim of both political parties in Canada for half a century. It had secured an agreement which opened a market in the United States for Canadian natural products without giving the Canadian manufacturer any legitimate and substantial ground for complaint. It had provided that in no case would there be discrimination against Britain. That Canada would not welcome this triumph of diplomacy seemed incredible.[45]

It was, Laurier insisted, "almost word for word the tariff agreement which was offered to the United States by Sir John Macdonald."[46] Not only did the agreement promise Canada nothing but gain, Laurier believed, but the *rejection* of the agreement threatened significant loss. "In my judgement," he wrote shortly after his defeat,

> the manufacturers made a great mistake in refusing to give way to the very legitimate demand of the farmers, especially the Western farmers who, being balked in their effort to get the American market for their products, will now work for the free entrance into Canada of American manufactured products and especially agricultural implements. . . . If the Democrats carry out their policy and open their markets to Canadian natural products, we shall never hear any more of reciprocity, but if the present American tariff is continued as it is now, we must be prepared for a serious agitation from the Western farmers.[47]

A young Liberal minister who lost his seat in the election—William Lyon Mackenzie King—drew his own conclusions. "The moral," he wrote in his diary on September 26, "is to make no appeal in good times for something better. It is only when people are hard up that they see the advantage of change."[48]

---

[45] Skelton, *Life and Letters of Sir Wilfrid Laurier*, p. 369.

[46] Quoted in Schull, *Laurier*, pp. 521–522.

[47] 24 October 1911; Skelton, *Life and Letters of Sir Wilfrid Laurier*, p. 391.

[48] National Archives of Canada, "The Diaries of William Lyon Mackenzie King," 26 September 1911, p. 2 (transcript); hereafter King Diaries.

KING AND THE RECIPROCITY NONAGREEMENT OF 1948

It would be thirty-seven years before Canadian and American officials would again agree on the essentials of a sweeping free-trade deal. This time, however, there would be no formal accord. There would be no election. In fact, there would no public disclosure of the initiative. Mackenzie King—no longer a junior minister, but now the longest-serving Canadian prime minister in history, and in the twilight of his career—authorized and encouraged a group of officials to seek a deal in the fall of 1947, only to draw back four months later, at the eleventh hour, somewhat in shock and horror at what he himself had done. What was it that frightened him so? And if the prospect of bilateral free trade with the United States was so truly frightening, why had he flirted with it in the first place?[49]

The answers to these questions have a great deal to do with the rapid changes in the Canadian and world economies brought about by World War II. In the 1930s Canada's standard of living was lower than that of Britain, and much lower than that of the United States, owing in large part to a lack of export markets and plummeting commodity prices. The war itself gave the Canadian economy an unprecedented boost. To supply the war effort, the Canadian manufacturing sector expanded dramatically and ran at full capacity; resource industries boomed; and unemployment virtually disappeared. Unlike Europe, Canada suffered no physical damage during the war. Living standards rose dramatically even as war production itself limited the availability of consumer goods, essentially forcing Canadians to save at a high rate. This, coupled with rapid demobilization at the end of the war and the inevitable shift from wartime to peacetime production, led to an explosion of pent-up consumer demand.

The difficulty, however, was that Canada's newfound prosperity threatened to collapse if Canada could not continue to sell in overseas markets. The war all but bankrupted Britain, Canada's second-biggest customer in 1939, who desperately needed Canadian goods but could not pay for them. The United States had no undercapacity of its own for Canada to satisfy and stood creditor to much of the world, with little or no hope of

[49] The best accounts of the negotiations are Robert D. Cuff and J. L. Granatstein, "The Rise and Fall of Canadian-American Free Trade, 1947–8"; Cuff and Granatstein, *American Dollars—Canadian Prosperity*; and Michael Hart, "Almost but Not Quite." For relevant documents, see Canada, Department of External Affairs, *Documents on Canadian External Relations*, vol. 14, docs. 642–661. Mackenzie King's diaries provide invaluable insight into his own deliberations and are available in full online; see King Diaries. A very useful edited collection, with some interstitial commentary, is J. W. Pickersgill and Donald F. Forster, *The Mackenzie King Record*, vol. 4. For a brief overview, see Granatstein and Hillmer, *For Better or for Worse*, pp. 170–175.

cashing in over the short run. Mainland Europe and Japan lay in ruins. There was no prospect of significant new export markets in Latin America, Asia, Africa, or Australia. Canadian officials were desperate to cultivate stable demand for Canadian exports and actively explored every option.[50]

All other things being equal, Canadian officials preferred multilateral arrangements to bilateral ones. As King told Parliament in December 1947, "The character of our trade, with surpluses of exports to certain countries and excesses of imports from other countries, requires a condition in which surpluses on one account can be converted to offset deficiencies on another account. This means that a bilateral approach to trade is not enough."[51] Thus Canada initially endorsed efforts to build an International Trade Organization (ITO) and strongly supported what was supposed at the time to be a stopgap measure on the road to an ITO, the General Agreement on Tariffs and Trade (GATT).[52] But progress toward a sustainable postwar multilateral trade regime was agonizingly slow, and Canada found itself confronted with a serious foreign exchange crisis that would prompt King, in desperation, to look south of the border for a bilateral solution before it was too late.

The exchange crisis had four main causes.[53] The first was the inconvertibility of the British pound, which meant that Canada built up large, and largely useless, Sterling balances in London.[54] Second, British demand for North American goods was much greater than expected, particularly for food. Canada had to finance much of its exports to Britain on credit, which Britain drew down much more quickly than anyone in Ottawa had expected. Third, the explosion of pent-up consumer demand in Canada generated a huge trade deficit with the United States that increasingly had to be paid out of reserves. Fourth, in July 1946 Canada revalued its currency, putting it on par with the U.S. dollar. While the Bank of Canada had what it considered sound reasons for revaluation, an unintended consequence was to increase the drain on reserves as Canadian exports became more expensive, Canadian debtors paid off their bills in the United

[50] Robert Bothwell and John English, "Canadian Trade Policy in the Age of American Dominance and British Decline, 1943–1947," pp. 60–63.

[51] Quoted in Cuff and Granatstein, "The Rise and Fall of Canadian-American Free Trade, 1947–8," p. 460.

[52] For background, see Hart, *A Trading Nation*, pp. 125–144. For a detailed history, see Kathleen Britt Rasmussen, "Canada and the Reconstruction of the International Economy, 1941–1947."

[53] Hart, "Almost but Not Quite," pp. 28–29.

[54] See also Cuff and Granatstein, "The Rise and Fall of Canadian-American Free Trade, 1947–8," p. 463. One option, of course, was to join the Sterling bloc, but the opportunity cost of such a move would be enormous. Britain was weak, the United States was strong, and Canada could ill afford to isolate itself from the world's largest and healthiest economy.

States, and American investment in Canada dried up.[55] Between May 1946 and November 1947, the hemorrhage averaged more than $65 million per month, and it peaked near $100 million a month. During that period, Canada's U.S. dollar reserves dropped from $1.67 billion to $480 million.[56] Within months they would disappear. Only better access to the U.S. market, devaluation, import controls, credits, or some combination of these could avert disaster.

With no multilateral relief in sight, Canadian officials turned to the United States for help. King met with U.S. President Harry Truman in April 1947 and laid bare Canada's predicament.[57] Truman was sympathetic. Canada would be an important friend and ally in the looming Cold War with the Soviet Union. Moreover, with multilateral trade talks at a delicate stage, American officials did not fancy the precedents Canada might set by devaluing its currency or arbitrarily restricting trade. If other countries followed suit, the precarious postwar recovery could falter, raising the prospect of precisely what world leaders feared most: a repeat of the disastrous interwar global depression. But the mood in Congress was not promising. Loans to Canada, and concessionary access for Canadian goods—particularly primary goods—were a hard sell to American voters.

Secretary of State George Marshall's Harvard Commencement speech on June 5, 1947, heralding what would later come to be known as the "Marshall Plan," provided Canadian officials with a glimmer of hope. If the U.S. administration put its political capital behind a major effort to stimulate postwar reconstruction abroad, Canada might find a way to benefit, and congressional obstacles might be surmounted. The Marshall Plan, however, was slow to gel. One State Department official likened it to a flying saucer: "[N]obody knows what it looks like, how big it is, in what direction it is moving, or whether it really exists."[58] Meanwhile, Canada's foreign exchange difficulties were fast approaching the point of crisis. In September King despatched his deputy minister of finance, Clifford Clark, to find a solution in Washington.

Clark and Canadian Ambassador Hume Wrong met a team of State Department officials, led by Deputy Assistant Secretary of State Tyler Wood and Paul Nitze, then a key member of the department's economic planning group, on September 18. Clark pledged that Ottawa would not devalue the Canadian dollar but signaled that his government would impose import restrictions if there were no other way to ease the drain,

---

[55] Cuff and Granatstein, *American Dollars–Canadian Prosperity*, p. 27.

[56] Cuff and Granatstein, "The Rise and Fall of Canadian-American Free Trade, 1947–8," p. 463.

[57] Cuff and Granatstein, *American Dollars–Canadian Prosperity*, pp. 33–34.

[58] Roy Jenkins, *Truman*, p. 170.

suggesting rather hopefully that Canada might become an offshore sup-
plier for Marshall Plan aid. Wood was unhelpful, and both sides came
away from the meeting "annoyed."[59] The unproductive encounter
spurred a series of deliberations among American officials that led to no
constructive proposals. Douglas Abbott, the Canadian minister of finance, became convinced that Washington's inaction was a result of the
fact that multilateral trade talks in Geneva were at a critical stage. Moreover, Canada simply did not loom large in Washington's view. "[T]hey
don't know we're here at all," Max Freedman of the *Winnipeg Free Press*
reported Abbott telling him in mid-October. "Therefore if we punched
them in the nose they would become aware of us and would realize that
we are trying to solve our dollar problem. He thought this would be very
helpful as a beginning to trade negotiations."[60]

The punch came in the form of two options Clark took to Washington
in late October. Both plans called for a $350 million Export-Import Bank
loan and rationing of pleasure travel, but Plan A called for draconian
import restrictions, including outright bans on most American consumer
goods, and quotas on most of the rest. Plan B was milder and less discriminatory, but Clark made clear that cabinet would be forced to choose Plan
A if no concessions were forthcoming on Marshall Plan purchasing. The
ruse worked, and with some false starts, Clark received vague assurances
that American officials would do what they could. On November 13 the
cabinet endorsed Plan B, which Abbott announced to the country four
days later. It met with a pleasantly mild reaction, both at home and
abroad, in part because it coincided with Princess Elizabeth's wedding to
Prince Philip, which dominated the headlines of the day.[61]

Plan B was, however, nothing more than a stopgap. King particularly
feared that consumer frustration with import and travel restrictions
would mount, imperiling his slender majority in Parliament.[62] Hence,
even before the announcement of the restrictions, King had authorized
his officials to sound out their American counterparts on the idea of a
much farther-reaching, longer-term bilateral arrangement. As Robert Cuff
and Jack Granatstein put it, "In their desperation the Canadians had indicated their willingness to shift direction substantially."[63]

On October 29 Hector McKinnon, chairman of the Canadian Tariff
Board, and John Deutsch, director of the International Economic Relations
Division of the Department of Finance, met with Clair Wilcox, director of

[59] Cuff and Granatstein, *American Dollars–Canadian Prosperity*, p. 48.
[60] Quoted in ibid., pp. 53–54.
[61] Ibid., pp. 56–60; Pickersgill and Forster, *The Mackenzie King Record*, vol 4, chap. 3.
[62] Cuff and Granatstein, "The Rise and Fall of Canadian-American Free Trade, 1947–
8," p. 465.
[63] Ibid., p. 469.

the Office of International Trade Policy at the Department of State; Andrew Foster, head of the Canadian Desk in the British Commonwealth Division; Woodbury Willoughby of the Commercial Policy Division; and Paul Nitze. The American minutes of the meeting record McKinnon proposing "a comprehensive agreement involving, wherever possible, the complete elimination of duties. . . . They feel that Canada must either integrate her economy more closely with that of the United States or be forced into discriminatory restrictive policies involving greater self-sufficiency, bilateral trade bargaining and an orientation toward Europe with corresponding danger of friction with the United States, if not economic warfare."[64] The Canadians were clear that they were not proposing a full customs union, which would be "politically impossible in Canada because it would be interpreted as abandoning the Empire and constituting a long step in the direction of political absorption by the United States."[65] The difficulty, however, was that neither the recently concluded GATT nor the draft ITO Charter permitted preferential arrangements of this kind.[66]

As American officials wrestled with the difficulty, Willoughby thought there might be some prospect for a "special form of customs union under which there would be substantially free trade between the two countries but each would retain its separate tariff vis-à-vis third countries."[67] Nitze floated the idea with Wilcox, who was leading the U.S. delegation trying to put the final touches on the ITO Charter in Havana. Fortuitously, a number of Middle Eastern and Central American countries were pushing for changes to the charter to permit "free trade areas," arguing that they did not have the institutional capacity for, and required more flexibility than would be allowed by, true formal customs unions.[68] This was exactly the arrangement Canada was looking for. Willoughby put the idea to Deutsch on December 31, strictly confidentially, as he had not yet cleared it with his superiors, and Deutsch promised to get back to him within two weeks.[69]

Back in Ottawa, Deutsch encountered some skepticism from certain quarters, but surprisingly strong support from three very powerful play-

---

[64] Quoted in ibid. Michael Hart argues, in slight contrast, that as late as December 1947, Canada was looking not for free trade as such, but essentially for improved access to the American market for a particular range of goods. Hart, "Almost but Not Quite," pp. 38–39. In his diary, King recorded Abbott telling him on January 13 that it was the Americans who proposed a complete reciprocity treaty, strongly suggesting a miscommunication concerning who was proposing what. King Diaries, 13 January 1948, p. 9.

[65] Cuff and Granatstein, *American Dollars–Canadian Prosperity*, p. 66.

[66] Both the GATT and Article 44 of the draft ITO Charter permitted orthodox customs unions but treated bilateral preferences as a violation of the most favored nation principle.

[67] Quoted in Cuff and Granatstein, *American Dollars–Canadian Prosperity*, p. 69.

[68] Hart, "Almost but Not Quite," p. 41.

[69] Cuff and Granatstein, *American Dollars–Canadian Prosperity*, p. 70.

ers: Abbott, Minister of Trade and Commerce C. D. Howe, and King himself. And so the heavy lifting began. Officials in both capitals began hammering out the details of an agreement, and Wilcox got to work ensuring that the draft ITO Charter would permit it. By March the pieces had largely fallen into place, leaving only questions of timing. The Canadians noted that the prime minister would almost certainly have to call an election on the issue but would take that risk only if the Senate had already ratified the deal, or if the Democrats and Republicans both embraced it in their platforms for the upcoming fall election. This meant a fairly tight timetable to move the deal through the American political system. Willoughby briefed his superior, Undersecretary of State Robert Lovett, and sat back to await the final green light from his Canadian counterparts so that the interdepartmental coalition building and Beltway politicking could begin.[70]

With everything ready to go, King got cold feet. At the beginning of March he had been enthusiastic. By the end of March he had decided against it. Why?

King's diaries shed considerable light on the issue. Essentially, he changed his mind about the balance of political risks and benefits. In January he wrote confidently, "If a treaty of complete reciprocity, such as in Sir Wilfrid's day, was before the country, [it] would . . . meet with a different kind of reception. The country had learned they had made a mistake in not accepting the treaty in Sir Wilfrid's day. What we had achieved in [limited] reciprocity would have prepared the public mind for a complete reciprocity."[71] In February he wrote that "the measure was of such advantages to Canada that we should not risk the chance of having an agreement of the kind [not] made."[72] As late as March 6 he was still on board.[73] But by March 22 he had begun to have serious doubts:

> I admitted that the agreement, if it could be brought into being, could be of tremendous benefit to Canada. The point to be considered still was the element of timing. That my experience in politics had taught me that no matter how good a thing might be, if the people were taken by surprise [sic] in its presentation, there was bound to be opposition to it. That they had to be led gradually into the appreciation of what it would mean. I felt perfectly sure that if this agreement

---

[70] Ibid., pp. 72–77. The Americans wanted to go public with the agreement by May 15; King Diaries, 22 March 1948, p. 2.

[71] King Diaries, 13 January 1948, p. 9.

[72] Ibid., 13 February 1948, p. 2.

[73] "I strongly advised Abbott to let us clear up all matters concerning the U.S. trade as rapidly as we can so as to have them out of the way before this new transaction [i.e., the free-trade deal] comes up in Parliament." Ibid., 6 March 1948, pp. 1–2.

were announced in the H. of C. [House of Commons], something which had already been arranged, and had to be approved by Parlt. [Parliament], there would be instant opposition from the Conservatives, and they would keep up that opposition very strongly. The cry would be raised at once that it was commercial union that we were after. So far as I was concerned, I would be a liability rather than an asset in the picture inasmuch as the Tories would say this is Mr. King's toy. He has always wanted annexation with the States. Now he is making his last effort toward that end. The press would not grasp the details. I doubted myself whether I had the mental energy and physical strength to make an explanation in the H. of C. such as had been made to us by Deutsch. If that explanation had to be gotten over to the public from the Commons, I did not know how that would be gotten with the details what they were. The size of the agreement what it was, etc.

It would be represented that we were seeking to separate from Britain. I said I would feel no matter what happened that we would have to offer Britain the same rights in our market as we were offering the Americans. All present agreed that it was so.

I concluded by saying that if the matter had to be settled in so short a space of time in relation to trade alone, I certainly felt pretty doubtful that we should give our consent to it.[74]

This statement is interesting because of its multifaceted sense of dread. While King seems still to have felt that the idea had economic merit—"I admitted that the agreement, if it could be brought into being, could be of tremendous benefit to Canada"—he lacked both the stomach and the stamina for a political battle the intensity and nature of which he was only now beginning to foresee. Why were these difficulties coming into focus only in March? Why not in January?

One of the things that had helped focus his attention was a March 15 editorial in *Life* magazine strongly endorsing the idea of a "customs union," to which more than two-thirds of Canadians polled reacted negatively.[75] "[W]hile it might be sound economically," King recorded telling his Québec lieutenant Louis St. Laurent, "I believed it would be fatal politically. Quite impossible of carrying out at this time in the limited time that was being suggested. It was the sort of thing that would require months, if not years

---

[74] Ibid., 22 March 1948, p. 2.

[75] "Customs Union with Canada: Canada Needs Us and We Need Canada in a Violently Contracting World [Editorial]," *Life*, 15 March 1948, p. 40; Cuff and Granatstein, *American Dollars–Canadian Prosperity*, p. 77. Some 69 percent of respondents to a *New Liberty* poll opposed economic union with the United States in the wake of the *Life* editorial; Hart, "Almost but Not Quite," p. 43.

of education. . . . I could think of nothing that would destroy my name and reputation more than to be made the spearhead of a political fight which would be twisted into a final endeavour to bring about economic union with the U.S. which would mean annexation and separation from Britain."[76] At the same time, he began to worry more that reciprocity might indeed *lead to* annexation—or, at any rate, he began to suspect that the Americans so hoped.[77]

King was now thinking very strongly about 1911. Convinced that reciprocity made economic sense in 1911, he nevertheless felt Laurier had erred in proposing such a dramatic change in a time of relative prosperity. He recalled how Laurier had underestimated the passions the issue would arouse. He could see those very same passions stirring once again.[78] His own government was popular. "Mr. St. Laurent said that he thought so far as our chances and the electorate of Canada were concerned, we did not need this issue to help us win," King wrote in his diary on March 22. "The public felt we were the best government that Canada could have, and that the govt. would be returned on that score. To make a new issue was not necessarily going to be an aid to us as a govt. . . . This, I think, is very true."[79] Electorally, in other words, reciprocity offered no opportunities, only risks. While the Liberals were likely to win the next election in any case, a quick and emotional campaign on reciprocity, as he later told Lester Pearson, "might throw the Liberal Party of Canada, into oblivion."[80] Arnold Heeney, clerk of the Privy Council and secretary to the cabinet, put it thus: "The terms were tempting and, if embodied in an agreement, would no doubt have been beneficial. But he would have none of it. He was not going to be responsible for a second 1911 and disaster for a Liberal government."[81]

Thus King began to see the proposal as something profoundly dangerous—to his health; to his name and reputation; to Canada's identity and autonomy; and to his party's electoral fortunes.[82] These dangers began to

---

[76] King Diaries, 25 March 1948, p. 5. See also Louis Balthazar, "Les Relations Canado-Américains," p. 252.

[77] "I believed the Americans in their attitude were carrying out what I felt was really their policy and had been so over many years, of seeking to make this Continent one. . . . I would rather have Canada within the orbit of the British Commonwealth of Nations than to come within that of the U.S." King Diaries, 22 March 1948, p. 4.

[78] Joy E. Esberey, *Knight of the Holy Spirit*, p. 195.

[79] King Diaries, 22 March 1948, p. 5.

[80] Ibid., 6 May 1948, p. 1.

[81] Arnold Heeney, *The Things That Are Caesar's*, pp. 92–93.

[82] Sealing his opposition to the proposal was a mystical experience of the kind to which, historians were somewhat surprised to discover when his diaries became public, King was prone: "I now want to record a quite extraordinary experience which I took to be a perfect evidence of guidance from Beyond. This morning, a propos of nothing, but feeling I ought to look at some book, I drew out from my shelves a volume entitled 'Studies in Colonial Nation-

loom large in his mind just as the desperate conditions that had made the idea seem attractive in the first place began to wane. The import restrictions were working. In fact, much to everyone's surprise, Canada's U.S. dollar reserves were beginning to rise again. A nearly catastrophic loss of $743 million in 1947 turned into a gain of $496 million in 1948. Moreover, in the spring of 1948, after some difficult bilateral bargaining, Washington finally authorized offshore Marshall Plan purchases in Canada.[83] At about the same time, serious discussions began on a North Atlantic security pact that would ultimately become NATO. King had visions of broadening it into a larger economic community. There was some chance, King mused, that Canada might reap all the benefits of bilateral reciprocity with the United States in a multilateral context.[84] Now that the foreign exchange crisis had eased, why not wait and see?

A comprehensive bilateral trade agreement, in other words, seemed the best hope for averting a painful loss in the fall of 1947. Within a few months, the loss having been averted otherwise, the agreement itself now seemed to pose the threat.

Mulroney and the Canada-U.S. Free Trade Agreement, 1988

By any standard, the Canadian economy did very well in the forty years following King's abortive flirtation with free trade. Incomes rose, stan-

---

alism' by [Richard] Jebb. A book I have not looked at in 20 years. Did not like the title—either Colonial or Nationalism and had forgotten having read it with care. Looked first at page 124—reference to Sir Wilfrid. I found myself looking with interest to the last chapter of all which was entitled The Soul of Empire. When I had read them, I had felt they were significant in reference to the proposals being made to me to support the programme of complete freedom of trade between the U.S. and Canada. . . . I did not believe it could be successful but for me to be placed in the position of being the spearhead of furthering a commercial union as the last act of my career would be to absolutely destroy the significance of the whole of it. The Tory party would make out that from the beginning my whole vision had been to further annexation. I was really at heart anti-British, etc. Everything opposite of the truth. . . . Each thing that happened today . . . seemed to bring confirmation of what I had felt about the whole business when I read the article on Colonial Nationalism. I felt wholly convinced that the taking out of that book, and reading that chapter was no matter of chance but had been inspired from some source in the Beyond." King Diaries, 24 March 1948, pp. 2–3.

[83] See especially Cuff and Granatstein, *American Dollars–Canadian Prosperity*, pp. 83–110.

[84] King Diaries, 22 March 1948, pp. 2–3. Canadian negotiators did succeed in convincing their NATO partners to approve Article 2 of the North Atlantic Treaty: "The Parties will contribute toward the further development of peaceful and friendly international relations by strengthening their free institutions, by bringing about a better understanding of the principles upon which these institutions are founded, and by promoting conditions of stability and well-being. They will seek to eliminate conflict in their international economic policies and will encourage economic collaboration between any or all of them." The so-called Canadian Article, however, ultimately proved otiose.

dards of living rose, and the economy diversified. In per capita terms, Canada surpassed Britain in wealth and came to rival the United States. At the same time, Canada created a social safety net that was the envy of the world.

Some of the credit for this happy situation must go to the creation of a stable global trade regime, the pillar of which was the GATT. While the International Trade Organization ultimately proved stillborn, the GATT itself persisted and evolved, succeeding to quite a remarkable degree, if unevenly, in reducing tariff barriers. Throughout this period, Canada's dependence on international trade increased. Canadian resource industries continued to do well in global markets, but increasingly Canada exported high value-added goods. The American market became steadily more important. Sectoral free-trade arrangements in automobiles, automobile parts, and defense production were especially significant to the Canadian economy, as they generated large numbers of well-paying jobs and attracted capital, technology, and knowledge.[85]

While the United States and Canada became the world's largest trading partners, and while leaders on both sides of the 49th parallel readily and routinely invoked the platitudinous image of the world's longest undefended border, U.S.-Canadian relations were far from perfectly harmonious. In addition to substantive disagreements on various specific high-policy issues, many of which reflected ideological differences (e.g., Vietnam, arms control, détente), bilateral relations were frequently complicated by personality conflicts at the highest level.[86] For the most part, however, economic ties were strong and stable. An attitude of pragmatism prevailed on both sides. As Social Credit leader Robert Thompson pithily put it: "The United States is our friend whether we like it or not."[87]

This economic concord began to erode under Prime Minister Pierre Elliott Trudeau, a nationalist who became increasingly uncomfortable with Canada's growing dependence upon the United States, and whose penchant for regulation repeatedly put him at odds with his American counterparts. Particularly irritating, from Washington's perspective, were his attempts to screen foreign investment through the Foreign Investment Review Agency (FIRA), protect Canadian cultural industries, and Canadianize the energy sector through the National Energy Program (NEP).[88] Trudeau's nationalism had both principled and tactical elements. He gen-

---

[85] See n. 6 above.

[86] The most entertaining account is Martin, *The Presidents and the Prime Ministers*.

[87] Quoted in ibid., p. 204.

[88] FIRA was established in 1973, the NEP in 1980. Various milestones in the protection of Canadian culture include the creation of the Canadian Radio-television and Telecommunications Commission (CRTC) in 1968; the tightening of Canadian content rules in broadcasting in 1971; and protections for Canadian magazines in 1976.

uinely sought to protect a distinctive Canadian society by resisting the pressures of Americanization, but to some extent he was also merely reacting to the increasing vulnerability of Canada to American economic unilateralism, a lesson painfully learned during the "Nixon shocks" of 1971, when Treasury Secretary John Connolly sought to impose a 10 percent import surcharge on foreign goods—including Canadian goods—as part of an attempt to correct a serious balance-of-payments problem. The net result, however, was that by the end of the Trudeau period, Canadian-American relations were at a low ebb, and economic issues were becoming increasingly divisive, just as Canada's economic dependence upon the United States was at an all-time high.

The 1980s looked to be heading toward a moment of truth. Several trends were converging toward possible disaster. First, the recently completed Tokyo Round of the GATT dramatically, if unintentionally, increased trade remedy actions, particularly in the United States. Though the Tokyo Round succeeded in reducing tariffs, by broadening the agreement to cover nontariff barriers such as subsidies, standards, government procurement programs, customs valuations, and import licensing, it stimulated countervailing and antidumping claims. Litigation began to replace negotiation as the dispute resolution mechanism of choice.[89] What was meant to be a further step along the path of trade liberalization, in short, inadvertently became a step along the path toward managed trade.[90] Second, in 1980 the American economy suffered a serious downturn, threatening Canadian exporters (owing to a weakened U.S. dollar) and exacerbating the bilateral conflict over Canadian energy and investment policies.[91] Third, developing countries were becoming tougher competitors for Canadian resource products, which were commanding lower prices in any case owing both to oversupply and decreasing demand. Fourth, as tariff levels dropped and production processes globalized, Canada's relatively inefficient manufacturers faced stiffer competition both at home and abroad.[92]

---

[89] Canada and the United States tended to make use of trade remedies in roughly equal proportion, in terms of numbers of cases, but the value of Canadian exports affected by U.S. measures dwarfed the value of American exports affected by Canadian measures (during the 1980s, by a ratio of more than 12:1). Ernie Stokes, "Macroeconomic Impact of the Canada-U.S. Free Trade Agreement," pp. 226–227.

[90] For an excellent discussion, see Hart, *A Trading Nation*, pp. 339–366. Cf. also Nelson Michaud and Kim Richard Nossal, "Necessité Ou Innovation?"

[91] G. Bruce Doern and Brian W. Tomlin, *Faith and Fear*, pp. 15, 17.

[92] Economic Council of Canada, *Looking Outward*, pp. 2–3; Michael Hart, "The Future on the Table," pp. 70–71; Hart, *A Trading Nation*, p. 361; Richard G. Lipsey and Murray G. Smith, *Taking the Initiative*. As Denis Stairs put it, the problem was that Canadian tariffs were no longer high enough to serve a nation-building function but were too high to allow Canadian producers to enjoy the stimulus of world competition. Denis Stairs, Gilbert R.

The Trudeau government decided that the time was ripe for a full review of Canadian trade policy. The Royal Commission on the Economic
Union and Development Prospects for Canada, chaired by former Liberal
cabinet minister Donald Macdonald, conducted extensive public hearings
and commissioned an enormous body of research on Canada's options.
Partway through its mandate, in September 1984, the Conservatives
swept into office under their new leader, Brian Mulroney—who, ironically, had campaigned against the idea of bilateral free trade with the
United States, one of the options then under discussion. But his own government's review of Canada's trade predicament, led by Minister for International Trade Jim Kelleher,[93] and the Macdonald Commission's surprisingly strong endorsement of bilateral free trade, led to a change of
heart. Mulroney and his American counterpart President Ronald Reagan
laid the foundation for negotiations at the famous March 1985 "Sham-
rock Summit" in Québec City, perhaps best known as a turning point in
the tone of U.S.-Canadian relations (news footage showed Reagan and
Mulroney arm in arm, hoisting pints, singing "When Irish Eyes are Smil-
ing"). There they issued the Québec Declaration on Trade in Goods and
Services, charging their trade ministers "to establish immediately a mechanism to chart all possible ways to reduce and eliminate existing barriers
to trade and to report back to us within six months."[94]
This time the effort bore fruit.
The Reagan administration obtained fast-track authority, by which
Congress committed itself to voting the package up or down, without
amendments, as long as the administration reported that a basis for
agreement existed by midnight, October 3, 1987. The two countries assembled their negotiating teams. Veteran trade negotiator Simon Reisman
led the Canadian team, supported by an enormous virtual bureaucracy
within a bureaucracy dedicated solely to the task at hand. A relatively
junior official, Peter Murphy, led the American team, operating out of the
Office of the United States Trade Representative (USTR), with what was,
in effect, a skeleton staff. The negotiations were difficult, painful, often
tense, and more than once seemed doomed to fail. The main difficulty,
from the Canadian perspective, was that the American team was under-
prepared, unimaginative, and lacking in political clout. Indeed, the Canadian delegation's frustration at what it perceived as the American team's
unwillingness to engage the Canadian agenda prompted Reisman to sus-

---

Winham, and the Royal Commission on the Economic Union and Development Prospects
for Canada, *The Politics of Canada's Economic Relationship with the United States*, Collected Research Studies Vol. 29, p. 9.
    [93] The discussion paper kicking off the review was Canada, Department of External Af-
fairs, *How to Secure and Enhance Access to Export Markets*.
    [94] Hart, *A Trading Nation*, p. 374.

pend negotiations at the eleventh hour. Only a last-minute flurry of high-level political activity brought the negotiations back on track, and literally only minutes before the deadline of midnight on October 3 did the negotiators shake hands on the essentials of a deal. On December 11 the two countries released the text for public consumption; on January 2, 1988, Reagan and Mulroney signed it.

While the history of the negotiation is detailed, complex, and as full of high drama as trade negotiation can be, it is neither necessary nor possible to rehearse it here.[95] The central questions for our purposes are simply these: What prompted the Canadian government to seek a bilateral free-trade deal with the United States? What in particular did it seek to achieve? What did it seek to avoid? What does the episode tell us about dramatic foreign policy change?

The central players on the Canadian side were the prime minister, Finance Minister Michael Wilson, Secretary of State for External Affairs Joe Clark, and successive ministers for international trade (James Kelleher, Pat Carney, and John Crosbie). John Turner and Ed Broadbent, leaders of the opposition Liberals and New Democrats respectively, played important roles in the unfolding of events, as did various provincial premiers; but the crucial decisions were taken by the cabinet, of whom these were the key figures.[96] The principles of cabinet solidarity and confidentiality limit what we can know about the ins and outs of their deliberations, but studies based upon extensive off-the-record interviews,[97] coupled with publicly available background materials and inferences from the statements, recollections, and behavior of Canadian negotiators who were in close contact with their political principals, enable us to arrive at usefully accurate characterizations. It is somewhat more difficult to interpret those characterizations in ways that enable us to make very strong judgments about how decision makers framed their options, as I discuss in the final section of the chapter, but I believe the evidence allows us to do so with tolerable confidence.

---

[95] The best account by far is Michael Hart, Bill Dymond, and Colin Robertson, *Decision at Midnight*, which includes an excellent bibliographic essay, pp. 433–439. A good, relatively brief overview is Hart, *A Trading Nation*, pp. 367–397. See also Canada, Department of External Affairs, *Canada-U.S. Trade Negotiations*; Ross McKitrick, *The Canada-U.S. Free Trade Agreement*; Gordon Ritchie, *Wrestling with the Elephant*. On the agreement itself, see Canada, Department of External Affairs, *The Canada-U.S. Free Trade Agreement*; *The Canada-U.S. Free Trade Agreement: Synopsis*; and *The Canada-U.S. Free Trade Agreement: Tariff Schedule*. For overviews, see Daniel Trefler, *The Long and Short of the Canada-U.S. Free Trade Agreement*; Paul Wonnacott, *The United States and Canada*. A particularly good treatment of the relationship between the FTA and the GATT is Richard G. Dearden, Debra P. Steger, and Michael Hart, eds., *Living with Free Trade*.

[96] Cf. Hart, Dymond, and Robertson, *Decision at Midnight*, p. xii.

[97] The most significant is Doern and Tomlin, *Faith and Fear*.

While the structural problems of the Canadian economy were reasonably clear to all in the early 1980s, bilateral free trade with the United
States was not the obvious solution. Indeed, even those who would later
become the staunchest proponents of bilateral free trade initially held out
hope that Canada's difficulties could be resolved multilaterally—through
the GATT, for example, or, failing that, through comprehensive trade
agreements that included Europe and/or Japan—reflecting a mild general
Canadian philosophical preference for multilateralism.[98] The Trudeau
government, having been disappointed in its efforts at trade diversifica-
tion,[99] toyed with expanding the roster of sectoral free-trade deals, an
option that resurfaced in the discussion paper that kicked off Kelleher's
review, *How to Secure and Enhance Canadian Access to Export Markets*.[100] The glacial pace of GATT rounds, coupled with the unfortunate
GATT-sanctioned trend toward trade remedy action, undermined faith in
full-blown multilateralism. Raging trade wars between the United States,
on the one hand, and Europe and Japan, on the other, made trilateral
or four-way deals unlikely. Indeed, to the extent that Canada was being
sideswiped by others' trade disputes, multilateralism, in the context of the
early 1980s, seemed rather more like a problem than a solution. To some
extent, a bilateral deal with the United States was the only option that
seemed to hold out any hope for addressing Canada's problems, and it
was largely for this reason that the Mulroney government embraced it.[101]

What, specifically, were those problems? The Macdonald Commission,
pro-free-trade economists, and much of the Canadian business community fingered two in particular: the uncompetitiveness of Canadian industry, and the American protectionist threat. The Macdonald Commission
and academic economists tended to stress the former; businessmen and
ministers tended to stress the latter.[102] But these were related problems
because American protectionism threatened the security of access to a
large market that Canadian industry needed to justify the investment re-

[98] Economic Council of Canada, *Looking Outward*. This preference is somewhat mythi-
cal as it is honored as often as not in the breach; see A. Claire Cutler and Mark W. Zacher,
eds., *Canadian Foreign Policy and International Economic Regimes*; Tom Keating, *The
Multilateralist Tradition in Canadian Foreign Policy*.

[99] Peter Dobell, "Reducing Vulnerability."

[100] The other three options were (1) the status quo; (2) a comprehensive trade agreement
with the United States (the Tories studiously avoided the phrase "free trade" at this point);
and (3) a framework agreement for further consultations and negotiations—what Michael
Hart and his colleagues call "the reddest of red herrings." Hart, Dymond, and Robertson,
Decision at Midnight, p. 66.

[101] See, e.g., Michael Wilson's comment in "The Negotiating Process," p. 21.

[102] Doern and Tomlin, *Faith and Fear*, pp. 10, 25, 34; Hart, Dymond, and Robertson,
Decision at Midnight, p. 65.

quired to realize productivity-boosting economies of scale.[103] Hence Canada's "key goal from the outset was to gain secure access to the U.S. market" by seeking exemptions from antidumping actions and countervailing duties, clearer rules to govern subsidies, and a binding dispute resolution mechanism.[104] Mulroney came to embrace free trade for two additional reasons as well: first, since it would reduce trade frictions with the United States, it would serve one of the central goals of his agenda, namely, improving relations with United States; and second, because it was popular in the West, in the East, and, rather surprisingly, in Robert Bourassa's Québec, which, along with Ontario, was part of the inefficient Canadian industrial heartland where labor was strong and could be expected to fear enhanced competition. Thus the project offered a chance to help serve Mulroney's national reconciliation agenda.[105] Finally, although perhaps not surprisingly there is little trace of this in the available record, it stands to reason that free trade was attractive both to business and to the Mulroney government for ideological reasons.[106] It would quite simply make a return to Trudeau-style industrial policy impossible. A bilateral agreement would surely bind future Canadian governments to the mast, unable to respond to the siren songs of nationalist intervention and regulation.[107]

There was, of course, opposition to the idea. While most studies showed that most industries stood to benefit from free trade, some would not (e.g., agriculture, food processing, and textiles).[108] Organized labor feared a loss of high-paying industrial jobs. Some feared that free trade with the United States would inevitably lead to political union, or at least cost Canada an independent foreign policy.[109] Many, like Trudeau, feared that it would undermine Canada's ability to define its own future, or to

[103] As Riesman put it in March 1986: "freer trade would allow us to overcome our deficiencies by having access to a bigger market and being able to use more up-to-date technology and having longer production runs and getting greater volume. That's the bottom line. The major benefit you expect to get from a free-trade arrangement will be to increase our productivity." Quoted in Hart, Dymond, and Robertson, *Decision at Midnight*, p. 155. Department of Finance studies indicated a long-term productivity gain of approximately 2.3 percent. Stokes, "Macroeconomic Impact of the Canada-U.S. Free Trade Agreement," p. 231.

[104] Konrad von Finckenstein, "Dispute Settlement under the Free Trade Agreement," p. 101.

[105] See, e.g., Derek H. Burney, "Present at the Creation," pp. 13–14; Doern and Tomlin, *Faith and Fear*, p. 32; Hart, *A Trading Nation*, p. 386; Hart, Dymond, and Robertson, *Decision at Midnight*, p. 62.

[106] John W. Warnock, *Free Trade and the New Right Agenda*.

[107] This theme is extensively explored, with particular reference to post-FTA developments, in Stephen Clarkson, *Uncle Sam and Us*.

[108] Gilbert R. Winham, *Canada-U.S. Sectoral Trade Study*.

[109] Hart, Dymond, and Robertson, *Decision at Midnight*, p. 65.

defend its character. The strongest opponents argued that free trade with the United States would destroy Canada's culture, social programs, health care system, multicultural character, relative gender equality, and environment.[110] Fully aware that there were several hot-button issues that could derail an agreement, the government took pains to argue that certain things were simply not on the table. Thus, for example, in the House of Commons on March 16, 1987, the government offered this particularly crafty motion designed to discomfit the opposition: "[T]hat this House supports the negotiation of a bilateral trading arrangement with the US, as part of the government's multilateral trade policy, while protecting our political sovereignty, social programs, agricultural marketing systems, the auto industry, and our unique cultural identity."[111]

While opposition to free trade materialized early and organized fairly effectively, its center of gravity was in civil society, not in Parliament. Groups such as the Council of Canadians, founded in 1985 precisely to fight free trade, and the Pro-Canada Network, an umbrella group of anti–free trade organizations founded at the Council of Canadians' 1987 summit, led the charge.[112] John Turner's Liberals waffled, riven by internal tensions, and torn between their desire to oppose the government and their leader's inability to betray his Bay Street roots. Ed Broadbent's New Democrats opposed the deal consistently but had no credible alternative to offer.[113] The relative weakness of the political opposition, coupled with

[110] Barlow, *Parcel of Rogues*; Mel Hurtig, *The Betrayal of Canada*; James Laxer, *Leap of Faith*; Pranlal Manga, *The Canada-U.S. Free Trade Agreement*; John Urquhart and Peggy Berkowitz, "Northern Angst"; Mel Watkins, "The U.S.-Canada Free Trade Agreement." Fears about the FTA's impact on Canada's social programs have proven unfounded and were based upon misunderstandings of the provisions and misperceptions of the scale and nature of Canada's social programs; K. A. Frenzel and Douglas J. McCready, "Canada-United States Free Trade." Cf. also Glenn Drover, ed., *Free Trade and Social Policy*.

[111] Hart, Dymond, and Robertson, *Decision at Midnight*, p. 229. Accordingly, beer—but not wine—was grandfathered from the agreement, beer being central to Canadian identity in a way that wine simply is not.

[112] Doern and Tomlin, *Faith and Fear*, pp. 208–213.

[113] Ibid., pp. 230–238. Doern and Tomlin also flag institutional incapacity as a cause of the opposition parties' ineffectiveness: "For all of Canada's political parties, the post–World War II consensus on a multilateral GATT-based approach to trade had removed trade policy from the arena of conventional politics. The trade policy field was left to a small band of trade professionals in the bureaucracy who spun out their policies in relative obscurity. Sheltered by the GATT consensus, both government and opposition parties became increasingly illiterate about trade developments. As a result, when the national agenda was seized by the free trade issue, the two opposition parties in particular were left scrambling, trying to learn trade policy on the run, and without the bureaucratic expertise available to the Mulroney government. Neither was able to successfully develop politically credible trade alternatives, harking back instead to the conventional, and comfortable, doctrines of multilateralism" (p. 229).

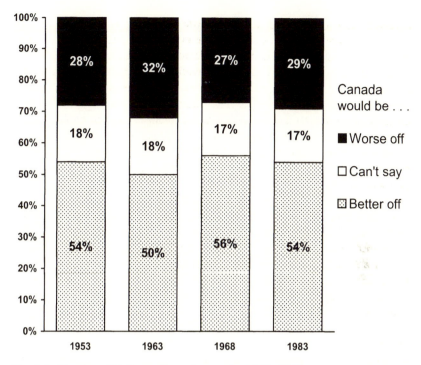

Fig. 5.5. Results of Gallup polls on free trade, 1953–1983
Source: Michael Hart, Bill Dymond, and Colin Robertson, *Decision at Midnight*, p. 72.

largely permissive polls (as figure 5.5 shows, a steady majority of Canadians had favored free trade in principle for thirty years), emboldened the Tories to press ahead with what everyone acknowledged to be a risky venture, particularly when seen against the background of Canada's two flirtations with free trade earlier in the century. "As students of Canadian history, we knew the issue would be politically sensitive," Mulroney's Chief of Staff Derek Burney recalled; "after all, free trade had been attempted twice before. It defeated one [L]iberal government in 1911. It intimidated another from going beyond very private, exploratory discussions in 1948." But the government was both banking on, and fearing, trends:

> What made it politically more palatable for us in the mid 1980s were, first of all, the increasing importance of trade with the United States, and the particular success of the Auto Pact. Forty years of GATT negotiations provided an umbrella for a steady liberalization of Canada-U.S. trade. This meant that the concept of free trade was, in fact, a logical, and certainly not a radical extension of the prevailing trend.

TABLE 5.1
Import duties by industrial sector, 1987.

	Canada	United States
Textiles	16.9%	7.2%
Clothing	23.7%	18.4%
Leather products	4.0%	2.5%
Footwear	21.5%	9.0%
Wood products	2.5%	0.2%
Furniture	14.3%	4.6%
Paper products	6.6%	0.0%
Printing and publishing	1.1%	0.3%
Chemicals	7.9%	0.6%
Rubber products	7.3%	3.2%
Nonmetal mineral products	4.4%	0.3%
Glass products	6.9%	5.7%
Iron and steel	5.1%	2.7%
Metal products	8.6%	4.0%
Nonelectrical machinery	4.6%	2.2%
Electrical machinery	7.5%	4.5%
Transportation equipment	0.0%	0.0%

Source: Paul Wonnacott, The United States and Canada, p. 4.

Equally, this trend placed a higher premium on the need for Canada to protect and preserve our existing access to the U.S. market, and to dampen concerns about U.S. trade remedy actions.[114]

The rocky history of the negotiations clearly shows that securing market access was a vital Canadian objective. Tariff reduction was not. Canadian tariffs were higher than American tariffs (see table 5.1), and so the prospect of eliminating them without some kind of relief from unilateral trade action was not, as Burney put it, "affecting."[115] The American nego-

[114] Burney, "Present at the Creation," pp. 11–12.

[115] Ibid., p. 10. In addition to rising protectionist sentiment in Congress, Canada was particularly concerned about the proliferation of U.S. nontariff barriers (NTBs). Peter Morici cites as examples federal and state procurement practices as embodied in various domestic preferences for defense procurement, the Surface Transportation Assistance Act of 1978, the Amtrak Improvement Act of 1977, the Public Works Act of 1977, and the re-energized

tiating team, more interested in cherry-picking issue-specific irritants, passively resisted all Canadian attempts to discipline domestic trade remedy law. Even as the two countries were allegedly negotiating a free-trade agreement, events illustrated both the urgency and the difficulty of making headway on this particular front. In May 1986, for example—right in the middle of negotiations—U.S. lumber producers sought a billion dollars' worth of new penalties on Canadian softwood imports; Congress passed an omnibus trade bill bolstering the U.S. lumber producers' case; and, with no warning, the Reagan administration slapped a 35 percent duty on Canadian shakes and shingles. Mulroney was beside himself. "[A]ctions like this," he complained, "make it extremely difficult for anyone, including Canadians, to be friends with the Americans."[116]

The lack of movement on trade remedies is precisely what prompted the Canadian delegation's walkout on September 22, 1987.[117] By all accounts, this was "key to the final success."[118] It energized high-level political action on the American side, as the administration—which had assumed that Canada would accommodate American demands in view of the fact that Canada was the supplicant—suddenly faced the prospect of failure on a project on which it had staked a good deal of its own prestige. The American attitude "changed dramatically. Driven by the desire not to fail, US officials became prepared to make compromises in areas in which previously they had only reluctantly considered Canadian demands." They dropped their insistence on writing intellectual property into the agreement, accommodated a Canadian demand on procurement, excluded beer, resolved a dispute over the fate of the Auto Pact with new rules of origin, and accepted less ambitious provisions for opening up investment and financial services than they had originally sought.[119] Trade remedy issues continued to prove the hardest problem to solve, however. Of the three main issues—subsidies and countervailing duties, dumping and antidumping duties, and safeguards—only the last was close to resolution. The Americans insisted on retaining domestic countervail law and

---

Clean Water Act of 1936, many of which shut out Canadian goods that enjoyed comparative advantages. The United States sought to roll back certain Canadian NTBs as well, particularly federal and provincial procurement policies, trade-related performance requirements placed on foreign companies, duty drawbacks, incentives such as low-interest loans, and regional development subsidies. Morici, "U.S.-Canada Free Trade Discussions." See also White, *Fur Trade to Free Trade*, p. 148.

[116] Hart, Dymond, and Robertson, *Decision at Midnight*, pp. 161–162.

[117] "The major sticking point for us at that time was the issue of dispute settlement, or, more generally, relief from unilateral trade remedy actions." Burney, "Present at the Creation," p. 10.

[118] Peter McPherson, "A Reunion of Trade Warriors from the Canada-U.S. Trade Negotiations," p. viii.

[119] Hart, Dymond, and Robertson, *Decision at Midnight*, p. 341.

were simply unprepared to accept the Canadian vision of a binding bilateral authority. Knowing this to be a deal breaker from the Canadian perspective, the Americans proposed an ingenious finesse: both countries would continue to apply their own trade law, and would retain the right to change it, but would have to state clearly that changes applied to the other party, and any changes they made would be subject to bilateral review to ensure that they were consistent both with the agreement and with the GATT. In addition, binational panels, rather than national courts, would review applications of domestic law, using domestic legal standards. Finally, the two countries would continue to try to negotiate a completely new regime to replace this temporary arrangement over the course of the next five years.[120]

Realizing that this was the best deal available, the Canadians decided it was good enough. "We knew . . . that an agreement which did not temper the unilateral, if not arbitrary, nature of U.S. trade remedy actions would not be saleable in Canada," Burney recalled. "As it was, there were expectations of total immunity which were impossible to attain, so we sought a respectable compromise."[121]

Critics of the agreement would argue that this compromise fell far short of providing the security of access and immunity from arbitrary American trade action that the government said was its sine qua non. And to some extent, the critics are correct. Neither the FTA nor NAFTA, for example, put an end to American harassment of Canadian softwood exports, which for years continued as "the *most* important trade irritant between the two countries."[122] But proponents of the agreement argue that while it fell short of what Canada had hoped for, nevertheless it represented significant progress toward making "the application of US trade remedy law more predictable and less capricious."[123] Certainly the record of success Canada enjoyed with the binational panels has caused some observers to wonder why the United States—by far the more powerful party—would have agreed to something so disproportionately favoring the weaker.[124]

There was very nearly no record to judge. With an agreement in hand, Mulroney proceeded to move the necessary legislation through Parliament. Passage of the bill was assured in the House of Commons, where the Tories had a strong majority, but the normally quiescent Senate, dominated by Liberal appointees, refused its assent and forced Mulroney to call an election on the issue. The campaign was an eerie reminder of

---

[120] Ibid., pp. 284, 298–300, 333–332.
[121] Burney, "Present at the Creation," p. 11.
[122] Paul Wonnacott, "The Canada-U.S. Free Trade Agreement," p. 75.
[123] Hart, Dymond, and Robertson, *Decision at Midnight*, p. 298.
[124] Judith Goldstein, "International Law and Domestic Institutions."

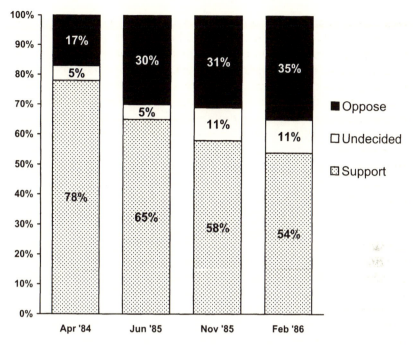

Fig. 5.6. Attitudes toward free trade with the United States (Environics polls)
Source: Hart, Dymond, and Robertson, *Decision at Midnight*, p, 131.

1911—this time with the parties' roles reversed. Throughout the negotiation of the FTA, the opposition's attempts to fan the flames of fear had eroded voter support (see figure 5.6). As election day approached, it seemed as though the Liberals might actually ride the issue back into office. Free trade dominated the campaign and provided Turner with an opportunity finally to demonstrate some spirit and some passion. He handily won an important leaders' debate. Liberal ads attacking the agreement made Canadians pause. A particularly clever and effective one showed a Canadian and an American negotiator haggling over the final details of the agreement, whereupon the American negotiator said, "There's just one line I would like to remove." "What's that?" asked his Canadian counterpart. "This one," said the American, erasing the U.S.-Canadian border.

But the federal election of 1988 was a three-party race, not a two-party race, and when the dust settled on November 21, the Conservatives were back in office with 170 seats in the House of Commons to the Liberals' 82 and the NDP's 43. The fact that the Conservatives garnered only 43 percent of the popular vote, as against a combined 52 percent for the two main opposition parties who had campaigned against the agreement, has led many commentators to conclude that the Canadian electorate in fact rejected free trade in 1988. "Had the vote been strictly a referendum on the free trade issue," Randall White characteristically asserts, "the Canada-U.S. Free Trade Agreement would have been defeated."[125] More detailed studies, however, show that a majority of voters cast their ballots neither for nor against free trade. Most voted for other reasons, and a significant proportion simply had mixed feelings about it. The vote itself was not a referendum on free trade as such, but by the norms of elections in a parliamentary democracy, it was tantamount to a public endorsement.[126]

ANALYSIS

Canada's three flirtations with free trade in the twentieth century provide an interesting variety of significant policy changes and nonchanges. In the 1911 case, we have an example of a governing party embracing a dramatic change as a matter of policy, but ultimately failing to effect the change on behalf of the country as a whole because of what amounted to an electoral veto. In the immediate postwar case, we have two dramatic changes within the span of a few months—a decision to seek a comprehensive trade agreement with the United States, and a subsequent decision not to carry through with it—that effectively canceled each other out and had no practical effect on the business of the country. In the case of the FTA, we have an example of a governing party embracing a dramatic change, seeking to implement it without running the risk of an electoral veto, being thwarted in that endeavor by an unelected legislative body, but ultimately winning the subsequent election and proceeding to carry the change into effect. Do our three hypotheses help us understand this pattern?

Hypothesis 1 states that foreign policy change should be less frequent in highly bureaucratic states with democratic regimes than in less bureaucratic states with autocratic regimes. By any reasonable standard, Canada qualifies as a democracy—and indeed, the Polity project scores Canada a robust +9 on the POLITY variable for the first two decades of the twentieth century, and a full +10 since 1921. However, compared to governments in countries such as the United States, France, Japan, or Germany, the Canadian government is relatively unconstrained by domestic political or bureaucratic considerations. Particularly when the government en-

---

[125] White, *Fur Trade to Free Trade*, p. 219.

[126] Doern and Tomlin, *Faith and Fear*, pp. 238–242. Cf. also Graham Fraser, *Playing for Keeps*; Alan Stewart Frizzell, Jon H. Pammett, and Anthony Westell, eds., *The Canadian General Election of 1988*; Granatstein and Hillmer, *For Better or for Worse*, pp. 306–311.

joys a majority in the House of Commons, the executive is relatively unfettered in its ability to change policy through legislation or order-in-council. Party discipline more or less ensures legislative compliance with executive will. While the Senate technically has the power to act as something of a check on the executive, by exercising its role as a chamber of "sober second thought," as a practical matter, in keeping with long-standing norms, the Senate almost never thwarts the will of a majority government in the House of Commons. Its insistence that Mulroney go to the people on the issue of free trade was a very rare example of the Senate playing an active role in shaping national policy. The Canadian bureaucracy has grown over the years, of course. Foreign Affairs Canada, for example, now headquartered in the magnificent Lester B. Pearson building on Sussex Drive—home to more than three thousand public servants—is a far cry from the original Department of External Affairs, which began life above a barber shop on Bank Street with a handful of clerks in 1909.[127] But compared to other large industrial democracies, the federal organizational chart is relatively simple; those at the top have a relatively free hand; and they enjoy a considerable degree of central control. In most policy areas, the most significant institutional check on the government's freedom of action is federalism itself: the provinces enjoy significant areas of jurisdictional competence.[128] The Canadian case is thus the one significant exception to the generally good fit between the Polity project codings and the regime and state characteristics of interest here: the POLITY scores of +9 and +10, and the XCONST score of 7 throughout the twentieth century, seem to exaggerate the constraints on the Canadian government's actual freedom of maneuver (see figure 6.1).

In none of the three cases was the government significantly constrained by internal governmental dynamics from embarking on a dramatic change in trade policy. Democracy itself provided the only real constraint. In one of the three cases, the voters thwarted the government when they had the opportunity to do so, and in another they did not. King never put the question to the voters in 1948, but it is clear from the record that his anticipation of the difficulties the voters would give him if he were to do so played a significant role in his decision to abandon the project. Mulroney was fortunate to have two parties splitting the opposition vote in 1988; the fact that both were generally seen as being to the left of his own party strongly suggests that in a two-party race, Mulroney would have lost. Whether this would have doomed the FTA is an interesting question.

---

[127] John Hilliker, *Canada's Department of External Affairs*, vol. 1.

[128] While foreign affairs and trade policy fall to Ottawa, there are increasingly strong consultation norms in Canadian politics, so that without having a critical mass of provinces in every region on their side, even majority federal governments shy away from dramatic policy changes.

Certainly it would have been difficult for either of the two opposition parties to carry through on an agreement that had Mulroney's fingerprints all over it, and against which they had campaigned so vigorously. But there is an argument to be made that the lack of plausible alternatives to Canada's particular predicament might have brought a Liberal government, at any rate, back to the table. Indeed, once back in office in 1993, the Liberals enthusiastically embraced the Conservatives' free trade agenda.

The relevant thought experiment for assessing what these three cases say about Hypothesis 1 is this: if Canada had been an autocratic state, or even merely a more highly bureaucratic democracy, would we have witnessed a different pattern, all other things being equal? The answer, I believe, is relatively straightforward for the autocracy counterfactual. Laurier appears to have had no doubts whatsoever about the merits of reciprocity in 1911. He consistently dismissed as unfounded all of the fears articulated by opponents of the deal. He evidently had no doubt that it strongly served the national interest. If it had been solely up to him, he would have proceeded. The same can be said of Mulroney in 1988. In these two cases, a change in national policy would have followed as a matter of course from a change in governing party policy. The 1948 case is the one case where it is difficult to be certain one way or the other. King evidently shared some of the fears that opponents to free trade articulated both in 1911 and in 1988. Whether they were more or less important than his fears of electoral defeat is difficult to say, but my impression, based upon his evident suspicions of American motives, his emotional attachment to the British Empire, and his fears for Canadian identity and independence, is that he would have abandoned the project all the same. At any rate, it is difficult to imagine the argument that free trade with the United States would have been anything other than more likely if Canada had been an autocracy in any of the three cases, even if, in one of the three, the government ultimately decided not to proceed of its own accord.

Similarly, it is difficult to imagine the argument that free trade would have been anything other than less likely in all three cases if the Canadian state had been more highly bureaucratic. Opposition both within the government and without would have had greater opportunity to bear on decision making at every stage. Conceivably, the horse-trading and side payments necessary to put together an intragovernmental consensus would have delayed, if not derailed completely, the formulation of coherent negotiating positions, and reduced the scope for agreement by constraining negotiating flexibility. A fairly clear indication of this tendency is the simple fact that Canada has, over the years, experienced far less difficulty than the United States in concluding and ratifying international agreements, precisely because competing interests have had less opportunity to thwart the executive. Certainly asymmetries in bureaucratic constraints go quite some distance in explaining the difference between the focused, organized, energetic Canadian approach to negotiating the FTA, and the distracted, piecemeal, cautious American approach.

All things considered, then, these three cases seem to provide considerable additional support for Hypothesis 1.

What of Hypothesis 2—that, all other things being equal, foreign policy change will be most likely when policy fails either repeatedly or catastrophically, or when leaders become convinced that it will imminently do so? Here the 1948 and 1988 cases provide strong support, while 1911 is in significant respects disconfirming.

Laurier's decision to embrace reciprocity in 1911 did not take place against the backdrop of policy failure. Canada was doing very well. Although Laurier understood himself to be pro–free trade as a matter of principle, and repeatedly said as much, he was, in fact, a defender of the National Policy in practice, and an architect of imperial preferences. He did not understand his policy to be failing Canada at all, let alone repeatedly or catastrophically. Thus Hypothesis 2 does not shed light on Laurier's decision, and the decision does not fit with the expectations of Hypothesis 2, other than, perhaps, in the utterly untestable possibility of being one of the rare unlikely changes that Hypothesis 2 permits by virtue of being stated in terms of likelihood. To the extent that the voters understood that Laurier's policy had *not* been failing repeatedly and catastrophically, however, they refused to embrace his proposed change. This comports with the hypothesis at hand rather better.

In 1947 Canada was in acute difficulty. The status quo was untenable. Without a significant change somewhere, Canada would run out of foreign exchange. Something had to be done. A change in trade policy was not the only available option, but as most of the other attractive options required altruistic action on the part of the U.S. Congress—which seemed unlikely at the time—Canadian leaders looked to trade policy to provide a long-term solution.

The difficulty was not yet acute in the 1980s, but the trends were clear, and the government anticipated that the status quo would shortly prove untenable. In their view, trade policy had to change somehow in order to avoid a future catastrophic failure. Again, bilateral free trade was not the only option available in theory, but decision makers, rightly or wrongly, came to regard it as the best option available in practice.

Taken together, these cases seem to fit with the pattern that Hypothesis 2 would lead us to expect tolerably well. There are, however, interesting tensions between some of these cases and the psychological dynamics undergirding Hypothesis 2. The expectation that foreign policy change will be most likely when policy fails either repeatedly or catastrophically arises from insights in cognitive and motivational psychology, which suggest that people are generally loath to admit that their beliefs and judgments about the world are wrong, to shoulder responsibility for bad news, or to embrace the risks inherent in change. Laurier, in embracing reciprocity, did not experience any psychological discomfort, and Mulroney, by all accounts, embraced free trade remarkably dispassionately.[129] Only King agonized over free trade, and he understood his agony to be situationally induced. His troubles were not his fault. In none of the three cases was the prime minister's embrace of free trade (temporary, in King's case) driven by an acknowledgment of error. This provocatively suggests that the dynamics captured by Hypothesis 2 may be more powerful and more evident in emotionally charged circumstances. I will return to this issue in the conclusion.

Hypothesis 3 states that, all other things being equal, leaders are more likely to pay the inherent costs of (and embrace the inherent risks in) foreign policy change to avoid perceived losses than to realize anticipated gains of equivalent magnitude; as a corollary, only prospects of disproportionate gain are likely to motivate foreign policy change. The 1911 and 1948 cases speak to this hypothesis very straightforwardly. The FTA case is more complex. All three, I believe, provide strong confirmation, but they do so from interestingly different angles.

The 1911 case is the only case we have examined in any domain in which a prospect of gain motivated a significant foreign policy change. Laurier and the Liberals understood the status quo to be completely acceptable and saw the reciprocity agreement as a no-lose proposition. So did most of the rest of the country, on first blush—including Borden, if his first diary entry on the subject is any indication. Those sectors of the Canadian economy clamoring for better access to the American market would get it; most sectors of the Canadian economy nervous about American competition would continue to be shielded from it. While there are no objective metrics for such things, it is clear that subjectively, at any rate, Laurier and the reciprocity enthusiasts understood the potential gains to be very great indeed. The deal offered no mere marginal benefit: it look like a genuine coup. The downside risks seemed negligible. There might be some small dislocation in the meat packing industry, for example, and in one or two

---

[129] Finance Minister Michael Wilson captured the mood well when he later recalled, "Brian Mulroney and I, in the leadership campaign in 1983, had both come out against free trade. So that there was a change of heart on the road to Damascus, but it wasn't a result of a major debate. Rather it was more by osmosis that we came around to thinking that maybe this is something we should try. It was a gradual shift, until we suddenly saw that this is the way we have to go, especially in light of the protectionist pressures." "The Negotiating Process," p. 21.

other sectors, but nothing of consequence in the grand scheme of things. Once the deal was there for the taking, moreover, *not* proceeding with it seemed to pose a serious prospect of loss: Western farmers would react with outrage, aggravating regional tensions, and tearing at the delicate fabric of the still relatively new Canadian confederation.

Both rational choice and prospect theory would predict that someone would choose an option that offered a sure prospect of gain over either the status quo or an option that offered a sure prospect of loss. The present theory suggests that if the prospect of gain were marginal, Laurier would have been insensitive to it. Since he did not understand it as marginal, his choice does not serve as evidence for or against Hypothesis 3 in a simple two-way runoff against a stylized standard rational choice explanation. Laurier's choice, in other words, is less interesting for our purposes than what happened after he made it. The largely successful battle the conservatives waged to reframe the choice as one between an acceptable status quo and a prospect of serious loss eroded support for reciprocity not only among the voters, but also within the Liberal party itself, which split on the issue very publicly.[130] The strongest argument defenders of reciprocity could make was that it offered prospects of economic gain; opponents successfully countered with the argument that it offered prospects of political loss. Borden played on emotionally charged fears of annexation, loss of independence, and danger to the British imperial connection. The best that Laurier could do was to argue that these fears were unfounded. But an essentially cerebral defense of the prospect of economic gain proved ineffective against a visceral fear for the very fate of the country.

The second case is a straightforward example of an initiative and an about-face both driven by fear of loss. The status quo being untenable in 1947, King rather desperately reached for a solution that in the ordinary course of events he almost certainly would have shunned. But once the foreign exchange crisis eased, and once he began to see multilateral possibilities for solving Canada's longer-term trade difficulties, the very same political and emotional fears Borden had played on in 1911 began to take over. In fact, in an interesting illustration of how prior events can shape leaders' understandings of risk, the 1911 precedent, in which potential high-politics losses trumped potential low-politics gains, weighed very heavily on King's mind in the endgame of 1948. He had learned his lesson then, and he did not forget it.

The FTA case is more difficult to relate to Hypothesis 3, because proponents of free trade embraced two discourses: realizing gains *and* avoiding

---

[130] Granatstein and Hillmer, *For Better or for Worse*, p. 49.

losses. This makes it difficult to nail down exactly how key players framed the problem and understood their prospects.

The two-discourse problem has both a rhetorical and a conceptual dimension. The rhetorical dimension quite simply reflects the political advantage to be had from prevailing on all possible battlefields at once. In seeking to persuade an audience to embrace a policy change, it is useful to be able to argue that the change is desirable for many reasons, not just one or a few. Similarly, it is useful to be able to argue that the change will simultaneously generate benefits and avoid costs. In this way, one might persuade both the risk-averse and the risk-acceptant as one simultaneously preempts or defeats counterarguments. While a lucky throw might be able to kill two birds with one stone, a cannon full of grapeshot is much more likely to get the job done. Proponents of free trade fired grapeshot with abandon.

The conceptual problem follows from the fact that when economic measures of welfare are salient, absolute growth can nevertheless appear as loss if the appropriate reference point is a particular *rate* of growth. Indeed, an absolute loss can appear as a gain if the operative reference point is a larger *expected* loss. While proponents of free trade clearly worried about prevailing political and economic trends in the 1980s, they had available to them a number of different reference points in terms of which they could compare the future under free trade against the future without free trade. Clearly persuaded that the Canadian economy would be better off with free trade, they could simultaneously argue that free trade held out prospects of gain, if the relevant comparison were with things such as absolute levels of investment in Canada, export earnings, or productivity without free trade. At the same time, they could argue that free trade held out the prospect of avoiding loss of market share to foreign competitors, loss of export opportunities, or loss of opportunities to attract investment. Canada could *gain* secure access to the U.S. market, or *avoid* arbitrary and costly American trade remedy actions. Both frames were available for the taking at will. Thus, for example, free-trade proponents such as Harry Eastman, Richard Harris, and Ronald Wonnacott could insist that "[t]he arguments in favour of a Canada-U.S. free trade arrangement hinged largely on the *gains* to Canada from improved access to the large US market resulting from lowered US trade barriers under a bilateral agreement," while the Economic Council of Canada argued that it would be very *costly to forgo* such a deal.[131]

While most of the analysis on the basis of which free-trade proponents rested their case freely indulged in both the language of gain and the language of avoiding loss—including, notably, the Macdonald Commission

---

[131] John Whalley with Roderick Hill, *Canada-United States Free Trade*, vol. 11, p. 44; Economic Council of Canada, *Looking Outward*, p. 117 (my emphasis).

report[132]—by all accounts, avoiding loss was the dominant trope. Free trade was attractive to its proponents largely because it would salvage a bad situation, not because it would make a good situation better. Michael Hart and his colleagues captured the sentiment well in their account of the consultations conducted in the wake of Trade Minister Jim Kelleher's options paper:

> The consultations demonstrated widespread dissatisfaction with the status quo: a high level of unemployment, especially among youths, limited optimism about the future, an inadequate investment performance, and few incentives for growth and new employment opportunities. The impatience was expressed despite the fact that Canada had a large merchandise trade surplus with the United States; many Canadian firms had become painfully aware of Canada's vulnerability to US protectionism. At the same time, there was a growing number of firms which were confident of their ability to compete in the larger North American market but felt threatened by the US protectionist surge.[133]

The status quo was unacceptable in large part because it would clearly lead to more protectionism, threatening even Canada's most successful sectors.[134] It was fear, Doern and Tomlin concluded, that led to "a turning point for Canada in its relations with the United States. The U.S. had openly threatened the security of Canadian access to a market on which Canada was overwhelmingly dependent. The implications for employment and investment in Canada were profound."[135]

Negotiating free trade with the United States was, of course, a risky business. Even Donald Macdonald, in endorsing free trade, candidly characterized it as a "leap of faith."[136] As Doern and Tomlin put it, Brian Mulroney "was not a prime minister inclined to take large risks, and free trade carried a substantial potential risk."[137] If the talks failed, the exercise would further damage U.S.-Canadian relations, which he very strongly thought had already deteriorated to an unacceptable level. Indeed, the prospect of undoing what he understood as Trudeau's damage both to U.S.-Canadian relations and to national unity was among the things that attracted him to free trade in the first place.

Even if the talks succeeded, an agreement was sure to prompt a divisive and nasty domestic debate. To minimize the risks, the Mulroney govern-

[132] Donald S. Macdonald, *Report of the Royal Commission on the Economic Union and Development Prospects for Canada.*

[133] Hart, Dymond, and Robertson, *Decision at Midnight*, p. 76.

[134] *Access USA*, pp. 35–36.

[135] Doern and Tomlin, *Faith and Fear*, p. 17. Cf. also White, *Fur Trade to Free Trade*, p. 151.

[136] Doern and Tomlin, *Faith and Fear*, pp. 53–54.

[137] Ibid., p. 9.

ment instructed its negotiators to keep certain things off the table. Social policy was one.[138] Culture was another. "[I]t was understood that unless we took culture out of the agreement there would be no agreement," negotiator Bill Dymond recalled:

> Canadians would be prepared to forego the benefits of an FTA [N.B. the interesting choice of frame] if there were not an exception for Canadian culture. . . . While wheat or softwood lumber disputes are generally confined to their constituencies, cultural issues generate waves of national feeling, which make them especially tricky to handle. We have great difficulty in persuading the United States of these points. The Americans don't get the point that our measures, modest as they are, to defend Canadian cultural industries are the necessary price for Canadian participation in trade agreements.[139]

Doern and Tomlin, whose study is grounded in the best access to decision makers that any scholars have enjoyed, have an interesting and provocative take on the importance of framing to Mulroney's own decision to seek a free-trade deal. It is worth quoting at length:

> For ministers, the central problem facing Canada was security of access to the country's major market. A comprehensive trade agreement with the United States offered an appealing, if politically sensitive, trade policy solution to the problem. Had the problem been defined primarily in terms of an uncompetitive manufacturing sector, however, then it is likely that a proposal for an industrial policy to subject the economy to a sudden cold shower through free trade would have been viewed as a considerably more risky venture. But these hard economic facts were not laid out for the prime minister, because he never received a comprehensive briefing from his senior trade officials on the economics of bilateral free trade. The way the problem was framed for Mulroney helps explain why this otherwise cautious prime minister would take such a leap of faith. As a trade policy, free trade offered the prospect of secure access to the American market. Although it carried some domestic political risk, the prospect of reducing protectionist harassment in Canada's dominant trade market would make the risk worthwhile. As an industrial policy, however, the removal of barriers to trade offers the potential for market gains, but at the risk of potential industry losses. Since the free trade option was framed as a means to avoid the loss of secure market access, it offered a more palatable choice to policy-makers who are naturally averse to taking major risks.[140]

---

[138] Cf. Drover, ed., *Free Trade and Social Policy.*

[139] William A. Dymond, "Cultural Issues," p. 114; Duncan Cornell Card, "Canada-U.S. Free Trade and Canadian Cultural Sovereignty."

[140] Doern and Tomlin, *Faith and Fear,* p. 34.

If this analysis is correct, the fact that Mulroney's advisers framed free trade as offering the prospect of reducing protectionist harassment (avoiding a loss) rather than improving Canadian competitiveness (a gain) made the option appear significantly more attractive.[141]

All things considered, the Conservatives' pursuit of free trade buttresses Hypothesis 3.[142] What, if anything, do we learn from opposition to free trade? Although defenders of the deal dismiss the critics as largely ill-informed (both about the FTA in particular and about trade policy in general), and while they insist that the critics' fears were unfounded, there is little reason to suspect that their fears were insincere. Those who feared free trade in the 1980s feared it for reasons not very different from those who feared it in 1911—or even from King, who came to fear it in 1948. Worries about Canada's social programs, health care system, and environment may have replaced worries about the British tie, which had long since weakened to the point of irrelevance in any case; but the underlying issue—Canada's very existence and character as a political community distinct from that of the United States—was as salient as ever.

Two important differences, however, distinguished the great free-trade debates of 1911 and 1988. First, Laurier tried to persuade Canadians to take a leap of faith when the status quo was perfectly acceptable to the country as a whole. Mulroney's task was much easier. He sought to persuade Canadians to take a leap of faith when the status quo looked grim. Second, relatively few Canadians in the 1980s feared that free trade jeopardized the country's very existence as such. Canada was experiencing hard times and looked to be headed for even harder times, but there was no Champ Clark in 1988, nor had there been for a very long time. Canadians at long last had the self-confidence to trust the Americans with free trade once again.

And so, among the many ironies of Canadian history, it was Brian Mulroney and the Conservatives—the heirs of Sir John A. Macdonald, architect of the National Policy—who finally realized Sir Wilfrid Laurier's dream of reciprocity, boldly embracing truck and trade with the Yankees.

---

[141] Gilbert Winham, in his review of Doern and Tomlin, finds their argument implausible because it suggests that Canada should not have settled for a compromise dispute settlement mechanism. The outcome, Winham suggests, is more consistent with the assumption that improving Canadian competitiveness was a major motivation. Winham, "Faith and Fear." The objection is deductive, however; Doern and Tomlin's account is based on interview data. It is also supported by the recollections of Michael Wilson (n. 129).

[142] American trade policy is not our concern at the moment, but it is worth recalling the important role a sudden prospect of serious loss played in catalyzing fairly frantic American activity to salvage the FTA in September 1987.

Chapter 6

CONCLUSION

> Theories about international relations never account
> for 100 percent of what happens in the world. In fact,
> a good academic theory might account for only about
> half of what goes on in the world.
> —Kenneth Pollack, *The Threatening Storm*

IN THE SPACE REMAINING, I would like to assess the performance of the theory as a whole, reflect upon its strengths and weaknesses, comment on its implications for international relations theory more broadly, and briefly discuss some of its practical implications for policy makers. In so doing, I will, of course, provide additional confirmation for Kenneth Pollack's eminently sensible claim that no international relations theory explains everything. Indeed, I am unaware of any international relations theory that explains even half of what goes on in the world, which may simply lead to the conclusion that there are no good academic theories of international relations. But I would like to suggest that if this is an appropriate benchmark, and if my cases are representative, the theory at hand may well qualify.[1]

In keeping with my contention that the subject matter determines the degree of rigor to which we can aspire, I believe it is most appropriate to seek fairly broad characterizations of the fit between the individual cases and the three hypotheses, and from there attempt to reach a general characterization of the theory's performance. Since the cases are complex, their interpretation inevitably invites a degree of debate that would make a refined scale for goodness-of-fit inherently contentious. Such contention would distract attention from the larger point, which is simply to determine whether the cases, on balance, bear out the expectations of the theory tolerable well. To this end it is satisfactory, I believe, merely to classify them as confirming, disconfirming, or ambiguous/undecidable. Table 6.1 presents my assessments. In making them, I have followed the conservative principle that, when in doubt, I should classify a case as either discon-

---

[1] I make no claims about the representativeness of my cases, of course. Any representativeness would be entirely fortuitous.

TABLE 6.1
Overall Performance

Hypothesis	Disconfirming	Ambiguous/ Undecidable	Confirming
1. State characteristics		• Vietnam 1973	• Falklands/Malvinas • Northern Territories • Vietnam 1965 • Reciprocity 1911 • Free trade 1948 • FTA 1988
2 Perceived failure	• Reciprocity 1911 (executive)	• Northern Territories	• Falklands/Malvinas • Vietnam 1965 • Vietnam 1973 • Reciprocity 1911 (electorate) • Free trade 1948 • FTA 1988
3 Losses vs. gains		• Northern Territories	• Falklands/Malvinas • Vietnam 1965 • Vietnam 1973 • Reciprocity 1911 • Free trade 1948 • FTA 1988

firming or ambiguous, so as not to risk overstating the success of the theory. Let me elaborate upon my classifications here.

Hypothesis 1 holds that foreign policy change should be less frequent in highly bureaucratic states with democratic regimes than in less bureaucratic states with autocratic regimes. Judgments of degree of bureaucratization are at best imprecise and are perhaps best made relatively (there being no clear metric to use, an issue to which I will return). An imperfect proxy is available in the Polity IV Project data set—the XCONST variable—but for both conceptual and interpretive reasons, which I discuss in chapter 2, it must be treated with a grain of salt. The POLITY variable is a widely accepted measure of how democratic or authoritarian a regime is in any given year, though it, too, may occasionally give an inaccurate impression of a government's freedom of maneuver, as our Canadian cases show. Clearly there are limits on how precise we can be in our judgments. But in case comparisons it is possible, by tracing the processes behind foreign policy decisions, or by identifying the forces underwriting foreign policy inertia, to draw conclusions about how state and regime characteristics enabled or constrained change.

In the cases I have presented in this book, we have examples of dramatic changes that happened in part because they *could* happen quite easily, there being insufficient constraints in the mechanics of government to prevent them; an example of a dramatic change that did not happen, arguably because bureaucratic and domestic political constraints were too strong to permit it; and cases where bureaucratic and domestic political constraints thwarted change for long periods of time but ultimately permitted change to occur.

The cases that fall into the first category are the Argentine decision to use force to resolve the sovereignty dispute with Britain over the Falkland/ Malvinas Islands in 1982, and the Canadian embrace of bilateral free trade with the United States in 1988. The Argentine Junta was essentially a free agent in setting Argentine foreign policy. It was answerable to no governmental or domestic constituency. Only *after* the occupation did interservice politics play a role, frustrating the negotiation of a peaceful solution as the British task force bore down upon the hapless Argentine garrison, and this was as a result of the Junta's conscious decision to engage the entire officer corps in negotiations.[2] It is difficult to imagine a clearer example of an autocratic regime free of bureaucratic fetters. The Canadian embrace of the FTA is interestingly different. The Canadian state is clearly more highly bureaucratic than the Argentine state, but dramatically less so than the American or Japanese state. Indeed, Canada is probably the least bureaucratic of G8 countries, and, for its size, among the least bureaucratic of developed Western liberal democracies. Democratic it is, however, and it was a curious feature of Canadian democracy that permitted the successful conclusion of the FTA: namely, the fact that it was at the time a three-party, first-past-the-post system. In contrast to 1911, opposition to the FTA in 1988 was divided between two parties, enabling the governing party favoring free trade to sweep back into office with a majority despite winning only 43 percent of the popular vote. Since it is difficult to argue that Argentina would have been as likely or more likely to resort to force to solve its sovereignty dispute with Britain had a greater number of actors and interests borne on the decision, I have classified the Falklands/Malvinas case as confirming—indeed, I would argue, strongly confirming. As I discuss in chapter 5, all three free-trade cases provide support for Hypothesis 1, but because of the somewhat quirky effects Canadian democracy had on the denouement in all three cases, I am inclined to be more cautious in asserting the strength of the confirmation.

---

[2] The purpose here, of course, was to legitimize the outcome of negotiations, whatever it may be, not to legitimize the process of negotiation itself. It is a safe interpretation that, by doing this, the Junta was maneuvering to spread responsibility for potential failure. Haig, *Caveat*, p. 289; *Times of London*, 5 May 1982, p. 10.

The Northern Territories case is an example of a dramatic change that did not happen, arguably because it could not, partly for bureaucratic and domestic political reasons. Japan was a weak state constrained by powerful domestic norms against dramatic foreign policy change, particularly those involving even a distant potential use of military force, and Japanese leaders were unwilling to entertain options other than energetic lobbying to secure the return of the disputed islands. Thus this case also confirms Hypothesis 1. But it is important to note that Japanese inertia on the Northern Territories issue had many causes, of which state and regime characteristics were only two. Arguably, inertia in this case was overdetermined. A Constructivist analysis of the dispute would point to the important role of norms with deep historical roots in constraining Japanese options. Memories of Japanese militarism and imperialism solidified a regional and domestic "logic of appropriateness" that ruled out not only the kinds of options Argentine leaders found irresistible, but a much milder set of options as well. A Realist analysis would point to Japan's position as a front-line Cold War state under the protection of an American defense umbrella to explain Japan's unwillingness to rock the boat over the Northern Territories issue. There is merit in both of these analyses.

The Vietnam cases largely confirm Hypothesis 1 because they illustrate the "stickiness" of American policy changes once they were made. The Americanization of the war was a significant change, but one that took place only after an agonizingly long period of attempting to muddle through by bolstering Saigon with economic aid, political and diplomatic support, military advice, and matériel. The American political system militated against both earlier Americanization and what Lyndon Johnson liked to characterize derisively as "cutting and running." Once committed, the very same bureaucratic and domestic political forces that had made it hard to abandon an obviously failing policy before 1965 conspired to make it difficult to abandon a new obviously failing policy until 1973. The framers of the U.S. Constitution went out of their way to design a system of government that made dramatic policy changes difficult, and Vietnam suggests that they succeeded. The one confounding feature of the Vietnam cases, from the perspective of Hypothesis 1, is the urgency to effect change that Nixon felt as the 1972 election approached. It is difficult to know whether, in the absence of domestic political or bureaucratic constraints, Nixon would have cut and run earlier, or stuck to his guns even longer. But since it is at least possible that democracy spurred rather than hindered dramatic policy change in this instance, I have scored it ambiguous/undecidable.

While table 6.1 gives the impression that Hypothesis 1 is a resounding success, my own interpretation of the cases is that they collectively suggest

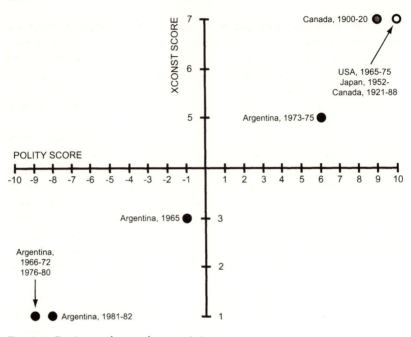

Fig. 6.1. Regime and state characteristics

that it is the least interesting and least valuable element of the theory. In admitting this I do not mean to disavow it: I believe the cases collectively do suggest that the mechanics of government bear on the ease with which leaders can overcome the forces of inertia. It seems fruitful indeed to ask questions about state and regime characteristics when attempting to gauge the likelihood of dramatic foreign policy change. But the bodies of theory inspiring Hypothesis 1 are more important and more interesting as parts of an explanation of the inertia itself than of deviations from it. The second and third hypotheses provide handles for explaining the deviations; the first does not. Moreover, we are not in a good position to draw the kinds of strong conclusions about likelihood that we would ideally like to be able to draw if we were to pass the kind of judgment on Hypothesis 1 that we would ideally like to pass. In the first place, my cases provide very limited variation on the dimensions of interest to us. As figure 6.1 illustrates, most of the cases cluster in the high democracy/ high executive constraint quadrant, and even if we were to score Canada as less bureaucratic than either Japan or the United States, as a nuanced understanding of the political systems in all three countries would suggest is appropriate, we would still have but one autocratic case to consider (Argentina). Third, while the cases allow us to make judgments of the "ease" or "difficulty" a government experienced in effecting foreign policy change, as long as we allow relying upon counterfactual thought experiment to do so, these are imperfect proxies for the concept of frequency in terms of which the hypothesis is stated. In other words, by clustering so many of the cases in the "confirming" column in table 6.1, I do not mean to suggest that it is in Hypothesis 1 that we find the theory's main value added. Quite the contrary.

Hypothesis 2 states that foreign policy change will be most likely when policy fails either repeatedly or catastrophically, or when leaders become convinced that it will imminently do so. It is grounded in insights from cognitive and motivational psychology suggesting that people resist admitting error, taking responsibility for disaster, or risking change in the face of uncertainty. Great pain, experienced or expected, is required to overcome psychologically reinforced inertia. Five of our cases provide confirmation, one is ambiguous or undecidable, and one requires special treatment.

The Falklands/Malvinas case provides strong support because the Argentine Junta clearly drew the conclusion that the diplomatic route had failed repeatedly, would continue to fail repeatedly, and that this failure was, and would continue to be, absolutely intolerable. Their sense of urgency was particular heightened by what they perceived as a crucial looming liminal date (the sesquicentennial of the British occupation), and by their perception of a limited window of opportunity. The two Vietnam cases also dramatically illustrate the importance of a long record of failure in motivating policy change. Faced with undeniable evidence that things were going from bad to worse, LBJ in 1965 opted for what he understood to be the least bad of a generally bad set of alternatives. Convinced that the war could not be won and that it was costing America dearly, Richard Nixon ultimately cut and ran. The painful experience of a disastrous balance of payments crisis pushed a desperate Mackenzie King into contemplating what otherwise might have been unthinkable—bilateral free trade with the United States—and the sudden easing of the crisis, combined with the twin prospects of new alternatives to solve Canada's economic woes and a potential replay of Laurier's 1911 disaster, pushed him away again. The Mulroney government's great fear that Canadian uncompetitiveness and capricious American trade actions would lead to economic disaster in the 1980s drove the quest for a free-trade deal.

The Northern Territories case is ambiguous. On the one hand, there is no question that Japanese leaders, and indeed the Japanese citizenry, understand current policy on the issue as ineffective. From the perspective of Hypothesis 2, it is therefore surprising that there is, and was, essentially no interest in policy change. This lack of interest can be explained in various ways, the most important of which I have just referred to above. Nonetheless, it seems that this is a case where the theory would predict at least the exploration of significant policy change, and we simply do not see it. On the other hand, while Japanese policy on the Northern Territories is, and always has been, an obvious failure—and is generally recognized as such—it is, curiously, not generally seen as catastrophic, and there is no popular or elite sense of looming disaster. This is rather more consistent with the expectations of Hypothesis 2.

The 1911 case is the one that requires special treatment. Here we have, in effect, two separable decisions: Laurier's decision to pursue reciprocity, and the Canadian electorate's decision not to ratify it. Laurier's decision is disconfirming because we see a dramatic policy change in the absence of any perception of failure whatsoever. The electorate's decision to reject Laurier and reciprocity, in contrast, is broadly confirming. The Canadian people agreed with Laurier that times were good and that current policy was working well. Hypothesis 2 in effect predicts the attitude, "If it ain't broke, don't fix it."

Thus Hypothesis 2 fares quite well overall. However, it is worth recalling that not all of the confirming cases give strong evidence of the often potent psychological dynamics that undergird it. Only in the cases involving the actual use of force and the 1948 free-trade case do we see decision makers experiencing the full psychological pain of confronting ongoing or imminent disaster. This suggests that Hypothesis 2 may in fact be of more use in explaining and helping us anticipate dramatic foreign policy changes in the security domain, or with respect to issues that touch hot-button high-political issues. These are the issues that tend to confront decision makers more directly and more suddenly with painful choices—choices involving significant stakes and significant potential payoffs or costs—that engage emotions at least as profoundly as they engage the intellect. In large part, the trade cases did not do this. When they did—when decision makers began to see trade policy as touching fundamental questions of autonomy or political identity—they engaged emotions that bore on their deliberations in precisely the way Hypothesis 2 suggested they should. It may be, then, that high-politics and low-politics cases have different sensitivity thresholds that Hypothesis 2 as currently stated does not recognize and cannot accommodate. Further study would be required to determine whether this is so, and whether refinements are in order.

My own reading of the cases is that they collectively suggest Hypothesis 3 is the most interesting and the most important. Hypothesis 3 states that, all other things being equal, leaders are more likely to pay the inherent costs of (and embrace the inherent risks in) foreign policy change to avoid losses than to realize gains of equivalent magnitude; as a corollary, only prospects of disproportionate gain are likely to motivate foreign policy change. As such, it both speaks to the expectation of inertia and provides an explanation for sudden departures. Here we have six confirming cases, and one case that does not clearly confirm or disconfirm. There are no disconfirming cases.

It is important to recall that while Hypothesis 3 is inspired by prospect theory's insights into risk-taking propensities, it is not, in fact, a derivation from, or strict application of, prospect theory. The "prospects" leaders faced in all of our cases were subjective judgments—typically impressionistic ones—of likely gains or losses from a subjectively identified reference point defining an acceptable state of affairs. They were not objectively knowable prospects to which we could assign meaningful numbers. For this reason, none of the cases in this book represent "tests" of prospect theory in any interesting sense. They do, however, collectively illustrate the soundness of prospect theory's key insight that people evaluate their options in terms of gains and losses from some reference point or other, and prospect theory's general claim that people will more readily take risks to avoid losses than to secure gains.

The Falklands/Malvinas case nicely illustrates risk-acceptance on the part of Argentine leaders, although, interestingly, what we know about their deliberations suggests that they grossly underestimated the risks they were taking, perhaps as a result of wishful thinking, or simply because of their parochial worldview, which made it difficult for them to anticipate others' reactions to their resort to force. But they did understand their actions as a gamble, and they felt the game well worth the candle precisely because they were operating so deeply in a loss frame. Avoiding, stanching, or recouping loss was the dominant trope in deliberations in both Vietnam cases, and in the latter two free trade cases. Indeed, we find the language of "potential gain" only in the 1911 reciprocity case and in the 1988 FTA case, and in the latter we find it primarily in the presentation of the public case for free trade, which freely employed the grapeshot strategy of trying to sell something in all conceivable ways at once. In the two Vietnam cases and the latter two trade cases, decision makers chose what they understood as risky courses of action to try to turn an unacceptable status quo into an acceptable one, as Hypothesis 3 would lead us to expect.

The 1911 case is worth particular attention here because it is the only case I have examined in which a decision maker opted for a significant policy change because of a prospect of gain. Since the hypothesis does not rule out significant policy choice in pursuit of gain—it merely predicts aysmmetric insensitivity to marginal prospects of gain—Laurier's perception that reciprocity offered the prospect of a genuine coup clears the hurdle.[3] Hypothesis 3 also renders intelligible the Canadian electorate's unwillingness to endorse Laurier's judgment. The Conservatives suc-

---

[3] As I argued in the previous chapter, however, this is an example of a case where both Hypothesis 3 and a stylized version of rational choice theory would predict the same behavior.

ceeded in reframing reciprocity as offering prospects of serious political loss. The voters simply did not see the benefit of altering the status quo, except with respect to which party would form the next government.

The Northern Territories case does not appear to confirm Hypothesis 3 on first glance, because, while clearly operating in a subjective loss frame, Japanese leaders have taken relatively few risks. During the peak of excitement at the prospect of recovering the islands in the early 1990s, Japanese leaders did squander political capital and irritate other important countries (most notably, Russia and the United States) in their zealous quest for a resolution, but they never abandoned diplomacy, and they never explored, let alone embraced, even mild coercion. Indeed, we might hold that the case is disconfirming. But two considerations suggest that the most appropriate classification here would be that the fit is undecidable. First, while the Japanese were (and are) clearly operating in a loss frame on this issue, it never had the acute urgency that the Falklands/Malvinas had for the Argentine Junta in 1982. The loss is one the Japanese have borne unhappily but fairly stoically for more than fifty years, and there is no perception that, unless soon redeemed, the prize will be forever beyond reach. The absence of a liminal event, in other words, makes biding one's time with an acknowledged ineffective policy tolerable, in the light of the absence of good alternatives, in a way that it might not otherwise be. In comparison to the subjective perceptions of Argentine leaders, Japanese leaders have not felt the loss of *their* useless islands quite so painfully. Second, Hypothesis 1 helps us understand why, even with a comparable perception of the intolerableness of the status quo, Argentine leaders would have more readily run the risks of a dramatic policy change. Taken together, and using the hypothetical probability curves from figure 2.2 as our heuristic (modified and rechristened as figure 6.2), we can see how, in fact, *both* cases might confirm Hypothesis 3. But since the Falklands/ Malvinas case is the clearer of the two, and since there is greater scope for debate about the proper interpretation of the Northern Territories case, it is safer to score the former confirming and the latter ambiguous.

On the whole, then, the theory performs rather well. Most of the cases are confirming in most relevant respects. They vindicate the expectation of inertia, illustrate the punctuated equilibrium of foreign policy, and demonstrate that these tendencies are rendered intelligible by a combination of organizational and psychological considerations. The third hypothesis appears to have the most "bang for the buck," and the first the least, but each contributes something of value to our understanding of the patterns we observe.

Having said as much, however, I would like to emphasize certain gaps the cases point up in the theory and highlight as well some of the limits on its rigor, precision, and practical applicability. As I have touched upon

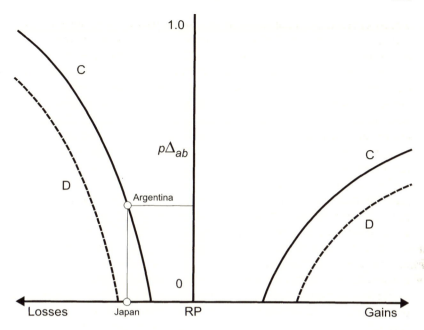

Fig. 6.2. Hypothetical probability curves

all these subjects *en passant,* I do not believe it is necessary to belabor them, but I do wish to paint them in fairly stark colors here, as it is important to appreciate them when attempting to form realistic expectations about the scientific approach to international relations, and about the usefulness of general IR theory to policy makers.

To begin with the gaps, it is plain that the theory exogenizes a number of things that ideally one would like to be able to bring under the theoretical tent. Leaders' particular conceptions of interest (or preferences, if one prefers that representation); their subjective identification of reference points; the frames they adopt for describing the status quo with respect to their operative reference points—all of these have to be brought to the theory, and none of them can be found in the theory itself. Obviously, this raises the information requirements for making use of the theory and poses a challenge to operationalization. Elsewhere, my colleague Masato Kimura and I have argued that this is unavoidable: these various things are simply not amenable to assumption or generalization.[4] Nevertheless, it is a gap, and it is the kind of gap that prevents this *general* theory from being a *comprehensive* one.

[4] Kimura and Welch, "Specifying 'Interests.' "

Second, the particular perceptions, attributions, and judgments that play crucial roles in leaders' deliberations are not themselves captured by the theory, although in limited ways some of the general patterns and processes behind them help undergird the expectation of inertia. In both the Falklands/Malvinas case and the Vietnam cases, for example, we found that the particular historical analogies leaders invoked to help them make sense of the otherwise ambiguous and uncertain situations they faced had an important effect on the choices they made (Suez and Rhodesia in the case of the Malvinas, for example, and Korea and Munich in the case of Vietnam). To some extent the selection of these analogies in particular was arbitrary; others were available that might have led to quite radically different judgments. Arguably, crucial decisions in all of the cases exhibited path dependencies and conscious reactions to earlier episodes of interaction. None of these is part of the theory, which is stated in fairly formal, abstract terms. Bringing them into the analysis when attempting to make use of the theory is vital and unavoidable, but, again, raises the information requirements and poses operational challenges.

Third, a particularly powerful datum, I would argue, is the salience of liminal events, which affect leaders' senses of urgency and shape their timetables for action. While this consideration orbits the theory, it is not part of the formal specification of any of the hypotheses, and I do not see how it might be made so. Again, it is part of the set of exogenous data one needs to bring to the theory to help it perform.

Finally, the logic of the theory is, one might say, somewhat economistic, mechanistic, and utilitarian. It attempts to provide handles on the likelihood of dramatic policy change that may be articulated in the language of gains, losses, costs, benefits, successes, failures, constraints, and opportunities. An alternative theory might seek to exploit a more sociological or semiotic logic, providing handles on the likelihood of dramatic policy change that may be articulated in the language of norms, intersubjective meanings, symbols, grammars, and logics of appropriateness.[5] Indeed, I suggested in chapter 3 that these considerations may well have played an important role in explaining Japanese passivity in contrast to Argentine activity in their respective territorial disputes. This at least raises the possibility that an alternative theory of foreign policy change with roots more firmly in the Constructivist camp might, in fact, perform even better than the theory at hand.

So much for gaps. What about other limitations, both conceptual and practical?

---

[5] Particularly suggestive to my mind in this respect, although they do not themselves have exactly this objective in mind, are Jennifer Milliken, *The Social Construction of the Korean War*; and Wendt, *Social Theory of International Politics*.

An obvious place to begin here is by noting the problem of metrics. I have articulated the theory in terms of "long" periods of inertia, perceptions of "significant" losses or gains, "relatively" bureaucratic regimes, and so forth. Indeed, what some might be tempted to call the theory's "dependent variable"—the likelihood of significant foreign policy change—is not, strictly speaking, measurable on either of its two crucial dimensions: likelihood, or significance. Without meaningful, objective metrics, it is not possible to formalize or test the theory in the most scientifically desirable way. How serious a limitation is this? Is it debilitating?

I believe it is important to concede that this is a serious limitation that must, at the end of the day, incline us to be cautious about exactly what we can claim for this theory in particular, and for explanatory/anticipatory IR theory in general. But there are two reasons why I do not believe it to be debilitating. First, the problem of objective metrics is a general problem that plagues IR theory at every turn, and unless we are willing to give up on the entire enterprise as insupportable for this particular reason, it does not count more heavily against the theory at hand than it does against any other theory. Even theories given formal mathematical representation and tested quantitatively commonly have metrics problems. Theories about alliances, arms races, wars, institutions, regimes, and cooperation all depend upon treating as reliable things about which one cannot really be perfectly confident. How do we know what a balance of power really is?[6] Do numbers of weapons systems ever really accurately reflect military capabilities? Can we ever meaningfully attach a number to the "democraticness" of democracies? Imprecision is part of the background radiation of International Relations. We simply do the best we can to cope with it, and we attempt to be realistic about our expectations of what we can achieve in light of it.

Of course, the metrics problem may debilitate this particular theory even if it does not debilitate others. Fortunately, the theory at hand actually relies upon judgments of relative degree or magnitude, not absolute ones, and for this the metrics problem is far less serious. Many of the relevant judgments are subjective—leaders' own assessments, in other words, not the analyst's—and those are available to us, quite reliably, in the form of self-reports accessible through careful historical investigation. A "significant" period of policy stability, or what I characterize as inertia, is simply one that is longer than a fully informed, unconstrained, rational actor would choose. A "significant" foreign policy change is one that

[6] The most ingenious attempts at quantifying power of which I am aware—Ray Cline's—have obvious metric problems in addition to conceptual ones. Ray S. Cline, *World Power Assessment 1977*; Cline, *World Power Assessment*; Cline, *World Power Trends and U.S. Foreign Policy for the 1980s.*

leaders' themselves understand as a radical break from the past, rather than as a tinkering or incremental adjustment. A painful loss, or a significant cost, is simply one that leaders obviously care about, and stands in contrast to minor losses, or minor costs, readily expressed in the language of annoyances or irritations. A highly bureaucratic state is visible as highly bureaucratic when seen in relief against a simpler one. When relative judgments do the heavy lifting, the absence of meaningful cardinal measures becomes tractable. It still represents a constraint, but not a debilitating one.

The complement to metric is measurement, and so the metrics problem leads naturally to the question of how confident we can be in the reliability of the particular judgments we must make to assess and exploit the theory. If no two analysts would reach similar judgments, then the interpretation of cases would become idiosyncratic and the theory-building exercise pointless. The so-called intercoder reliability problem is one that has always plagued case study research in political science, and it has also plagued, in a less obvious way, historical research through the ages, where interpretations and judgments sometimes strike readers as unacceptably impressionistic. Again, I believe it is important to concede that there is a real limitation here. My case studies, without question, are my interpretations of the evidence, and the question of whether they are the best possible interpretations is one that probably cannot be answered definitively in the affirmative. They are not, for the most part, idiosyncratic; I have freely reached out broadly to others with acknowledged expertise. But at the end of the day my interpretations, to the extent that they are mainstream, will inevitably reflect the biases and errors of the mainstream, and to the extent that they are iconoclastic, will inevitably reflect my own biases and errors. We can never be perfectly confident that we have rid ourselves of bias and error—and, of course (this goes without saying), even if we were immune to bias and error, we almost never have exactly the kind of information we would need to have perfect confidence in our interpretations. Although this, too, is part of the background radiation of uncertainty, it is neither more nor less debilitating in this particular case than it is with respect to any other work in social science, and I am content to allow my presentations of the cases stand or fall on their merits.

During the behavioral revolution there were those who had high expectations for IR theory, and who saw in the natural sciences the model for political science to emulate. Those expectations were unrealistic. We do not enjoy the luxury of the precision available to natural scientists, nor the luxury of the passive tractability of their subject matter. (Arguably, natural science itself never enjoyed these luxuries to the extent that natural scientists hoped.) We must acknowledge the important differences between the natural world and the social world, and the more significant obstacles social scientists face. But despite those obstacles, and notwithstanding the rather more significant limitations and constraints, I believe the fairly impressive performance of the theory at hand does indeed vindicate the quest for general, portable IR theory. There is indeed a benefit to asking whether there is anything we can say about international politics in general, and in looking for tools that we can bring to the analysis of a general set of problems with a hopeful expectation that those tools will prove useful. Our frustration with past attempts should not lead us to abandon the enterprise wholesale: the key, quite simply, was to look for the general patterns not in what states *sought*, or in what they *did*, but in *the conditions under which they were likely to do something different*, and in *how they decided*, whatever it was they sought. If table 6.1 is a reliable indicator, there is reason indeed to hope that there are "good academic theories" that can account for at least half of what goes on in the world.

Finally, what are the practical implications of the theory? In and of itself, this is a potentially large subject, and my discussion throughout the book speaks to it fairly straightforwardly in any case, so I will confine myself to relatively brief, suggestive closing remarks, rather than attempt to be exhaustive. I believe it will be useful to distinguish implications for intelligence analysts from implications for negotiators. My remarks on the former head will be of greater utility in the security domain, as they bear principally on strategic warning.[7] My remarks on the latter head bear principally on assessing ripeness and resistance points, which are applicable to international negotiation in any domain.[8]

The theory predicts that dramatic policy change will be rare and will be more likely the result of perceived losses—ongoing or prospective—than perceived opportunities for gain. As I explained in chapter 2, its scope conditions exclude opportunists, adventurers, risk-seekers, megalomaniacs, or madmen. It is a theory about run-of-the-mill decision makers, who make up the vast majority. (This is the one significant constraint on the generality of the theory; it is an *almost-general* theory for this particular reason.) The first task an intelligence analyst must discharge when attempting to harness the insights of the theory to anticipate a

---

[7] The literature on strategic warning is curiously limited, but particularly important works include Richard K. Betts, "Surprise Despite Warning"; Lebow, "Deterrence and Threat Assessment"; Leonard S. Spector, "Strategic Warning and New Nuclear States"; Roberta Wohlstetter, *Pearl Harbor*. My colleague James Blight and I reflect somewhat more deeply on the subject than is possible here, with particular attention to the case of the Cuban missile crisis, in "The Cuban Missile Crisis and Intelligence Performance."

[8] The literature on ripeness is more extensive. See, inter alia, Diane B. Bendahmane and John W. McDonald, eds., *Perspectives on Negotiation*; Conflict Research Consortium, University of Colorado, "Good Timing"; Christopher R Mitchell, "Cutting Losses"; I. William Zartman and Maureen R. Berman, *The Practical Negotiator*.

dramatic change is to determine whether the target is a target of the appropriate kind. Intelligence services regularly profile foreign leaders and attempt to assess their basic personality traits. The theory is ill-suited to anticipating the behavior of a Hitler, for whom one must work with rather different indicators. Indeed, the actions of a decision maker such as this are likely to be especially difficult to anticipate precisely because, as a risk-seeking opportunist interested in radically overthrowing the existing order, he or she would be especially keen not to telegraph intentions.

A run-of-the-mill decision maker may well also be interested in avoiding telegraphing intentions, particularly if he or she becomes convinced that a radical change in policy is required, unavoidable, and will be resisted. From deception and surprise flow obvious strategic advantages. Nevertheless, a run-of-the-mill decision maker, in contrast to a Hitler, should not be expected to have settled on a bold stroke as an appropriate démarche early in the game. Inclined toward inertia in the first place, such a decision maker will normally signal dissatisfaction, deliberately or inadvertently, in an attempt to redeem a perceived difficulty through diplomacy or some other relatively low-cost modality. Thus Argentine leaders stuck with diplomacy to resolve their territorial dispute with Britain for decades before finally entertaining the option of military force seriously. Saddam Hussein badgered and cajoled Kuwaiti leaders for months in an attempt to get them to write off his debts from the Iran-Iraq War, to cede the islands of Warba and Bubiyan in the Shatt al-'Arab waterway, and to stop pumping oil from the Ramallah oil field straddling the border. During these extended periods, Argentine and Iraqi leaders, as well as their spokesmen, quite clearly articulated their grievances in fairly strident terms. Both spoke of their limited patience, and both evinced a crescendo of desperation.[9] In both cases, intelligence analysts appear to have missed the significance of the stridency and desperation because of mirror-imaging and their confidence in deterrence. British analysts felt certain that Argentina would not resort to force because they assumed Argentine leaders saw the world as they did and would appreciate just how intolerable acquiescence in such a move would be. Unable to empathize with the Junta, British analysts assumed the bluster was tactical rather than sincere. Western analysts drew similar conclusions about Saddam in 1990, for essentially similar reasons.

---

[9] In Saddam's case, the articulation of grievances against Kuwait reflected an increasingly obvious paranoia. Indeed, it seems that his claims on Kuwait had a great deal to do with his mounting fear of the United States and Israel. I discuss details with respect to the Argentine case in chapter 3. For the Iraqi case, see, e.g., Pollack, *The Threatening Storm*, pp. 26–36; Stein, "Deterrence and Compellence in the Gulf, 1990–91."

What clues would the present theory suggest an analyst should look for in order to assess the likelihood of a resort to arms? The following questions provide some operational guidance:

1. Do leaders in the target state describe their concerns in the language of need (in contrast to desire)?

2. Do they freely employ the language of ongoing or prospective loss (in contrast to the language of prospective gain)?

3. Do they describe the status quo as intolerable or unacceptable (in contrast to merely disadvantageous)?

4. Do they evince stridency, desperation, or limited patience?

5. Do they speak of a forthcoming liminal event? In particular, do they characterize it as a deadline for the satisfaction of their grievances?

6. Are their demands categorical?

7. Do probes for compromise, partial satisfaction of their grievances, or side-payments elicit anger (as opposed to interest)?

8. Are they relatively free agents, or are they operating under severe bureaucratic and/or domestic political constraints?

Questions such as these help analysts reconstruct targets' subjective viewpoints, and in particular help identify reference points and operative frames (gains/losses). They encourage attempts at genuine empathy and discipline dismissals grounded in deductions from abstract heuristics (such as rational deterrence theory) that invite, rather than combat, mirror-imaging problems. They also help analysts gauge the ease with which leaders will be able to move boldly should they choose to do so.

Intelligence analysts always face the difficulty of distinguishing sincere from insincere claims and representations, of course, and no theory will provide a magic bullet. But the long history of intelligence failure suggests that discrediting sincerity is more commonly a source of error than crediting insincerity, and that self-conscious attempts to cultivate empathy—and in particular to reconstruct others' perspectives on international disputes—result in more accurate and more useful assessments than deductions from first principles. To the extent that the present theory encourages such attempts in addition to offering general, portable insights into behavioral tendencies, it would seem to make two potentially important contributions to strategic warning simultaneously.

The present theory does not add to negotiation theory so much as reaffirm what negotiation theorists have known for quite some time: namely, that if one wishes to know whether the time is ripe for a negotiated settlement, and if one wishes to conclude the most advantageous settlement possible, it is useful to be able to reconstruct the other party's viewpoint in detail, and it is particularly useful to be able to know when the other party is very highly motivated to deal.[10] An ongoing or imminent painful loss certainly provides motivation to negotiate. It may also spur another party to accept terms somewhat less advantageous than he or she would accept if the status quo were somewhat better, or indeed perfectly acceptable. Put another way, an ongoing or imminent painful loss might shift his or her "resistance point" defining the worst acceptable deal.[11] The same kinds of questions that could helpfully prime an intelligence analyst working on problems of strategic warning can help negotiators assess the prospects for negotiation.

The asymmetry of the loss and gains frames, coupled with the evident importance of the outcome of a battle over which frame to adopt (as the trade cases in the previous chapter nicely illustrate), suggest that negotiators should be particularly concerned to try to frame possible deals in the way most likely to secure agreement. Good negotiators, in other words, are often talented framers.[12] Again, this is not a new insight for negotiation theory, which long ago assimilated the most significant insights from the very same bodies of theory informing and inspiring my explorations in this book.

Indeed, it is perhaps the practical successes these bodies of theory have enjoyed in the field of negotiation and mediation that provide the best possible argument for attempting to bring their insights to bear on the general problem of foreign policy change. Notwithstanding the constraints and limitations inherent in the enterprise, I see no reason why the art of statecraft cannot benefit from the science of international politics, and I hope my exploration in this book will encourage us to reconsider the growing skepticism about that very project within the field. That skepticism, I suggested at the beginning of the book, was a reaction to frustration about the quest for general theories of state *behavior*. With respect to that particular quest, the skepticism is well founded. But while explaining and anticipating state behavior is an intractable problem, for very good reasons, it is also, at the end of the day, an unimportant one. We do not need to explain and anticipate state behavior. We need only explain and anticipate the deviations. Sometimes the best antidote to skepticism is simply to ask a slightly different question.

---

[10] Zartman and Berman, *The Practical Negotiator*, pp. 66–78.

[11] For relevant discussion with respect to international negotiation, see., e.g., Gordon Alexander Craig and Alexander L. George, *Force and Statecraft*, pp. 163–178.

[12] Welch, *Decisions, Decisions*, pp. 138–141.

WORKS CITED

"A Gentle Breeze of Change Blows through Japanese Defence," *Jane's Defence Weekly*, 15 July 1995, pp. 20–21.

Access USA: Setting the Agenda for Negotiating a New Trade Pact, Financial Post Conferences in Association with Air Canada, the Prince Hotel, Toronto, Thursday, April 25, 1985 (Toronto: Financial Post, 1985).

Achen, Christopher, and Duncan Snidal. "Rational Deterrence Theory and Comparative Case Analysis," *World Politics*, vol. 41, no. 2 (January 1989), pp. 143–169.

Adler, Emanuel, and Michael Barnett. *Security Communities* (Cambridge: Cambridge University Press, 1998).

Adler, Emanuel, and Peter M. Haas. "Conclusion: Epistemic Comunities, World Order and the Creation of a Reflective Research Program," *International Organization*, vol. 46, no. 1 (Winter 1992), pp. 367–390.

Akaha, Tsuneo, and Takashi Murakami. "Soviet/Russian-Japanese Economic Relations," in *Russia and Japan: An Unresolved Dilemma between Distant Neighbors*, ed. Tsuyoshi Hasegawa, Jonathan Haslam, and Andrew C. Kuchins (Berkeley: University of California Press, 1993), pp. 161–186.

Allison, Graham T. *Essence of Decision: Explaining the Cuban Missile Crisis* (Boston: Little, Brown, 1971).

"Alternatively, Harakiri," *Economist*, 4 July 1992, pp. 33–34.

Ambrose, Stephen E. *Nixon* (New York: Simon & Schuster, 1987).

Anaya, Jorge I. "Malvinas: La Guerra Justa," *Boletin del Centro Naval*, vol. 110, no. 766 (April 1992), pp. 252–293.

Anderson, Craig A. "Abstract and Concrete Data in the Perseverance of Social Theories: When Weak Data Lead to Unshakable Beliefs," *Journal of Experimental Social Psychology*, vol. 19, no. 2 (March 1983), pp. 93–108.

Anderson, Craig A., Mark R. Lepper, and Lee Ross. "Perseverance of Social Theories: The Role of Explanation in the Persistence of Discredited Information," *Journal of Personality and Social Psychology*, vol. 39, no. 6 (November 1980), pp. 1037–1049.

Archer, Jules. *Ho Chi Minh: Legend of Hanoi* (New York: Crowell-Collier, 1971).

Arrow, Kenneth J. *The Limits of Organization* (New York: Norton, 1974).

Axelrod, Robert M. *The Evolution of Cooperation* (New York: Basic Books, 1984).

Axelrod, Robert, and Robert Keohane. "Achieving Cooperation under Anarchy: Strategies and Institutions," *World Politics*, vol. 38, no. 1 (October 1985), pp. 226–254.

Bajanov, Evgueni. "Assessing the Politics of the Korean War, 1949–51," *Cold War International History Project Bulletin*, no. 6–7 (Winter 1995/1996), pp. 54, 87–91.

Baldwin, David A., ed. *Neorealism and Neoliberalism: The Contemporary Debate* (New York: Columbia University Press, 1993).

Ball, George W. *The Past Has Another Pattern: Memoirs* (New York: Norton, 1982).

———. "Top Secret: The Prophecy the President Rejected," *Atlantic Monthly*, January 1972, pp. 36–49.

Balthazar, Louis. "Les Relations Canado-Américains," in *De Mackenzie King à Pierre Trudeau: Quarante Ans de Diplomatie Canadienne, 1945–1985*, ed. Paul Painchaud (Québec: Les Presses de l'Université Laval, 1989), pp. 251–274.

Barlow, Maude. *Parcel of Rogues: How Free Trade Is Failing Canada* (Toronto: Key Porter Books, 1990).

Beaulieu, Eugene, and J. C. Herbert Emery. "Pork Packers, Reciprocity, and Laurier's Defeat in the 1911 Canadian General Election," *Journal of Economic History*, vol. 61, no. 4 (December 2001), pp. 1083–1101.

Beck, Peter. *The Falkland Islands as an International Problem* (London: Routledge, 1988).

Bell, Nancy E. "Negotiating on Precedent: An Analysis of the Nexus between Auto Pact Success and FTA Implementation," *International Studies Notes*, vol. 23, no. 2 (Spring 1998), pp. 17–28.

Bellah, Robert N. "Legitimation Processes in Politics and Religion," *Current Sociology*, vol. 35, no. 1 (Summer 1987), pp. 89–99.

Bendahmane, Diane B., and John W. McDonald, eds. *Perspectives on Negotiation: Four Case Studies and Interpretations* (Washington, DC: Center for the Study of Foreign Affairs, 1986).

Berger, Thomas U. "From Sword to Chrysanthemum: Japan's Culture of Anti-Militarism," *International Security*, vol. 17, no. 4 (Spring 1993), pp. 119–150.

Berman, Larry. *Planning a Tragedy: The Americanization of the War in Vietnam* (New York: Norton, 1982).

Bernstein, Steven F. *The Compromise of Liberal Environmentalism* (New York: Columbia University Press, 2001).

Bernstein, Steven, et al. "God Gave Physics the Easy Problems: Adapting Social Science to an Unpredictable World," *European Journal of International Relations*, vol. 6, no. 1 (March 2000), pp. 43–76.

Berti, Anna Emilia. "The Development of Political Understanding in Children between 6–15 Years Old," *Human Relations*, vol. 41, no. 6 (June 1988), pp. 437–446.

Berton, Pierre. *The National Dream: The Great Railway, 1871–1881* (Toronto: McClelland and Stewart, 1970).

———. *The National Dream: The Last Spike* (Toronto: McClelland and Stewart, 1974).

Beschloss, Michael R. *Taking Charge: The Johnson White House Tapes, 1963–1964* (New York: Simon & Schuster, 1997).

Betts, Richard K. "Surprise Despite Warning: Why Sudden Attacks Succeed," *Political Science Quarterly*, vol. 95, no. 4 (Winter 1980–81), pp. 551–572.

Bird, Kai. *The Color of Truth: McGeorge Bundy and William Bundy: Brothers in Arms* (New York: Simon & Schuster, 1998).

Black, Duncan. *Voting in Committees and Elections* (Cambridge: Cambridge University Press, 1958).

Blainey, Geoffrey. *The Causes of War* (New York: Free Press, 1973).

Blight, James G. "Red, White and Blue Blood," *Washington Post Book World*, 1 November 1998, pp. 1, 11.

———. *The Shattered Crystal Ball: Fear and Learning in the Cuban Missile Crisis* (Savage, MD: Rowman & Littlefield, 1990).

Blight, James G., Bruce J. Allyn, and David A. Welch. *Cuba on the Brink: Castro, the Missile Crisis, and the Soviet Collapse* (New York: Pantheon, 1993).

Blight, James G., and David A. Welch. "The Cuban Missile Crisis and Intelligence Performance," in *Intelligence and the Cuban Missile Crisis*, ed. James G. Blight and David A. Welch (London: Frank Cass, 1998), pp. 173–217.

———, eds. *Intelligence and the Cuban Missile Crisis* (London: Frank Cass, 1998).

———. *On the Brink: Americans and Soviets Reexamine the Cuban Missile Crisis*, 2nd ed. (New York: Noonday, 1990).

Blyth, Mark. "Structures Do Not Come with an Instruction Sheet: Interests, Ideas, and Progress in Political Science," *Perspectives on Politics*, vol. 1, no. 4 (December 2003), pp. 695–706.

Boettcher, William A., III. "Context, Methods, Numbers, and Words: Prospect Theory in International Relations," *Journal of Conflict Resolution*, vol. 39, no. 3 (September 1995), pp. 561–583.

———. "The Prospects for Prospect Theory: An Empirical Evaluation of International Relations Applications of Framing and Loss Aversion," *Political Psychology*, vol. 25, no. 3 (June 2004), pp. 331–362.

Booth, Ken. "Security and Emancipation," *Review of International Studies*, vol. 17, no. 4 (October 1991), pp. 313–326.

"Boris, about Our Islands," *Economist*, 31 August 1991, pp. 30–31.

Bothwell, Robert, and John English. "Canadian Trade Policy in the Age of American Dominance and British Decline, 1943–1947," *Canadian Review of American Studies*, vol. 8, no. 1 (Spring 1977), pp. 52–65.

Bridges, Brian. "Japan: Waiting for Gorbachev," *Pacific Review*, vol. 4, no. 1 (1991), pp. 56–62.

Bueno de Mesquita, Bruce, David Newman, and Alvin Rabushka. *Forecasting Political Events: The Future of Hong Kong* (New Haven: Yale University Press, 1985).

Bullitt, William. "The Saddest War," *Life*, 29 December 1947, p. 64.

Bullock, Alan. *Hitler: A Study in Tyranny*, abr. ed. (New York: Harper & Row, 1971).

Bundy, McGeorge. *Danger and Survival: Choices about the Bomb in the First Fifty Years* (New York: Random House, 1988).

Bundy, William. *The Tangled Web: The Making of Foreign Policy in the Nixon Presidency* (New York: Hill and Wang, 1998).

Burney, Derek H. "Present at the Creation: The Canadian Side," in *Building a Partnership: The Canada-United States Free Trade Agreement*, ed. Mordechai E. Kreinin (East Lansing: Michigan State University Press, 2000), pp. 9–18.

Burns, Jimmy. *The Land That Lost Its Heroes: The Falklands, the Post-War, and Alfonsin* (London: Bloomsbury, 1987).

Buttinger, Joseph. *A Dragon Defiant: A Short History of Vietnam* (New York: Praeger, 1972).

———. *Smaller Dragon: A Political History of Vietnam* (New York: Praeger, 1958).

———. *Vietnam: A Dragon Embattled* (New York: Praeger, 1967).

Buzan, Barry, Ole Wæver, and Jaap de Wilde. *Security: A New Framework for Analysis* (Boulder: Lynne Rienner, 1998).

Caldwell, Dan. "Bureaucratic Foreign Policy-Making," *American Behavioral Scientist*, vol. 21, no. 1 (October 1977), pp. 87–110.

———. *Henry Kissinger, His Personality and Policies* (Durham, NC: Duke University Press, 1983).

Call, Keith A. "Southern Kurils or Northern Territories? Resolving the Russo-Japanese Border Dispute," *Brigham Young University Law Review*, vol. 1992, no. 3 (Summer 1992), pp. 727–758.

"Calmer Waters: Ambitious Plans May Transform Contested Islands," *Far Eastern Economic Review*, 30 August 1990, pp. 28, 30.

Calvert, Peter. "The Malvinas as a Factor in Argentine Politics," in *International Perspectives on the Falklands Conflict: A Matter of Life and Death*, ed. Alex Danchev (New York: St. Martin's, 1992), pp. 47–66.

Camerer, Colin F. "Individual Decision Making," in *The Handbook of Experimental Economics*, ed. John H. Kagel and Alvin E. Roth (Princeton: Princeton University Press, 1995), pp. 587–703.

Canada, Department of External Affairs. *Canada-U.S. Trade Negotiations: A Chronology* (Ottawa: External Affairs Canada, 1987).

———. *Documents on Canadian External Relations*, vol. 14 (Ottawa: Queen's Printer, 1948).

———. *How to Secure and Enhance Access to Export Markets* (Ottawa: External Affairs Canada, 1985).

———. *The Canada-U.S. Free Trade Agreement* (Ottawa: External Affairs Canada, 1987).

———. *The Canada-U.S. Free Trade Agreement: Synopsis* (Ottawa: External Affairs Canada, 1987).

———. *The Canada-U.S. Free Trade Agreement: Tariff Schedule* (Ottawa: External Affairs Canada, 1987).

Canada, Parliament. *House of Commons Debates, 1910–1911*, vol. 2 (Ottawa: Queen's Printer, 1911).

Card, Duncan Cornell. "Canada-U.S. Free Trade and Canadian Cultural Sovereignty," LL.M. thesis, University of Toronto (1987).

"Carrots for Gorbachev: Japan Finds Its Voice on Soviet Aid Issue," *Far Eastern Economic Review*, 25 July 1991, p. 13.

Chan, Steve. "Rationality, Bureaucratic Politics and Belief Systems: Explaining the Chinese Policy Debate, 1964–66," *Journal of Peace Research*, vol. 16, no. 4 (1979), pp. 333–347.

Charlton, Michael. *The Little Platoon: Diplomacy and the Falklands Dispute* (London: Basil Blackwell, 1989).

Clark, Gregory. "Japanese Emotionalism Surfaces in the Northern Territories Issue," *Tokyo Business Today*, vol. 60, no. 11 (November 1992), pp. 12–14.

Clarke, Richard A. *Against All Enemies: Inside America's War on Terror* (New York: Free Press, 2004).

Clarkson, Stephen. *Uncle Sam and Us: Globalization, Neoconservatism, and the Canadian State* (Toronto: University of Toronto Press, 2002).

Clifford, Clark. "A Vietnam Reappraisal: The Personal History of One Man's View and How It Evolved," *Foreign Affairs*, vol. 47, no. 4 (July 1969), pp. 603–622.

Cline, Ray S. *World Power Assessment: A Calculus of Strategic Drift* (Washington, DC: Center for Strategic and International Studies, Georgetown University, 1975).

———. *World Power Assessment 1977: A Calculus of Strategic Drift* (Boulder: Westview, 1977).

———. *World Power Trends and U.S. Foreign Policy for the 1980s* (Boulder: Westview, 1980).

Clippingdale, Richard. *Laurier, His Life and World* (Toronto: McGraw-Hill Ryerson, 1979).

Cloughley, Brian. "Bring the Boys Home from the Kuriles, Too," *Far Eastern Economic Review*, 7 July 1988, pp. 28–29.

Cohen, Raymond. *Threat Perception in International Crisis* (Madison: University of Wisconsin Press, 1979).

Committee on the Present Danger. *Can America Catch Up? The U.S.-Soviet Military Balance* (Washington, DC: The Committee on the Present Danger, 1984).

Conflict Research Consortium, University of Colorado. "Good Timing: Identifying 'Ripe' Times for Negotiations." http://www.colorado.edu/conflict/peace/treatment/idripe.htm (1998).

Conover, Pamela J., and Stanley Feldman. "How People Organize the Political World: A Schematic Model," *American Journal of Political Science*, vol. 28, no. 6 (February 1984), pp. 95–126.

Cooper, Chester L. *The Lost Crusade: America in Vietnam* (New York: Dodd, Mead, 1970).

Craig, Gordon Alexander, and Alexander L. George. *Force and Statecraft: Diplomatic Problems of Our Time*, 2nd ed. (New York: Oxford University Press, 1990).

Crocker, Jennifer. "Judgment of Covariation by Social Perceivers," *Psychological Bulletin*, vol. 90, no. 2 (September 1981), pp. 272–292.

Crocker, Jennifer, Darlene B. Hannah, and Renee Weber. "Person Memory and Causal Attributions," *Journal of Personality and Social Psychology*, vol. 44, no. 1 (January 1983), pp. 55–66.

Cuff, Robert. "The Conservative Party Machine and Election of 1911 in Ontario," *Ontario History*, vol. 57, no. 3 (September 1965), pp. 149–156.

Cuff, Robert D., and J. L. Granatstein. *American Dollars–Canadian Prosperity: Canadian-American Economic Relations, 1945–1950* (Toronto: Samuel Stevens, 1978).

———. "The Rise and Fall of Canadian-American Free Trade, 1947–8," *Canadian Historical Review*, vol. 58, no. 4 (December 1977), pp. 459–482.

"Customs Union with Canada: Canada Needs Us and We Need Canada in a Violently Contracting World [Editorial]," *Life*, 15 March 1948, p. 40.

Cutler, A. Claire, and Mark W. Zacher, eds. *Canadian Foreign Policy and International Economic Regimes* (Vancouver: UBC Press, 1992).

Cyert, Richard Michael, and James G. March. *A Behavioral Theory of the Firm* (Englewood Cliffs, NJ: Prentice-Hall, 1963).

Daalder, Ivo H., James M. Lindsay, and James B. Steinberg. *The Bush National Security Strategy: An Evaluation* (Washington, DC: The Brookings Institution, 2002), pp. 1–9.

Dabat, Alejandro, and Luis Lorenzano. *Argentina: The Malvinas and the End of Military Rule*, trans. Ralph Johnstone (London: Verso, 1984).

Dallek, Robert. *Flawed Giant: Lyndon Johnson and His Times, 1961–1973* (New York: Oxford University Press, 1998).

Dalyell, Tam. *One Man's Falklands . . .* (London: Cecil Woolf, 1982).

De Vita, Alberto A. *Malvinas 82: Como Y Por Que* (Buenos Aires: Instituto de Publicaciones Navales, 1994).

Dearden, Richard G., Debra P. Steger, and Michael Hart, eds. *Living with Free Trade: Canada, the Free Trade Agreement and the GATT* (Halifax: Institute for Research on Public Policy, 1989).

Desmond, Edward W. "The Screen of Steel: Russia's Military Still Considers the Kuriles Indispensable, Even with the End of the Cold War," *Time*, 25 October 1993, p. 26.

Dessler, David. "What's at Stake in the Agent-Structure Debate?," *International Organization*, vol. 43, no. 3 (Summer 1989), pp. 441–474.

Deutsch, Karl W. *Political Community and the North Atlantic Area: International Organization in the Light of Historical Experience* (Princeton: Princeton University Press, 1957).

deVillafranca, Richard. "Japan and the Northern Territories Dispute: Past, Present, Future," *Asian Survey*, vol. 33, no. 6 (June 1993), pp. 610–624.

Dobell, Peter. "Reducing Vulnerability: The Third Option, 1970s," in *Canadian Foreign Policy: Selected Cases*, ed. Don Munton and John J. Kirton (Scarborough, ON: Prentice-Hall Canada, 1992), pp. 237–258.

Doern, G. Bruce, and Brian W. Tomlin. *Faith and Fear: The Free Trade Story* (Toronto: Stoddart, 1992).

Dower, John W. *Embracing Defeat: Japan in the Wake of World War II* (New York: The New Press, 1999).

Downs, George W. "The Rational Deterrence Debate," *World Politics*, vol. 41, no. 2 (January 1989), pp. 225–238.

Doyle, Michael. "Liberalism and World Politics," *American Political Science Review*, vol. 80, no. 4 (December 1986), pp. 1151–1169.

Drover, Glenn, ed. *Free Trade and Social Policy* (Ottawa: Canadian Council on Social Development, 1988).

Duiker, William J. *Ho Chi Minh* (New York: Hyperion, 2000).

Dulles, John Foster. *War or Peace* (New York: Macmillan, 1950).

Dymond, William A. "Cultural Issues," in *Building a Partnership: The Canada-United States Free Trade Agreement*, ed. Mordechai E. Kreinin (East Lansing: Michigan State University Press, 2000), pp. 113–115.

Economic Council of Canada. *Looking Outward: A New Trade Strategy for Canada* (Ottawa: Economic Council of Canada, 1975).

Eddy, Paul, et al. *The Falklands War* (London: André Deutsch, 1982).

Ehrlichman, John. *Witness to Power: The Nixon Years* (New York: Simon & Schuster, 1982).

Ellerby, Clive. "The Role of the Falkland Lobby," in *International Perspectives on the Falklands Conflict: A Matter of Life and Death*, ed. Alex Danchev (New York: St. Martin's, 1992), pp. 85–108.

Esberey, Joy E. *Knight of the Holy Spirit: A Study of William Lyon Mackenzie King* (Toronto: University of Toronto Press, 1980).

Escudé, Carlos. *Education, Political Culture, and Foreign Policy: The Case of Argentina*, Occasional Paper 4 (Durham: Duke-University of North Carolina Program in Latin American Studies, 1992).

Evans, Peter B., Harold K. Jacobson, and Robert D. Putnam, eds. *Double-Edged Diplomacy: International Bargaining and Domestic Politics* (Berkeley: University of California Press, 1993).

Fall, Bernard B. *The Two Viet-Nams: A Political and Military Analysis*, 2nd ed. (Boulder: Westview, 1984).

Farnham, Barbara, ed. *Avoiding Losses/Taking Risks: Prospect Theory and International Conflict* (Ann Arbor: University of Michigan Press, 1994).

Feaver, Peter, Takako Hikotani, and Shaun Narine. "Civilian Control and Civil-Military Gaps in the United States, Japan, and China," paper presented to the Fifth Shibusawa Seminar, Aomori Prefecture, Japan, 21 June 2004.

Feldman, David Lewis. "The U.S. Role in the Malvinas Crisis, 1982: Misguidance and Misperception in Argentina's Decision to Go to War," *Journal of Interamerican Studies and World Affairs*, vol. 27, no. 2 (Summer 1985), pp. 1–22.

Ferns, H. S., and Bernard Ostry. *The Age of Mackenzie King* (Toronto: J. Lorimer, 1976).

Fettweis, Christopher J. "Evaluating IR's Crystal Balls: How Predictions of the Future Have Withstood Fourteen Years of Unipolarity," *International Studies Review*, vol. 6, no. 1 (March 2004), pp. 79–104.

Fiegenbaum, Avi, and Howard Thomas. "Attitudes toward Risk and the Risk/Return Paradox: Prospect Theory Explanations," *Academy of Management Journal*, vol. 31, no. 1 (March 1988), pp. 85–106.

Finckenstein, Konrad von. "Dispute Settlement under the Free Trade Agreement," in *Building a Partnership: The Canada-United States Free Trade Agreement*, ed. Mordechai E. Kreinin (East Lansing: Michigan State University Press, 2000), pp. 101–108.

Fischer, Beth A. *The Reagan Reversal: Foreign Policy and the End of the Cold War* (Columbia: University of Missouri Press, 1997).

Fiske, Shelley T. "Schema-Based Versus Piecemeal Politics: A Patchwork Quilt, but Not a Blanket, of Evidence," in *Political Cognition*, ed. Richard R. Lau and David O. Sears (Hillsdale, NJ: Lawrence Erlbaum and Associates, 1986), pp. 41–53.

Fiske, Shelley T., and Susan E. Taylor. *Social Cognition*, 2nd ed. (New York: McGraw-Hill, 1991).

"Four Bones of Contention: Moscow Recognises Japan's Northern Islands Problem," *Far Eastern Economic Review*, 18 August 1988, pp. 24–25.

Franchini, Philippe. *Les Guerres D'Indochine* (Paris: Pygmalion/G. Watelet, 1988).

Franks, The Rt. Hon. Lord, Chairman. *Falkland Islands Review: Report of a Committee of Privy Counsellors* (London: Her Majesty's Stationery Office, 1983).

Fraser, Graham. *Playing for Keeps: The Making of the Prime Minister, 1988*, rev. & exp. ed. (Toronto: McClelland & Stewart, 1990).

Freedman, Lawrence, and Virginia Gamba-Stonehouse. *Signals of War: The Falklands Conflict of 1982* (London: Faber and Faber, 1990).

Frenzel, K. A., and Douglas J. McCready. "Canada-United States Free Trade: Concern over Social Programs," *The American Journal of Economics and Sociology*, vol. 51, no. 3 (July 1992), pp. 349–359.

Friedman, Milton. "The Methodology of Positive Economics," in *Essays in Positive Economics*, ed. Milton Friedman (Chicago: University of Chicago Press, 1953), pp. 3–43.

Frizzell, Alan Stewart, Jon H. Pammett, and Anthony Westell, eds. *The Canadian General Election of 1988* (Ottawa: Carleton University Press, 1990).

Frolich, Norman, and Joe Oppenheimer. "Beyond Economic Man: Altruism, Egalitarianism, and Difference Maximizing," *Journal of Conflict Resolution*, vol. 28, no. 1 (March 1984), pp. 3–24.

Funabashi, Yoichi. "Japan and the New World Order," *Foreign Affairs*, vol. 70, no. 5 (Winter 1991/92), pp. 58–74.

Fursenko, Aleksandr, and Timothy Naftali. *'One Hell of a Gamble': Khrushchev, Castro and Kennedy, 1958–1964* (New York: Norton, 1997).

———. "Soviet Intelligence and the Cuban Missile Crisis," in *Intelligence and the Cuban Missile Crisis*, ed. James G. Blight and David A. Welch (London: Frank Cass, 1998), pp. 64–87.

Gaddis, John Lewis. "International Relations Theory and the End of the Cold War," *International Security*, vol. 17, no. 3 (Winter 1992/93), pp. 5–58.

Galbraith, John Kenneth. *How to Get Out of Vietnam: A Workable Solution to the Worst Problem of Our Time* (New York: New American Library, 1967).

Gallicchio, Marc. "The Kuriles Controversy: U.S. Diplomacy in the Soviet-Japan Border Dispute, 1941–1956," *Pacific Historical Review*, vol. 60, no. 1 (February 1991), pp. 69–101.

Gardner, Lloyd C. "Review of David Kaiser, *American Tragedy: Kennedy, Johnson, and the Origins of the Vietnam War*." http://www.h-net.msu.edu/reviews/showrev.cgi?path=31585950218853 (2000).

———. "Review of Jeffrey P. Kimball, *Nixon's Vietnam War*." http://www.h-net.msu.edu/reviews/showrev.cgi?path=8099958758287 (2000).

Garthoff, Raymond L. *Détente and Confrontation: American-Soviet Relations from Nixon to Reagan* (Washington, DC: Brookings, 1985).

———. *Reflections on the Cuban Missile Crisis*, rev. ed. (Washington, DC: Brookings, 1989).

———. "US Intelligence in the Cuban Missile Crisis," in *Intelligence and the Cuban Missile Crisis*, ed. James G. Blight and David A. Welch (London: Frank Cass, 1998), pp. 18–63.

Geiss, Immanuel, ed. *July 1914: The Outbreak of the First World War: Selected Documents* (New York: Charles Scribner's Sons, 1967).

Gelman, Harry. *Russo-Japanese Relations and the Future of the U.S.-Japanese Alliance* (Santa Monica, CA: RAND, 1993).

George, Alexander. "Case Studies and Theory Development: The Method of Structured, Focused Comparison," in *Diplomacy: New Approaches in History, Theory, and Policy*, ed. Paul Gordon Lauren (New York: Free Press, 1979), pp. 43–68.

George, Alexander L., and Juliette L. George. *Woodrow Wilson and Colonel House* (New York: John Day Co., 1956).

George, Alexander L., and Timothy J. McKeown. "Case Studies and Theories of Organizational Decision Making," in *Advances in Information Processing in Organizations*, vol. 2 (Greenwich, CT: JAI, 1985), pp. 21–58.

Germany, Auswärtiges Amt. *Documents on German Foreign Policy, 1918–1945*, vol. 1, Ser. D (Washington, DC: United States Government Printing Office, 1949–).

Gilbert, Marc Jason, and William P. Head. *The Tet Offensive* (Westport, CT: Praeger, 1996).

Gilpin, Robert G. "The Richness of the Tradition of Political Realism," in *Neorealism and Its Critics*, ed. Robert O. Keohane (New York: Columbia University Press, 1986), pp. 301–321.

———. "The Theory of Hegemonic War," *Journal of Interdisciplinary History*, vol. 18, no. 4 (Spring 1988), pp. 591–613.

———. *War and Change in World Politics* (Cambridge: Cambridge University Press, 1981).

Goertz, Gary. *International Norms and Decision Making: A Punctuated Equilibrium Model* (Lanham, MD: Rowman & Littlefield, 2003).

Goldstein, Judith. "International Law and Domestic Institutions: Reconciling North American 'Unfair' Trade Laws," *International Organization*, vol. 50, no. 4 (Autumn 1996), pp. 541–564.

Goodfellow, Troy S. "An Empirical Test of the Theory of Compellence," Ph.D. dissertation, Department of Political Science, University of Toronto (2000).

Gowa, Joanne S. *Ballots and Bullets: The Elusive Democratic Peace* (Princeton: Princeton University Press, 1999).

Granatstein, J. L., and Norman Hillmer. *For Better or for Worse: Canada and the United States to the 1990s* (Toronto: Copp Clark Pitman, 1991).

Grieco, Joseph M. "Anarchy and the Limits of Cooperation: A Realist Critique of the Newest Liberal Institutionalism," *International Organization*, vol. 42, no. 3 (Summer 1988), pp. 485–507.

———. *Cooperation among Nations: Europe, America, and Non-Tariff Barriers to Trade* (Ithaca, NY: Cornell University Press, 1990).

Gromyko, Andrei. *Memories*, trans. Harold Shukman (London: Hutchinson, 1989).

Gruening, Ernest Henry, and Herbert Wilton Beaser. *Vietnam Folly* (Washington: National Press, 1968).

Gulick, Edward Vose. *Europe's Classical Balance of Power* (New York: Norton, 1967).

Gustafson, Lowell S. *The Sovereignty Dispute over the Falkland (Malvinas) Islands* (New York: Oxford University Press, 1988).

Haas, Peter M. "Do Regimes Matter? Epistemic Communities and Mediterranean Pollution Control," *International Organization*, vol. 43, no. 3 (Summer 1989), pp. 377–403.

———. "Introduction: Epistemic Comunities and International Policy Coordination," *International Organization*, vol. 46, no. 1 (Winter 1992), pp. 1–35.

Haig, Alexander M., Jr. *Caveat: Realism, Reagan, and Foreign Policy* (New York: Macmillan, 1984).

Halberstam, David. *The Best and the Brightest* (New York: Random House, 1972).

———. *Ho* (New York: Random House, 1971).

Haldeman, H. R. *The Haldeman Diaries: Inside the Nixon White House* (New York: G. P. Putnam's Sons, 1994).

Halperin, Morton H. *Bureaucratic Politics and Foreign Policy* (Washington, DC: Brookings, 1974).

Halperin, Morton H., and Arnold Kanter, eds. *Readings in American Foreign Policy: A Bureaucratic Perspective* (Boston: Little, Brown, 1973).

Hammel, Eric M. *Fire in the Streets: The Battle for Hue, Tet 1968* (Chicago: Contemporary Books, 1991).

Hannan, Michael T., and John Freeman. *Organizational Ecology* (Cambridge: Harvard University Press, 1989).

———. "The Population Ecology of Organizations," *American Journal of Sociology*, vol. 82, no. 5 (March 1977), pp. 929–964.

Hart, Michael. "Almost but Not Quite: The 1947–48 Bilateral Canada-U.S. Negotiations," *American Review of Canadian Studies*, vol. 19, no. 1 (Spring 1989), pp. 25–58.

———. *A Trading Nation: Canadian Trade Policy from Colonialism to Globalization* (Vancouver: UBC Press, 2002).

———. "The Future on the Table: The Continuing Negotiating Agenda under the Canada-United States Free Trade Agreement," in *Living with Free Trade: Canada, the Free Trade Agreement and the GATT*, ed. Richard G. Dearden, Debra P. Steger, and Michael Hart (Halifax: Institute for Research on Public Policy, 1989), pp. 67–131.

Hart, Michael, Bill Dymond, and Colin Robertson. *Decision at Midnight: Inside the Canada-U.S. Free Trade Negotiations* (Vancouver: UBC Press, 1994).

Hasegawa, Tsuyoshi. "Rocks and Roles," *Far Eastern Economic Review*, 10 September 1992, p. 15.

———. "The Gorbachev-Kaifu Summit: Domestic and Foreign Policy Linkages," in *Russia and Japan: An Unresolved Dilemma between Distant Neighbors*, ed. Tsuyoshi Hasegawa, Jonathan Haslam, and Andrew C. Kuchins (Berkeley: University of California Press, 1993), pp. 49–82.

Hastings, Max, and Simon Jenkins. *The Battle for the Falklands* (New York: Norton, 1984).

Heeney, Arnold. *The Things That Are Caesar's: Memoirs of a Canadian Public Servant*, ed. Brian D. Heeney (Toronto: University of Toronto Press, 1972).

Helmers, Henrik O. *The United States-Canadian Automobile Agreement: A Study in Industry Adjustment* (Ann Arbor: Institute for International Commerce, Graduate School of Business Administration, University of Michigan, 1967).

Henderson, William Darryl. *Why the Vietcong Fought: A Study of Motivation and Control in a Modern Army in Combat* (Westport, CT: Greenwood Press, 1979).

Herring, George C. *America's Longest War: The United States and Vietnam, 1950–1975* (New York: Knopf, 1986).

———. *LBJ and Vietnam: A Different Kind of War* (Austin: University of Texas Press, 1994).

———. "Review of David Kaiser, *American Tragedy: Kennedy, Johnson, and the Origins of the Vietnam War*." http://www.h-net.msu.edu/reviews/showrev.cgi ?path=10580964721262 (2000).

Hersh, Seymour M. *The Price of Power: Kissinger in the Nixon White House* (New York: Summit Books, 1983).

Hershberg, James G. "Before 'the Missiles of October': Did Kennedy Plan a Military Strike against Cuba?," *Diplomatic History*, vol. 14, no. 12 (Spring 1990), pp. 163–198.

Higgins, E. T., and J. A. Bargh. "Social Cognition and Social Perception," in *Annual Review of Psychology*, ed. M. R. Rosenzweig and L. W. Porter, vol. 38 (Palo Alto, CA: Annual Reviews, 1987), pp. 369–425.

Hilliker, John. *Canada's Department of External Affairs*, vol. 1, *The Early Years, 1909–1946* (Kingston, ON: McGill-Queen's University Press, 1990).

Hilsman, Roger. *The Politics of Policy Making in Defense and Foreign Affairs: Conceptual Models and Bureaucratic Politics*, 3rd ed. (Englewood Cliffs, NJ: Prentice Hall, 1993).

Hirt, Edward R., and Steven J. Sherman. "The Role of Prior Knowledge in Explaining Hypothetical Events," *Journal of Experimental and Social Psychology*, vol. 21, no. 6 (November 1985), pp. 519–543.

Hitchens, Christopher. "The Case against Henry Kissinger, Part One: The Making of a War Criminal," *Harper's*, February 2001, pp. 33–58.

Hitler, Adolf. *Mein Kampf* (New York: Reynal & Hitchcock, 1939).

Hoff-Wilson, Joan. *Nixon Reconsidered* (New York: Basic Books, 1994).

Hoffmann, Fritz L., and Olga Mingo Hoffmann. *Sovereignty Dispute: The Falklands/Malvinas, 1493–1982* (Boulder: Westview, 1984).

Hollis, Martin, and Steve Smith. "Beware of Gurus: Structure and Action in International Relations," *Review of International Studies*, vol. 17, no. 4 (October 1991), pp. 393–410.

———. *Explaining and Understanding International Relations* (Oxford: Clarendon Press, 1991).

———. "Structure and Action: Further Comment," *Review of International Studies*, vol. 18, no. 2 (April 1992), pp. 187–188.

Holloway, David. *Stalin and the Bomb* (New Haven: Yale University Press, 1994).

Holsti, Kalevi J. *Peace and War: Armed Conflicts and International Order, 1648–1989* (Cambridge: Cambridge University Press, 1991).

Holsti, Ole R. "Cognitive Dynamics and Images of the Enemy," in *Image and Reality in World Politics*, ed. John Farrell and Asa Smith (New York: Columbia University Press, 1989), pp. 16–39.

———. "Cognitive Dynamics and Images of the Enemy: Dulles and Russia," in *Enemies in Politics*, ed. David Finlay, Ole Holsti, and Richard Fagen (Chicago: Rand McNally, 1967), pp. 25–96.

———. *Crisis, Escalation, War* (Montreal: McGill-Queen's University Press, 1972).

———. "The 1914 Case," *American Political Science Review*, vol. 59, no. 2 (June 1965), pp. 365–378.

Hoopes, Townsend. *The Limits of Intervention: An Inside Account of How the Johnson Policy of Escalation in Vietnam Was Reversed* (New York: D. McKay, 1969).

Hopf, Ted. "Getting the End of the Cold War Wrong," *International Security*, vol. 18, no. 2 (Fall 1993), pp. 202–210.

———. *Peripheral Visions: Deterrence Theory and American Foreign Policy in the Third World, 1965–1990* (Ann Arbor: University of Michigan Press, 1994).

Horelick, Arnold L. "The Cuban Missile Crisis: An Analysis of Soviet Calculations and Behavior," *World Politics*, vol. 16, no. 3 (April 1964), pp. 363–389.

Hosmer, Stephen T. *Constraints on U.S. Strategy in Third World Conflicts* (New York: Crane, Russak, 1987).

Hoyenga, Katharine Blick, and Kermit T. Hoyenga. *Motivational Explanations of Behavior: Evolutionary, Physiological and Cognitive Ideas* (Monterey, CA: Brooks/Cole, 1984).

Hume, David. "Treatise of Human Nature," in *Hume's Moral and Political Philosophy*, ed. Henry D. Aiken (New York: Hafner Press, 1948), pp. 49–69.

Hurtig, Mel. *The Betrayal of Canada* (Toronto: Stoddart, 1991).

Huth, Paul, and Bruce Russett. "Testing Deterrence Theory: Rigor Makes a Difference," *World Politics*, vol. 42, no. 4 (July 1990), pp. 466–501.

———. "What Makes Deterrence Work? Cases from 1900 to 1980," *World Politics*, vol. 36, no. 4 (July 1984), pp. 496–526.

Ikenberry, G. John. "Creating Yesterday's New World Order: Keynesian 'New Thinking' and the Anglo-American Postwar Settlement," in *Ideas and Foreign Policy: Beliefs, Institutions, and Political Change*, ed. Judith Goldstein and Robert O. Keohane (Ithaca: Cornell University Press, 1993), pp. 57–86.

Ikenberry, G. John, and Charles Kupchan. "Socialization and Hegemonic Power," *International Organization*, vol. 44, no. 3 (Summer 1990), pp. 283–316.

International Institute for Strategic Studies. *The Military Balance* (London: International Institute for Strategic Studies, 1963 et seq.).

Isaacson, Walter. *Kissinger: A Biography* (New York: Simon & Schuster, 1992).

Ito, Kenichi. "Japan and the Soviet Union: Entangled in the Deadlock of the Northern Territories," *Washington Quarterly*, vol. 11, no. 1 (Winter 1988), pp. 34–44.

Iyengar, Shanto. *Is Anyone Responsible? How Television Frames Political Issues* (Chicago: University of Chicago Press, 1991).

Iyengar, Shanto, and William J. McGuire. *Explorations in Political Psychology* (Durham: Duke University Press, 1993).

Janis, Irving L. *Crucial Decisions: Leadership in Policymaking and Crisis Management* (New York: Free Press, 1989).

———. *Groupthink: Psychological Studies of Policy Decisions and Fiascoes* (New York: Houghton Mifflin, 1982).

Janis, Irving L., and Leon Mann. *Decision Making: A Psychological Analysis of Conflict, Choice, and Commitment* (New York: Free Press, 1977).

Japan, Ministry of Foreign Affairs. *Diplomatic Blue Book 1999: Japan's Diplomacy with Leadership toward the New Century*. http://www.mofa.go.jp/policy/other/bluebook/1999/I-c.html#2 (1999).

———. *Japan's Policy on the Russian Federation*. http://www.mofa.go.jp/region/europe/russia/russia_policy.html.

Japan, Ministry of Foreign Affairs. *Tokyo Declaration on Japan-Russia Relations (Provisional Translation)*. http://www.mofa.go.jp/region/n-america/us/q&a/declaration.html (1993).

Jebb, Richard. *Studies in Colonial Nationalism* (London: Edward Arnold, 1905).

Jenkins, Roy. *Truman* (London: Collins, 1986).

Jervis, Robert. "Deterrence and Perception," *International Security*, vol. 7, no. 3 (Winter 1982/83), pp. 3–30.

———. "Domino Beliefs and Strategic Behavior," in *Dominoes and Bandwagons*, ed. Robert Jervis and Jack Snyder (New York: Oxford University Press, 1991), pp. 20–50.

———. "The Future of World Politics: Will It Resemble the Past?," *International Security*, vol. 16, no. 3 (Winter 1991/92), pp. 39–73.

———. "Rational Deterrence Theory," *World Politics*, vol. 41, no. 2 (January 1989), pp. 183–207.

Jervis, Robert, Richard Ned Lebow, and Janice Gross Stein. *Psychology & Deterrence* (Baltimore: Johns Hopkins University Press, 1985).

Johnson, Lyndon B. *The Vantage Point: Perspectives of the Presidency, 1963–1969* (New York: Holt, Rinehart and Winston, 1971).

Jones, Edward E., and Richard E. Nisbett. "The Actor and Observer: Divergent Perceptions of the Causes of Behavior," in *Attribution: Perceiving the Causes of Behavior*, ed. Edward E. Jones et al. (Morristown, NJ: General Learning Press, 1971), pp. 79–64.

Jukes, Geoffrey. *Russia's Military and the Northern Territories Issue* (Canberra: Strategic & Defence Studies Centre, Australian National University, 1993).

Kahin, George McTurnan. *Intervention: How America Became Involved in Vietnam* (New York: Knopf, 1986).

Kahneman, Daniel, Jack L. Knetsch, and Richard H. Thaler. "Fairness and the Assumptions of Economics," *Journal of Business*, vol. 59, no. 4 (October 1986), pp. S285–S300.

———. "The Endowment Effect, Loss Aversion, and the Status Quo Bias," *Journal of Economic Perspectives*, vol. 5, no. 1 (Winter 1991), pp. 193–206.

Kahneman, Daniel, Paul Slovic, and Amos Tversky, eds. *Judgment under Uncertainty: Heuristics and Biases* (Cambridge: Cambridge University Press, 1982).

Kahneman, Daniel, and Amos Tversky. "Prospect Theory: An Analysis of Decisions under Risk," *Econometrica*, vol. 47, no. 2 (March 1979), pp. 263–291.

Kaiser, David E. *American Tragedy: Kennedy, Johnson, and the Origins of the Vietnam War* (Cambridge: Belknap Press of Harvard University Press, 2000).

Kaiser, David. "Review of Jeffrey P. Kimball, *Nixon's Vietnam War.*" http://www2.h-net.msu.edu/reviews/showrev.cgi?path=8107958758290 (2000).

Kameda, Tatsuya, and James Davis. "The Function of the Reference Point in Individual and Group Risk Taking," *Organizational Behavior & Human Decision Processes*, vol. 46, no. 1 (June 1990), pp. 55–76.

Karnow, Stanley. *Vietnam: A History* (New York: Viking, 1983).

Katzenstein, Peter J., ed. *Between Power and Plenty: Foreign Economic Policies of Industrial States* (Madison: University of Wisconsin Press, 1978).

———. *Cultural Norms and National Security: Police and Military in Postwar Japan* (Ithaca: Cornell University Press, 1996).

Katzenstein, Peter J., and Nobuo Okawara. "Japan's National Security: Structures, Norms, and Policies," *International Security*, vol. 17, no. 4 (Spring 1993), pp. 84–118.

———. *Japan's National Security: Structures, Norms, and Policy Responses in a Changing World* (Ithaca: Cornell University East Asia Program, 1993).

Kearns, Doris. *Lyndon Johnson and the American Dream* (New York: Harper & Row, 1976).

Keating, Tom. *The Multilateralist Tradition in Canadian Foreign Policy* (Toronto: McClelland & Stewart, 1993).

Kelley, Harold H. "Attribution Theory in Social Psychology," in *Nebraska Symposium on Motivation*, ed. D. Levine (Lincoln: University of Nebraska Press, 1967), pp. 192–240.

———. *Causal Schemata and the Attribution Process* (Morristown, NJ: General Learning Press, 1972).

Kennedy, Paul M. *The Rise and Fall of British Naval Mastery* (Houndmills, Basingstoke: Macmillan, 1976).

Keohane, Robert O. *After Hegemony* (Princeton: Princeton University Press, 1984).

———. "Neoliberal Institutionalism: A Perspective on World Politics," in *International Institutions and State Power: Essays on International Relations Theory*, ed. Robert O. Keohane (Boulder: Westview, 1989), pp. 1–20.

Khadduri, Majid. *The Gulf War: The Origins and Implications of the Iraq-Iran Conflict* (New York: Oxford University Press, 1988).

Khong, Yuen Foong. *Analogies at War: Korea, Munich, Dien Bien Phu, and the Vietnam Decisions of 1965* (Princeton: Princeton University Press, 1992).

Khrushchev, Nikita S. *Khrushchev Remembers: The Glasnost Tapes*, trans. Jerrold L. Schecter and Vyacheslav V. Luchkov (Boston: Little, Brown, 1990).

Khrushchev, Sergei. *Nikita Khrushchev and the Creation of a Superpower* (University Park: Pennsylvania State University Press, 2000).

Kimball, Jeffrey. "Debunking Nixon's Myths of Vietnam," *The New England Journal of History*, vol. 56, nos. 2–3 (Winter 1999–Spring 2000), pp. 31–46.

———. *Nixon's Vietnam War* (Lawrence: University Press of Kansas, 1998).

———. "Review of Fredrik Logevall, *Choosing War: The Lost Chance for Peace and the Escalation of War in Vietnam.*" http://www.h-net.msu.edu/reviews/showrev.cgi?path=31585950218853 (2000).

Kimura, Masato, and David A. Welch. "Specifying 'Interests': Japan's Claim to the Northern Territories and Its Implications for International Relations Theory," *International Studies Quarterly,* vol. 42, no. 2 (June 1998), pp. 213–244.

Kingwell, Mark. *Dreams of Millennium: Report from a Culture on the Brink* (Toronto: Viking, 1996).

Kinney, Douglas. *National Interest/National Honor: The Diplomacy of the Falklands Crisis* (New York: Praeger, 1989).

Kirton, John J. "Consequences of Integration: The Case of the Defence Production Sharing Agreements," in *Continental Community? Independence and Integration in North America,* ed. W. Andrew Axline (Toronto: McClelland and Stewart, 1974), pp. 116–136.

———. "The Politics of Bilateral Management: The Case of the Canada-United States Automotive Trade," *International Journal,* vol. 36, no. 1 (Winter 1980), pp. 39–69.

Kissinger, Henry A. *American Foreign Policy* (New York: Norton, 1977).

———. *Diplomacy* (New York: Simon & Schuster, 1994).

———. *Nuclear Weapons and Foreign Policy* (New York: Harper, 1957).

———. "The Viet Nam Negotiations," *Foreign Affairs,* vol. 47, no. 2 (January 1969), pp. 211–234.

———. *White House Years* (Boston: Little, Brown, 1979).

———. *A World Restored: Metternich, Castlereagh and the Problems of Peace, 1812–1822,* new ed. (New York: Grosset & Dunlap, 1964).

———. *Years of Upheaval* (Boston: Little, Brown, 1982).

Knetsch, Jack L. "The Endowment Effect and Evidence of Nonreversible Indifference Curves," *The American Economic Review,* vol. 79, no. 5 (December 1989), pp. 1277–1284.

Knetsch, Jack L., and J. A. Sinden. "Willingness to Pay and Compensation Demanded: Experimental Evidence of an Unexpected Disparity in Measures of Value," *Quarterly Journal of Economics,* vol. 99, no. 3 (August 1984), pp. 507–521.

Kozak, David C., and James M. Keagle, eds. *Bureaucratic Politics and National Security: Theory and Practice* (Boulder: Lynne Rienner, 1988).

Krasner, Stephen. *Defending the National Interest: Raw Materials Investments and U.S. Foreign Policy* (Princeton: Princeton University Press, 1978).

Kruglanski, Arie W. *Basic Processes in Social Cognition: A Theory of Lay Epistemology* (New York: Plenum, 1986).

———. "Lay Epistemologic-Process and Contents: Another Look at Attribution Theory," *Psychological Review,* vol. 87, no. 1 (January 1980), pp. 70–87.

Kuhl, Julius. "Motivation and Information Processing: A New Look at Decision Making, Dynamic Change, and Action Control," in *Handbook of Motivation and Cognition: Foundations of Social Behavior,* ed. Richard M. Sorrentino and E. Tory Higgins (New York: Guilford, 1986), pp. 404–434.

Kulik, James A. "Confirmatory Attribution and the Perpetuation of Social Beliefs," *Journal of Personality and Social Psychology*, vol. 44, no. 6 (June 1983), pp. 1171–1181.

Kupchan, Charles A., and Clifford A. Kupchan. "Concerts, Collective Security, and the Future of Europe," *International Security*, vol. 16, no. 1 (Summer 1991), pp. 114–161.

Lacouture, Jean. *Ho Chi Minh: A Political Biography*, trans. Peter Wiles (New York: Random House, 1968).

Lakatos, Imre. *The Methodology of Scientific Research Programmes*, vol. 1 (Cambridge: Cambridge University Press, 1978).

Lakatos, Imre, and Alan Musgrave, eds. *Criticism and the Growth of Knowledge* (Cambridge: Cambridge University Press, 1970).

LaPierre, Laurier L. *Sir Wilfrid Laurier and the Romance of Canada* (Toronto: Stoddart, 1996).

Lau, Richard R., and David O. Sears. "Social Cognition and Political Cognition: The Past, Present, and Future," in *Political Cognition*, ed. Richard R. Lau and David O. Sears (Hillsdale, NJ: Lawrence Erlbaum and Associates, 1986), pp. 347–366.

Laxer, James. *Leap of Faith: Free Trade and the Future of Canada* (Edmonton: Hurtig, 1986).

Lebovic, James H. "Riding Waves or Making Waves? The Services and the U.S. Defense Budget, 1981–1993," *American Political Science Review*, vol. 88, no. 4 (December 1994), pp. 839–852.

Lebow, Richard Ned. *Between Peace and War: The Nature of International Crisis* (Baltimore: Johns Hopkins University Press, 1981).

———. "Deterrence and Threat Assessment: The Lessons of 1962 and 1973," paper prepared for a Conference on Strategic Warning, National War College, Fort McNair, 27–28 September 1993.

———. "What's So Different about a Counterfactual?," *World Politics*, vol. 52, no. 4 (July 2000), pp. 550–585.

Lebow, Richard Ned, and Thomas Risse-Kappen, eds. *International Relations Theory and the End of the Cold War* (New York: Columbia University Press, 1995).

Lebow, Richard Ned, and Janice Gross Stein. "Afghanistan, Carter, and Foreign Policy Change: The Limits of Cognitive Models," in *Diplomacy, Force, and Leadership: Essays in Honor of Alexander L. George*, ed. Dan Caldwell and Timothy J. McKeown (Boulder: Westview, 1993), pp. 95–128.

———. "Deterrence: The Elusive Dependent Variable," *World Politics*, vol. 42, no. 3 (April 1990), pp. 336–369.

———. "Rational Deterrence Theory: I Think, Therefore I Deter," *World Politics*, vol. 61, no. 2 (January 1989), pp. 208–234.

———. *We All Lost the Cold War* (Princeton: Princeton University Press, 1994).

———. *When Does Deterrence Succeed and How Do We Know?* (Ottawa: Canadian Institute for International Peace and Security, 1990).

Leffler, Melvyn P. "Inside Enemy Archives: The Cold War Reopened," *Foreign Affairs*, vol. 75, no. 4 (July/August 1996), pp. 120–135.

Leites, Nathan. *The Operational Code of the Politburo* (New York: McGraw-Hill, 1951).

Lentin, Antony. *Lloyd George, Woodrow Wilson and the Guilt of Germany: An Essay in the Pre-History of Appeasement* (Baton Rouge: Louisiana State University Press, 1985).

Lerner, Melvin J. "The Justice Motive in Human Relations," in *The Justice Motive in Social Behavior: Adapting to Times of Scarcity and Change*, ed. Melvin J. Lerner and Sally C. Lerner (New York: Plenum Press, 1981), pp. 11–35.

Levin, Norman D., Mark A. Lorell, and Arthur J. Alexander. *The Wary Warriors: Future Directions in Japanese Security Policies* (Santa Monica, CA: RAND, 1993).

Levy, Jack S. "Contending Theories of International Conflict: A Levels-of-Analysis Approach," in *Managing Global Chaos: Sources of and Responses to International Conflict*, ed. Chester A. Crocker and Fen Osler Hampson (Washington, DC: United States Institute of Peace, 1996), pp. 3–24.

———. "Loss Aversion, Framing, and Bargaining: The Implications of Prospect Theory for International Conflict," *International Political Science Review*, vol. 17, no. 2 (April 1996), pp. 179–195.

———. "Prospect Theory and the Cognitive-Rational Debate," in *Decision-Making on War and Peace: The Cognitive-Rational Debate*, ed. Nehemia Geva and Alex Mintz (Boulder: Lynne Rienner, 1997), pp. 33–50.

———. "Prospect Theory, Rational Choice, and International Relations," *International Studies Quarterly*, vol. 41, no. 1 (March 1997), pp. 87–112.

———. *War in the Modern Great Power System* (Lexington: University Press of Kentucky, 1983).

Levy, Jack S., and Lily I. Vakili. "Diversionary Action by Authoritarian Regimes: Argentina in the Falklands/Malvinas Case," in *The Internationalization of Communal Strife*, ed. Manus I. Midlarsky (London: Routledge, 1992), pp. 118–146.

Lind, Michael. *Vietnam, the Necessary War: A Reinterpretation of America's Most Disastrous Military Conflict* (New York: Free Press, 1999).

Link, Arthur S., ed. *Woodrow Wilson and a Revolutionary World, 1913–1921* (Chapel Hill: University of North Carolina Press, 1982).

Lipsey, Richard G., and Murray G. Smith. *Taking the Initiative: Canada's Trade Options in a Turbulent World* (Toronto: C. D. Howe Institute, 1985).

Logevall, Fredrik. *Choosing War: The Lost Chance for Peace and the Escalation of War in Vietnam* (Berkeley: University of California Press, 1999).

———. "Vietnam and the Question of What Might Have Been," in *Kennedy: The New Frontier Revisited*, ed. Mark J. White (London: Macmillan, 1998), pp. 19–62.

Lomperis, Timothy J. *The War Everyone Lost—and Won: America's Intervention in Viet Nam's Twin Struggles*, rev. ed. (Washington, DC: CQ Press, 1993).

Longley, Jeanne, and Dean G. Pruitt. "Groupthink: A Critique of Janis' Theory," in *Review of Personality and Social Psychology*, ed. Ladd Wheeler, vol. 1 (Beverly Hills: Sage, 1980), pp. 74–93.

Lyon, Peyton V., and David Leyton-Brown. "Image and Policy Preference: Canadian Elite Views on Relations with the United States," *International Journal*, vol. 32, no. 3 (Summer 1977), pp. 640–671.

Macdonald, Donald S. *Report of the Royal Commission on the Economic Union and Development Prospects for Canada* (Ottawa: Minister of Supply and Services Canada, 1985).

Machiavelli, Niccolò. *Discourses on Livy*, ed. Harvey C. Mansfield and Nathan Tarcov (Chicago: University of Chicago Press, 1996).

Machina, Mark J. "Decision-Making in the Presence of Risk," *Science*, vol. 236 (May 1987), pp. 537–543.

Mack, Andrew, and Martin O'Hare. "Moscow-Tokyo and the Northern Territories Dispute," *Asian Survey*, vol. 30, no. 4 (April 1990), pp. 380–394.

MacMillan, Margaret. *Paris 1919: Six Months That Changed the World* (New York: Random House, 2002).

Maechling, Charles, Jr. "The Argentine Pariah," *Foreign Policy*, no. 45 (Winter 1981–82), pp. 69–83.

Manga, Pranlal. *The Canada-U.S. Free Trade Agreement: Possible Implications on Canada's Health Care Systems*, Discussion Paper No. 348 (Ottawa: Economic Council of Canada, 1988).

Mansourov, Alexandre Y. "Stalin, Mao, Kim, and China's Decision to Enter the Korean War, September 16–October 15, 1950: New Evidence from the Russian Archives," *Cold War International History Project Bulletin*, no. 6–7 (Winter 1995/1996), pp. 94–119.

Maoz, Zeev. *National Choices and International Processes* (Cambridge: Cambridge University Press, 1990).

March, James G., and Johan P. Olsen. *Ambiguity and Choice in Organizations* (Bergen, Norway: Universitetsforlaget, 1976).

March, James G., and Herbert A. Simon. *Organizations* (New York: Wiley, 1958).
———. *Organizations*, 2nd ed. (Cambridge, MA: Blackwell Business, 1993).

Markus, Hazel, and Robert B. Zajonc. "The Cognitive Perspective in Social Psychology," in *Handbook of Social Psychology*, ed. Gardner Lindzey and Elliot Aronson, 3rd ed., vol. 1 (New York: Random House, 1985), pp. 137–230.

Martin, Joanne. *Cultures in Organizations* (New York: Oxford University Press, 1992).

Martin, Lawrence. *The Presidents and the Prime Ministers: Washington and Ottawa Face to Face: The Myth of Bilateral Bliss, 1867–1982* (Toronto: Doubleday Canada, 1982).

Martin, Lisa. *Coercive Cooperation* (Princeton: Princeton University Press, 1992).

Mayall, James. *Nationalism and International Society* (Cambridge: Cambridge University Press, 1990).

Mazlish, Bruce. *In Search of Nixon: A Psychohistorical Inquiry* (New York: Basic Books, 1972).

McAuliffe, Mary S., ed. *CIA Documents on the Cuban Missile Crisis* (Washington, DC: Central Intelligence Agency History Staff, 1992).

MccGwire, Michael. "The Rationale for the Development of Soviet Seapower," in *Soviet Strategy*, ed. John Baylis and Gerald Segal (London: Croom Helm, 1981), pp. 210–254.

McGuire, Timothy, Sara Kiesler, and Jane Siegal. "Group and Computer-Mediated Discussion Effects in Risky Decision Making," *Journal of Personality and Social Psychology*, vol. 52, no. 5 (May 1987), pp. 917–930.

McKeown, Timothy J. "The Limitations of 'Structural' Theories of Commercial Policy," *International Organization*, vol. 40, no. 1 (Winter 1986), pp. 43–64.

McKitrick, Ross. *The Canada-U.S. Free Trade Agreement: An Annotated Bibliography of Selected Literature* (Kingston, ON: Industrial Relations Centre, Queen's University, 1989).

McNamara, Robert S. *In Retrospect: The Tragedy and Lessons of Vietnam* (New York: Times Books, 1995).

McNamara, Robert S., et al. *Argument without End: In Search of Answers to the Vietnam Tragedy* (New York: PublicAffairs, 1999).

McPherson, Peter. "A Reunion of Trade Warriors from the Canada-U.S. Trade Negotiations: Remembering How It Happened," in *Building a Partnership: The Canada-United States Free Trade Agreement*, ed. Mordechai E. Kreinin (East Lansing: Michigan State University Press, 2000), pp. vii–ix.

Mendl, Wolf. "Japan and the Soviet Union: Toward a Deal?," *The World Today*, vol. 47, no. 11 (November 1991), pp. 196–200.

Menon, Rajan, and Daniel Abele. "Security Dimensions of Soviet Territorial Disputes with China and Japan," *Journal of Northeast Asian Studies*, vol. 8, no. 1 (Spring 1989), pp. 3–19.

Mercer, Jonathan. "Anarchy and Identity," *International Organization*, vol. 49, no. 2 (Spring 1995), pp. 229–252.

Michaud, Nelson, and Kim Richard Nossal. "Necessité ou Innovation? Vers une Redefinition de la Politique Étrangère Canadienne, 1984–1993," *Études Internationales*, vol. 31, no. 2 (June 2000), pp. 237–346.

Middlebrook, Martin. *Operation Corporate: The Falklands War* (London: Viking, 1985).

Miller, Dale T., and Neil Vidmar. "The Social Psychology of Punishment Reactions," in *The Justice Motive in Social Behavior: Adapting to Times of Scarcity and Change*, ed. Melvin J. Lerner and Sally C. Lerner (New York: Plenum Press, 1981), pp. 145–172.

Miller, Judith, and Laurie Mylroie. *Saddam Hussein and the Crisis in the Gulf* (New York: Times Books, 1990).

Milliken, Jennifer. *The Social Construction of the Korean War: Conflict and Its Possibilities* (Manchester: Manchester University Press, 2001).

Mineshiga, Miyuki. "In the Way," *Look Japan*, July 1991, p. 7.

Mitchell, Christopher R. "Cutting Losses: Reflections on Appropriate Timing," Institute for Conflict Analysis and Resolution Working Paper no. 9, George Mason University. http://www.ciaonet.org/wps/mic01/ (1996).

Mochizuki, Mike M. "The Soviet/Russian Factor in Japanese Security Policy," in *Russia and Japan: An Unresolved Dilemma between Distant Neighbors*, ed. Tsuyoshi Hasegawa, Jonathan Haslam, and Andrew C. Kuchins (Berkeley: University of California Press, 1993), pp. 125–160.

Moïse, Edwin E. *Tonkin Gulf and the Escalation of the Vietnam War* (Chapel Hill: University of North Carolina Press, 1996).

Moravcsik, Andrew. "Taking Preferences Seriously: A Liberal Theory of International Politics," *International Organization*, vol. 51, no. 4 (Autumn 1997), pp. 513–553.

Morgenthau, Hans J. *Politics among Nations: The Struggle for Power and Peace*, 5th ed. (New York: Knopf, 1978).

Morici, Peter. "U.S.-Canada Free Trade Discussions: What Are the Issues?," *American Review of Canadian Studies*, vol. 15, no. 3 (Fall 1985), pp. 311–323.

Moro, Rubén O. *The History of the South Atlantic Conflict*, trans. Michael Valeur (New York: Praeger, 1989).

Most, Benjamin A., and Harvey Starr. "International Relations Theory, Foreign Policy Substitutability, and 'Nice' Laws," *World Politics*, vol. 36, no. 3 (April 1984), pp. 383–406.

Mouritzen, Hans. *Bureaucracy as a Source of Foreign Policy Inertia* (Copenhagen: Institute of Political Studies, University of Copenhagen, 1985).

National Archives of Canada. "The Diaries of William Lyon Mackenzie King." http://king.archives.ca/EN/.

National Commission on Terrorist Attacks upon the United States. *The 9/11 Commission Report: Final Report of the National Commission on Terrorist Attacks upon the United States*, authorized ed. (New York: Norton, 2004).

"National Security Strategy of the United States of America." http://www.whitehouse.gov/nsc/nss.pdf (2002).

"The Negotiating Process: A Panel Discussion Led by Roger Porter," in *Building a Partnership: The Canada-United States Free Trade Agreement*, ed. Mordechai E. Kreinin (East Lansing: Michigan State University Press, 2000), pp. 19–37.

Neumann-Hoditz, Reinhold. *Portrait of Ho Chi Minh: An Illustrated Biography*, trans. John Hargreaves (New York: Herder and Herder, 1972).

Neustadt, Richard E., and Ernest R. May. *Thinking in Time: The Uses of History for Decision-Makers* (New York: Free Press, 1986).

Nimmo, William F. *Japan and Russia: A Reevaluation in the Post-Soviet Era* (Westport, CT: Greenwood Press, 1994).

Nixon, Richard M. *No More Vietnams* (New York: Arbor House, 1985).

———. *Peace in Vietnam [Text of a Radio and Television Address from the White House, May 14, 1969]*, East Asia and Pacific Series 180 (Washington, DC: Department of State Publication 8467, 1969).

———. *RN: The Memoirs of Richard Nixon* (New York: Simon & Schuster, 1990).

———. *Six Crises* (Garden City, NY: Doubleday, 1962).

Nye, Joseph S., Jr. "The Case for Deep Engagement," *Foreign Affairs*, vol. 74, no. 4 (July/August 1995), pp. 90–102.

Oberdorfer, Don. *Tet!* (New York: Da Capo Press, 1984).

"Off Again: Second Cancelled Trip Strains Tokyo-Moscow Ties," *Far Eastern Economic Review*, 20 May 1993, p. 13.

O'Neill, Barry. "Risk Aversion in International Relations Theory," *International Studies Quarterly*, vol. 45, no. 4 (December 2001), pp. 617–640.

Orchard, David. *The Fight for Canada: Four Centuries of Resistance to American Expansionism* (Toronto: Stoddart, 1993).

Organski, A.F.K., and Jacek Kugler. *The War Ledger* (Chicago: University of Chicago Press, 1980).

Orr, Robert M., Jr. "Japan Pursues Hard Line on the Northern Territories Issue," *Tokyo Business Today*, November 1992, p. 15.

Ostry, Bernard. "Conservatives, Liberals, and Labour in the 1870s," *Canadian Historical Review*, vol. 41, no. 2 (June 1960), pp. 93–127.

O'Sullivan, Chris S., and Francis T. Durso. "Effect of Schema-Incongruent Information on Memory for Stereotypical Attributes," *Journal of Personality and Social Psychology*, vol. 47, no. 1 (July 1984), pp. 55–70.

Owen, John M., IV. *Liberal Peace, Liberal War: American Politics and International Security* (Ithaca: Cornell University Press, 1997).

Oye, Kenneth A., ed. *Cooperation under Anarchy* (Princeton: Princeton University Press, 1986).

Patti, Archimedes L. A. *Why Viet Nam? Prelude to America's Albatross* (Berkeley: University of California Press, 1980).

Payne, John W., James R. Bettman, and Eric J. Johnson. "Behavioral Decision Research: A Constructive Processing Perspective," *Annual Review of Psychology*, vol. 43 (1992), pp. 87–131.

Pelletiere, Stephen C. *The Iran-Iraq War: Chaos in a Vacuum* (New York: Praeger, 1992).

Pickersgill, J. W., and Donald F. Forster. *The Mackenzie King Record*, vol. 4 (Toronto: University of Toronto Press, 1960).

Polity IV Project. Dataset and *User's Manual*. Integrated Network for Societal Conflict Research (INSCR) Program, Center for International Development and Conflict Management (CIDCM), University of Maryland, College Park. http://www.cidcm.umd.edu/inscr/polity.

Pollack, Kenneth M. *The Threatening Storm: The Case for Invading Iraq* (New York: Random House, 2002).

Porter, Gareth, ed. *Vietnam: A History in Documents* (New York: New American Library, 1979).

Post, Jerrold M. "Saddam Hussein of Iraq: A Political Psychology Profile," in *The Psychological Assessment of Political Leaders: With Profiles of Saddam Hussein and Bill Clinton*, ed. Jerrold M. Post (Ann Arbor: University of Michigan Press, 2003), pp. 335–366.

"Presidential Debate between Democratic Candidate Vice President Al Gore and Republican Candidate Governor George W. Bush, Clark Athletic Center, University of Massachusetts, Boston, MA, 3 October 2000." http://www.cspan.org/campaign2000/transcript/debate_100300.asp (2000).

"Presidential Debate between Democratic Candidate Vice President Al Gore and Republican Candidate Governor George W. Bush, Wait Chapel, Wake Forest University, Winston-Salem, NC, 11 October 2000." http://www.c-span.org/campaign2000/transcript/debate_101100.asp (2000).

Price, Glen W. "Legal Analysis of the Kurile Island Dispute," *Temple International and Comparative Law Journal*, vol. 7, no. 2 (Fall 1993), pp. 395–422.

Purdum, Todd S. *A Time of Our Choosing: America's War in Iraq* (New York: Times Books/Henry Holt, 2003).

Putnam, Hilary. *Reason, Truth, and History* (Cambridge: Cambridge University Press, 1981).

Putnam, Robert. "Diplomacy and Domestic Politics: The Logic of Two-Level Games," *International Organization*, vol. 42, no. 3 (Summer 1988), pp. 428–460.

Quattrone, George A., and Amos Tversky. "Contrasting Rational and Psychological Analyses of Political Choice," *American Political Science Review*, vol. 82, no. 3 (September 1988), pp. 719–736.

Rasmussen, Kathleen Britt. "Canada and the Reconstruction of the International Economy, 1941–1947," Ph.D. dissertation, Department of History, University of Toronto (2001).

Raynor, Joel O., and Dean B. McFarlin. "Motivation and the Self-System," in *Handbook of Motivation and Cognition: Foundations of Social Behavior*, ed. Richard M. Sorrentino and E. Tory Higgins (New York: Guilford, 1986), pp. 315–349.

Record, Jeffrey. *The Wrong War: Why We Lost in Vietnam* (Annapolis: Naval Institute Press, 1998).

Reder, Lynne M., and John R. Anderson. "A Partial Resolution of the Paradox of Inference: The Role of Integrating Knowledge," *Cognitive Psychology*, vol. 12, no. 4 (October 1980), pp. 447–472.

Redlick, Fritz. *Hitler: Diagnosis of a Destructive Prophet* (New York: Oxford University Press, 1999).

Rees, David. *The Soviet Seizure of the Kuriles* (New York: Praeger, 1985).

Reeve, Simon. *The New Jackals: Ramzi Yousef, Osama Bin Laden, and the Future of Terrorism* (London: André Deutsch, 1999).

Regan, Dennis T., Ellen Straus, and Russell H. Fazio. "Liking and the Attribution Process," *Journal of Experimental Social Psychology*, vol. 10, no. 4 (July 1974), pp. 385–397.

Rhodes, Edward. "Do Bureaucratic Politics Matter? Some Disconfirming Findings from the Case of the U.S. Navy," *World Politics*, vol. 47, no. 1 (October 1994), pp. 1–41.

Ricks, Thomas E. "Containing Iraq: A Forgotten War," *Washington Post*, 25 October 2000, p. A01.

Riker, William H. "The Political Psychology of Rational Choice Theory," *Political Psychology*, vol. 16, no. 1 (March 1995), pp. 23–44.

Ritchie, Gordon. *Wrestling with the Elephant: The Inside Story of the Canada-US Trade Wars* (Toronto: Macfarlane Walter & Ross, 1997).

Rock, Stephen R. *Appeasement in International Politics* (Lexington: University Press of Kentucky, 2000).

Rock, William R. *British Appeasement in the 1930s* (London: Edward Arnold, 1977).

Rorty, Richard. *Philosophy and the Mirror of Nature* (Princeton: Princeton University Press, 1979).

Rosenau, James, ed. *Domestic Sources of Foreign Policy* (New York: Free Press, 1967).

Ross, Lee. "The Intuitive Psychologist and His Shortcomings: Distortions in the Attribution Process," in *Advances in Experimental and Social Psychology*, ed. Leonard Berkowitz, vol. 10 (New York: Academic Press, 1977), pp. 174–177.

Ross, Lee, and Craig R. Anderson. "Shortcomings in the Attribution Process: On the Origins and Maintenance of Erroneous Social Assessments," in *Judgment under Uncertainty: Heuristics and Biases*, ed. Daniel Kahneman, Paul Slovic, and Amos Tversky (Cambridge: Cambridge University Press, 1982), pp. 129–152.

Ross, Lee, Mark R. Lepper, and Michael Hubbard. "Perseverance in Self Perception and Social Perception: Biased Attributional Processes in the Debriefing Paradigm," *Journal of Personality and Social Psychology*, vol. 32, no. 5 (November 1975), pp. 800–892.

Ross, Lee, and Constance Stillinger. "Barriers to Conflict Resolution," *Negotiation Journal*, vol. 7, no. 4 (October 1991), pp. 389–404.

Rusk, Dean. *As I Saw It* (New York: Norton, 1990).

Russett, Bruce M. *Grasping the Democratic Peace: Principles for a Post–Cold War World*, 2nd ed. (Princeton: Princeton University Press, 1995).

Sagan, Scott. "History, Analogy, and Deterrence Theory: A Review Essay," *Journal of Interdisciplinary History*, vol. 22, no. 1 (Summer 1991), pp. 79–88.

Sainteny, Jean. *Ho Chi Minh and His Vietnam: A Personal Memoir*, trans. Herma Briffault (Chicago: Cowel, 1972).

Sanger, David E. "In Russia and Japan, Once Again, National Egos Block Cooperation," *New York Times*, 13 September 1992, p. E4.

Savranskaya, Svetlana, and David A. Welch, eds. *SALT II and the Growth of Mistrust: Transcript of the Proceedings of the Musgrove Conference of the Carter-Brezhnev Project, Musgrove Plantation, St. Simon's Island, GA, May 7–9, 1994* (Providence: Thomas J. Watson Jr. Institute for International Studies, Brown University, 1994).

Schank, Roger, and Robert Abelson. *Scripts, Plans, Goals, and Understanding: An Inquiry into Human Knowledge Structures* (Hillsdale, NJ: Lawrence Erlbaum, 1977).

Schaubroek, John, and Elaine David. "Prospect Theory Predictions When Escalation Is Not the Only Chance to Recover Sunk Costs," *Organizational Behavior & Human Decision Processes*, vol. 57, no. 1 (January 1994), pp. 59–82.

Schelling, Thomas C. *Arms and Influence* (New Haven: Yale University Press, 1966).

———. *The Strategy of Conflict* (London: Oxford University Press, 1960).

Schmemann, Serge. "Little Isles, Big Fight," *New York Times*, 11 September 1992, p. A6.

———. "Yeltsin Cancels a Visit to Japan as Dispute over Islands Simmers," *New York Times*, 10 September 1992, pp. A1, A6.

Schoenbaum, Thomas J. *Waging Peace and War: Dean Rusk in the Truman, Kennedy, and Johnson Years* (New York: Simon & Schuster, 1988).

Schull, Joseph. *Laurier: The First Canadian* (Toronto: Macmillan of Canada, 1965).

Schwartz, Morton. *Soviet Perceptions of the United States* (Berkeley: University of California Press, 1978).

Sciolino, Elaine. *The Outlaw State: Saddam Hussein's Quest for Power and the Gulf Crisis* (New York: Wiley, 1991).

Segal, Gerald. "Gorbachev in Japan: The Territorial Issue," *The World Today*, vol. 47, no. 4 (April 1991), pp. 59–61.

———. "Moscow Adopts a New Realistic Line on Japan," *Far Eastern Economic Review*, 6 October 1988, pp. 28, 30.

———. *Normalizing Soviet-Japanese Relations* (London: Royal Institute of International Affairs, 1991).

Semmel, Bernard, ed. *Marxism and the Science of War* (New York: Oxford University Press, 1984).

Shackleton, Lord. *Economic Survey of the Falkland Islands* (London: Economist Intelligence Unit, 1976).

———. *Falkland Islands: Economic Study 1982 (Cmnd. 8653)* (London: Her Majesty's Stationery Office, 1982).

Shackleton, Lord, R. J. Storey, and R. Johnson. "Prospects of the Falkland Islands," *The Geographical Journal*, vol. 143, part 1 (March 1977), pp. 1–13.

Shafir, Eldar. "Prospect Theory and Political Analysis: A Psychological Perspective," *Political Psychology*, vol. 13, no. 2 (June 1992), pp. 311–322.

Shawcross, William. *Sideshow: Kissinger, Nixon, and the Destruction of Cambodia* (New York: Simon & Schuster, 1979).

Sheehan, Neil, et al., eds. *The Pentagon Papers* (New York: Bantam, 1971).

Short, Anthony. *The Origins of the Vietnam War* (London: Longman, 1989).

Short, Philip. *Mao: A Life* (London: Hodder & Stoughton, 1999).

Simon, Herbert. *Administrative Behavior: A Study of Decision-Making Processes in Administrative Organization*, 3rd ed. (New York: Free Press, 1976).

———. *Models of Bounded Rationality* (Cambridge: MIT Press, 1982).

———. "Rationality in Political Behavior," *Political Psychology*, vol. 16, no. 1 (March 1995), pp. 45–61.

Singer, J. David. "The Levels of Analysis Problem in International Relations," in *International Politics and Foreign Policy*, ed. James N. Rosenau (New York: Free Press, 1969), pp. 20–29.

Singer, J. David, and Paul F. Diehl, eds. *Measuring the Correlates of War* (Ann Arbor: University of Michigan Press, 1990).

Skak, Mette. "Post-Soviet Foreign Policy," *Journal of East Asian Affairs*, vol. 7, no. 1 (Winter/Spring 1993), pp. 137–185.

Skelton, Oscar Douglas. *Life and Letters of Sir Wilfrid Laurier*, vol. 2 (Toronto: Oxford University Press, 1922).

Slovic, Paul, and Sarah Lichtenstein. "Preference Reversals: A Broader Perspective," *American Economic Review*, vol. 73, no. 4 (September 1983), pp. 596–605.

Small, Melvin. *The Presidency of Richard Nixon* (Lawrence: University Press of Kansas, 1999).

Small, Melvin, and J. David Singer. *Resort to Arms: International and Civil Wars, 1816–1980* (Beverly Hills, CA: Sage, 1982).

Smith, George W. *The Siege at Hue* (Boulder: Lynne Rienner, 1999).

Smith, Jean Edward. *George Bush's War* (New York: Henry Holt, 1992).

Smith, Michael Joseph. *Realist Thought from Weber to Kissinger* (Baton Rouge: Louisiana State University Press, 1986).

Smith, R. B. *An International History of the Vietnam War*, vol. 2 (New York: St. Martin's Press, 1983).

Smith, Steve. "The Concept of Security in a Globalising World," paper presented to the 37th Otago Foreign Policy School, Dunedin, New Zealand, 29 June 2002.

Smith, Steve, Ken Booth, and Marysia Zalewski, eds. *International Theory: Positivism and Beyond* (Cambridge: Cambridge University Press, 1996).

Snyder, Jack. *Myths of Empire* (Ithaca: Cornell University Press, 1991).

Snyder, Richard C., H. W. Bruck, and Burton Sapin, eds. *Foreign Policy Decision-Making: An Approach to the Study of International Politics* (New York: Free Press of Glencoe, 1962).

Sorensen, Theodore C. *Kennedy* (New York: Harper & Row, 1965).

Spector, Leonard S. "Strategic Warning and New Nuclear States," *Defense Intelligence Journal*, vol. 7, no. 2 (Fall 1998), pp. 45–63.

Srull, Thomas K., and Robert S. Wyer. "Person Memory and Judgment," *Psychological Review*, vol. 96, no. 1 (January 1989), pp. 58–83.

Stairs, Denis, Gilbert R. Winham, and the Royal Commission on the Economic Union and Development Prospects for Canada. *The Politics of Canada's Economic Relationship with the United States*, Collected Research Studies, vol. 29 (Toronto: University of Toronto Press, 1985).

Starr, Harvey. *Henry Kissinger: Perceptions of International Politics* (Lexington: University Press of Kentucky, 1984).

Staudinger, Hans. *The Inner Nazi: A Critical Analysis of Mein Kampf*, ed. Peter M. Rutkoff and William B. Scott (Baton Rouge: Louisiana State University Press, 1981).

Stein, Janice Gross. "Deterrence and Compellence in the Gulf, 1990–91: A Failed or Impossible Task?," *International Security*, vol. 17, no. 2 (Fall 1992), pp. 147–179.

Stein, Janice Gross, and Louis W. Pauly, eds. *Choosing to Co-Operate: How States Avoid Loss* (Baltimore: Johns Hopkins University Press, 1993).

Stein, Janice Gross, and David A. Welch. "Rational and Psychological Approaches to the Study of International Conflict: Comparative Strengths and Weaknesses," in *Decision-Making on War and Peace: The Cognitive-Rational Debate*, ed. Nehemia Geva and Alex Mintz (Boulder: Lynne Rienner, 1997), pp. 51–77.

Stern, Eric, and Bertjan Verbeek. "Whither the Study of Governmental Politics in Foreign Policymaking? A Symposium," *Mershon International Studies Review*, vol. 42, no. 2 (November 1998), pp. 205–255.

Stevens, Paul, ed. *The 1911 General Election: A Study in Canadian Politics* (Toronto: Copp Clark, 1970).

Stokes, Ernie. "Macroeconomic Impact of the Canada-U.S. Free Trade Agreement," *Journal of Policy Modeling*, vol. 11, no. 2 (Summer 1989), pp. 225–245.

"Stuck on the Rocks: Japan Miffed as Yeltsin Cancels Visit," *Far Eastern Economic Review*, 24 September 1992, pp. 14–16.

Suedfeld, Peter, and A. Dennis Rank. "Revolutionary Leaders: Long-Term Success as a Function of Changes in Conceptual Complexity," *Journal of Personality and Social Psychology*, vol. 34, no. 3 (August 1976), pp. 169–178.

Suedfeld, Peter, and Philip Tetlock. "Integrative Complexity of Communication in International Crisis," *Journal of Conflict Resolution*, vol. 21, no. 1 (March 1977), pp. 169–184.

Summers, Anthony. *Arrogance of Power: The Secret World of Richard Nixon* (New York: Viking, 2000).

Summers, Harry G. *On Strategy: A Critical Analysis of the Vietnam War* (Novato, CA: Presidio, 1982).

Sylvan, David, and Stephen Majeski. "A Methodology for the Study of Historical Counterfactuals," *International Studies Quarterly*, vol. 42, no. 1 (1998), pp. 79–108.

Szulc, Tad. *The Illusion of Peace: Foreign Policy in the Nixon-Kissinger Years* (New York: Viking Press, 1978).

Takagi, Yoji. "Getting on Track," *Look Japan*, December 1992, pp. 8–11.

Taliaferro, Jeffrey. "Cognitive Realism: Risk Taking and the Psychology of Loss Aversion in Foreign Policy," Ph.D. dissertation, Harvard University, 1997.

Tanaka, Takahiko. *Nisso Kokko Kaifuku no Shiteki Kenkyu: Sengo Nisso Kankei no Kiten, 1945–1956* (Soviet-Japanese Normalization 1945–1956: A History) (Tokyo: Yuhikaku, 1993).

Taubman, William. *Khrushchev: The Man and His Era* (New York: Norton, 2003).

Taylor, Maxwell D. *Responsibility and Response* (New York: Harper & Row, 1967).

Terrill, Ross. *Mao: A Biography*, rev. and exp. ed. (Stanford: Stanford University Press, 1999).

Tesser, Abraham. "Some Effects of Self-Evaluation Maintenance on Cognition and Action," in *Handbook of Motivation and Cognition: Foundations of Social Behavior*, ed. Richard M. Sorrentino and E. Tory Higgins (New York: Guilford, 1986), pp. 435–464.

Tetlock, Philip E. "Integrative Complexity of American and Soviet Foreign Policy Rhetorics: A Time-Series Analysis," *Journal of Personality and Social Psychology*, vol. 49, no. 6 (July–September 1985), pp. 1565–1585.

Tetlock, Philip E., and Aaron Belkin, eds. *Counterfactual Thought Experiments in World Politics: Logical, Methodological, and Psychological Perspectives* (Princeton: Princeton University Press, 1996).

Thaler, Richard H. *The Winner's Curse: Paradoxes and Anomalies of Economic Life* (New York: Free Press, 1992).

———. "Toward a Positive Theory of Consumer Choice," *Journal of Economic Behavior and Organization*, vol. 1, no. 1 (March 1980), pp. 39–60.

't Hart, Paul. *Groupthink in Government: A Study of Small Groups and Policy Failure* (Amsterdam: Swets & Zeitlinger, 1990).

"The Rising Sun in Russia's Sky," *Economist*, 25 November 1989, pp. 35–36.

The United States and Japan in 1994: Uncertain Prospects, Edwin O. Reischauer Center for East Asian Studies, Nitze School of Advanced International Studies. http://www.gwjapan.com/ftp/pub/policy/sais/1994/sais94-6.txt (1994).

Thompson, W. Scott. *Power Projection: A Net Assessment of U.S. and Soviet Capabilities* (New York: National Strategy Information Center, 1978).

Thorndyke, Perry W., and Barbara Hayes-Roth. "The Use of Schemata in the Acquisition and Transfer of Knowledge," *Cognitive Psychology*, vol. 11, no. 1 (January 1979), pp. 82–105.

Thornton, Richard C. *The Nixon-Kissinger Years: Reshaping America's Foreign Policy* (New York: Paragon House, 1989).

Tompson, William J. *Khrushchev: A Political Life* (New York: St. Martin's Press, 1995).

Trefler, Daniel. *The Long and Short of the Canada-U.S. Free Trade Agreement* (Ottawa: Industry Canada, 1999).

Trevor-Roper, H. R. "The Mind of Adolf Hitler," introductory essay to *Hitler's Secret Conversations, 1941–44* (New York: Farrar, Straus & Young, 1953).

Trope, Yaacov, and Zvi Ginossar. "On the Use of Statistical and Nonstatistical Knowledge: A Problem-Solving Approach," in *The Social Psychology of Knowledge*, ed. Daniel Bar-Tal and Arie W. Kruglanski (New York: Cambridge University Press, 1986), pp. 209–230.

Tuchman, Barbara W. *The Guns of August* (New York: Macmillan, 1962).

Tversky, Amos, and Daniel Kahneman. "Advances in Prospect Theory: Cumulative Representation of Uncertainty," *Journal of Risk and Uncertainty*, vol. 5, no. 4 (October 1992), pp. 297–323.

———. "Loss Aversion in Riskless Choice: A Reference-Dependent Model," *The Quarterly Journal of Economics*, vol. 106, no. 4 (November 1991), pp. 1039–1061.

———. "Rational Choice and the Framing of Decisions," *Journal of Business*, vol. 59, no. 4 (October 1986), pp. S251–S277.

———. "The Framing of Decisions and the Psychology of Choice," *Science*, no. 211 (30 January 1981), pp. 453–458.

Tversky, Amos, and Itamar Simonson. "Context-Dependent Preferences," *Management Science*, vol. 39, no. 10 (October 1993), pp. 1179–1189.

Tversky, Amos, and Richard H. Thaler. "Preference Reversals," *Journal of Economic Perspectives*, vol. 4, no. 2 (Spring 1990), pp. 201–211.

Tversky, Amos, and Peter Wakker. "Risk Attitudes and Decision Weights," *Econometrica*, vol. 63, no. 6 (November 1995), pp. 1255–1280.

Tyroler, Charles. *Alerting America: The Papers of the Committee on the Present Danger* (Washington, DC: Pergamon-Brassey's, 1984).

United Nations Conference on Trade and Development Division on Transnational Corporations and Investments. *World Investment Report 1994: Transnational Corporations, Employment and the Workplace* (New York: United Nations, 1994).

United States, Department of State. *Foreign Relations of the United States*, various volumes (Washington, DC: U.S. Government Printing Office, 1988–2003). http://www.state.gov/r/pa/ho/frus/.

United States Senate. *Hearings before the Preparedness Investigating Subcommittee of the U.S. Senate Armed Services Committee* (Washington, DC: Government Printing Office, 1967).

United States Senate, Committee on Foreign Relations. *Background Information Relating to Southeast Asia and Vietnam*, 5th ed. (Washington, DC: U.S. Government Printing Office, 1969).

Urquhart, John, and Peggy Berkowitz. "Northern Angst: Canada Worries Anew over Loss of Identity to Its Big Neighbor," *Wall Street Journal*, 22 September 1987, p. 1.

Usowski, Peter S. "John McCone and the Cuban Missile Crisis: A Persistent Approach to the Intelligence-Policy Relationship," *International Journal of Intelligence and Counterintelligence*, vol. 2, no. 4 (Winter 1988), pp. 547–576.

Vennema, Alje. *The Viet Cong Massacre at Hue* (New York: Vantage Press, 1976).

Vertzberger, Yaacov. *Misperceptions in Foreign Policymaking: The Sino-Indian Conflict, 1959–1962* (Boulder: Westview, 1984).

———. *The World in Their Minds: Information Processing, Cognition, and Perception in Foreign Policy Decisionmaking* (Stanford: Stanford University Press, 1990).

Volkan, Vamik D., Norman Itzkowitz, and Andrew W. Dod. *Richard Nixon: A Psychobiography* (New York: Columbia University Press, 1997).

Waite, Robert G. L. "Adolf Hitler's Anti-Semitism: A Study in History and Psychoanalysis," in *The Psychoanalytic Interpretation of History*, ed. Benjamin B. Wolman (New York: Basic Books, 1971), pp. 192–230.

Walker, Stephen G. "The Impact of Personality Structure and Cognitive Processes upon American Foreign Policy Decisions," paper delivered at the Annual Meeting of the American Political Science Association, Washington, DC, 1988.

Wallerstein, Immanuel. *The Politics of the World Economy* (Cambridge: Cambridge University Press, 1984).

———. "The Rise and Future Demise of the World Capitalist System: Concepts for Comparative Analysis," *Comparative Studies in Society and History*, vol. 16, no. 4 (September 1974), pp. 387–415.

Waltz, Kenneth N. *Man, the State and War* (New York: Columbia University Press, 1959).

———. *Theory of International Politics* (New York: Random House, 1979).

Warnock, John W. *Free Trade and the New Right Agenda* (Vancouver: New Star Books, 1988).

Watkins, Mel. "The U.S.-Canada Free Trade Agreement," *Monthly Review*, September 1988, pp. 34–42.

Weathersby, Kathryn. "Korea, 1949–50: To Attack or Not to Attack? Stalin, Kim Il Sung, and the Prelude to War," *Cold War International History Project Bulletin*, no. 5 (Spring 1995), pp. 1–9.

———. "New Russian Documents on the Korean War: Introduction and Translations," *Cold War International History Project Bulletin*, no. 6–7 (Winter 1995/1996), pp. 30–40, 42–84.

Welch, David A. "Crisis Decision-Making Reconsidered," *Journal of Conflict Resolution*, vol. 33, no. 3 (September 1989), pp. 430–445.

———. "Culture and Emotion as Obstacles to Good Judgment: The Case of Argentina's Invasion of the Falklands/Malvinas," in *Good Judgment in Foreign Policy: Theory and Application*, ed. Stanley A. Renshon and Deborah W. Larson (Lanham, MD: Rowman & Littlefield, 2003), pp. 191–215.

————. *Decisions, Decisions: The Art of Effective Decision Making* (Amherst, NY: Prometheus Books, 2001).

————. *Justice and the Genesis of War* (Cambridge: Cambridge University Press, 1993).

————. "Morality and 'the National Interest'," in *Ethics in International Affairs: Theory and Cases*, ed. Andrew Valls (Lanham, MD: Rowman & Littlefield, 2000), pp. 3–12.

————. "The Organizational Process and Bureaucratic Politics Paradigms: Retrospect and Prospect," *International Security*, vol. 17, no. 2 (Fall 1992), pp. 112–146.

————. "The Politics and Psychology of Restraint: Israeli Decision-Making in the Gulf War," in *Choosing to Co-Operate: How States Avoid Loss*, ed. Janice Gross Stein and Louis W. Pauly (Baltimore: Johns Hopkins University Press, 1993), pp. 128–169.

————. Review of Richard Wyn Jones, *Security, Strategy, and Critical Theory* (Boulder, CO: Lynne Rienner, 1999), *American Political Science Review*, vol. 92, no. 2 (June 2000), pp. 522–524.

Welch, David A., and James G. Blight. "The Eleventh Hour of the Cuban Missile Crisis: An Introduction to the ExComm Transcripts," *International Security*, vol. 12, no. 3 (Winter 1987/88), pp. 5–29.

Wendt, Alexander. "The Agent-Structure Problem in International Relations Theory," *International Organization*, vol. 41, no. 3 (Summer 1987), pp. 335–370.

————. "Anarchy Is What States Make of It: The Social Construction of Power Politics," *International Organization*, vol. 46, no. 2 (Spring 1992), pp. 391–425.

————. "Bridging the Theory/Meta-Theory Gap in International Relations," *Review of International Studies*, vol. 17, no. 4 (October 1991), pp. 383–392.

————. "Collective Identity Formation and the International State," *American Political Science Review*, vol. 88, no. 2 (June 1994), pp. 384–396.

————. "Levels of Analysis vs. Agents and Structures: Part III," *Review of International Studies*, vol. 18, no. 2 (April 1992), pp. 181–185.

————. *Social Theory of International Politics* (Cambridge: Cambridge University Press, 1999).

Westad, Odd Arne, et al. "77 Conversations between Chinese and Foreign Leaders on the Wars in Indochina, 1964–1977," Cold War International History Project Working Paper No. 22 (Washington, DC: Woodrow Wilson International Center for Scholars, 1998).

Whalen, Richard J. *Catch the Falling Flag: A Republican's Challenge to His Party* (Boston: Houghton Mifflin, 1972).

Whalley, John, research coordinator, with Roderick Hill. *Canada-United States Free Trade*, Collected Research Studies/Royal Commission on the Economic Union and Development Prospects for Canada, vol. 11 (Toronto: University of Toronto Press, 1985).

White, Mark J. *The Cuban Missile Crisis* (Basingstoke, Hampshire: Macmillan, 1996).

White, Ralph K. *Nobody Wanted War: Misperception in Vietnam and Other Wars* (Garden City, NY: Doubleday, 1968).

White, Randall. *Fur Trade to Free Trade: Putting the Canada-U.S. Trade Agreement in Historical Perspective*, 2nd ed. (Toronto: Dundurn Press, 1989).

Whyte, Glen. "Escalating Commitment in Individual and Group Decision Making: A Prospect Theory Approach," *Organizational Behavior & Human Decision Processes*, vol. 54, no. 3 (April 1993), pp. 430–455.

———. "Escalating Commitment to a Course of Action: A Reinterpretation," *Academy of Management Review*, vol. 11, no. 2 (April 1986), pp. 311–321.

———. "Groupthink Reconsidered," *Academy of Management Review*, vol. 14, no. 1 (January 1989), pp. 40–56.

Winham, Gilbert R. *Canada-U.S. Sectoral Trade Study: The Impact of Free Trade: A Background Paper* (Halifax: Centre for Foreign Policy Studies, Dalhousie University, 1986).

———. "Faith and Fear: The Free Trade Story," *Canadian Public Administration*, vol. 34, no. 4 (Winter 1993), pp. 656–658.

Winston, Mark L. *Killer Bees: The Africanized Honey Bee in the Americas* (Cambridge: Harvard University Press, 1992).

Wirtz, James J. *The Tet Offensive: Intelligence Failure in War* (Ithaca: Cornell University Press, 1991).

Wohlforth, William Curti. *The Elusive Balance: Power and Perceptions in the Cold War* (Ithaca: Cornell University Press, 1993).

Wohlstetter, Roberta. *Pearl Harbor: Warning and Decision* (Stanford: Stanford University Press, 1962).

Wonnacott, Paul. "The Canada-U.S. Free Trade Agreement: The Issue of Assured Access," in *Building a Partnership: The Canada-United States Free Trade Agreement*, ed. Mordechai E. Kreinin (East Lansing: Michigan State University Press, 2000), pp. 65–79.

———. *The United States and Canada: The Quest for Free Trade: An Examination of Selected Issues* (Washington, DC: Institute for International Economics, 1987).

Wood, Patricia K. "Defining 'Canadian': Anti-Americanism and Identity in Sir John A. Macdonald's Nationalism," *Journal of Canadian Studies*, vol. 36, no. 2 (Summer 2001), pp. 49–69.

Woodward, Bob. *Bush at War* (New York: Simon & Schuster, 2002).

———. *Plan of Attack: The Road to War* (New York: Simon & Schuster, 2004).

Wu, Samuel S. G., and Bruce Bueno de Mesquita. "Assessing the Dispute in the South China Sea: A Model of China's Security Decision Making," *International Studies Quarterly*, vol. 38, no. 3 (September 1994), pp. 379–403.

Wyer, Robert S., Jr., and Sallie E. Gordon. "The Recall of Information about Persons and Groups," *Journal of Experimental Social Psychology*, vol. 18, no. 2 (March 1982), pp. 128–164.

Wyn Jones, Richard. *Security, Strategy, and Critical Theory* (Boulder: Lynne Rienner, 1999).

Yamakage, Susumu. "Japan's National Security and Asia-Pacific's Regional Institutions in the Post-Cold War Era," in *Network Power: Japan and Asia*, ed. Peter J. Katzenstein and Takashi Shiraishi (Ithaca: Cornell University Press, 1997), pp. 275–305.

"Yeltsin's Yoke: Japan Strives for G-7 Backing in Islands Dispute," *Far Eastern Economic Review*, 16 July 1992, p. 11.

Zagare, Frank C. "Rationality and Deterrence," *World Politics*, vol. 42, no. 2 (January 1990), pp. 238–260.

Zagorskii, Alexei. "Russian Security Policy toward the Asia-Pacific Region: From USSR to CIS," in *Russia and Japan: An Unresolved Dilemma between Distant Neighbors*, ed. Tsuyoshi Hasegawa, Jonathan Haslam, and Andrew C. Kuchins (Berkeley: University of California Press, 1993), pp. 399–416.

Zagorsky, Alexei. "Kuriles Stumbling Block," *Far Eastern Economic Review*, 20 August 1992, p. 21.

Zartman, I. William, and Maureen R. Berman. *The Practical Negotiator* (New Haven: Yale University Press, 1982).

Zubok, Vladislav, and Constantine Pleshakov. *Inside the Kremlin's Cold War: From Stalin to Khrushchev* (Cambridge: Harvard University Press, 1996).

Zukier, Henri. "The Paradigmatic and Narrative Modes in Goal-Guided Inference," in *Handbook of Motivation and Cognition: Foundations of Social Behavior*, ed. Richard M. Sorrentino and E. Tory Higgins (New York: Guilford, 1986), pp. 465–502.

INDEX

9/11, 2–4, 35

Abbott, Douglas, 188, 190
Acheson, Dean, 123–24
actors. *See* behavior
Adler, Emanuel, 30n1
Afghanistan, 2, 4
Alberta, 182
Alexandroff, Alan, 172n4
al-Qaeda, 2–3, 35
Alsace-Lorraine, 54
Amtrak Improvement Act of 1977, 201n115
Anaya, Jorge Isaac, 77, 84, 87n45, 88n46, 93–94
anti-submarine warfare (ASW), 97
Argentina, 69–70, 132, 220, 224; Chile and, 83, 93, 94n66; Dirty War and, 83–84; Falklands/Malvinas Islands and, 72–95; irredentism and, 82–83; Junta and, 77–81, 217, 230; Perón and, 75; Project Alpha and, 78n23; state characteristics and, 89; Uruguay and, 82–83
ARVN, 130–33, 135, 137, 146, 148
Ascension Island, 87n45
Austria, 26
Austria-Hungary, 11
autarky, 168

Bacevich, Andrew, 7
Bahía Buen Suceso (naval transport), 78–79
balance-of-power politics, 12
Ball, George, 141–42, 164
Bank of Canada, 186–87
Barents Sea, 97
Beagle Channel islands, 83, 93, 94n66
behavior: cognitive psychology and, 36–41; decision-based theory and, 18–23; entitlements and, 54–55; expectations and, 52–56; foreign policy change and, 23–29; International Relations [IR] theory and, 23–30 (*see also* International Relations [IR] theory); loss-aversion theory and, 42, 45–51, 67–68 (*see also* loss-aversion theory); parsimony and, 20–21;

positivism and, 18–23; power and, 23–29; predicting state, 10–18; prospect theory and, 41–45; Skinnerian, 20; status quo and, 53–56; uncertainty conditions and, 47–48
behavioral revolution, 5n18
belief change, 39n23
Bernhardt, Gaston de, 74n4
bin Laden, Osama, 2–3
Blaine, James G., 176
Blainey, Geoffrey, 24
Borden, Robert, 178, 180–84, 211
Bosnia, 11n3
Bourassa, Robert, 199
Britain, 11, 21, 230; Crimean War and, 21–22; Falklands and, 53–54, 69, 72–95; free trade and, 176; Hong Kong and, 53–54, 76; national interest and, 53–54; Reciprocity Treaty of 1854 and, 174; Ten Year Rule and, 35; Thatcher and, 11, 76, 78–79, 85, 87; World War I and, 35
British Commonwealth Division, 189
Broadbent, Ed, 197, 200
Brown, George, 175
Buchanan, Patrick, 153
Bueno de Mesquita, Bruce, 29n57, 166–67
Bundy, McGeorge (Mac): air war and, 148; "Fork in the Road" memorandum and, 145–46; Vietnam policy and, 130, 136–40, 142, 145–46, 148
Bundy, William P., 130, 141–47
Burney, Derek, 201
Burns, Jimmy, 84
Bush, George H. W., 11
Bush, George W., 1–4

Cambodia, 119, 132
Canada, 60–61; British Columbia and, 175; Bureaucracy of, 207, 217–18, 220; Confederation and, 172, 174–75; Conservative Party and, 175, 180–84, 205; cultural concerns and, 200; currency revaluation and, 186–88; demographics of, 169–70; Dingley Tariff of 1897 and,